Successful Marriage
A Principles Approach

THE DORSEY SERIES IN SOCIOLOGY

Editor   ROBIN M. WILLIAMS, JR.
Cornell University

Successful Marriage

A Principles Approach

WESLEY R. BURR

*Professor of Child Development and Family Relationships
and Professor of Sociology
Brigham Young University*

1976

THE DORSEY PRESS   Homewood, Illinois   60430

Irwin-Dorsey International   Irwin-Dorsey Limited
Arundel, Sussex   Georgetown, Ontario
BN18 9AB   L7G 4B3

Photographs by Jean-Claude Lejeune

First Printing, January 1976

ISBN 0-256-01789-1
Library of Congress Catalog Card No. 75–26103
Printed in the United States of America

To Ruth and our successful marriage

Preface

SOME marriage and family textbooks are written for "institutional" courses where the major goal is to learn theories and research about the family as an institution. In these courses there is little concern with practical relevance. Other textbooks are written for "functional" courses where the primary goal is to learn information that can be used to improve the quality of marriage and family relationships. This book belongs to the latter group because its primary objectives are (1) to identify a number of ideas that can help readers obtain their marital goals better than if they had not read this book, (2) to describe and illustrate these ideas in language that can be understood without any prior training in the social sciences, and (3) to identify ways to increase the skills or abilities that are needed in applying these ideas in one's personal life situation.

This book introduces a new dimension in marriage education by taking advantage of several recent advances in fields that focus on marriage and family. This new dimension can be called a *principles approach,* and it is the process of identifying general principles in the social sciences that are potentially useful and helping people learn what these ideas are and how to use them in their personal lives. This approach de-emphasizes moralistic or normative information since the principles can be used in widely different cultural groups. It also de-emphasizes descriptive information such as discussing the proportion of couples that have difficulty in various aspects of their marriage, the average length of engagements, the percentage of couples who want high amounts of companionship, or the recent changes in divorce.

One of the advantages of the principles approach can be illustrated by a brief example. All married couples encounter situations where decisions have to be made. They have to decide where to live, who is to accomplish which daily tasks, how to relate to in-laws, and so on. If some general principles about "decision making" could be identified, and if these principles provided information about how to maximize the efficiency of the decision-making process, these principles would provide valuable information that couples could use throughout their marriages. By learning the general principles and applying them, the couples will have acquired knowledge that is far more valuable than knowing what to do in several dozen specific situations. The principles approach is sufficiently different from traditional texts that some new terms and ways of thinking need to be learned. These new terms are all introduced in the second chapter, and that chapter should be read before trying to understand the later chapters.

Readers will note that different kinds of type and colors of ink are used in different sections. This is done to help readers move between the information and application sections of the book. When the type is set like this the text is presenting information about principles or research about the principles.

However, when the type is like this the text is dealing with ways to apply or use principles. These sections also begin with a line across the page.

No single book can be all things to all people, and an emphasis on one type of information creates a proportional de-emphasis on other ideas, phenomena, or literature. Since the emphasis in this volume is on how to use general principles that have more than a little scientific justification, there is a relative ignoring of sensational issues that have recently arisen in the field, in which the research is still trying to identify the issues and trends. We have not yet progressed to the point of having any general principles. Thus, if readers are expecting this volume to be a thorough discussion of the "hot topics" in the field they will be disappointed and view the book as not knowing what's really going on. In my opinion this lack of attention to polemic and philosophical issues is a defensible and complementary specialization, and students in marriage courses can get access to these other useful bodies of literature by reading volumes such as those by Cuber and Harroff (1966), Otto (1970), O'Neill and O'Neill (1971), Bernard (1972), Casler (1973), and Wells (1975).

There are many individuals who are directly or indirectly involved in the preparation of a book such as this and I appreciate them. I am grateful for the influence of Reuben Hill and Murray

Straus who were very important to me in graduate school and whom I continue to learn from as colleagues. I also appreciate Boyd Rollins, Darwin Thomas, Gene Mead, Owen Cahoon, Joel Moss, Elmer Knowles, Kenneth Cannon, Lynn Scoresby, and Blaine Porter who have provided various combinations of stimulation, reaction, ideas, friendship, and administrative support. Without these contributions this book would never have been written. I am also grateful to three graduate students, Margaret Jensen, Glen McClure, and John Miller who spent a great deal of time and energy working with me on what material to put into this book and how to present it. Appreciation is also expressed to Rick Cantrell, Robin Williams, Robert E. Wilson, Rebecca M. Smith, Greer Litton Fox, and Richard K. Kerckhoff for their very helpful suggestions after reading the manuscript.

And last but certainly not least, Ruth and our four children, Ken, Steve, Rob, and Nicole, are an integral part of this book. Interacting with them has convinced me that many of the ideas in this book are not only true—they work. Living with them also provides meaning and purpose, and that's what books like this are all about.

Provo, Utah   Wesley R. Burr
December 1975

Contents

Using principles in other chapters to enrich marriage as the years pass: *Interaction. Using principles about communication and decision making.* One additional principle.

Introduction

The two chapters in the introductory section of this volume lay a foundation for the later parts of the book. The first chapter discusses ten of the many different "styles of marriage" that are becoming available in contemporary society, and tries to help readers further crystallize their opinions about which style they prefer. Chapter 1 is essential because most of the information in the later sections deals with things individuals or couples can do to help attain their own marital goals, and that information is most useful when the individuals or couples have a fairly clear picture of the style of marriage they want. The second chapter describes what "general principles" are and how they can be used in practical, everyday ways. Those who have some background in contemporary social science literature will be able to cover Chapter 2 quickly, but those who do not have this background will need to go through the information in the chapter carefully before they can get the maximum value from the later chapters.

1

Alternative styles of marriage and marital success

I N A BOOK that tries to help people attain success in their marriage or marriagelike relationships the first issue that should be addressed is what is viewed as marital "success." If this book had been written 20 or 30 years ago it would have been relatively easy to describe a successful marriage because there was then a great deal of consensus in the American society about what an ideal marital relationship was supposed to be. In such a relationship spouses developed an intimate and enduring love for each other, had a fairly equalitarian method of making decisions, experienced a great deal of companionship, reared children, and, especially for the wife, confined sexual activity to the marriage. The husband was the "head" of the family and had the primary responsibility for providing the income, and the wife had the primary responsibility for rearing the children. Separation or divorce was to be resorted to only if a marital relationship was a complete failure.

In recent years, however, a large number of people have become dissatisfied with the traditional style of marriage, and a number of new styles have begun to emerge. These alternative marriage styles include such innovative practices as temporarily living together, swinging, and "open" marriage. They also include a number of marriage forms that have been used in other cultures, such as trial marriage, polygamy, group marriage, communes, and living together permanently without a legally sanctioned ceremony (common-law marriage).

These innovations have made it more difficult to define marital success than was the case several decades ago because it is no longer defensible to describe one style of life or one type of marital relationship as the *best* type of marriage and then say that achieving it is marital success while not achieving it is marital failure. That rather provincial view of marital success was, however, the one that dominated the study of the family from the 1930s to the 1960s. The view was initially developed by Burgess and Cottrell (1939) and Terman (1938), and their conceptualization and measuring instruments were widely used in research about marital and family processes for decades. Their narrow view of marital success was widely criticized in the scientific literature (Waller and Hill, 1951, chap. 17; Kirkpatrick, 1963; Burr, 1967; and Lively, 1969), and it has now become apparent to social scientists and large segments of the public that this earlier view of marital success is so culture-specific and rigid that it is indefensible. Because of this, if the term *marital success* is to be useful it has to be defined in such a way that it can be applied to many different styles of marriage.

To lay a foundation for a definition of marital success that is appropriate for the many alternative styles of marriage being advocated in contemporary society, it seems useful to first describe some of these alternatives. It would be impossible to describe all of them, so a few illustrative alternatives are discussed here. The ten styles treated have been selected because they provide a broad sampling of the styles that Americans seem to prefer and because they include some of the more recent innovations and some of the traditional styles.

Before the descriptions of these various styles of marriage are read, it should be realized that these various styles of marriage are not exclusive categories or nonoverlapping sets. The styles are all more similar to one another than different, and the uniqueness of each style is that it has a few characteristics that are different from any of the others. It is, of course, possible to develop additional unique styles of marriage by selecting some of the unique characteristics of one alternative and combining them with some characteristics of another alternative.

ALTERNATIVE FORMS OF MARRIAGE

The Intrinsic marriage

Cuber and Harroff (1966) conducted a study of over 400 upper middle-class marriages, and they subsequently divided the couples into a number of different marital types. Some of the types they identified were viewed by the researchers and by the couples they studied as undesirable, but two types were viewed as desirable. The *Intrinsic* marriage was one of the desirable types. This style of marriage is a relationship in which couples have intense feelings about each other, and each considers the other person, as a person, to be of central importance. The Intrinsic marriage is a merging of two people that is so intimate and encompassing that it is the pervasive concern and source of pleasure in their lives. People who prefer Intrinsic marriages also have other concerns in life, such as careers, kin, friends, and their own individuality, and these other concerns are almost always sufficiently important that they do not want to neglect them. In some manner, however, these other aspects of life tend to be subordinate to the husband-wife relationship. Several of the quotations from couples studied by Cuber and Harroff (1966, pp. 133–34) illustrate the Intrinsic type of marriage:

Well, we've got a marriage-type marriage. Do you know what I mean? So many people—and me in my first marriage—just sort of touch on the edges of existence—don't *really* marry. It's funny, but my cookbook distinguished between marinating and marrying of flavors. You know—the marinated flavors retain their identity—just mix a little—or the one predominates strongly over the other. But the married ones blend into something really new and the separate identities are lost. Well, a lot of people that I know aren't married at all—just marinated!

I'll admit I'd rather have run for elective office. But my wife isn't comfortable with all the campaign dishonesty . . . and a full life together is more important to me than being Senator. It's no sacrifice really. I just don't want to jeopardize or weaken the major satisfaction of my life for a minor one, even if it is important too. What would it profit me to try for a Senate seat and make it, if afterwards I found that our close and deeply sustaining life had been damaged in the process? How can any success be worth that?

From the time I was a child I never thought of it any other way. The first and central thing even in my adolescent fantasies was a close couple. I don't know how I came to see it this way because my parents certainly weren't close and I can't recall any particular pair who have set the model for me. It seems to come from the inside. . . . As I told you, I've had more than one marriage but the common element each time is this complete merging of myself, what I want in the personality of my woman and what she wants and does. I haven't the slightest interest in doing anything that I can't share with her or that she can't participate in with me. . . .

Now that doesn't mean that we haven't differences—sometimes sharp ones—or that I haven't inhibited some desires because she doesn't want to share them. All I mean is that I just don't have or want to have any separate existence that amounts to anything. I do my work as well as I can—but—I'm a little ashamed when I realize it—it doesn't have the importance to me that people think it does. As far as I'm concerned the whole corporation can go to hell any time if it infringes unduly on her, and especially on *us,* and the things that are precious to us.

All Intrinsic marriages are not alike because within this general style of marriage it is possible to have many variations. For example, some couples want considerable intellectual stimulation and others want little, and in some Intrinsic marriages the couples are extremely active sexually while in others the sexual aspect of life is less important. The key ingredients of Intrinsic marriages are that the marital relationship is a very high-priority aspect of life, that there is great commitment to one's spouse, that deeply felt satisfactions are expected from the marriage, and that the marital experience is considered intrinsically valuable. Couples who want this style of life cannot be passive about their marriage, as it takes continual attention, devoted care, and a great deal of energy to develop and maintain this type of relationship. Some people would find these demands overwhelming, stifling, and undesirable, but others seem to find them fulfilling, actualizing, and pleasant.

Utilitarian marriage

The other major type of marriage that emerged in the Cuber and Harroff (1966) study was what they termed the *Utilitarian* marriage. They describe Utilitarian marriages as those which are "established or maintained for purposes other than to express an intimate, highly important personal relationship between a man and a woman. The absence of continuous and deep empathetic feeling and the existence of an atmosphere of limited companionship are natural outcomes since the purposes for its establishment or maintenance are not primarily sexual and emotional ones" (p. 109). The Utilitarian style of marriage is one in which the marriage is desirable and useful, but is subservient to other aspects of life that have greater value. In most cases this relationship is also one in which only selected parts of the individuals' lives are shared. Other parts, and frequently these are most important aspects of the individuals' lives, are viewed as separate concerns that are shared with others and not the spouse. Cuber and Harroff found that many couples who do not want a Utilitarian type of marriage when they are first married later find that it is really the one that suits them best. As one woman of 38 commented after realizing that the glamour and excitement of her earlier relationship had changed:

Now we have it worked out perfectly. He travels—the whole southwest now that he's been promoted—and only gets home alternate weekends. And I teach—well, really, I'm the principal in a pretty exclusive girls' school. We've moved to the country now and Joey can have his horses and Ellen has her boating and swimming close by.

At first it seemed like such a compromise—and I did consider getting a divorce, but that's foolish—you just get into the same bind again.

Anyway, there's a lot of nothing between me and Bob—we might as well face it. When he comes home it's exciting at first but after a while . . . . Really, there's no sentiment or closeness there. I don't know whether he's got someone or something on the road—but what's the difference. I'm not losing anything. And he's had to forgive (or anyway not divorce me over) an affair or two. So you just balance it out.

Anyway, we've worked it all out—equally and fairly. When we go to visit our families in the summer, we spend half of the time with each set of grandparents—minus the time for travel. We work it out as exactly as we can. We both want to be *fair* about everything (pp. 107–8).

Other couples realize they want a Utilitarian marriage before they are married, and they deliberately plan for it as they select a mate and prepare for marriage. As one of Cuber and Harroff's more verbal husbands commented:

I can tell you why I got married! I was getting to the place where I had to. I'd gone up in the corporation as far as I could as a single man. Why they're so prejudiced in favor of married men, I'll never know. Maybe it's those psychological adjustment guys in personnel. Anyway, I wanted Carl's job so bad I could taste it and I knew he was moving on in a year or so. So I looked around. None of the girls I was sleeping with quite filled the bill. So I looked around some more. And then I lit on Charmaine. Now I know it's sort of a "married the boss's daughter" routine, but really it's not quite so bad. She wanted to join up with a marriage as bad as I did. She'd had enough of this career stuff and she was ready for maternity wards and rose gardens. So we did it. . . .

Now we've got ten years' perspective on it and three kids. . . . But neither of us has welshed on the bargain. We stay out of each other's lives all we can, but we cooperate in every way with what the other one wants. She's been a sweety about it—and I don't think I've let her down either. I told her before we were married that she could have fifty percent of my income after taxes to run the house and spend on herself and no questions asked. We leave each other's private lives alone—and not because either of us has anything to hide—it's just a principle. . . . Now don't ask me if I love her, or if she loves me. That doesn't mean anything anyway. We have fun together if we don't see too much of each other. I'm kind of proud of her—a dish, really, for her age. And I know she's proud as hell to be married to the executive vice-president. That ought to be enough for anybody! (pp. 108–9).

There is, of course, great variability in Utilitarian marriage. Some couples have considerable affection while others have none, and some build their lives around their parental roles while others build them around careers, art, or social life. Some couples find that they can live together only in a Utilitarian relationship because they are highly concerned about their independence and individuality. Other couples design their marriages with careful attention to the welfare and rights of others. This latter type is illustrated by the following wife's comments:

The key to our marriage is respect. We really respect each other's individuality. I don't smother him and he doesn't smother me. The only time we really had any trouble was when he first started the business. He made home his office and I nearly went crazy with him underfoot. These gals that wish they could share in their husband's work can have

it! I'd been in the laboratory with him before we got married, but
when he was home all the time and I had other things to do, it was a
different story, I can tell you! Now it's perfect. He's on the road a
little more than half the time and when he's been gone a week or so I
really miss him and look forward to seeing him again. We have one hell
of a reunion! Then after he's home four or five days, we're starting
to get on each other's nerves again. Mostly when he's here I have a
wonderful time with him. And when he's gone I have a wonderful time
with others. I'm happy either way (pp. 115–16).

Cuber and Harroff found that Utilitarian marriages seemed to be
the most functional or appropriate type for the majority of their
upper-class respondents. As they noted, this type is shaped

by a series of related, often unconscious, yet impelling choices. Once one
sets his personal sights primarily on goals which lie outside the pair,
once he thus devalues the private sphere in deference to some other, he
commits himself, whether he realizes it or not, to an almost inexorable
sequence of actions which culminate sooner or later in a full-fledged
Utilitarian marriage. . . . *chiefly, they do not want to reverse it;* they
are content with the current order of things (pp. 130–31; italics added).

Open marriage   The bestselling paperback by O'Neill and O'Neill (1972) describes a third style of married life, which they term *Open* marriage. This style of marriage involves a unique balance of intimacy,
interpersonal commitment, and flexibility. One of the most important aspects of this alternative is a recognition that individuals
change throughout their lives, and the marital relationship is viewed
as sufficiently flexible to permit both members of the couple to
change and grow, yet retain a meaningful relationship with each
other. This style includes a rather large commitment to marriage in
general and to one's spouse in particular, but the nature of the
marital relationship is always subject to discussion. The negotiation
that results from this communication process is always open to new
possibilities for growth or change in either spouse, and the marriage can include radical departures from the established husband-
wife conventions that have traditionally existed in society.

Other main ingredients in an Open marriage, as described by the
O'Neills, are living for now, realistic expectations, privacy, role
flexibility, open companionship, equality, identity, and trust; and
the O'Neills describe each of these in some detail in their book.
Living for now involves giving a high priority to the present rather
than being primarily guided by past events or traditions or by
long-term future goals. Implicit in this too is the idea that a present
orientation tends to deal more with emotional and intellectual
aspects of life—which the O'Neills value in marriage. Both partners
have areas of life that are their own private concern, and these are

used for self-renewal, self-actualization, discovery, and growth. The Open style of marriage thus capitalizes on the individualistic values that exist in the United States culture even though the individuality is couched in a long-term, important interpersonal relationship.

Open companionship implies that both spouses are free to develop deep, involved, and important interpersonal relationships with other individuals. These relationships can be with persons of either sex, temporary or permanent, and limited to very narrow aspects or very broad and inclusive. The main purpose of such non-marital relationships is consistent with the overall themes of individual growth, gleaning from the here and now experiences that are emotionally rewarding, and yet having a home-base relationship that one can count on. Equality and mutual trust are essential components, and these imply a view of the spouse as a peer rather than a master or servant, and a respect for the spouse's role or social status.

The flexibility, variety, and innovation that are involved in the Open style of marriage make it a form that would be difficult to live with for people who want constancy, routine, and stability. This form also demands that a large amount of time and energy be committed to the marital relationship. It requires extensive communication about desires, future options, and alternatives, and negotiation is necessary in maintaining intimacy yet avoiding jealousies and in periodically restructuring the relationship. The concern, emotional commitment, and psychic energy this form demands would only be wanted by individuals who rank their marital relationship fairly high in their priorities. Individuals who opt for the Open style of marriage usually get their satisfactions from a broader array of things than do individuals who opt for Intrinsic marriages, in which the husband-wife relationship is more the central aspect of life. Couples in Open marriages may not value their marriages more highly than do some couples in Utilitarian marriages, but they usually turn to their marital relationship for more of their personal satisfactions. It is likely that very few modern Americans have been attaining the goals sought in Open marriage, but judging from the response to the O'Neills' ideas there are probably a large number of couples who are working toward these goals.

One of the styles of marriage that has been recently increasing in popularity is *Swinging*.[1] This style is a new version of the age-old practice of married couples exchanging partners for sexual activity.

Swinging marriage

---

[1] Considerable research has recently been conducted on swinging as a life-style. The descriptions here rely primarily on studies by Bartell (1970, 1971), Breedlove and Breedlove (1964), Lewis (1969), O'Neill and O'Neill (1970), Palson and Palson (1970), and Smith and Smith (1970).

It has recently, however, become more prevalent, advocated, and socially acceptable, as many of the traditional taboos and mores about sexuality have become more relaxed. This form of marriage usually seems to involve a fairly traditional marital relationship except for sexual behavior. Usually the couples who engage in swinging have high commitment to permanence in their marital relationship, and most of the time they are fairly conventional in the other roles they occupy. In regard to sexual behavior, however, they adopt a style of life that is markedly different from the traditional system. They use periodicals, social activities, and informal contacts to locate other couples who want to exchange marital partners, and they then usually engage fairly regularly in sexual activity with those couples. The actual form of the sexual activity differs considerably with different couples and groups. Some groups participate only in "open" sex, in which everyone is always in the same room. Other variations are "closed" or "closet" versions, in which couples are free to go into separate rooms. Also, on some occasions the sexual activity may be with large groups of couples. Swinging almost always begins with heterosexual activity, but frequently homosexual activity occurs later. However, the homosexual participation is usually more common for women than for men.

Swinging as a style of marriage in contemporary society does not usually occur until several years after the wedding, when it is begun for such reasons as revitalizing the marital relationship, providing excitement and adventure, or providing an alternative to secretive affairs. There is, however, variation from this general pattern, as some couples adopt the Swinging style prior to or from the beginning of their marriage. In contemporary society most swinging couples adopt this style of marital relationship for only a short period of time, but some swing for long periods. Some swinging couples are careful to keep their contacts with their swinging associates purely sexual and to avoid long-term relationships. Others form small cliques of couples that swing only with one another. For still other couples swinging is only a minor part of more involved friendships and permanent emotional and social ties.

The distinguishing characteristic of this marital alternative is the unique form of sexual activity. Since sex is only one aspect of the total marital relationship it is possible to combine the Swinging style of marriage with one or several of the other alternatives. For example, swinging is compatible with Utilitarian or Open marriage. It is, however, incompatible with such other styles of marriage as the Judaic-Christian style.

Two-step marriage

A number of types of multiple-step marriage have been advocated in the United States in recent years, and various types of multiple-step marriage have been practiced in other cultures.[2] The first time multiple-step marriage received wide attention in the United States was when a judge (Lindsey, 1927) advocated a form of marriage that he referred to as Companionate marriage. He argued, and such scholars as Russell (1929) echoed approval, that many of the problems in the marriage system would be solved if young couples would (a) have quasi-permanent relationships to determine how compatible they were, (b) have legally sanctioned sexual accessibility, and (c) defer parenthood until a later, more appropriate time. Subsequently numerous scholars advocated various forms of trial marriage, even though they used slightly different labels to describe this style of marriage. Mead (1966), for example, referred to this system as "two-step" marriage, and Satir (1967) referred to it as a "statutory five year renewable contract." Packard (1968) separated the stages by advocating that the first two years of marriage be a "conformation period."

The distinguishing characteristics of multiple-step marriage are that there is more than one type of marital relationship and that these types occur in sequential order. In the first marital relationship the individuals usually live together, cohabit sexually, and form one economic unit, but they do not have children. The second relationship involves a more permanent commitment and includes the bearing and rearing of children. It is usually assumed that the first relationship can be easily terminated if the couple find it unsatisfactory. The first relationship also seems to have a testing or "try it out to see if it is what we want" connotation about it, and there is usually no social pressure for the couples to stay together if things do not work out. The first relationship thus tends to be viewed as a prelude to a more enduring commitment. This is in contrast to the Temporary type of marriage discussed later, in which there is no connotation that the marriage is "leading to" something else. The Temporary marriage is regarded as an end in itself, and the couples expect to have as many Temporary marriages as they find desirable and appropriate.

The advocates of Two-Step marriage have specified little about the nature of the later, parental marriage, so it seems feasible to combine the Two-Step style of marriage with several of the other forms of marriage. Certain types of marriage, however, are not compatible with the Two-Step alternative. For example, the sacred nature and high emphasis on stability of the Judaic-Christian style of marriage are incompatible with the trial-and-error philosophy of

---

[2] One form of trial marriage was practiced by the Trobrianders (Malinowski, 1929). Another form has been used for centuries by several South American Indian tribes (Price, 1965; MacLean, 1941). A third form has been used in parts of Europe (Gibney, 1948).

the Two-Step alternative. At present there are no legal provisions for the Two-Step form of marriage, but many couples are in effect adopting this style of marriage because of the way they define their marital relationship.

Temporary marriage

One innovative style of marriage that has been emerging in contemporary society has not yet been given a distinctive label. Some, such as Slater (1968) and Ramey (1972), refer to it as the *Temporary* style. Others refer to it as heterosexual cohabitation (Macklin, 1972). Some have used the term *living together* (Firestone, 1970), and others have termed it *unmarried marriage* (Karlen, 1969). Whitehurst (1969) coined the term *unmalias* to refer to one version of this form of marriage by contracting the words *unmarried college liaisons*. No one term has yet been widely used to label this style of marriage. One reason for this is that it is probably the least marriagelike form of all the alternative life-styles that are currently advocated. Nonetheless, it is sufficiently distinctive from conventional forms of marriage and the other alternatives to be included here under the label Temporary marriage.

The Temporary style of marriage is one in which the couple enter into the relationship for the satisfactions and rewards that are inherent in the relationship at the given time, and have the expectation that as they change or as they encounter different situations or circumstances the relationship may not last. They may then enter into another fairly permanent, pair-bonded relationship, live singly, or enter into a different type of marital relationship. They may or may not resume their "marriage" at a later time, depending on the circumstances. Temporary couples usually seem to value a monogamous relationship, but they do not want to be restricted by a host of legal obligations, long-term expectations, parental responsibilities, or financial obligations. However, their relationship occasionally evolves into a more long-term, conventional style of marriage.

Some scholars prefer that this type of pair-bonding not be labeled as marriage, but if it is not a type of marriage it is very similar to marriage in many ways. Usually Temporary couples live together much, if not all, of the time. They have unrestricted sexual activity, and they invariably form some type of division of household tasks. The couple are also usually one financial unit, though Temporary college couples are frequently not economically independent and hence often do not form an economic unit. Moreover, the relationship is usually entered into to meet intimate emotional needs which for all practical purposes are essentially the same as the needs met by most of the other forms of marriage.

One unique aspect of Temporary marriages is that frequently

there are no explicit commitments either when the marriages begin or when they end. A Temporary relationship may develop in a very spontaneous undeliberate manner, and it may dissolve in much the same way. Many of the couples in these relationships never explicitly discuss whether they ought to start living together. This just happens with staying together several weekends and then for longer periods until they have evolved into a Temporary "marriage."

Another important way in which the Temporary style of marriage differs from more conventional marriage styles is that both couple members expect the relationship to be short-term. It will last as long as they want it to and will be dissolved as circumstances and relationships change. Most Temporary couples practice contraception and want to defer the birth of children, so the Temporary style is a marital relationship rather than a spouse-parent arrangement. It is possible, however, that in the future some segments of society may adopt the same degree of spontaneity, freedom from commitment, and temporary characteristics and also attempt to raise children. If such a pattern is occurring now, however, it does not yet have the visibility of the purely "marital" Temporary style.

A marriage style that is desired by a large segment of the American population is what Martinson (1960, Chap. 3) has termed the Judaic-Christian model. As he pointed out, this style of marriage has deep cultural roots that are millennia old and was the dominant type in the Western world for centuries.

The Judaic-Christian marriage

The advocates of this system believe that since the essential ingredients of the marital institution have a divine origin they should not be changed or taken lightly. These essential ingredients include the belief that marriage should be a lifelong relationship unless extenuating circumstances, such as infidelity, prevent it from achieving this ideal. The marital relationship is viewed as the one place in which intimate sexual activity is appropriate, and marriage is viewed as a sacrament rather than as a civil contract. Other essential aspects of marriage according to this perspective are that it is designed to meet intimate emotional and spiritual needs through such activities as companionate interaction and emotional support. Advocates of this system view marriage as the only social institution that should be used for the bearing and rearing of children, and hence would oppose the assumption of these functions by other social institutions. It is also explicitly advocated in this system that the male should be the "head" of the home, though it is usually pointed out that this should not be in a tyrannical or absolute sense. Most contemporary thinkers advocate that this be done with a democratic or equalitarian method of decision making, but traditionally the Judaic-Christian approach to marriage has resulted in patriarchal family relationships. Martinson summarized the Judaic-Christian style of marriage in the following manner:

> These, then are the essential elements of the Judaic-Christian marriage model: It is an institution created by God for man's good and His glory. When two persons marry they become one—"one flesh"—a mysterious union understood only in the mind of God. This union, once established, is permanent and not to be set aside by man. The purposes of marriage are unity, procreation and education of children, and an outlet for sexual desire (1960, p. 41).

Eternal marriage

A unique subtype of the Judaic-Christian style of marriage occurs in the Mormon culture. This subtype is called *Eternal* marriage.[3] Mormons believe that when marriages are solemnized in special temples and the couples conform rather rigorously to the principles and tenets of the Mormon faith the marriages will continue in a postmortal life. The Eternal style of marriage is thus in one way at an opposite pole from the Temporary style because couples plan to live together forever.

Mormons also believe that those individuals who "endure to the end in righteousness" can progress in their postmortal life to a point at which they eventually become "Gods" and create other earths. This progression and Godlike condition cannot, however, be achieved by individuals. It must be achieved by married couples. This means that the marital relationship has an otherworldly orientation in many ways, since routine daily events are seen as preparation for what is believed to be an exalted future.

Another characteristic of this marriage style is that parents and children expect to have a parent-child relationship in their postmortal life. They believe that they will all be adults in their postmortal life and expect the postmortal relationship between parents and children to be much like the relationship between adult married children and their not-yet-aged parents. One effect of this belief is that having children and creating permanent relationships with them is an integral part of the marital relationship. The belief also has the side effect of maintaining a rather close-knit kinship network.

Another aspect of the Eternal marriage alternative is that one form of polygamy is permissible. This form is the one in which one husband is married to more than one wife. A legal struggle between the Mormon church and the federal government in the late 19th century eventually forced Mormons to stop contracting polygamous marriages. However, many modern Mormon couples expect to live in polygamous marriage in the postmortal life because if a wife

---

[3] Descriptions of Eternal marriage are found in Widtsoe (1945), Brown (1960), and Porter (1968).

dies before her husband it is possible for the husband to contract a second Eternal marriage with another woman.

The religious beliefs of the Mormon subculture influence the day-to-day interaction in the Eternal style of marriage in several other ways. Sexual interaction is supposed to be confined to the marital relationship, and sexual intercourse outside that relationship is viewed as a moral offense second in seriousness only to murder. Marital and family life are also closely tied to social and service activities in the church, and family life is thus a part of a more inclusive religious experience. This includes, among those committed to this style of life, such things as having the family spend at least one evening each week in a "family home evening" at which they plan religious lessons and recreational activities as a family. It also includes viewing the marital contract as a sacred arrangement rather than as a legal contract that can be easily modified or broken. Divorce is permitted, but it is usually viewed as a serious measure that should be used only as a last resort.

Group marriage

A Group marriage is defined in modern literature as a group of three or more persons in which the individuals consider themselves pair-bonded or married to at least two other members of the group (Constantine and Constantine, 1971; Ramey, 1972). Group marriages include such combinations as a couple and a single person, two couples, two couples and a single person, three couples, and so on. Group marriages have been reported in several anthropological studies,[4] but until very recently they were fairly uncommon in the United States. With the recent relaxation of many social taboos, however, it has become apparent that a number of couples prefer this style of marriage even though it is not currently legal. Usually Group marriages are begun by couples who have already established a monogamous marriage and then either join with other couples or add a third person. Occasionally, however, especially in communal living arrangements, Group marriages do not have "couples" as the basic unit when they begin. There is some evidence (Ramey, 1972) that these groups usually number fewer than seven individuals and that the most common number is three.

Group marriages have several characteristics that are uniquely

---

[4] Linton (1936, pp. 181–82) describes Group marriage among the Marquesan Islanders, and Henry (1964) describes another form of marriage among an Indian tribe in South America. Murdock (1949, pp. 24–25) argues that no society has ever been discovered in which Group marriage was the predominant form of marriage, but he too, describes several societies in which a small minority of marriages are Group marriages. Westermarck (1922, vol. 1, p. 103) argues that most prehistoric marriages were probably closer to a Group form of marriage than to any of the other forms known.

different from those of the other styles of marriage. Usually, but not always, intimate sexual activity, such as sexual intercourse, occurs in all of the cross-sex relationships and, occasionally homosexual relationships develop in the same-sex relationships. The homosexual relationships seem to be more common among the female than the male pairs, and, apparently, female homosexual combinations are less disruptive than male combinations (Constantine and Constantine, 1971). Also, Group marriage demands considerably more commitment, time, energy, and effort than do the simpler forms of marriage, and the larger the group the more demanding the interpersonal relationships. This is partly the case just because of the increased complexity of the relationships. When three are married there are three possible pair combinations, and when six are married, there are 21 possible pair combinations as well as a number of other possible clique combinations. Given the tendency of humans to have such reactions as jealousy, feeling left out, resentments, and a need for esteem, group arrangements can become extremely complex. Many of the couples who opt for the Group style, however, argue that the satisfactions, joys, and advantages—in other words, what you get out of Group marriage—are proportional to what you put into it. They recognize the complexities and the demands that Group marriage makes on them, and they still consciously and deliberately choose this style of life. Some believe that Group marital relationships are a more mature or advanced type than the less complex marital relationships, and the following example illustrates this view:

My ideal of marriage is a union of more than three adults with a total equalitarian position and shared social and economic responsibilities. I would not limit the number of people that can be involved, but there should be at least four. To have a marriage of less than four would tend to regenerate some of the same problems that occur in the monogamous marriage. The members of this union should be sexually compatible and not limited to just the opposite sex. Bisexuality would be practiced not only in sexual relations, but in the attitudes toward raising children.

The roles each member assigns himself are to be of his own choosing. Any role may be adopted so long as it is fulfilling to the individual and not destructive to the family unit. The release of frustrations and tensions would be an organized function of the group. The number of adults in the household offers the possibility for a better parent-child relationship. The child could interact with a larger number of adults. The sharing of the economic responsibility is a major step toward lessening the tension in the home. My type of marriage would spread the cost of living across all members thus reducing financial problems. Each member would give as much as possible and share equally in the security and comforts with the group (Cox, 1974, p. 3).

One other characteristic of the Group style of marriage is that most of the people who seem to be choosing and remaining with this style in contemporary society are older adults. Seldom are individuals under 30 found in group relationships (Ramey, 1972). Some groups of individuals live together for a few weeks or even several months when they are younger, but these younger groups usually tend to be very short-term arrangements and are closer to being Temporary marriages than Group marriages. Marriagelike groups also occur in some of the communal arrangements associated with college campuses, but these arrangements are generally a unique style of dormitory living in which a group of individuals live together and are sexually available to one another while in a temporary living arrangement. The individuals concerned seldom view this as even a semipermanent pair-bonding, let alone a marital arrangement.

Traditional marriage

My ideal man-woman relationship would be the traditional marriage. When I marry, I want a formal wedding. I have always dreamed of having a big wedding. This type of wedding is normal to me since my family has always talked about it. Although my husband-to-be doesn't like everything about a big wedding, he has told me that if I want it he will go along with it.

I am not a strong person who easily makes decisions. No matter what I want, I will let him tell me what he wants. If I don't have anything special I want to do, then we will do what he wants. I will love waiting on him and doing special things for him to show my love. An ideal man-woman relationship to me means total open communication, being able to express yourself and knowing that he will listen and not turn you off. It also means being able to put your husband first before yourself, giving him encouragement when he is down, building his ego and showing him your love which will in turn bring thoughtfulness and considerations back to me (Cox, 1974, p. 2).

There is some risk in trying to identify a "traditional style of marriage" because most of us tend to read different things into the established, typical, old-fashioned style of life. This selective definition of the past is documented by research by Furstenburg (1966) and Lantz (1968, 1974), who have demonstrated that many of the views we have of "traditional" courtship and marriage are distortions. For example, many people think that in bygone times in America the parents chose the mates for their children, women did not really have much power over their husbands, people married for economic reasons rather than for personal happiness, "romantic" love was not really very important to couples, parents were restrictive rather than permissive, and men and women were content with the roles that fate seemed to give them. Furstenberg and

Lantz have demonstrated that there is excellent evidence that all of these beliefs about traditional life in America are unfounded. Perceptions of Traditional marriage forms are also distorted because individuals who want to return to the "good old days," are likely to select only a few of the most preferred aspects of the old style of life as characterizing their ideal. This, of course, describes the approach of many older people who are concerned about what is happening with the younger generation. On the other hand, younger individuals who want to abandon the established patterns in favor of better ways also frequently select only part of the Traditional forms and try to change them. Nevertheless, at the risk of identifying a style of marriage that is not really preferred by anyone, it seems useful to go out on a limb and try to describe a fairly Traditional style of marriage.

The Traditional couple probably experience a great deal of excitement, optimism, euphoria, and love at the beginning of their marriage. They are firmly convinced that their love is different from the type of love that most married couples experience and that they will not encounter the apathy or many of the difficulties and monotonies that characterize the marriages of the masses. Divorce is something that happens to couples who "don't have what we have." Traditional couples usually struggle economically in the initial years of marriage. They plan on having several children, but they don't want a large family. They don't view their marriage as a particularly religious experience or as a mere contract that is easily broken. Rather, they simply assume that it is *the* way to live. They are not sure just what their marriage will be like in many ways, but they are able to communicate and work things out well enough to be sure that their marriage will be a deeply rewarding experience.

The husband and wife roles will be fairly different in that the husband will be the primary source of income. The wife will assume the primary responsibility for running the household even though the husband will be expected to help out somewhat. If the wife works it will probably not be to have a career. She will work because they need money or because she needs to get out of the house. The couple will find in the first few years of their marriage that their relationship will become fairly routine, with such things as watching TV, taking care of the kids, reading the paper, fixing something in the house, getting the kids to the doctor, and other daily tasks occupying most of the time. The euphoria of the first few months will disappear as practical concerns such as house payments, vaccinations, frayed cuffs, pay raises, strikes, insurance, dripping taps, promotions, PTA, Little League, buying shoes, and getting dishes done take its place. Life will not be unpleasant, but the couple will gradually realize that they are getting older, that they aren't going to revolutionize the world, and that life is really quite ordinary. Their sexual activity, social life, and companionship will become routine, and sex will be confined primarily to the marriage even though both individuals will have exotic sexual fantasies.

As the years pass the couple will spend less time going out. They will still do some things together, and both will have important relationships outside the marriage. In fact, in many ways the persons who understand them best will be persons other than the spouse. Married life will have its share of surprises, excitements, joys, and satisfactions, but most of the time it will be quite ordinary and routine.

It is possible to identify several basic *dimensions* of marital relationships and to use these dimensions to compare and contrast the alternative forms of marriage. In doing so it becomes evident that some of the alternatives are similar to others on some of the dimensions and that each of the alternatives is uniquely different from all of the others on at least one of the dimensions. Fourteen dimensions are identified and discussed below and Table 1–1 is an attempt to briefly summarize how the various alternatives differ on these dimensions.

Dimensions in the alternative styles

1. *The value of stability.* This dimension deals with how important it is for a marriage to be a permanent or lasting relationship. In some alternatives couples want their marriage to be a lifelong relationship, and in others couples expect to have short-term relationships and to change partners once or more in their lifetime. The alternative in which stability is valued least is the Temporary marriage, and the forms in which stability is valued most are the Judaic-Christian, Eternal, Intrinsic, and Traditional styles. The amount of stability is not an issue in Utilitarian, Open, and Group marriages.

2. *The disruptiveness of divorce.* In some of the marital alternatives divorce is extremely traumatic, and in others the process of terminating a marital relationship is less difficult. Divorce is probably most traumatic in the Intrinsic, Judaic-Christian, Eternal, and Traditional styles. It is probably least disruptive in the Temporary and Utilitarian styles and in the first stage of the Two-Step style.

3. *The amount of companionship expected.* This dimension refers to the amount of friendly, companionate interaction that individuals expect in their marital relationship. Some individuals want the spouse to be their best friend, and others expect to find the main sources of companionship outside their marriage. Couples who have Intrinsic and Temporary styles of marriage seem to expect the

greatest amounts of companionship, and couples with Utilitarian marriages seem to expect the least. Traditional couples probably expect considerable companionship in their marriage when they are first married but frequently find later that they have little. The amount of companionship expected probably varies a great deal from couple to couple in the Open style of marriage, and this also seems to be the case with most of the other styles.

4. *Equality of the sexes.* The Open, Temporary, and Swinging styles of marriage seem to expect the most equality of the sexes. The Traditional, Judaic-Christian, and Eternal types probably have the most rigidly defined sex roles, and the net effect of these definitions is to create patriarchal dominance. There seems to be great variability from couple to couple in the other types.

5. *Desire for children.* Children are highly desired in the Traditional, Judaic-Christian, and Eternal types of marriage and in the second stage of the Two-Step marriage. Children are definitely not wanted in the first stage of the Two-Step marriage, and they may or may not be wanted in the other styles of marriage.

6. *Approval of extramarital sexual activity.* Intimate sexual interaction outside the marital relationship, such as petting and coitus, is desired in some styles and prohibited in others. Swinging is the style that encourages extramarital sex the most, but many who want to have an Open style of marriage are probably also open to extramarital sexual activity. Extramarital sex is viewed as the most undesirable in the Judaic-Christian and Eternal forms of marriage, but most couples with an Intrinsic marriage probably also prefer marital fidelity. Consistent with traditional practices, couples in the Traditional type of marriage probably view extramarital sexual activity as more serious for the wife than for the husband.

7. *The importance of legal sanction of the marriage.* Most couples with Intrinsic, Utilitarian, Judaic-Christian, Eternal, Traditional, and Two-Step marriages probably view legal approval of their marriage as important. Couples in the United States who have Temporary and Group marriages, however, do not seem to define legal sanction as important. Most couples with a Swinging style of marriage have a legally sanctioned marriage, even though the swinging may not be legal.

8. *The importance of marriage.* Couples differ in the importance they attach to the marital part of their life as compared to other aspects, such as personal development, a profession, interaction with friends, and leisure-time pursuits. Couples with Intrinsic and Eternal marriages define the marital relationship as among the most important aspects of their life. Couples with other forms, such as Utilitarian and Temporary marriages, usually define the marital relationship as subservient to many other things.

9. *The intensity of the affect toward the spouse.* In some marital relationships, such as Intrinsic marriages and the beginning of the Traditional marriage, it is usually expected that couples will have an intense love for each other. In other styles the same degree of affect is seldom, if ever, expected. The Utilitarian type probably values affect the least, but affect is also probably not important to many couples with Traditional, Judaic-Christian, and Eternal marriages, especially later in the marriage. Couples who have Open marriages probably vary considerably in the amount of affect they want.

10. *The complexity of the marital relationship.* Some marital styles have very complex interrelationships, and others have relatively simple and uncomplicated ways of interacting. The Group marriage is probably the most complex, and the Utilitarian and Temporary marriages the least complex. The relationships are also probably more complex in Eternal, Intrinsic, and Open marriages than in other marital styles because more is demanded from such marriages.

11. *The amount of change expected in the relationship.* The Open style of marriage includes the expectation that the nature of the relationship will probably change dramatically as new situations and developmental interests are encountered. Other styles, however, such as the Traditional and Intrinsic types, seem to expect fairly stable ways of relating.

12. *The amount individuality or personal development is valued.* The Open style of marriage values individual development extremely highly, and the Utilitarian and Temporary styles also seem to give it high priority. The Traditional, Judaic-Christian, and Intrinsic forms seem to give the least priority to individuality.

13. *Amount of involvement with kin.* In the Traditional, Judaic-Christian, and Eternal types of marriage the couples are usually highly involved with kinship relationships. In the Temporary type of marriage, however, there often seems to be little, if any, involvement with kin. In most of the other styles of marriage there seems to be considerable variation from couple to couple in the amount of interaction with kin.

14. *Intensity of the bonds that tie the couple.* The Intrinsic, Eternal, Traditional, and Judaic-Christian types of marriage have many different bonds that tie the individuals together, and these bonds tend to be complex and intense. Other types, however, such as Temporary and Utilitarian marriages and the first stage of the Two-Step types, have fewer and less complex bonds.

This analysis of the dimensions of ten marital alternatives has several practical consequences. One consequence is that it provides some order to what would otherwise be a hodgepodge collection of

Table 1–1

Dimensions in the ten alternative styles of marriage discussed in Chapter 1

	Intrinsic	Utilitarian	Open	Swinging
1. Value of stability.....................	Very high	Varies*	Varies	High
2. Disruptiveness of divorce............	Very high	Low	Low	†
3. Amount of companionship expected..	Very high	Limited amount	Varies	
4. Equality of the sexes.................	Varies	Varies	Equal	Equal
5. Desire for children...................	Probably	Varies	Varies	
6. Approval of extramarital sexual activity...............................	Usually no	Varies	Yes	Yes
7. Importance of legal sanction.........	High	Varies	High	High
8. Importance of marriage compared to other aspects of life..................	Very high	Low	High	Usually high
9. Intensity of the affect................	Very high	Usually not high	Varies	Varies
10. Complexity of the marital relationship..........................	High	Lowest	High	High
11. Amount of change expected in marital relationship..................	Low	Varies	High	High
12. Amount personal development is valued..............................	Varies	High	Very high	
13. Amount of involvement with kin......				Low
14. Intensity of marital bonds............	Very high	Low	High	Usually high

* "Varies" means that there is considerable variation in this style of marriage on this particular dimension. Some want the marriage to be one way and some another.

† Column is left blank if the trait is not a distinguishing characteristic of a particular style of marriage and if the literature describing the style of marriage doesn't necessarily state that there is variation on this dimension.

Two-Step	Temporary	Judaic-Christian	Eternal	Group	Traditional	My preferred Style
Low/High	Very low	Very high	Very high	Varies	High	_____
Low	Very low	High	High	Varies	High	_____
High	Very high	Varies	Varies	High	Seldom high	_____
	Equal	Unequal	Unequal	Varies	Unequal	_____
No/Yes	No	Yes	Yes	Usually	Yes	_____
		No	No	Varies	No	_____
Ideally high	Low	High	High	Low	High	_____
	Varies	High	Very high	Usually high	Varies	_____
	High	Varies	Varies		High then low	_____
Low/High	Low	High	High	Highest	High	_____
		Low	Low		Low	_____
	Varies	Varies	Varies	Varies	Low	_____
	Low	High	Very high		High	_____
	Very low	High	High	Varies	Usually high	_____

unique styles of marriage. Another is that it enables us to evaluate each of these dimensions and to use them to help us describe the style of marriage that we want in our own life. Most of us can describe our own preferred style of marriage better by paying attention to the different dimensions than we can by merely identifying which of the various alternatives is closest to our preferred style of life. The far right column in Table 1–1 illustrates a useful way to do this by describing what we would want on each of these 14 dimensions. This description would be far from complete because there are many other factors most of us would want to take into account, but it would be a start.

In conclusion   Each of the ten marital life-styles discussed above is advocated by one or more cultural groups as the preferred style of marriage, and there are *many* other styles, such as the Two-Career Family, Child-Centered, Contractual, Permissive Matrimony (Casler, 1974), and Symmetric styles of marriage. The ten styles discussed here were selected because they illustrate the broad spectrum of choices available, not because they are an exhaustive list of all the desired possibilities. In addition it is, of course, also possible to identify many other marital life-styles that are common but not preferred. Cuber and Harroff (1966), for example, identify several less than ideal types that they label the Conflict-Habituated, Passive-Congenial, Devitalized, and Misalliance styles of marriage. These terms are fairly descriptive of the relationships that occur in them. The Conflict-Habituated style is a relationship with tension, differences of opinion that interfere with the relationship, and usually a continual struggle for power. The Passive-Congenial relationship is one of resignation to one's situation, and the Devitalized relationship is one in which there is a clear discrepancy between what the marriage once was and what it eventually evolved into. Usually couples in Devitalized relationships say that they were "deeply in love" and highly companionate during the early years of the marriage, but that their relationship degenerated into one in which most of their interaction became "duty time" or fulfilling obligations. The Misalliance is a relationship in which the couple are clearly mismated but for a number of reasons consider it best not to terminate the marriage. The conclusions that emerge are that there is a virtually infinite variety of marital styles and that it would be impossible to get consensus about which style is really in any absolute or ultimate sense the best type for everyone.

SO . . . WHAT IS MARITAL SUCCESS?

This description of some of the different styles of marriage that are available in contemporary society makes it unavoidably clear that a description of marital "success" that is limited to only one or a few of these styles would be inappropriate as it would not be valid for most or all of the others. Because of this the view of marital "success" used in this book is that such success is something that occurs from the point of view of the participants in a marriage rather than from the point of view of society, social scientists, or one particular subcultural attitude toward marriage. Marital success is therefore defined as the *degree to which an individual's marital goals are attained.* Those individuals who attain more of their goals in marriage are more successful than those who attain fewer goals.

People enter into legal forms of marriage and into various non-legal marital arrangements because they want to attain certain ends or goals. Sometimes, as in some Utilitarian marriages, there may be only a few goals, such as wanting to maintain a certain social image, to obtain help in entertaining, or to conform to the expectations of a family. In other styles of marriage, such as In-trinsic marriage, couples have many goals, such as wanting to acquire a deeply experienced intimacy with another person, to meet complex emotional needs, to become genuinely one in purpose, style, and feeling. In all marital styles, however, *there are GOALS.*

People may not have a very accurate or thorough awareness of their goals, but nonetheless the goals exist, and as far as this book is concerned the success of a marriage is the degree to which those goals are met. The goals are not the objectives of a society, a social class, an organization, a subculture, or any other social unit. They are the goals of the individual couples themselves, and each married couple has its unique set of goals. Some of these goals are widely shared in society or in subcultural groups, but each couple also has some unique goals, and each couple's total set of goals is undoubtedly always unique.

Thus, in this book no attempt is made to describe the style of marriage that is the "ideal" or "best" style. Any attempt to do so would be provincial, narrow, and limited to a unique culture or group of cultures. This is the case because what one group views as ideal is frequently rejected by another and because what one group views as irrelevant is important to another. In addition to this "cultural" objection to defining a particular style of courtship and marriage as "ideal" or "best," there is another reason why it is in-appropriate and impossible to describe the one "best" style of marital life. There is evidence that people make substantial changes (Brim, 1966; Duvall, 1967; Foote, 1956) and encounter new and different situations in the course of their life cycle. At the beginning of adulthood most people are busily courting and marrying, and they have a set of goals unique to that particular stage of life. Sixty years later, however, they are coping with very different situations and have very different goals. The ideal form of marriage at age 80 may be very different from the ideal form at age 20. To illustrate the point that developmental changes make it impossible to describe any one form of marriage as the ideal style, let us see how a couple might want one thing at age 20 and just the opposite at age 80. At age 20 most people are trying to grow close to someone else and to build what are termed close "bonds" with that person. At this stage of life one goal of marriage might be to *increase* the marital bonds. However, when these same people are considerably older and their spouses have recently died, or even when they are somewhat older and a divorce is imminent, they may want to learn ways to decrease the "bonds" that tie them to the marital partner.

How can this book help individuals attain such a variety of goals?

If individuals are unique in their goals, and if there are such very different goals in the alternative styles of marriage, how can one book be useful in helping people achieve success (attain goals) in their marital experience? Part of the answer to this question is that *this book deals with only a selected group of marital goals and simply ignores many other marital goals.* The goals that are dealt with here tend to fall into two general types. The first type consists of a few goals that are common to all the styles of marriage. In virtually all, if not all, of the various styles of marriage (1) we want to have effective communication and (2) we want to develop the ability to make efficient and satisfying decisions. Few couples, if any, want to become the best communicators or decision makers in the world. This would take too much energy, time, and resourcefulness, and expending effort in becoming excessively good at these two things would detract from other valued aspects of life. However, most, if not all, couples have a goal of acquiring and maintaining an adequate level of proficiency in both communication and decision making. It also happens that these are two areas in which the social sciences have considerable information. A number of general principles have been discovered about communication and decision making, and some of these principles are discussed in later chapters. As couples learn these principles and then use them they can better attain the goals of adequate communication and efficient decision making.

Another goal that is common to all of the marriage styles is that of attaining the ability to cope with the inevitable tragedies and stresses of life. Unfortunate events, such as the death of a spouse or child, serious injury from an automobile accident, or a crippling illness, occur in and to families; and one of the goals in most marriages is learning how to cope with such events in ways that minimize their unpleasant aspects and their disruptive effects on other aspects of life. This too is an area in which the social sciences have learned a great deal, and many of the related principles are discussed in Chapter 16.

The second type of marital goal that is included in the following chapters has to do with some of the dimensions in Table 1–1. As illustrated in that table, the goals in regard to these dimensions are frequently very different in the alternative styles of marriage, but the *dimensions* occur in all forms of marriage. One example of how this book can help couples attain goals about these dimensions has to do with the affectionate feeling or sentiment that we refer to as "love." Most, if not all, couples want to have some form of love in their marital relationship. The difference in the alternative lifestyles is that some individuals want one amount of love and others want a different amount. For example, most of the people who want an Intrinsic type of marriage want intense and encompassing love feelings in their marriage, but in several of the other styles of marriage, such as the Utilitarian and Traditional types, couples frequently do not want to engage in the rather demanding behaviors that would create these intense love feelings. The point here is that the *dimension* of love exists in all marital relationships, and that most, if not all, people have the goal of attaining a certain amount of this dimension. The way this book is useful in helping couples attain their goals in regard to this dimension is that it identifies general principles that couples can use to increase, decrease, or just maintain the amount of sentiment (love feelings) they have.

A number of dimensions of marital interaction other than the love dimension are discussed in the following chapters. One is the "bondedness" of relationships. This refers to the strength of the ties that bind the members of a couple or hold them together. A strong feeling of love toward one's spouse is one source of bondedness, but love and bondedness are two different dimensions, and there are many things other than love that hold married people together. This volume identifies a number of general principles about bondedness which couples can use to increase, decrease, or maintain their bondedness.

No book can be all things to all people, and this one will not be useful in helping couples attain many of the unique goals in some of the alternative styles. The principles identified here are applicable to at least several of the marital alternatives, and there tends to be a bias toward identifying principles that are useful in the most dominant and widely preferred alternatives.

One way to increase the usefulness of this book is to develop a fairly clear definition of one's own marital goals. This is valuable because the principles that are identified in the following chapters provide only information about *how* to attain a variety of goals, and

Table 1–2

Other dimensions of marriage on which couples may have
goals

Amount of intimacy with friends
Amount of intellectual stimulation
Will it be a dual-career or a single-career marriage?
Amount of affection
Amount of "romance"
How much will "personal development" be emphasized?
How much do you want to travel?
Will you have a "close to nature" style of life?
Will you have a small-town—rural—cosmopolitan style of life?
Will you have equal say when disagreements arise?
Amount of privacy

Marriages tend to have certain "themes." What will yours be?
Some examples of themes are:
    Outdoorish
    Leisure oriented
    Intellectual
    Work oriented
    Religious
    Sports oriented
    Centered on cultural events

the principles are of no value until we have determined *what* our
personal goals are. The dimensions in Table 1–1 provide some
things to think about in determining the type of marriage we want,
and the additional aspects listed in Table 1–2 identify some additional dimensions. The following exercise describes one way to
think through and write down our own preferred marital goals.

WHAT DO I WANT IN MARRIAGE?

Goal: To develop a clearer and more comprehensive definition of
        my own marital goals.

1.   Write a description of what I want my own marriage to be. It
     should be several pages long, and it should include:

     a. Goals that are absolutely essential.

     b. Characteristics of marriage that are completely unacceptable.

     c. Goals that would be desirable but are not absolutely essential.

SUMMARY

A wide variety of types of legal marriage and of nonlegal marriagelike relationships are available in the modern world. Several of

these types were reviewed in this chapter to illustrate the variety of these options and to demonstrate that there is no one BEST style of marriage for everyone. Each of us thus has to decide which alternative or group of alternatives is best for us in our life situation when our philosophy of life and the opportunities available to us are taken into account. Some styles of marriage that are desirable and moral when viewed from one particular system of values and beliefs are undesirable and immoral when viewed from a different set of values and beliefs. Fortunately, however (and this reveals one of the author's biases), society seems to be learning that styles that originate in and are consistent with divergent philosophical traditions ought to be more than just tolerated. These styles ought to be permitted in the recognition that the differences are honestly held and that no person or group should be in a position to determine by force or fiat which of the systems will remain or terminate.

The fact that these differences exist, however, does not mean that "success" in marital or marriagelike relationships is unique to these alternatives. There are commonalities among the alternatives, and it is possible to identify ways that general, scientific principles can be used to help us attain our goals. This book is an attempt to identify some of the goals that are important in a large number of the alternatives and then to identify some general principles that individuals and/or couples can use to help them attain those goals.

SUGGESTIONS FOR FURTHER STUDY

Bernard, Jessie   1972. *The Future of Marriage*. New York: World.

Bowman, Henry A.   1970. *Marriage for Moderns*. 6th ed. New York: McGraw–Hill, pp. 581–84.

Breedlove, William, and Breedlove, Jerrye   1964. *Swap Clubs*. Los Angeles: Sherbourne Press.

Brown, Hugh B.   1960. *You and Your Marriage*. Salt Lake City: Bookcraft.

Casler, Lawrence   1973. *Is Marriage Necessary?* New York: Human Sciences Press.

Cuber, John F., and Harroff, Peggy B.   1965. *The Significant Americans: A Study of Sexual Behavior among the Affluent*. New York: Appleton-Century-Crofts.

Kirkpatrick, Clifford   1963. *The Family as Process and Institution*. 2d ed. New York: Ronald Press, pp. 89–97.

Martinson, Floyd M.   1960. *Marriage and the American Ideal*. New York: Dodd, Mead, chaps. 3 and 4.

Mead, Margaret   1935. *Sex and Temperament in Three Primitive Societies*. New York: Morrow.

O'Neill, George C., and O'Neill, Nena   1972. *Open Marriage*. New York: Evans.

Otto, Herbert A.   1970. *The Family in Search of a Future.* New York: Appleton-Century-Crofts.

Porter, Blaine R.   1968. *The Latter Day Saint Family.* Salt Lake City: Deseret.

Rogers, Carl R.   1972. *Becoming Partners: Marriage and Its Alternatives.* New York: Delacorte Press.

Wells, J. Gibson   1975. *Current Issues in Marriage and the Family.* New York: Macmillan.

2

How to use general principles

THE PRIMARY GOAL of this book is to identify some information we can use in our personal lives to help us attain our marital goals; and there are several different strategies that could be used to attain this rather ambitious goal. One strategy would be to present case histories that identify a large number of the day-to-day situations, problems, and issues in premarital and marital interaction and then to discuss various ways to cope with these specific concerns. This approach has several advantages, but since there is an infinite number of specific issues that could be discussed, and since there are many different ways each issue could be effectively dealt with, a discussion of these specific problems would be an endless and inefficient strategy. In addition the author's experience is that this strategy is interesting and pleasant but that it is usually difficult to identify what is learned from its use that can be applied in a situation other than the unique situation that has been discussed.

An alternative strategy, and it is the one used here, is to search the scientific literature for a number of "general principles" of human behavior that can be applied to marriage and then (1) to present those principles in nontechnical language and (2) to provide some experiences that will help us learn ways to use the principles to attain our unique, individual goals in marriage. If the general principles that are selected can be used in many different premarital and marital situations this will turn out to be an efficient and useful procedure. Before this can be done, however, it is necessary that we have a common understanding of what is meant by a "gen-

33

eral principle." If some of us think principles are one thing, and others think they are something else, the ideas presented here will be more confusing than useful.

WHAT ARE GENERAL PRINCIPLES?

The progress of the social sciences in recent years enables us to make some fairly accurate and useful statements about how certain behaviors or situations influence other situations or behaviors. An example of one such statement is that when something threatens our self-esteem or feelings of self-worth we will almost always react in a very predictable way. We will do something to defend our feelings of adequacy or our acceptability as a person.[1] One of the things that makes this idea a principle is that it states that there is a *co-variational relationship* between threats to self-esteem and defensive behavior. A covariational relationship is one in which changes in one variable or factor are accompanied by changes in a different variable or factor. This principle states that increases in the amount of threat to self-esteem are accompanied by increases in the amount of defensive behavior and that decreases in threat bring about decreases in defensiveness. Or, stated slightly differently, threats to self-esteem and defensiveness covary.

A second aspect of the above statement that makes it a general principle is that it is *general* enough not to be limited to a particular culture or to a certain time or social situation. If threats to self-esteem were to bring about defensiveness only in a certain specific situation, the statement would not be a general principle. The generality of the above principle is illustrated by the fact that threats create defensiveness in different cultures, with old and young, with male and female, and that the principle operates even when people do not want it to.

A third aspect of a general principle is that it refers to two or more *variables*. Variables are factors, phenomena, or properties that can change. In other words, variables can assume different values. The amount of threat to self-esteem and the amount of defensiveness are the two variables in the example cited above. Both are variables because they can range from being absent to being very high. A person can have no threat, slight threat, or large threat to self-esteem, and a person can have no defensiveness, some defensiveness, or a large amount of defensiveness. Most variables can be diagramed in some manner, and these two can be diagramed in the following way:

---

[1] This principle is discussed in detail in Chapter 3. There the terms are defined, the principle is carefully stated, and the references to appropriate literature are cited.

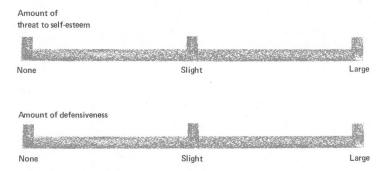

Amount of
threat to self-esteem

None   Slight   Large

Amount of defensiveness

None   Slight   Large

A fourth aspect of general principles is that they make an assertion about *how* two or more variables are related to each other. In the example cited above the greater the threat to self-esteem the greater the defensiveness and the less the threat the less the defensiveness. This type of relationship between variables is called a *positive* relationship because when one variable changes the other changes in the same direction. As one goes up, the other goes up; and as one goes down, the other goes down. This type of relationship can be diagramed by plotting the two variables on different axes, as is done in Figures 2–1 and 2–2. The horizontal axis is the amount of threat variable, and it is the causal factor. The vertical axis is the amount of defensiveness variable, and it is the variable that is influenced in a cause and effect statement. The terms that are usually used to refer to these variables are *independent* and *dependent variables*. The term *independent variable* is used to refer to the causal factor, and the term *dependent variable* is used to label the variable that is influenced. Figure 2–1 shows how the relationship can be diagramed with a bar graph, and Figure 2–2 shows the same relationship with a line graph. In Figure 2–2 the slanted line describes the relationship between the two variables since it shows that increases in threat are accompanied by increases in defensiveness, and vice versa.

A bar graph, such as the one in Figure 2–1, is the simplest way to diagram the relationships between variables, but other graphs communicate slightly more information. The same relationship that is diagramed in Figures 2–1 and 2–2 is also diagramed in a slightly different way in Figure 2–3, which uses lines to show the 10th, 50th, and 90th percentiles in a typical population. The center line shows that individuals who are at the 50th percentile in defensiveness have the same amount of control as the group depicted by the bar graph and the single-line graph. Their defensiveness goes up as the threat becomes high. The lines showing individuals who are at the 10th (low defensive reaction) and 90th (high defensive reaction) percentiles communicate some information that is not available in the bar graph or when just the 50th percentile line is used in a line

Figure 2–1

The relationship between threat to self-esteem and defensiveness as shown in a bar graph

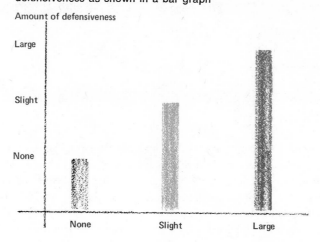

graph. These lines show that when threats are low there is a great deal of variability in the amount of defensiveness individuals have. Some people are very high in defensiveness, and some are very low. However, when the threat becomes large there is less variability, as virtually everyone is defensive. Since line graphs can communicate

Figure 2–2

The relationship between threat to self-esteem and defensiveness as shown in a line graph

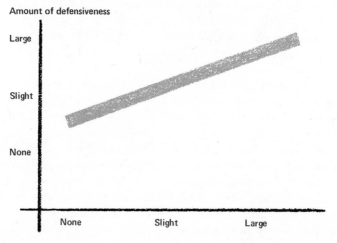

Figure 2–3

The relationship between threats to self-esteem and
defensiveness showing the 10th, 50th, and 90th
percentiles

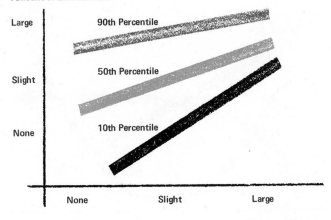

considerably more information about relationships than can bar
graphs, line graphs are used in the following chapters. Usually one
line is sufficient to describe a relationship, but occasionally "multiple line" graphs are necessary.

Another aspect of the relationship diagramed in these three figures is that it is *linear*. This means that the relationship or function
can be diagramed with a straight line. If the line describing the relationship were curved the relationship would be referred to as *curvilinear,* and lines *A, B,* and *C* in Figure 2–4 are examples of curvilinear relationships. The term *curvilinear* is not very specific since
all it says is that a relationship is not linear. It is therefore necessary
to describe the *shape* of a curvilinear relationship whenever one is
found. To illustrate this with the example of threat to self-esteem
and ensuing defensiveness, line *B* could describe a special population of people who show moderate defensiveness to threat until the
threat reaches a high level, whereupon those individuals *control*
their defensiveness at that level through various mechanisms.
It is possible to use mathematic symbols to describe the shape of
these relationships, but that would be too complex and unneces-
sarily technical for this book. Hence, a combination of verbal descriptions and line drawings, such as those in Figure 2–4, is used
here to describe the shape of nonlinear relationships.

Another type of relationship is called a *negative* relationship.
Here increases in one variable create or are associated with decreases in another variable, and, conversely, decreases in one vari-

Figure 2–4

Different shapes of relationships

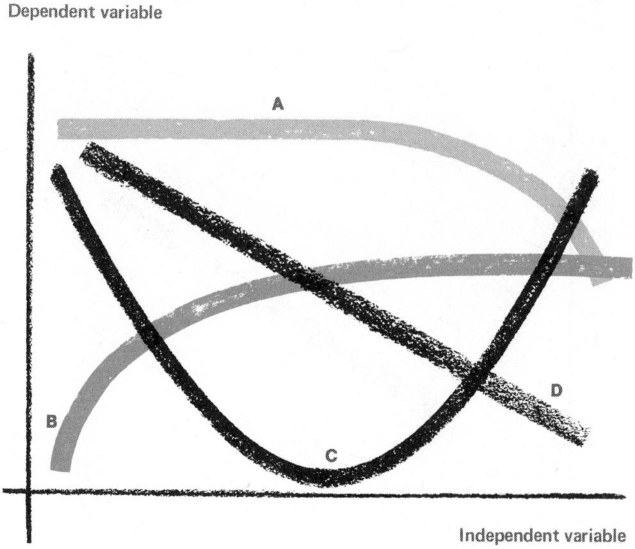

Dependent variable

Independent variable

able cause increases in another. A negative, linear relationship is diagramed in Figure 2–4, and line A shows a negative, curvilinear relationship.

Researchers and theorists in the sciences have identified a number of other characteristics of general principles, and if this book were a research monograph whose goals were to do such things as discover and test principles these other characteristics of principles would need to be explained. However, since the goal here is to understand principles and find ways to implement them in our personal lives, it is sufficient to understand the aspects of principles that have been discussed above.

It seems useful to review briefly the essential aspects of general principles. *General principles* are declarative sentences that have two or more *variables*. They identify that a *covariational relationship* exists between these variables, and they usually describe the nature of this relationship by identifying whether it is *positive* or *negative* and whether it is *linear* or *curvilinear*. If a relationship in a principle is curvilinear there is usually a description of the unique *shape* of the relationship. Principles are sufficiently *general* that they are not limited to certain events, situations, times, or places. If the meaning of the italicized words in the preceding sentences is understood there is enough understanding of general principles that the ideas presented in later chapters can be understood.

USING GENERAL PRINCIPLES

It is evident that learning general principles is one of the major goals of this book. An intellectual understanding of these principles, however, is only half of the process. The other half is learning how to *use* the principles in our personal life situations.

Using principles is not a process of consuming something, as we use a supply of pencils, and it is not a process of using something physically, as we use an electrical appliance or an automobile. General principles are ideas that identify the consequences of various actions or situations, and it is the *knowledge* that the principles provide that is used. The process of using principles can be illustrated with the principle that asserts that threats to self-esteem influence defensiveness. When people are aware of this principle *and* know how to manipulate threats to self-esteem, the principle gives them knowledge that they can use to increase or decrease the defensiveness in their interpersonal relationships. If they know how to decrease threats to self-esteem they can decrease defensiveness by decreasing threats to self-esteem. And if they want to increase defensiveness they can accomplish this by increasing threats to either their own or another person's self-esteem. What they are doing is using the knowledge provided by a general principle to effect change or to manipulate a variable in their life situation in order to bring about a particular consequence that they want in another variable. Stated slightly differently, when people decide which variable to change and how much to change it because they are aware of a general principle that identifies the consequences of their behavior, *they are using a general principle.*

Since the process of using principles involves more than just being aware of principles this book needs to do more than help readers acquire an intellectual understanding of the general propositions. It also needs to provide some suggestions about how to learn the skills or abilities that we need to know if we are to learn how to change the causal variables. Attempts are therefore made in the subsequent chapters to describe activities that will help us to *acquire* some of the skills we do not already have or to *increase* skills we do have.

Some of the activities suggested in the later chapters are real life situations we can do with someone else, such as a spouse, fiancé(e), date, parent, or friend. Other activities are simulated experiences, such as role playing and brainstorming, and hopefully these simulations will also help increase skills. Occasionally the suggested activities will seem artificial and unsophisticated, and some of them are; but readers might be interested in some comments of college students who have used these activities. A number of students have approached several of the activities with such comments as "You don't think I'm going to do that"; "You know, that seems awfully silly"; and "Do I *have* to do that?" A number of these same students, though, after having completed some of the exercises, made comments like the following: "You know, I really learned something from that"; "I didn't really understand the principle until after I did that corny exercise"; "I didn't for the life of me think it would make a difference, but it actually did"; "It works; I tried, and it really works; our relationship is really different."

These comments illustrate that it is sometimes difficult to determine the effect of the exercises until after they have been done. Afterward some that seemed as if they would be the most interesting turn out to be useless and some that at first seemed trite and irrelevant became real "Ah-ha!" experiences. Another aspect of the exercises is that the activities described in this book are only a sampling of the activities that can increase our ability to use the general principles discussed. The ones included are those that the author and several of his colleagues and students have devised, but there are undoubtedly many others that can help us attain the same skills. Hopefully, readers will invent original learning experiences when the ones provided are irrelevant or inappropriate. The author believes very strongly that merely having "book learning" about the principles will be of little value in our personal lives.[2] We have to actually *DO SOMETHING* with the principles before we will really understand them *or* be sure we have the ability to implement them. Learning what the principles are is half the job, and learning how to use them in our personal lives is the other half.

It is important to be tentative   Two criteria were used in determining which principles should be included in this book. The first criterion was that the author and his colleagues and students consider the principle to be useful in premarital and marital interaction in the contemporary United States. In order to meet this criterion a principle has to deal with something that is important in marriage and has to have an independent (causal) variable that can be manipulated or changed. The second criterion was that there be considerable evidence that the principle is valid. The first criterion is a matter of judgment, and there are undoubtedly many other principles not included here that are equally valuable in marriage. Only a finite number could be included, and hopefully readers will find many more in other places that they can also use to help make their marital and other relationships pleasant and rewarding.

The second criterion, however—that there be considerable evi-

---

[2] Those interested in literature dealing with this educational point of view will find Bloom (1956) useful.

dence that a principle is valid—is a much more complex matter, and it is something that readers and the author should be very sensitive about. The author has decided not to burden readers with all of the technical literature that assesses the pros and cons of each of the principles. Instead references are given in footnotes in the event that readers want to read further to find out how much evidence there is about the various principles. Readers will, however, want to realize that all of the principles are still very much in a "theoretical" stage. The social sciences are still so young that the principles cannot yet be viewed as social laws; and it is possible that additional thought and research will make it necessary to modify and qualify many of the principles in the future. Also, it may be that some of the principles will ultimately be shown to be incorrect. What this means is that these are the best principles the social sciences have to offer at this stage of their development and that they seem to most scholars in the field to have considerable credence. But the principles are not infallible, and all of us who use them should retain some tentativeness about their validity. Some are based on considerable empirical evidence, but others only have logical, rational, or intuitive justifications. The author hopes that this note of caution will not discourage readers from trying to use principles, but that it will encourage an appropriate degree of tentativeness and caution in using scientific ideas.

One aspect of this book that makes it appealing in some ways and problematic in other ways is that the scientific principles discussed in it are amoral. The principles do not advocate any particular style of life, philosophy of life, normative beliefs, or system of values. They say nothing about what a person "should" or "ought" to do in premarital and marital situations. They merely identify the consequences of behavior very much as laws in physics and astronomy identify the consequences of various physical and astronomical events. Those of us who elect to "use" the principles to help attain our goals do so on the basis of our unique, individual value systems, and those value systems can be religious or atheistic, traditional or innovative, legal or nonlegal. What we do is use our personal value systems to decide what we want to accomplish or attain and then implement the general principles to help us achieve those goals.

Utility without values

This process of identifying principles that are as free as possible from cultural values and then using them to attain our unique goals is one of the unique aspects of this book. It permits the principles (and hence the book) to be used by radically different groups of individuals. For example, the principles could be used by individuals in innovative communes to help them attain their goals; or they could be used by the most traditionally oriented segments of society. Couples in such divergent cultural groups as Mennonite, Jewish, Protestant, Indian, Black, Mormon, artistic, and aesthetic, could use the principles to help them attain their particular goals. Some of these groups will want to increase factors that other groups will want to decrease, and some will view as irrelevant aspects of this book which others will view as important, but the process of applying principles holds for all groups. All of us in our various cultural groups are influenced in the same way by physical laws of the universe, and as we become aware of those physical laws we can use them to help us attain our unique cultural goals. In the same sense we are also influenced by social and psychological laws, and as we gradually learn these laws we can also use them to help us attain our goals. The principles that are identified here are not "laws" in the sense that they are proven, but they include some of the most plausible ideas in the social sciences, and, hopefully, we can use them to help us attain more of our marital goals than we would if we did not have access to these principles.

SUMMARY

This chapter discussed the nature of general principles and how we can use them in our personal lives. Principles are declarative statements that identify how two or more variables are covariationally related to one another. These statements are general in the sense that they are not limited to a certain social situation, time, or historical period, and because of this they can be applied in many different social situations. The covariational relationships in principles can be positive or negative, linear or curvilinear, and some of them identify cause and effect relationships while others only identify that variables are correlated with each other.

The principles included in this book were selected because it was hoped that they would help us attain our own unique marital goals. The way we use the generalizations is to change certain variables or factors in our lives when a principle indicates that a change will tend to bring about a certain result in one or more other variables or factors. The principles are among the most defensible ideas in the modern social sciences, but they should all be viewed as tentative, theoretical ideas that do not yet have sufficient proof to be viewed as social laws. It is also, of course, to be expected that there will be exceptions to the general rules because the social sciences have not yet discovered all of the circumstances that determine when the relationships in the principles occur. Hopefully, however, the principles will provide enough information to help us attain our marital goals better than we would be able to without them.

SUGGESTIONS FOR FURTHER STUDY

Aldous, Joan 1970. "Strategies for Developing Family Theory." *Journal of Marriage and the Family* 32:250–57.

Blalock, Hubert M., Jr. 1969. *Theory Construction*. Englewood Cliffs, N.J.: Prentice-Hall, chaps. 1 and 2.

Braithwaite, R. B. 1959. *Scientific Explanation*. London: Cambridge University Press.

Burr, Wesley R. 1973. *Theory Construction and the Sociology of the Family*. New York: Wiley, chaps. 1 and 2.

Dubin, Robert 1969. *Theory Building*. Glencoe, Ill.: Free Press.

Hage, Jerald 1972. *Techniques and Problems of Theory Construction in Sociology*. New York: Wiley Interscience.

Hill, Reuben 1966. "Contemporary Developments in Family Theory." *Journal of Marriage and the Family* 28:10–25.

Stinchcombe, Arthur L. 1968. *Constructing Social Theories*. New York: Harcourt, Brace and World, chaps. 1 and 2.

Zetterberg, Hans L. 1965. *On Theory and Verification in Sociology*. 3d ed. Totowa, N.J.: Bedminster Press, chaps. 1–4.

Communication and decision making

Those of us who are able to communicate easily and effectively with others have a skill that is invaluable in dating and marital relationships. This skill can help us to avoid many difficulties and problems that would arise if we did not have it, to provide support when it is needed, and to experience the joys that are possible only in intimate, enduring human relationships. Those of us, on the other hand, who have difficulty in communicating with others have a serious handicap in dating and marital relationships. We find it difficult and sometimes impossible to work out differences in a satisfactory manner, to decide what to do, to get as close to others as we would like to, and to create lasting relationships. Since communication is basic to most of what occurs in marriage and is essential if a marriage is to be successful in all of the various alternative styles of marriage, the second major section of this book deals with information that can be used to promote effective communication.

Chapter 3 deals with ways that emotions influence verbal communication, and several principles are identified that can be used to eliminate undesired effects of emotions and to increase desired effects. Chapter 4 includes several ways that our feelings about "self" influence the quality of communication in marital relationships. Chapter 5 focuses on nonverbal communication and on several nonverbal processes that are potentially useful in intimate relationships. It also identifies a number of specific factors that influence the quality of communication, and suggests several ways to maximize the positive effects of these factors while minimizing the negative effects. Chapter 6 concludes the section with a discussion of ways to influence the quality of decision making and the extent to which we tend to be satisfied with our decisions. The ideas in this section of the book form a foundation upon which the rest of the book is built *because the ideas in the later chapters are continually tied back to the ideas in the four chapters in this section.*

3

Emotion and verbal communication

V ERBAL communication is the process of sharing information through sending and receiving spoken messages. This particular type of communication is an important part, but only a part, of the total process of communication. We also use many nonverbal methods to share information, such as facial expressions, touching, silence, posture, and gestures. A great deal of the interaction in dating and marital relationships is verbal communication, and because of this it is useful to discover new ways to eliminate problems and increase our efficiency in communicating verbally.

This chapter addresses the issue by discussing several ways in which emotion and communication are intertwined. The first section of the chapter differentiates between several different aspects of emotion and then identifies two general principles that can be used to keep feelings from interfering with verbal communication. One of the ideas developed is that at certain times emotions play an important role in communication—whether we want them to or not; and because of this it is frequently useful to communicate verbally about the emotions themselves. The second section of the chapter deals with the process of communicating about emotions by identifying three principles that can be used to facilitate the verbal communication of feelings.

THE NATURE OF EMOTION

A number of very different processes occur in the human body. Digestion of food and multiplication of body cells are examples of two quite different processes. One refers to the chemical breakdown

49

of food, and the other refers to ways the body grows. These two processes are indirectly related to each other since the division of cells is somewhat dependent on digestion—and digestion is somewhat dependent on the division of cells; but it would not be defensible to argue that they are the same process. The same is true for intellectual and emotional processes. These two processes are interrelated in a number of ways, but they are very different from each other. One refers to the cognitive, rational, thinking processes that occur in the mind, and the other refers to affective, sentimental feelings that are experienced.[1] In order to fully convey the *differences* and yet the *interrelationships* between intellectual and emotional processes it seems useful to analyze the nature of emotion in more detail.

There are at least five different aspects of emotion, and it is important to keep these aspects separate and not confuse them. These aspects are the intensity, source, effects, consciousness, and venting of emotions.[2] The *intensity* of an emotion refers to the level of strength or the degree of the emotion that is experienced. The intensity can be illustrated with the emotion of excitement. A person may at certain times feel only slightly excited while at other times he or she could be highly excited. This is a variable or continuum that ranges from no emotion at all to extremely high intensity, and this is illustrated by the continuum drawn below:

Intensity of emotion

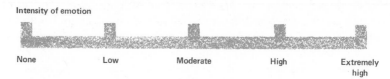

| None | Low | Moderate | High | Extremely high |

The *source* of an emotion refers to the situation, event, or process that leads to, creates, or gives rise to an emotion. There are, of course, a great many different events that can create emotional experiences. For example, something someone else does or says can create an emotional response. The decor of a room or such sounds

---

[1] This distinction between intellectual and emotional processes is not universally accepted in the scientific community. One different view of emotionality, which has come to be known as the James-Lange theory of emotion (James, 1890), argues that emotions are really somatic responses and that the perception of an emotion is the recognition of these physiological processes. Others, such as McDougall (1928, pp. 200–204), however, make even more precise distinctions than the one made here by differentiating between emotions and feelings. The distinction made here is consistent with the work of Allport (1961, chap. 11) and McClelland (1951), and it seems to be the most widely accepted view among contemporary scholars.

[2] This discussion is dependent on the work of Reymert (1950), Arnold (1960), Shibutani (1961), Allport (1961), Davitz (1969), and Dittman (1972).

as soft or loud music have systematic effects on emotions, and architects and interior decorators pay great attention to these effects. Other stimuli, such as odors, bodily stimulation, and thought processes, also influence emotions. Clearly, however, the intensity of an emotion is *different* from its source because the source is not the emotion itself but something that gives rise to the emotion. Interestingly, however, one emotion can be the source of a different emotion. For example, an individual who has a quick temper may show anger in a socially inappropriate situation and then experience other feelings, such as sorrow, sadness, or guilt, as a result of the prior emotion.

An aspect of emotion distinctly different from the two already discussed is the *effect* of emotion. The effect of an emotion is something other than the feeling that is influenced by the affective experience. This influence can be quite direct, such as an emotion of excitement leading to jumping up and down or embracing someone, or it can be indirect, as when the wife's boss gets after her and she, as a result of her feelings, yells at her husband who scolds the child who kicks the dog who chases the cat. . . . Indirectly the wife's emotion had an effect on the dog's behavior.

A fourth aspect of emotion is the *consciousness* or awareness of emotion. Psychiatrists have distinguished between the conscious, preconscious, and unconscious levels of this variable.[3] When something is conscious the person experiencing it is aware of it. With regard to emotion, consciousness means that the person knows what he is feeling. Preconsciousness lies between consciousness and unconsciousness. People are not fully aware of things that are preconscious, but can become aware of them by such processes as introspection or hearing someone make a related comment. When something is unconscious it exists in the mind, but people are not aware of it. In other words they do not know about it and cannot cognize, recognize, or perceive what it is. Unconscious emotions are emotions which a person experiences without being aware that they are being experienced. The above example of the boss getting after the wife would be an example of this if the wife were not aware of the emotions that were created in her by the boss. She could have such feelings as hurt or anger, but be so concerned with other

---

[3] Sigmund Freud (1893), the father of psychoanalysis, is usually credited with the "discovery" of the unconscious, and since Freud others, such as Cameron and Margaret (1951) and Allport (1961, chap. 7), have refined the conscious-unconsciousness dimension by pointing out that it is a continuum rather than a dichotomy. It is of course possible to accept the existence of the unconscious without accepting other ideas in psychoanalysis. Experiments such as Kolers (1957) have so conclusively demonstrated the role of unconscious processes in human behavior that their existence is almost beyond question.

things that the existence of these emotions never comes into her consciousness.

Thus, several conclusions about the consciousness of emotions seem reasonably well established. One is that emotions can exist and remain unconscious. Another is that consciousness is a different aspect of emotions than their existence, intensity, source, or effect. Also, as is pointed out later in this chapter, emotions frequently have especially disruptive influences on communication when they are unconscious.

The final characteristic of emotion discussed here is the process of *venting* emotion. This is the process of doing something to decrease the intensity of emotions. If emotions are positive emotions, such as joy, happiness, or excitement, we seldom want to consciously decrease their intensity. However, if they are negative emotions, such as anger, resentment, frustration, sadness, and jealousy, and they are fairly intense, most of us usually want to decrease their intensity. Sometimes we push an emotion out of our awareness and think we have eliminated it or at least decreased its intensity to a point where it is a very unimportant emotion. Frequently, however, all this does is make us unaware of the emotion, and there is an important distinction between this suppressive activity and genuinely venting an emotion. Venting an emotion actually changes its intensity rather than just our perception of how intense it is.

Hopefully, the differences between intellectual and emotional processes have gradually become apparent in this analysis of emotion. Emotions are affective experiences, and they tend to be felt rather than thought. It is possible for people to become aware of what they are feeling, and such awareness involves the intellect. This involvement of the intellect does not, however, justify the conclusion that intellectual and emotional experiences are identical. This analysis of some of the differences between intellectual and emotional processes provides some essential groundwork for two principles that can now be identified.

PRINCIPLES ABOUT THE EFFECTS OF EMOTION ON VERBAL COMMUNICATION

The first principle can be labeled the Emotionality principle, and it is:

THE EMOTIONALITY PRINCIPLE: When the intensity of emotions is high, the greater the intensity the less the amount of rational control people have over their behavior, and the less the intensity the greater the control.[4]

---

[4] This principle is a theoretical idea that is central to a great deal of literature in several disciplines. It is explicit in much of the literature of psychiatry, as illustrated by the writings in which Horney (1942, 1945) describes how

Before the Emotionality principle can be clearly understood or used it is necessary to define both of its variables. The *intensity of emotions* is one aspect of emotion discussed earlier, and it refers to the degree of strength or force of an emotion. As a variable it ranges between no emotion at all and very high intensity, and this factor was diagramed on page 50.

The *amount of rational control over behavior* refers to the amount that conscious, intellectual processes control what a person does. At certain times we seem to have complete or virtually complete control over what we do, and at other times a sizable portion of what we do is beyond our rational control. This variation in rational control can occur as a result of several different factors. Many drugs, for example, temporarily influence intellectual processes, and when this occurs the proportion of control that our intellect has over our behavior can be changed substantially. Hypnotism can also decrease the amount of rational control many of us have over our behavior. The amount that behavior is rationally controlled is a variable that ranges from situations in which the rational intellect has no control over our behavior to situations in which it has a very high amount of control over what we do, and this variable can be diagramed in the following way:

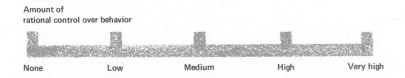

Amount of
rational control over behavior

None   Low   Medium   High   Very high

Figure 3–1 is an attempt to diagram the curvilinearity that is thought to occur in this relationship. The lines show that as long as the intensity of an emotion stays between low and moderately high there does not seem to be any predictable change in the amount of rational control. However, when the intensity varies between moderately high and high there is a slight change in the amount of rational control, and when the variation in the intensity of emotions is between high and very high there is a substantial variation in the amount of control. It is important to note that increases in intensity

---

people respond to what she terms *basic anxiety* by turning to neurotic needs and by Sullivan's (1953) analysis of how people respond to threats to what he terms their *self-esteem*. It is also implicit in the works of Adler (1929, 1930) which describe how people respond to inferiorities in developing their unique style of life. In sociology this relationship is discussed by Rose (1950, chap. 1) and Shibutani (1961, chap. 13), and in counseling literature it is described by Rogers (1951, chap. 11) and Hogan (1948). None of these writers are as explicit in diagraming the curvilinear relationship as is Figure 3–1, because that diagram is an attempt to formalize ideas that are implicit in this earlier literature.

Figure 3–1

The effect that the intensity of emotions has on rational control over behavior

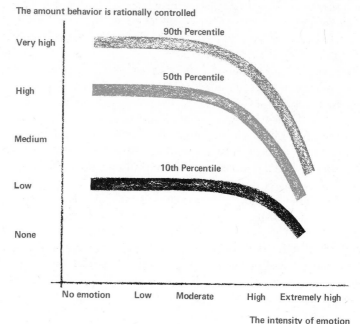

The amount behavior is rationally controlled

decrease the control *and* that decreases in intensity increase the control. Figure 3–1 uses three lines to show the 10th, 50th, and 90th percentiles in a typical population, and these lines show that individuals who are at the 10th, 50th, and 90th percentiles in rational control all tend to experience a decrease in control as emotions become intense. However, since there is greater space between the lines when emotions are low in intensity, these lines also show that when emotions are low to moderate there is a great deal of variability in the amount of control individuals have. Some people have high control and some have low control. However, when the intensity becomes extremely high there is less variability and very few people are able to retain high rational control over their behavior. Thus, changes in the intensity of emotion seem to have more effect on rational control when intensity is very high than when intensity is moderate to high.

It is important that we view the Emotionality principle with tentativeness. It is an idea that is widely accepted in the social sciences, but the research that led to its discovery was mostly clinical impressions, and virtually nothing is known about how other factors, such as intelligence or situational variables, influence the effect that the intensity of emotions has on rational control. Hopefully, future research will provide additional evidence about the principle's validity and will also discover how other factors influence when and how emotions affect rational control over behavior.

The second principle that is introduced here can be called the Control principle, and it asserts:

> THE CONTROL PRINCIPLE: The greater the rational control over behavior the greater the quality of verbal communication, and vice versa, and this is a curvilinear relationship.[5]

Before this principle can be fully understood it is necessary to define one new variable—the *quality of verbal communication.* It is possible to break the communication process into numerous small components and to talk about the quality of each of these parts. The components include such processes as deciding what idea one wants to communicate, selecting words to send the message, and transmitting the sounds as well as the decoding of the information received in the receiver's head (Garner and Hake, 1951; Fane, 1961). However, for the purposes of this chapter it seems more useful to group these processes into an overall general assessment of the quality of verbal communication. This assessment is an evaluation of how well two or more individuals are able to send and receive verbal information that brings about a shared understanding of the issues or topics they try to discuss. When there is good quality the communication tends to be accurate, efficient, and fairly easy to accomplish. When there is poor quality the individuals have a difficult time accurately understanding each other, or the communication is easily disrupted, inefficient, or ineffective. This rather global variable is not a dichotomy between poor and excellent communication. It is a continuum that ranges between the two extremes of poor and excellent communication. There are many degrees between these extremes, and the continuum can be diagramed in the following way:

Quality of verbal
communication in a relationship

Poor   Fair   Good   Excellent

---

[5] This principle is a central idea in Nirenberg's (1963) analysis of communication; and his clinical, consulting experience was the basis of the principle. The principle also has an inherent rationality, but it has not been tested with subsequent empirical research. It should thus be accepted tentatively until additional research is undertaken. Nirenberg does not plot the relationship shown in Figure 3–4, but the shape of the relationship that is suggested here is implicit in his work.

It is important to keep in mind that this variable deals with the quality of verbal communication and that a sizable portion of the communication in courtship and marital relationships, and in most other relationships for that matter, is nonverbal. We communicate, for example, with such nonverbal processes as gestures, body posture, speed of movement, and volume of speech. In addition there are several other aspects of communication, such as Ruesch and Bateson's (1951) distinction between the content and relationship aspects of communication and Watzlawick, Beavin, and Jackson's (1967) distinction between digital and analogic communication. These other aspects of communication are dealt with in Chapter 5.

Figure 3–2 is an attempt to diagram the curvilinearity that is thought to exist in the relationship between rational control and the quality of verbal communication. As the lines show, an increase or decrease in the amount of control has considerable effect on the quality of communication when the amount is fairly low. However, when the amount of control is above even a moderate level, variation in the amount of control has little effect on the quality of communication. In addition this principle asserts that as control decreases toward the absence of control almost everyone tends to have poor verbal communication.

When the Emotionality and the Control principles are put to-

Figure 3–2

The effect of rational control on quality of communication

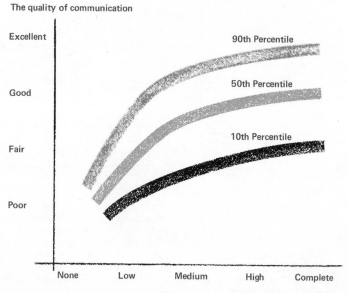

The amount of rational control over behavior

Figure 3–3

The chain sequence showing the effect of emotional intensity on rational control and the effect of rational control on the quality of communication

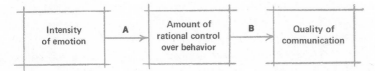

gether they form a chain sequence in which the intensity of emotion influences the amount of rational control and the amount of rational control influences the quality of communication. This is diagramed in Figure 3–3. The line that is marked with the letter *A* is the Emotionality principle, and the line that is marked with the letter *B* is the Control principle. As this figure shows, the intensity of emotion has an indirect influence on the quality of communication.

Applying the Emotionality and Control principles to courtship and marriage

The main way these principles are relevant for dating and marital relations is that the intensity of our emotions influences our ability to communicate verbally. When we have intense emotions we tend to be less able to share ideas effectively than when we are relatively calm. Apparently this is not an all-or-nothing situation in which having intense emotions automatically creates poor communication, and having less intense emotions creates good communication. It is more a gradual process in which the more intense the emotions the poorer the communication—when the emotions are extremely intense. Also, of course, there are many other factors that can influence the quality of verbal communication.

We can do several things to use these principles. One is to be aware of the effects that emotions—positive and negative—have on communication. If we are aware of this cause and effect relationship and we or our partner have intense feelings we can at least have the peace of mind that comes from knowing one of the reasons we can't—at that time—communicate very effectively. A second way to use these principles is to temporarily stop trying to communicate verbally when emotions are highly intense because the obstacles to verbal communication are then fairly high. This is, of course, not always possible but at certain times it is possible, and we can wait until the emotions are less intense before we try to communicate. A third way to use these principles is to be sensitive to when the intensity of emotion is having a detrimental effect on the quality of communication, and then, when it does have such an effect, to take the time to "vent" the emotion before it interferes too much with the communication.

The three ideas in the preceding paragraph seem to be valuable strategies in courtship and marital relationships, but they are not natural responses for many of us. Many times when we are trying to communicate about something and one or both individuals become highly emotional the natural thing to do is to try all the harder to communicate about the issue or problem that we were initially trying to discuss. In addition many of us view it as undesirable to have to stop communicating about the initial problem and to focus on the emotions one or both of us are experiencing. Also, many of us are taught that we should not reveal or discuss our emotions. For example, most men have been taught from toddlerhood that they need to be "tough" and "strong," and that they need to exert "leadership" in their relationships with others; and one of the things this usually means is that they are supposed to conceal their emotions. For many men this tradition also results in their believing that they should avoid even having strong emotions, and if they do have them that they are to hold them in so that no one is aware they exist. Women usually learn in our society that it is appropriate for them to have strong feelings, but even they frequently assume that it is inappropriate to interrupt a discussion in order to focus explicity and directly on what they are experiencing emotionally.

The result of these cultural patterns is that many of us have a difficult time using the ideas discussed earlier about stopping our attempts to communicate verbally when our emotions are intense and waiting until a later time to resume the verbal communication. In addition we frequently have an even more difficult time using the idea of continuing to communicate when the emotions become intense but changing the topic of the conversation so that the discussion is temporarily about the emotions themselves rather than about the initial topic.

Since many of us are trained in this way and the principles are also probably valid, it seems useful to identify several skills we can acquire to help us increase our ability to use these two principles in our lives. These skills are: (1) being able to recognize our own emotions—at least when they are intense; (2) being able to recognize emotional responses in others—at least when they are intense; (3) being able to "vent" emotions that are intense when these emotions are having undesirable effects; and (4) being able to discuss these feelings in courtship and marital relationships and to be comfortable with this type of discussion. This last skill is dealt with in the second section of this chapter, so no more is being said about it here. However, it seems useful to identify several exercises that we can use to help ourselves increase our skills of understanding our own emotions, understanding others' emotions, and venting feelings. First, improving our ability to recognize emotions . . .

Two reasons that many of us fail to recognize our emotional sensations are (1) that we just don't know how to recognize our inner feelings, and (2) that we know how but for some reason we just don't do it. One way to help with the second problem is to use some basic principles of psychological conditioning by somehow getting a "reward" or something pleasurable when we recognize an emotional experience. Psychologists have discovered that we usually can condition ourselves to do something more frequently when we're rewarded at about the same time we do it, and the following exercise makes use of this discovery.

REWARDING THE RECOGNITION OF EMOTIONS

Goal: To increase the amount we recognize emotions by getting a reward when we become aware of an emotion.

1. Find something that is pleasurable to you and relatively easy to either start or stop. Some examples might be having or not having dessert at dinner, carrying around a package of candies and eating one at a certain time, or putting money in a special bottle for something you want.

2. For the next week (or longer) reward yourself with one of the pleasures every time you consciously recognize an emotional sensation, such as happiness, anger, warmth, jealousy, or love. If you are interested in increasing your ability to recognize your own emotions, reward yourself when you become aware of an emotion you are experiencing. If you are interested in increasing your ability to recognize emotional experiences in others, reward yourself when you accurately recognize an emotion someone else has.

3. At the end of the time period assess the experience, and try to determine whether or not you are recognizing your emotions more. One alternative to this exercise is to have the rewards administered by someone else, such as your spouse or fiancé(e).

If we do not have the skill or ability to recognize emotions the former exercise cannot solve this problem because we wouldn't have any successful experiences to reward. There are, however, many different ways this skill can be acquired, and the following two exercises are strategies that can help us acquire it. The first exercise is useful for those who have trouble figuring out what emotions are, and the second exercise is a way to get help from someone else.

WHICH ARE EMOTIONS?

Goal: To recognize the difference between emotions and several things that are frequently confused with emotions.

1. Identify the following statements according to whether they acknowledge ownership of thought (T) or feeling (F), describe a physical or verbal act that is an effect of an emotion (E), or label or evaluate someone (L).

   Example:

      T   "I think we might be able to work together better if we knew more about each other."

      F   "I feel rejected and defensive after someone questions my ideas."

      E   Embraces someone when feeling warm.

      L   "You are a very considerate person."

   a. _____ Walks out—slams door.

   b. _____ "You've been a pest to every teacher you've ever had."

   c. _____ "I'm uncomfortable and nervous talking like this."

   d. _____ "Saturdays give me an enjoyable sense of freedom and relief from pressures."

   e. _____ "Shut up."

   f. _____ "I think that a teacher who feels threatened by the principal will not be free to innovate."

   g. _____ Suddenly becomes silent.

   h. _____ "You shouldn't talk that way; it's not very nice."

   i. _____ "I get a good feeling inside when the entire class is able to do something we've worked hard at learning."

   j. _____ "She certainly has a nice way of making one feel good."

   k. _____ "I think nobody cares what happens to me."

2. Think about or discuss with someone the following question: What characteristics differentiate the statements identified as owning a described thought (T) or feeling (F), describing an effect of an emotion (E), and labeling or evaluating others (L)?

(*Answers given at bottom of page 61.*)

Source: This exercise is adapted from Heaps and Rohde (1974).

RECOGNIZING CLUES TO EMOTIONS

Goal: To learn how to recognize emotions.

1. Select someone with whom you have a fairly close relationship, such as a spouse, fiancé(e), friend, or date.

2. Explain to the person that you are engaging in a project to increase your ability to recognize emotions, and ask if he or she will assist you for 15–30 minutes.

3. Have the person think back to one or two emotional sensations he or she has experienced when in your presence, and then both of you try to identify several things that might have given you "clues" about those emotions. It is important to listen "hard" to the person's descriptions of the clues.

4. If the other person can identify an emotion he or she has experienced while doing step 3, have him or her identify it and then discuss things that might have been "clues" about that emotion.

5. Can you now identify an emotion you have experienced while doing steps 3 or 4? If you are able to, can you also identify some ways you or someone else could recognize that emotion?

6. Hopefully, you have increased your ability to recognize emotions. Have you? If not, can you devise an exercise that would be more appropriate for you?

Another skill that is useful in applying the Emotionality and Control principles in our personal life is to be able to do something to "vent" emotions when they are interfering with other aspects of our life. Most of the time we are only interested in venting negative emotions, such as anger, resentment, frustration, discouragement, and hurt, because positive emotions, such as joy, felicity, love, euphoria, and excitement, are so pleasant that we usually want to prolong and enjoy them . . . unless they are interfering with other things that we also want—like getting something done. Most of us also usually have a number of things we can do to decrease the intensity of emotions, such as playing a musical instrument, reading, taking a walk, crying, engaging in physical exercise, watching TV, writing or reading poetry, pounding a pillow, and counting to ten, and many of these behaviors can be used without using violent (Straus, 1974; Steinmetz and Straus, 1973) or other socially undesirable methods.

Correct answers for exercise on page 60:
a (E); b (L); c (F); d (F); e (E); f (T); g (E); h (L); i (F); j (L); k (T).

Many of us may still find it useful to increase our repertoire of socially acceptable things we can turn to when we want to decrease uncomfortable emotions, and the following exercise is designed to help accomplish this.

INCREASING SOCIALLY DESIRABLE METHODS OF VENTING EMOTIONS

Goal: To increase the number of socially desirable ways we can vent our emotions.

1. Make a list of all the methods you now have to vent emotions. (The examples in the last paragraph will get you started.)

2. After you have written down all the methods you can think of— take four or five minutes to do it—engage in a conversation with several others (this can be done in a class) and try to make a *new* list of at least five socially acceptable methods you have never thought about.

3. Display both of your lists in some conspicuous spot. For example, tape them to the refrigerator door for two weeks and see how many times you can use the items on your new list in that time. You may want to reward yourself each time you use one.

It is probably useful to make a final comment about the use of these principles, because some readers may get the impression from this discussion that emotions are undesirable obstacles that get in the way and should be avoided. It seems to the author that this discussion should not be construed as an argument against emotionality in the human experience. The principles that have been discussed here could be used by someone who wants to have a fairly unemotional style of life, but they could also be used by those who tend to be and who want to be highly emotional. For one thing the Emotionality principle only suggests that emotions tend to get in the way when they are highly intense, and that leaves considerable room for emotional reactions that probably do not have any effect on verbal communication. Also, some of us may highly value intense emotional experiences, and may not want to forgo them to increase the "quality" of our verbal communication. Who is to say this is not desirable? Certainly not this author! This author believes that each of us ought to be able to select the style of life that is best suited to our life preferences—as long as we don't make inappropriate infringements on the rights of others. And those of us who want to experience intense emotions—particularly when they are pleasurable experiences—may not want to be "effective" verbal communicators when we are experiencing these feelings. The two principles discussed here suggest that if we do want to communicate verbally when we have intense emotions we will probably be disappointed, and they explain why we will probably be disappointed, but they do not, by themselves, advocate either high or low emotionality as a desirable style of life. They also say nothing about the nonverbal communication that can occur as a result of intense emotions. All they do is suggest that our emotions tend to have certain systematic effects on other phenomena, and we can use this information however we wish.

COMMUNICATING ABOUT EMOTIONS

One of the observations made in the first section of this chapter was that at certain times couples may want to focus their attention on their emotions and to communicate verbally about those emotions. Also, as Heaps and Rohde (1974, pp. 9–10) have suggested, the seven following consequences usually occur when we openly describe thoughts and feelings, and they provide some additional reasons for sharing our feelings:

1. A norm or expectation for open communication is established, so that the other person knows how to respond in the relationship.
2. Reciprocal attempts at open communication by others are more likely.
3. Misunderstandings are less likely, since your intentions do not need to be inferred.
4. Self-awareness is enhanced, since you need to be aware of your thoughts and feelings to be able to describe them.
5. Evaluative or judgmental statements are minimized, since ownership of your opinion is acknowledged. Ideas are shared as personal thoughts rather than as statements of fact.
6. Feelings of trust, comfort, and closeness frequently follow open expressions which acknowledge ownership and avoid placing responsibility for feelings on others.
7. An atmosphere is created which allows for open expression of problems and problem solving.

The times when we want to talk about feelings occur in a wide variety of situations. For example, they may be in very pleasant settings where we want to share a delicate and deeply felt affection or love for someone. Or, certain negative emotional sensations may be interfering with our efforts to solve a problem. Whatever the situation, verbal communication about important feelings is a different process than the type of communication that occurs when we are discussing objective or physical things, such as ideas, facts, experiences, opinions, or social problems. It is possible to discuss the latter phenomena in many different circumstances, and usually relatively little conscious attention has to be given to whether or not the situation is "appropriate" to discuss them. A conversation about deeply felt emotion, however, is an infinitely more delicate and intricate matter, and it demands different and more complex communication skills. The following series of comments illustrate how different couples are in their ability to talk about their feelings, and demonstrate the need of some couples to increase their ability to do this more involved type of communicating.

I've tried to tell him how I feel about it, but he just gets mad and makes some comment about my parents.

One of the things that has meant the most to me in my marriage is that when a problem comes up we can talk it out. And if one of us gets upset while we're trying to work things out it doesn't seem to get in the way. We talk about our feelings and get them calmed down, and then we can go back to solving the problem.

She never tells me how she feels, and she never lets on. I just never know where she sits unless she's mad, and, boy, when she's mad, that's it. All hell breaks loose! The rest of the time she's like a clam.

As soon as anything comes up that's the least bit upsetting, she turns on the tears and heads for the bedroom. We've got so many problems around here I've about had it, and she's about as good as nothing when it comes to working things out.

The members of only one of these four couples were able to communicate about their feelings, yet all of the others indicated or intimated that they would like to be able to. And it is likely that if they could communicate about their feelings they would be better able to solve some of their marital difficulties. Undoubtedly, however, all four of these couples were able to discuss more factual things, such as whether the daily paper had arrived, what they were having for dinner, or whether or not to buy a new vacuum cleaner. They were also probably able to discuss some of their less intimate emotional feelings, such as how they liked a ball game or whether the temperature in the room made them uncomfortable. The difference between the couples is that one of them was able to communicate about fairly sensitive emotional feelings, and the others were not. The ability to discuss delicate, intense, sensitive, or intimate emotional feelings is a skill that is fairly difficult to acquire, and it is this skill that is the main concern of the latter part of this chapter. The goals in this part are to identify three principles that deal with verbal communication about emotions and to describe several ways in which these principles can be used in dating and marital relationships.

Most people are able to identify verbally certain types of emotional reactions, such as their affective responses to impersonal things like the weather, TV programs, or a controversial political figure. In addition they are usually willing to do more than just identify what these feelings are. They will discuss why they feel the way they do, and they will even talk about the level of intensity of their feelings. There are, however, other feelings that most of us are more reluctant to discuss, and these are the feelings that tend to occur deep within ourselves. These feelings are very carefully guarded and are only discussed under certain types of situations. The difference between the two types of emotion is that some feelings are deeply felt, personal responses that are central to the "self," whereas other feelings are fairly superficial responses that are not intricately tied to ourselves as persons. We tend to be fairly willing to divulge and discuss our superficial emotions, but we are much more cautious and careful in talking about the more intensely felt, intimate, and central emotions.

The dependent variable

The main concern here is with the willingness people have to communicate about the emotions that are deeply important to them, and virtually no attention is paid to how to communicate about the more superficial emotions. Unfortunately there are no simple labels for the dependent variable that is relevant here, so it is referred to as *the willingness to communicate about important emotions*.[6] This variable is apparently a continuous factor that ranges between being completely unwilling to communicate about important emotions and being completely uninhibited about communicating about them. There is thus a gradualness in the shift between these two extremes, as is shown in the following continuum:

Willingness to communicate
about important emotions

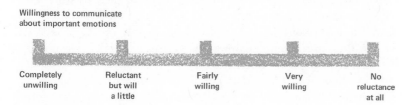

| Completely unwilling | Reluctant but will a little | Fairly willing | Very willing | No reluctance at all |

This concept is similar to what has come to be known as "self-disclosure," but self-disclosure is different in two ways. As Culbert (1967) and Jourard (1971) define self-disclosure, it is a broader

---

[6] Appreciation is expressed to Kenneth L. Cannon for his reactions, advice, and assistance when I was analyzing the literature and trying to figure out just what this variable is.

phenomenon in that it includes the process of revealing anything that is unique to oneself, and this includes opinions about impersonal things, thoughts, observations, and wishes in addition to feelings. The willingness to communicate about important emotions is more restricted in that it only deals with how willing we are to share affective experiences or feelings. Also, self-disclosure refers to the actual disclosing of something related to oneself, while the variable that is important here refers to our inclination to share our emotions rather than the actual sharing. The sharing of feelings can have many different effects in a relationship, and the following exercise may help you discover what some of these effects are in your own situation.

DISCLOSING FEELINGS

Goal: To discover more about the effects of disclosing feelings to others.

1. When you are having a pleasant experience with someone who knows you well, disclose some positive feeling about yourself that you would not normally disclose.

2. Having made this disclosure, note the reaction of the person to whom you communicated. And, more important, identify how you felt disclosing, including how the other person's response affected your feelings.

3. Summarize what you learned about the benefits and risks of disclosing feelings.

Appreciation is expressed to Terrence D. Olson for his help in designing this exercise.

The Trust principle

One idea that occurs over and over again in the literature about communication is that people are only willing to talk about or share important emotions when they can trust or rely on the others with whom they are communicating. In Harper's (1958) discussion of this generalization he describes this as an "atmosphere of safety," and his view of safety is that it is a situation in which the individuals believe they will not be hurt or taken advantage of if they express how they feel or in some other way discuss their emotional experiences. Deutsch (1962) and Johnson (1972, chap. 3) prefer the term *trust* to describe this factor, and they have suggested that the following elements are the essential components in a trusting situation.

1. You are in a situation in which trusting another person can lead to beneficial or harmful consequences for your needs and goals. Thus you realize that there is a risk involved in trusting.

2. You realize that whether the consequences are beneficial or harmful depends upon the future behavior of another person.
3. You feel relatively confident that the other person will behave in such a way that the beneficial consequences will result (Johnson, 1972, p. 44).

The causal variable here can be labeled the amount of trust that is sensed in the relationship, and apparently it can range from no trust to complete trust, as shown in the following continuum:

Amount of trust

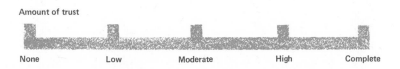

| None | Low | Moderate | High | Complete |

The relevant principle is:

THE TRUST PRINCIPLE: The greater the trust that an individual perceives in a relationship the greater the willingness to communicate about important emotions, and the less the trust the less the willingness.

Harper does not identify how much safety or trust is needed before individuals are willing to risk the exposure of their emotional feelings, but others, such as Rogers (1951, esp. pp. 139 f.), who have written about the same issue intimate that the greater the trust the greater the willingness. If this is the case, the relationship is a linear function like the one drawn in Figure 3–4. At present, how-

Figure 3–4

The effect a sense of trust has on the willingness to communicate about important emotions

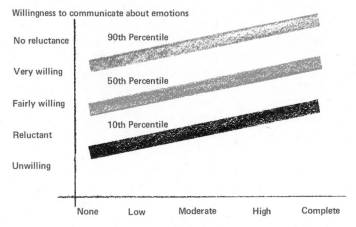

The amount of trust perceived in the relationship

ever, the social sciences have little information about the shape of this relationship, and this line is little more than an educated guess. The Trust principle has considerable acceptance among clinically oriented students of the family, but it has not yet been systematically tested with quantified empirical data. In addition to the clinical data that support this idea, however, it seems that the consistency of this principle with the experiences we routinely encounter in life also argues for its validity.

This principle has important implications for dating and marital relationships because it identifies one of the conditions that we apparently need to create if we are to communicate verbally about our important feelings. It is apparently a simple fact that if we do the things that create a sense of trust in a relationship we *might* be able to communicate about our important emotions, and if we don't create this type of atmosphere we won't. This leads to the very practical questions of how trust can be created and how it can be destroyed.

Trust is usually built in a series of small steps. We reveal some aspect of ourselves that is not very threatening, and others respond to it. If they respond with openness and acceptance, and if they also reveal part of themselves to us, this creates a certain amount of trust. We then feel free enough to reveal aspects of ourselves that are more personal and that involve greater personal risk, and if the other persons treat these in ways we are comfortable with, we learn we can trust more. Often in the early stages of becoming acquainted this process occurs many different times and in a variety of different ways, and it often occurs casually with little awareness of what is going on. Gradually, however, we develop a feeling of being able to trust or not trust our feelings, reactions, opinions, or problems with another person. Usually the nonverbal messages we receive tell us a lot about how much we can "trust" someone. Nonverbal messages, such as the way something is said or the fact that some things are not said that could be said, make a great deal of difference.

One reason it usually takes considerable time to develop a deep sense of trust is that we cannot be sure what others will do with information they have about us until we have seen them in a variety of situations in which they have a choice as to what they will do with the information they have. Gradually, however, we learn how trustworthy another person is, and the other person learns how much we can be trusted, and a certain level of trust evolves in a relationship.

Some behaviors tend to build a sense of trust in dating and marital relations, and other behaviors tend to destroy trust. Some trust-destroying ways to act are:

1. Treat emotions as irrelevant or unimportant when the individual who is experiencing them thinks they are important.
2. Ridicule or make fun of someone's feelings.
3. Use information about the feelings of others to later hurt or embarrass them.
4. Fail to recognize feelings in others.
5. Violate a trust that has been placed in you.

Some ways to behave that usually tend to create additional trust in dating and marital relationships are:

1. Be delicate, tactful, and sensitive in responding to emotions that are important to someone else.
2. Never violate trusts or confidences placed in you.
3. When an incident occurs that undermines trust, talk about it with the other person, as it may be the result of a misunderstanding, lack of information, or misperception rather than something that should decrease trust.
4. Share something about yourself with the other person.
5. Be a good listener when someone wants to talk about emotions.

Frequently the ability to create trust in a relationship can only be acquired over a lengthy period of time during which each member of the couple gradually exposes his or her "central" emotions to the other person and sees how the other responds. This means that usually the type of exercises used in this book are of little value in creating trust. However, it is occasionally possible to make small changes in this aspect of a relationship, and because of this the following exercise is designed to help develop a greater sense of trust in a relationship.

TRUST

Goal: To assess the level of trust in a relationship and to change it if a different level is desired.

1. Identify a person who is important to you, such as a spouse, parent, sibling, or fiancé(e) and ask the other person to help you with this exercise.

2. Try to describe to each other just how "safe" or "trusting" you both feel in discussing important feelings (not opinions, views, attitudes, or facts—you're discussing *emotions*). You may feel safer in discussing certain emotions than others, and if you are try to identify these differences.

3. Assess whether this is the level of trust you would like in your relationship. If it is, you have finished this exercise. If not, go on to steps 4 and 5.

4. Describe to each other two things that would be necessary for you to feel "slightly" more trusting of each other.

5. Implement at least one of the suggestions in step 4, and then go back to steps 2 and 3 again after implementing it.

One other aspect of this process of creating trust is that frequently individuals have little or no conscious control over the things that influence their emotions, and hence they have little control over the emotions they experience. If they are able to become conscious of those emotions and to deal with them, they can often influence how long they have the emotions and how they let the emotions influence their behavior. Frequently the only way a person can do this is to have someone else's help. If, however, the other person responds by doing such things as punishing or ridiculing him or her for the emotions, this type of response will gradually teach the person with the emotions that the other person is not one to whom he or she can safely expose emotions. The result will then be that many emotional feelings will not be communicated in that relationship. On the other hand, if the other person responds with patience, understanding, and other trust-building behaviors the individual with the emotions will learn that he or she can comfortably deal with emotions with this other person. A closely related point is that some of us think that when another person has emotions that are socially undesirable we should respond in ways that show our disapproval of those emotions, as this will help the other person stop experiencing the undesirable emotions. The result of these punishing responses, however, is frequently not at all what we want. The effect is frequently to have the person hide emotions from us and become less willing to share other emotions.

David Johnson (1972) has developed several exercises that use nonverbal methods to help individuals learn more about what interpersonal trust really is and how to create it. Two of his exercises seem sufficiently valuable to be repeated here. He introduces them by commenting that:

Taking a risk which makes you vulnerable to another person and receiving support can take place in a variety of nonverbal as well as verbal ways. One of the interesting aspects of the development of trust in a relationship is that sometimes the sense of physical support can be as powerful a developer of trust as a sense of emotional support. Your group may like to try some of the following nonverbal exercises. Each of them is related to the development of trust. Before you attempt the exercises, however, you should carefully consider the following points:

1. No one with a bad back or another physical condition that might be adversely affected should participate in an exercise in which they might be roughly handled.

2. Although these nonverbal exercises can be used as a form of play, they should be used only for educational purposes. That is, they should be done for a specific learning purpose, such as learning more about the development of trust, and they should be discussed thoroughly after they have been done.

3. Do not enter into an exercise unless you plan to behave in a trustworthy manner. If you cannot be trusted to support another person, do not enter into an exercise where you are responsible for physically supporting him. No one should be allowed to fall or to suffer any injury.

4. No group pressure should be exerted upon individuals to participate. Participation should be strictly voluntary. If you do not feel like volunteering, however, you may find it interesting to analyze why. You may learn something about yourself and your relationships with the other members of the group from such an analysis. A lack of trust in the group of other individuals might lead you to refuse to participate; on the other hand, a sense of adventure and fun might lead you to volunteer even though you do not trust the group or other individuals (Johnson, 1972, pp. 55–56).

TRUST CIRCLE

The group stands facing into a close circle. A person who wishes to develop more trust in the group is handed around the inside of the circle by the shoulders and upper torso. He should stand with his feet in the center of the circle, close his eyes, and let the group pass him around or across their circle. His feet should not move from the center of the circle. After as many people who want to try it have been passed around the circle, discuss the following questions:

1. How did it feel to be on the inside of the circle? What were you thinking about? What was the experience like?

2. How did it feel to be a part of the circle, passing others around? What were you thinking about? What were you experiencing?

   Did you feel differently with different people in the center? Did the groups behave differently when different people were in the center?

3. Some groups take a great deal of care in passing a person around and are very gentle; other groups engage in aggressive play and toss the person from side to side. What did your group do? What does it signify about the group and the members?

Source: The trust circle and the trust walk exercise are reprinted from Johnson, 1972.

TRUST WALK

Each member of the group pairs up with another person. One person is designated as the guide, the other as a blind person. The blind person should close his eyes, and the guide will lead him around the room. The guide should grasp the wrists of the blind person and either from the side or from behind guide the blind person around the room, planning as "rich" an experience as possible for the blind person using all the other senses besides sight. Touching experiences, such as feeling the wall, the covering of a chair, the hair or face of another person, are all interesting. If you can go outdoors, standing in the sun or the wind is enjoyable. In a large room trust in the guide can be tested by running across the room, the blind person keeping his eyes shut. After 15 minutes, reverse roles and repeat. After both individuals have been a guide and a blind person, discuss the following questions in the groups as a whole:

1. How did it feel to be the blind person?

2. What were some of the best experiences your guide gave you?

3. What did you learn about the guide?

4. What did you learn about the blind person?

5. How did it feel to be the guide?

6. At this point, how do the two of you feel about each other?

The Concern principle

Numerous writers in the family field (Burgess and Wallin, 1953, chap. 10; Waller and Hill, 1951, chap. 16) and in closely related fields, such as psychiatry (Saul, 1947) and counseling (Harper, 1958; Rogers, 1951), argue that another characteristic that is necessary if important emotional feelings are to be discussed is a sense of *concern* in a relationship. Different words, such as *love, caring,* and *unconditional positive regard,* are used to describe this factor. So there is some ambiguity about what this variable should be called. There is, however, considerable agreement on what these scholars are really describing, and the main ingredient seems to be a genuine and warmly felt concern about another person that leads to responding with care, interest, and involvement. One reason for the difficulty in finding a label for this variable is that there is no single term in the English language that adequately describes this phenomenon. The terms *care* and *concern* are fairly close when they are divested of negative, fearful, or anxious connotations, but the term *love* is not adequate at all because it has so many different connotations.

Fortunately the actual presence of this phenomenon in human interaction is much less difficult to identify than it is to label, and because of this the label used for it is not as important as understanding that it influences our willingness to communicate about emotions. The term *concern* is used here, but it should be recognized that it is used to denote an active rather than a passive concern and does not have the worrisome, anxious components that the term sometimes connotes. This factor can be viewed as a variable that ranges from low to high degrees, as shown in the following

Amount of concern

None   Low   Medium   High

continuum, and the principle that seems to be implicit in a great deal of literature and explicit in Harper's (1958) analysis is:

> THE CONCERN PRINCIPLE: The greater the concern an individual perceives another person has for him or her the greater the willingness of the individual to communicate about important emotions, and the less the concern the less the willingness.

Writers who have dealt with this principle have not concerned themselves with the shape of the relationship, even though there seems to be consensus that it is generally a positive relationship. It may be that little bits of concern make a great deal of difference, or it may be that there has to be a great deal of concern before it makes much difference. It may also be that the relationship is linear and that any variation in concern brings about a change in the emotional communication. We thus need to realize that we do not yet know much about *how* feelings of concern influence our willingness to communicate about emotions.

We also know very little about whether we can change the *concern* variable. It may be that it is very difficult to alter one's level of concern about another person. If this is the case, this principle is useful in that it helps provide insight into another factor that influences emotional communication, but it does not provide us with more control over our own situations. It may be, however, that there are ways to change the amount of concern for other individuals. Some of us, for example, may be so concerned about ourselves and how much others are putting us out that we devote little energy to a concern for the welfare of others; and this may be preventing the amount of emotional disclosure we may want in our marital relationship. In this type of situation it may be that focusing on the welfare of others more and on our own selves less would create a situation in which emotions would be discussed more.

Norms about emotional communication

Our willingness to communicate about emotions is undoubtedly also influenced by some of the social norms that we learn and internalize. The term *social norm* refers to the beliefs that each of us has about what we should or should not do in various social situations. These beliefs are a part of our culture, and they are learned from the individuals we interact with, such as parents, friends, and teachers. Some norms tend to be universal in that they are accepted by virtually everyone, and other norms are unique to certain subcultural groups. Still other norms are unique to very small groups of individuals. Social norms are relevant here because the norms we learn influence our behavior. For example, if the norms we learn state that we should wear clothes when we are in public we tend to wear clothes in public. If the norms state that we should not physically assault other people we will probably not do so unless there are extreme extenuating circumstances, such as desperation or military necessity. These norms are not so much abstract ideas that exist in society as they are beliefs that people have, which influence what people do (Bott, 1957).

One reason norms are relevant in the present context is because we acquire normative beliefs about experiencing and expressing our feelings. Some people learn, for example, that they should not admit to themselves that they are experiencing certain emotions, and as a result they become convinced that they are not experiencing them— even though they really are. A mother, for example, may be convinced that she is not jealous or angry when she really is, or a father may be deeply overjoyed to see a child after an absence but is unwilling to admit to himself or to anyone else that he has emotional responses. Another norm that has been internalized by many people in the contemporary United States society is the belief that it is inappropriate to talk about emotional feelings—even if one is aware that she or he has the emotions. This is a variable in that some people have internalized this norm and some have not. The variable can be labeled the amount norms proscribe communication about important emotions, and it ranges from norms not proscribing any emotional communication to norms proscribing communication about virtually all emotions. This variable can be shown in the following way, and the relevant principle is:

Amount norms proscribe
communication about important emotions

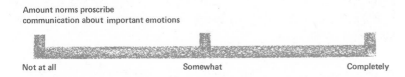

Not at all   Somewhat   Completely

THE NORMS-EMOTION PRINCIPLE: The more a person's norms proscribe communication about emotions the less willing the person is to communicate about important emotions, and vice versa.

The social sciences do not yet know what the shape of this relationship is. About all that is known is that it is an inverse relationship: the greater the proscription the less willing people are to discuss emotions. There is, however, a vast amount of scientific evidence about this one characteristic of the relationship.[7]

This principle has a number of important implications for dating and marital interaction because it is one that we can use to increase or decrease our ability to communicate about our emotions. The way it can be used is to devise some strategies to change our normative beliefs so that we will be either more or less willing to talk about emotions—depending on which we want. Since norms are not innate biological phenomena, but are beliefs that are acquired from the groups in which we live, it is often possible to change our norms by talking, usually at some length, about their appropriateness.

[7] Theory and research beginning with Sumner's (1906) analysis of the role of mores argue for the validity of this idea. Research in such divergent areas as sexual behavior (Christensen, 1969), mate selection (Kerckhoff, 1964), and power (Taysom, 1973) demonstrates the role of normative definitions on behavior. There are frequently many contingencies that determine how much impact these definitions have, but it is virtually axiomatic in modern sociology that the normative structure influences behavior (Davis, 1949). Ehrlich (1969) and Wicker (1969) are two reviews of research in this area, and Liska (1974) is a recent analysis of the issues in the research in this area.

The two following exercises are designed to help us do something about our personal normative beliefs. The first exercise is designed to help us gain a better understanding of what our beliefs really are. This is often useful because our normative beliefs are frequently vague feelings that we have not really articulated to ourselves. They are often nebulous feelings that we should or shouldn't *really* do something or act in certain ways. The second exercise is designed to help us decrease normatively caused reluctance to talk about emotions.

UNDERSTANDING PERSONAL "COMMUNICATION" NORMS

Goal: To better understand your personal beliefs about communicating about emotions.

1. Identify someone who knows you fairly well—such as a fiancé(e), spouse, or close friend—and ask him or her to help you with this exercise by having a conversation that would last at least 15 to 30 minutes.

2. Explain the goal of the exercise to the other person, and then try to determine what you *really* believe about verbally talking about emotions. Talking about some of the following questions may help:

    a. Do I think I would be less of a man or woman if I were to talk about my feelings more openly?

    b. Do I turn people off by talking about my own emotions too much?

    c. If two people I know who are very open and very closed about their own emotions are opposite extremes on a continuum, where do I think I should be on that continuum?

3. Write down what you learned about your own beliefs.

CHANGING PERSONAL "COMMUNICATION" NORMS

Goal: To change your personal norms so you are more willing to talk about emotions.

1. Find a person with whom you have a meaningful relationship (a close friend, date, or spouse) who believes that people should share their emotions more than you think they should. Ask that person to help you with this exercise.

2. Make two lists on a piece of paper. One should be the reasons that you think you should not talk about your feelings more than you do, and the other should be a list of the reasons the other person thinks people should share their emotions more than you do.

3. Try to identify situations in the past or relationships in the present which influenced your belief that you shouldn't be more open about your emotions. (Often our parents' opinions have influenced us, and sometimes women and men subtly hold each other to sex-typed, traditional communicator roles, such as the "strong and silent" or "highly emotional" type.)

4. Discuss the ideas you have identified in steps 2 and 3 to see whether you might want to change your opinions about talking about emotions. If you do want to, try to identify what you want to believe and why you now think you should believe it.

SUMMARY

This chapter has identified five principles that deal with emotions and communication. The first generalization discussed was the *Emotionality* principle, which states that the greater the intensity of emotions the less the ability to rationally control behavior. The second was the *Control* principle, which states that the greater the rational control we have over ourselves the better the quality of our verbal communication. These two principles are shown as arrows 1 and 2 in the diagram in Figure 3–5. The plus sign indicates a positive relationship. The minus sign indicates a negative relationship.

The other generalizations discussed in this chapter were the *Trust, Concern,* and *Norms-Emotion* principles. The Trust principle states that the amount we trust others in a relationship influences our willingness to communicate about important emotions. The Concern principle states that the more we perceive that others are concerned about us the greater our willingness to communicate verbally about our important feelings. The Norms-Emotion principle states that the presence of normative proscriptions against discussing emotions prevents the open discussion of emotions. These three principles are shown as arrows 3, 4, and 5 in Figure 3–5.

These last three principles identify factors that influence the willingness to communicate about emotions, and most of the time couples will probably want to use the principles to increase the amount they verbally communicate about emotions. The principles, however, can also be used to decrease communication about emotions, and there may be times when a person is not physically or emo-

Figure 3–5

Causal models of the principles in Chapter 3

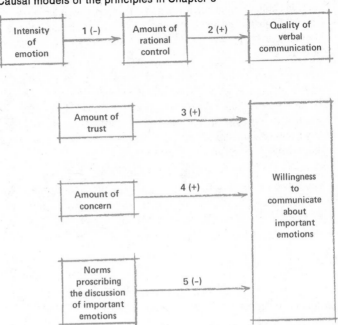

tionally able to deal with additional emotional issues, or when someone is making inappropriate intrusions about his or her feelings. At these times, decreasing such factors as safety and concern will probably change the relationship so that the individuals involved will be more reluctant to communicate about their feelings.

SUGGESTIONS FOR FURTHER STUDY

Arnold, Magda B.   1960. *Emotion and Personality*. New York: Columbia University Press.

Davitz, Joel R.   1969. *The Language of Emotion*. New York: Academic Press.

Dittman, Allen T.   1972. *Interpersonal Messages of Emotion*. New York: Springer.

Harper, Robert A.   1958. "Communication Problems in Marriage and Marriage Counseling." *Marriage and Family Living* 20:107–12 (May).

Hillman, James   1960. *Emotion: A Comprehensive Phenomenology of Theories and their Meaning for Therapy*. London: Routledge and Kegan Paul.

Horney, Karen   1945. *Our Inner Conflicts*. New York: Norton.

Johnson, David   1972. *Reaching Out: Interpersonal Effectiveness and Self-Actualization.* Englewood Cliffs, N. J.: Prentice-Hall, chaps. 5–6.

Lund, Frederick H   1939. *Emotions: Their Psychological, Physiological, and Educative Implications.* New York: Ronald Press.

Waller, Willard, and Hill, R. L.   1951. *The Family: A Dynamic Interpretation.* Rev. ed. New York: Dryden, chap. 3.

Young, Paul T.   1973. *Emotion in Man and Animal.* Huntington, N.Y.: Krieger.

4

The role of self-esteem in communication

THE LAST CHAPTER dealt with the effects of intense emotions on verbal communication and with ways to increase or decrease the open discussion of emotions. That chapter was very general, however, in the sense that all of the different types of emotions were grouped together rather than dealt with separately. This chapter is more precise in that it deals with the effects that a particular group of emotions—the feelings we have about ourselves—have on communication processes. Our feelings about ourselves influence our verbal communication in several ways. One way is that when we are in situations in which we feel comfortable about ourselves we usually tend to be more skillful at listening, being sensitive to the feelings of others, and sharing our own ideas than when we feel such emotions as embarrassment, inadequacy, or unimportance. The following case history illustrates a situation in which some of these emotions influenced the communication in a relationship.

"All he ever talks about is the women at his office," Gladys told the counselor. "He pays more attention to them than he does to me. A little secretary can have some trouble with her boyfriend and he listens for hours and then wants to come home and tell me about it. He never listens to me; he just buries his nose in the television. Other husbands talk to their wives about their work and about politics and business, but not Harold."

"I try to talk to her," Harold said. "At least I used to. But she's so sensitive that everything I say she takes personally. It's especially bad since she got older and put on a little weight. Now every time I mention something that concerns any other women, she has a fit. I work in an insurance office, and we employ a lot of young women. Most of the things that happen to me during the day have something to do with problems that the girls get into. I've found that it's easier to keep quiet at home and let her yell about my not talking than to talk to her and have a dramatic scene about the affairs she imagines I'm having with the office girls" (Klemer, 1970, p. 208).

Self feelings probably operated in this situation in several ways. The wife's feelings about herself apparently made her sensitive and difficult to talk with, and it may be that the husband's feelings about himself caused him to select certain topics that would be disruptive so he could escape the uncomfortable parts of the situation. Since our feelings about ourselves influence our ability to communicate, and effective communication is essential in most, if not all, of the alternative styles of marriage, it seems useful to identify several skills that can help us increase the feelings that aid communication and decrease the feelings that hinder communication. This is the main objective of this chapter, and this overall goal is sought by trying to attain the following more specific goals:

1. Define several terms so that we have the same thing in mind when we use such words as *self-concept, self-esteem,* or *anxiety.*
2. Identify several principles that explain how our feelings about ourselves influence communication.
3. Illustrate how these principles can be used in dating and marital relationships.
4. Identify several activities that we can use to acquire or increase the skills we need if we are to use these principles.

TERMINOLOGY

Four major terms should be defined before the principles are introduced. Each of these terms is uniquely different from the others, but two of them are frequently confused. The two that are easily mixed up are *self-concept* and *self-esteem.* The term *self-concept* is used here to refer to opinions that people have of what they think they are as persons.[1] The self-concept is usually very

---

[1] The term *self-concept* is a basic concept in several schools of thought. Its importance in Symbolic Interaction is illustrated by the fact that the most singularly important work in that field is Mead's (1934) *Mind, Self, and Society.* This concept is also used in every major work in the field, such as Rose (1962, chap. 1), Stryker (1964), and Goffman (1959). Rogers' (1951, chap. 11) theory of personality has come to be known as a "self" theory (Hall and Lindzey, 1957). It is also a central concept in what has come to be known as role theory (Biddle and Thomas, 1966; Sarbin, 1968). The term was initially developed in its present form by James (1890), and it is similar to several other terms, such as *identity* (Allport, 1961, pp. 114–17; Erikson, 1951) and *ego* (Warren, 1934). The use of the term *ego* as a synonym for *self-concept* should not, however, be confused with the very different meaning *ego* has in psychoanalysis.

complex, as it includes such varied components as height, sexuality, temperament, gender, weight, traits, inclinations, location in the social fabric, and habits. It is also primarily an intellectual process, as it consists of impressions, opinions, perceptions, and concepts. It is thus not an emotional process, as a self-concept is not a feeling, sentiment, or affective response. As the term is used here it also does not have evaluative components, such as judgments about the worth or value of a person's characteristics.

Some people do not make a distinction between self-concept and self-esteem, but when they fail to separate the two they confuse two very different human processes. The self-concept refers to what people think they are, and self-esteem refers to the evaluative judgments they make of this self-concept.[2] It refers to such judgments as a person viewing himself as acceptable or unacceptable, worthwhile or worthless, esteemable or unesteemable, and to many other similar evaluative assessments. The self-concept identifies what a person thinks he actually is, and self-esteem identifies how much he likes or dislikes what he thinks he is. The self-concept is so complex and has so many different facets that it does not have any dimensionality to it. Self-esteem, on the other hand, does have dimensionality because it can vary from low to high self-esteem, as shown below:

Self-esteem

Very low   Low   Adequate   High   Very high

Social scientists would probably be more precise if they did not refer to self-esteem as an overall assessment of worth, since it is probably many individual assessments of various traits. Yet many social scientists seem to lump all of these various evaluations together into a generalized, overall assessment of worth, and hence that is the way the term is used here. As will be seen later, the

[2] An example of a careful distinction between self-concept and self-esteem is Allport's (1961, chap. 6) analysis of the self. He distinguishes between the awareness and the evaluative aspects of the self. He later groups both of them with several other factors in his "proprium," but that does not negate their independence. It seems to this author that one of the reasons that symbolic interaction has been slow in advancing beyond the thinking of Mead is that it has not made such distinctions as the refinement between self-concept and self-esteem in the same way as they have been made in the closely related perspective known as role theory (see Jackson, 1966, as an example). Secord and Backman (1964, p. 579) distinguish between what are termed here as *self-concept* and *self-esteem* by labeling them the cognitive and affective aspects of the self.

self-esteem factor is a very crucial part of the principles that are introduced in this chapter.

A third term that should be defined is *anxiety.* This concept is defined here as an emotional condition of being worried, uneasy, or apprehensive.[3] It too is a variable because the amount of anxiety can vary from very small to very great. When individuals have a large amount of anxiety, they frequently exhibit such symptoms as sweaty palms, upset stomach, tenseness of muscles, and physical reactions, such as clenching the jaw, squeezing the fist, having a quivering upper lip or eyelid, or tapping the feet. As anxiety goes down, people tend to be proportionately more relaxed. The anxiety variable can also be diagramed as a continuum:

Anxiety about self-esteem

Very   Low   Medium   High   Very high

The fourth concept is *rational control.* This variable was defined in Chapter 3 as the amount of conscious, intellectual control that a person has over what he or she does. It varies between an absence of intellectual control over behavior and complete intellectual control over behavior; and this can also be diagramed as a continuum:

Amount of
rational control over behavior

None   Low   Medium   High   Complete

SELF-ESTEEM AND COMMUNICATION

There are several ways in which changes in our self-esteem influence communication. One way is that when events threaten to decrease our self-esteem we become anxious and defensive, and this defensiveness then frequently tends to interfere with the quality of verbal communication. The three principles that are involved in this process are called here the *Self-Esteem, Defensiveness,* and *Defense-Communication* principles. Because these principles are

---

[3] Analyses of anxiety as a scientific construct are contained in Baughman and Welsh (1962, pp. 419–54) and Sarason et al. (1960). In these analyses anxiety is broken down into several different types, but given the relatively limited use of the term in the present formulation it seems more useful to use the global construct than to be concerned about the complication introduced by dealing with the specific subtypes of anxiety.

important, and because they form a chain sequence, all three will be described before discussing their practical implications for dating and marriage or how to develop skills in using them.

THE SELF-ESTEEM PRINCIPLE: The amount of self-esteem influences the amount of anxiety that individuals experience, and this is an inverse, curvilinear relationship.[4]

This principle asserts that the amount of self-esteem that individuals experience has a causal effect on the amount of anxiety they experience. This relationship is illustrated in Figure 4–1, which

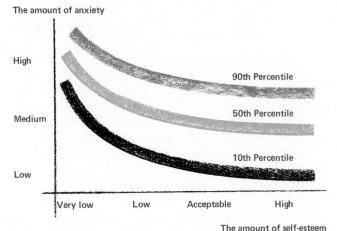

Figure 4–1

The relationship between self-esteem and anxiety

shows that when self-esteem decreases below a marginal level the decrease tends to create an increase in anxiety, and that further drops in self-esteem tend to bring about rather marked increases in anxiety. It is fairly important to recognize that this is a curvilinear relationship, and to realize that this curvilinearity makes a difference in the practical implications of this principle. If the relationship were an inverse, linear relationship, we would expect that any variation (increase or decrease) in self-esteem would have an influence on anxiety. The curvilinearity, however, creates a situation

---

[4]Rose's (1962, pp. 537–49) interactional theory of neurosis has a detailed discussion of this relationship. The relationship is also a basic proposition in Sullivan's (1953) interpersonal theory of psychiatry. This author does not know of any empirical studies that have tested the relationship; therefore, confidence in its validity at the present time rests on the fact that it is part of several very complex and widely respected theories in the social sciences and on the fact that it seems to be consistent with everyday observable behavior.

in which variation in the amount of self-esteem has no effect on anxiety unless the self-esteem is fairly low.

Another characteristic of this relationship that is suggested by Figure 4–1 is that there is considerable "range" in the amount of anxiety people have when their self-esteem is fairly high. In other words our anxiety can vary between low and high when we have relatively high self-esteem—apparently because anxiety is influenced by other factors. However, when we have low self-esteem, the amount of anxiety has a smaller range because few people, if any, have low anxiety when their self-esteem is threatened. This idea that there is a predictable variation in the range of anxiety is not explicit in the previous literature, but it seems to be sufficiently implicit in the prior theorizing to be included here as a tentative suggestion. It should be realized, however, that this principle has not been precisely stated before and has not yet been tested with quantified empirical research.

One of the ideas in this generalization is that when something happens to make people feel that they are less acceptable or less worthwhile than they like to think they are, this is not something that is taken lightly. It is something that usually generates intense emotional responses. People get anxious, upset, and tense, and are generally very uncomfortable inside. These feelings do not, of course, always show readily on the outside because many people are pretty effective at concealing their emotions, but the principle asserts that the feelings are usually still there.

The Defensive-ness principle   If people merely felt anxious when their self-esteem became uncomfortably low, this would probably have little relevance for dating and marital relationships, and it would hardly be worth mentioning in this book. Unfortunately, however, that is not where this chain of events stops. When individuals start feeling anxious as a result of threats to their self-esteem this anxiety usually has an influence on other processes. One of its effects is summarized in the Defensiveness principle.

> THE DEFENSIVENESS PRINCIPLE: The amount of anxiety due to lowered self-esteem influences the amount individuals use defensive behaviors called defense mechanisms.[5]

This principle asserts that increases in a certain type of anxiety tend to bring about defensiveness in people, and that, conversely,

---

[5] This principle was first developed as a part of psychoanalysis. See, for example, the work of Anna Freud (1946). Now, however, the idea has such wide acceptance that it is not viewed as being limited to psychoanalytic theory, as is illustrated by its use by Allport (1961, pp. 155–63) and Rogers (1951, 182–87) and by its prominent role in general texts on abnormal psychology (see Coleman, 1956, pp. 84–100, as an example).

decreases in this particular type of anxiety tend to decrease defensiveness. The principle thus introduces a new variable, and before the principle can be discussed in detail it is important to define this variable. The variable is *the amount people use defense mechanisms,* and it refers to a group of behaviors that seem to be fairly effective in defending self-esteem. These behaviors have come to be known as "defense mechanisms," but it is important to realize that they are really only one type of defensive behavior. They are acts that are designed to defend or protect one's self-esteem.

Some defense mechanisms are so commonly used and so widely known that they are a part of our everyday vocabulary. *Rationalization* is one of these defense mechanisms. It is the process of seeking out *false* justifications for something when the real reasons would be too threatening to our self-esteem. *Fantasy* is another common defense mechanism. It is the process of gratifying frustrated desires in imaginary achievements, such as a person imagining that he is a great sports hero when it would be too frustrating to his self-esteem to face his actual level of performance. We use many other behaviors to defend our self-esteem, and it seems useful to list and describe a number of them. Before doing that, however, it should be pointed out that there is nothing inherently bad about using defense mechanisms. We all use them, and they serve an extremely important function in helping us to salve our wounded egos. They only become serious problems when they are either (1) used so extensively that they distort reality enough to interfere with one's life, or (2) when they interfere with attaining certain desired goals. Defense mechanisms are important in dating and marital communication mostly for the second reason, and one thing they *frequently* interfere with is the quality of verbal communication. A number of commonly used defense mechanisms other than rationalization and fantasy are:

Projection: Inappropriately placing the blame for problems or difficulties on others or attributing one's own unethical desires to others.
Compensation: Covering up a weakness by emphasizing or concentrating on traits that are acceptable or making up for frustration in one area by turning to another area.
Regression: Retreating to behaviors that were appropriate at an earlier stage of development (such as childhood). Usually this involves less mature behavior, such as temper tantrums, throwing things, and crying.
Putting others down: Trying to depreciate the value, contributions, or traits of other persons so that we will be less inadequate when compared with them.

Denial: Refusing to perceive or face something by such behaviors as being preoccupied with other things, getting sick, selectively perceiving, etc.

Aggression: Attacking persons or things to get even, divert attention, "show" them, defeat them, etc. Aggression can be physical or verbal and is frequently covert rather than overt.

Reaction formation: Coping with dangerous or unacceptable feelings or desires by expressing exaggerated opposing attitudes and types of behavior.

Emotional insulation: Withdrawing emotional involvement by becoming passive, apathetic, or uninterested.

Repression: Preventing uncomfortable, dangerous, or threatening thoughts from becoming conscious.

Acting out: Reducing anxiety that is aroused by forbidden or uncomfortable thoughts or wishes by permitting their expression.

Diverting attention: Focusing on different issues so that our inadequacies will be less visible.

Escape: Departing either physically or mentally from a situation that is too hurtful.

These examples illustrate many of the common defense mechanisms, but many other behaviors can also be used to defend one's threatened self-esteem. These defensive behaviors should not be viewed as pathological or undesirable, and in the long run they are occasionally helpful in verbal communication because they can be used to reduce our anxiety enough for us to reconcentrate on the issues being communicated. However, they can also disrupt communication, and that brings us to the last of the three principles.

The Defense-Communica-tion principle

Defense mechanisms can interfere with the quality of verbal communication in several ways. One way is that occasionally one spouse is the source of a threat to the self-esteem of the other, and the offended spouse reacts by verbally attacking the one who initially caused the threat. The result of this type of defensive behavior can frequently be predicted by using the Self-Esteem principle. The verbal attacks will cause the first spouse to become threatened, and he or she will then also become defensive. The net result is a sequence of behaviors in which both individuals undermine each other's self-esteem and wind up with negative feelings toward each other. When this happens and the couple then try to continue to communicate about the initial topics they were discussing they will frequently use the situation to continue to defend themselves rather than to address and cope with the issues they are ostensibly discussing. Defensiveness thus prevents them from communicating about the issues that they really want to discuss. Often neither member of the couple will realize that this process is occurring because the defensive and attacking behaviors are frequently subtle or covert acts, such as a glance or a look that discredits the other person, a disrespectful or a snide comment, or a joke told at the other person's expense.

Another way in which defensive behaviors become problematic in marriages is that frequently one spouse feels threatened when the couple is coping with an important situation. When this occurs the threatened spouse will tend to become anxious and then defensive. The defensiveness will then frequently divert the couple from the initial situation they were trying to solve. At this point the spouse who was not threatened may still be so intent on coping with the initial situation that he or she does not realize what is going on and becomes frustrated at the diverting behavior of the threatened spouse. The net result is that one spouse is defensive and the other frustrated, and when this occurs the chances of their being able to continue to communicate about the initial problem are almost·nil.

Since high defensiveness frequently interferes with the quality of communication it seems sensible to state this idea in a formal principle. On the other hand, there is a danger in stating this as a general rule because many times defensiveness has no adverse effect on the communication process, and thus far research has not specified the circumstances in which defensiveness influences communication. At the risk of being premature the principle is stated here, but readers should be aware that there are probably many circumstances in which it does not operate. The generalization is:

THE DEFENSE-COMMUNICATION PRINCIPLE: The use of defense mechanisms frequently has an adverse effect on the quality of the verbal communication.

So little is known about this relationship that nothing can be said about the shape of the relationship. About all that can be said is that increases in defensiveness frequently seem to interfere with the quality of verbal communication.

In summary

These three principles can be viewed as a chain sequence, and this sequence is diagramed in Figure 4–2. The Self-Esteem principle is represented by the arrow labeled A; the Defensiveness principle is represented by the arrow labeled B; and the Defensive-Communication principle is represented by the arrow labeled C. When the principles are put together in this causal sequence, it can be seen that variation in the amount of self-esteem tends to indirectly influence the quality of communication. These principles

Figure 4–2

A chain sequence of propositions showing the effects of changes in self-esteem

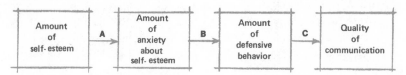

are probably most relevant when threats to self-esteem are fairly high, because that is when anxiety and defensiveness will also be highest.

How can these principles be used in marital interaction?

At least four different skills are involved in using the Self-Esteem principle in our personal lives. Some of these skills are more elementary than the others in the sense that they need to be mastered before the more complex skills can be acquired. Probably the most elementary of the four skills is being able to recognize the level of self-esteem that we have ourselves or the level that someone else has. This skill permits us to recognize whether or not persons have a sufficiently high level of self-esteem to be unthreatened and comfortable with themselves as opposed to having a lower level of self-esteem. This also includes the ability to determine whether or not a person is at the point of being threatened; and those of us who are proficient in this skill can distinguish between being slightly threatened as opposed to being highly threatened.

A skill that is slightly more complex is the ability to recognize changes in self-esteem. Changes occur when individuals are in situations in which their self-esteem is either increased or decreased, or they have at least a suspicion that they are more or less esteemworthy than they previously thought. This skill, like the first one mentioned, can be used to understand what is going on with one's own self and what is occurring with others' views of themselves.

A third skill is the ability to recognize factors that tend to bring about changes in self-esteem. There are many different situations that influence self-esteem, such as receiving a request for a date or a proposal of marriage, getting grades in school, making or not making a team, or being jilted, recognized, ignored, or insulted. It is likely that having this skill is not dependent on having the first two skills mentioned above. For example, a person might recognize that something will lower or raise someone's self-esteem but still not be aware of how much self-esteem the individual has or how much its level will be changed.

A fourth skill is being able to consciously *do* something that will influence someone's self-esteem, and this includes being able to manipulate one's own self-esteem or someone else's. It seems reasonable to believe that this skill is in at least some ways more advanced and complex than the three preceding skills. We could probably influence our own or someone else's self-esteem on rare occasions if we didn't have the ability to determine levels of self-esteem, to recognize changes in self-esteem, and to know what brings about changes, but if we were to become very proficient at influencing self-esteem we would probably also have to be fairly competent in the other three skills.

These four skills deal specifically with how to know something or do something about *self-esteem*. It takes only a slight change, however, to modify these same inter- and intrapersonal processes so that they can also apply to anxiety and defensiveness. For example, the first skill mentioned was the ability to recognize different levels of self-esteem. If this same basic skill of recognizing different levels of a variable is extended to the other two variables, then

Table 4–1

Twelve skills relevant for using the Self-Esteem, Anxiety, and Defense-Communication principles

Ability	Self-esteem	Amount of anxiety	Use of defense mechanisms
Recognize the level of the variable	A Recognize level of self-esteem	B Recognize level of anxiety	C Recognize use of defense mechanisms
Recognize changes in the variable	D Recognize changes in self-esteem	E Recognize changes in anxiety	F Recognize changes in use of defense mechanisms
Know what changes the variable	G Know what changes self-esteem	H Know what changes anxiety	I Know what changes use of defense mechanisms
Be able to consciously change the variable	J Be able to change self-esteem	K Be able to change anxiety	L Be able to change amount defense mechanisms are used

two other skills are identified. These are the ability to recognize different levels of anxiety and to recognize different levels of defensiveness. Table 4–1 shows these three skills, as cell *A* identifies the ability to recognize different levels of self-esteem, and cells *B* and *C* identify the ability to recognize different levels of the other two variables. The same extrapolation process can be applied to recognizing changes in the amount of anxiety and defensiveness, to knowing what changes them, and to being able to change them, and cells *D* through *L* identify these skills. This table is useful because it illustrates the complexity of the skills that are relevant for the three principles that have been discussed so far in this chapter, and it shows how some of these skills are related to one another.

The following four exercises are designed to help us increase some of the skills identified in Table 4–1. The first exercise is the most complex. It deals with four of the skills in Table 4–1 since it is designed to help increase skills *A, D, G* and *J*. The second exercise deals with skill *D,* and the third one deals with skills *A* and *J*. The last exercise deals with skills *C, F,* and *I*. These four exercises are, of course, not appropriate for all situations, and those of us who find them inappropriate may wish to modify them or to design more effective ways to determine how skillful we are and to improve our abilities.

IMPROVING SKILLS DEALING WITH SELF-ESTEEM

Goal: To increase your ability to (*a*) recognize the level of self-esteem in others, (*b*) recognize changes in their self-esteem, (*c*) recognize what causes these changes, and (*d*) know what you can do to change the self-esteem of others. (This exercise is more complex than most of the exercises.)

1. Think of a person with whom you have a close relationship—spouse, fiancé(e), friend, etc. Then do the four following things.

   a. Try to identify what "level" of self-esteem he or she has had in recent weeks in regard to several specific aspects of his or her life, such as physical appearance, conversationalist, ability to be a friend, adequacy as a companion, or adequacy as a sex partner. Commit yourself by writing your conclusions down on paper.

   b. Next, think of what changes have occurred in this person's self-esteem in the last several weeks or months. Remember that some changes may last only a few hours or days. List these in writing.

c. Identify in writing the events or situations that probably brought about the changes you identified in step *b.*

d. Identify in writing three or four things that you did or you could have done (1) to bring about the changes you identified in step *b* or (2) to bring about other changes in the other person's self-esteem.

2. Talk with the other person to determine how accurately you perceived what had been occurring in regard to her or his self-esteem. If there are aspects of steps *a, b, c,* or *d* on which you disagree about what happened, talk about why each of you perceived the situation the way you did and try to arrive at a consensus.

3. Discuss with the other person what you could have done to better understand the level of self-esteem, when changes occurred in self-esteem, what changed it, and what you could have done to change it.

4. Identify several specific things you will do in the future in this relationship to be better at these four skills.

Appreciation is expressed to Owen Cahoon for his assistance in developing this activity.

UNDERSTANDING AND IMPROVING SELF-ESTEEM

Goal: To better understand what influences your feelings of self-esteem and how much self-esteem you have.

An elementary exercise

1. Identify a situation after which you felt "better" about yourself than you did before the situation.

2. Identify what happened to make you feel better about yourself.

A more advanced exercise

1. List on a piece of paper five things that enhance your self-esteem that you use on a regular basis to convince yourself that you are an adequate, acceptable person. (Some can do this easily, and others have difficulty doing this. If you are a person who has difficulty doing this, discuss the problem with someone you are close to and see whether he or she can help you.)

2. List on the same piece of paper five things that tend to decrease your self-esteem periodically (or continually). These things will be

situations or events that contribute to uneasy, guilty, or uncomfortable feelings about yourself.

3. Think about the items on the two lists, and try to determine what your "net" feelings about yourself tend to be.

4. Identify two or three things you could do in the future to create a more positive image of yourself, and implement them.

RECOGNIZING CHANGES IN SELF-ESTEEM

Goal: To improve your ability to recognize changes, especially negative changes, in self-esteem during communication.

1. Get together with another person (spouse, fiancé(e), roommate, friend) and make a list of verbal and nonverbal signals which indicate a lowering of self-esteem in you or the other person during communication.

2. Put the list in a place where you can refer to it often until you know it fairly well.

3. After being conscious of these factors for a week or two, evaluate what effect this has had on the communication in this relationship.

RECOGNIZING DEFENSIVENESS

Goal: To increase your ability to recognize defensive behavior when communicating.

1. Get someone you live with to help you with this exercise. It will involve an initial discussion of 15–30 minutes and then being alert to several things for a week.

2. Review the list of defense mechanisms on pages 87–88 together with the other person so that you both understand what they are.

3. During the next week each of you point out to the other whenever either of you thinks someone is acting defensively. It may be wise to identify what kinds of statements would be "acceptable" ways to point this out, as moments when we are defensive also tend to be moments when we are less open-minded about having others telling us we are defensive.

4. Whenever possible in the situations in which someone is being defensive, try to identify the "reasons" for the defensiveness. This

type of analysis will probably also help you increase your ability (a) to see what influences self-esteem and feelings of anxiety and (b) to see what effects changes in self-esteem and anxiety have on defensiveness.

5. At the end of the week, evaluate the experience to determine what effect this exercise has had on your ability to communicate and on your feelings toward the other person.

It is very likely that after readers of this chapter complete several of the exercises they will be able to identify many different situations in their lives that will be even more useful in helping them increase their skill at recognizing and manipulating these variables. Hopefully, in the process they will become increasingly effective in their ability to communicate verbally with others.

THE ANXIETY PRINCIPLE

It seems useful to integrate the issues in this chapter with one of the principles in the previous chapter. This can be done by making a "logical" deduction from the Emotionality principle in the last chapter. The Emotionality principle stated that the intensity of our emotions influences the amount of control we have over our behavior. When we have emotions that are low to moderately high we can have considerable control over our behavior, but as our emotions become intense we tend to lose control over our behavior. The way that principle can be tied to the issues in this chapter is to specify the logical connection between the more general term *intensity of emotion* and the more specific term *anxiety*. Since anxiety is nothing more than one particular emotion it follows that, if the Emotionality principle is valid, variation in anxiety should influence the amount that behavior is rationally controlled. Thus, there is reason to accept:

THE ANXIETY PRINCIPLE: The amount of anxiety an individual experiences due to lowered self-esteem influences the amount the person's behavior is rationally controlled, and this is a positive, curvilinear relationship.

The relationship in this principle is diagrammed in Figure 4–3, and this figure shows that we usually have considerable control over our behavior when we have a moderate amount of anxiety. When we have very high levels of anxiety, however, we tend to have less control over what we do or say.

Figure 4–3

The effect of anxiety on rational control

Amount of rational control a person has over behavior

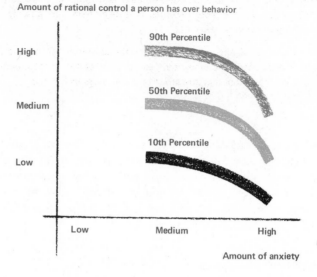

The main idea in this generalization can also be stated in less precise terms. What it means is that when individuals become upset because of threats to their self-esteem their behavior will be less sensible and more a product of their emotions. On the other hand, when individuals start to feel more positively toward themselves they tend to calm down and become more "sensible" or rational. It takes quite a bit of anxiety, however, before people's emotions tend to take over, and they do not have to be completely free from anxiety before they tend to get control over their behavior.

The addition of the Anxiety principle provides a more comprehensive picture of how threats to self-esteem influence the quality of verbal communication because the anxiety created by threats to self-esteem causes us to lose control *as well as* become defensive, and this particular combination of factors may have a more detrimental effect on the quality of communication than just becoming defensive.

SUMMARY

This chapter identified three new principles that form a fairly complex chain sequence. The *Self-Esteem* principle identifies the fact that changes in self-esteem, when esteem is fairly low, influence anxiety, and the *Defensiveness* principle identifies the fact that increases in this type of anxiety tend to bring about defensive behavior while decreases in this type of anxiety tend to decrease

defensive behavior. The *Defense-Communication* principle asserts
that frequently this type of defensive behavior influences the quality of verbal communication. This sequence is diagramed in Figure
4–4 with arrow 1 identifying the Self-Esteem principle, arrow 2
identifying the Defensiveness principle, and arrow 3 identifying
the Defense-Communication principle. The *Anxiety* principle was
then identified, and it is a more specific case of the Emotionality
principle discussed in Chapter 3. The Anxiety principle asserts that
variation in anxiety influences the amount of rational control people
have over their behavior, and this is shown in Figure 4–4 as arrow

Figure 4–4

Causal model of the principles in Chapter 4

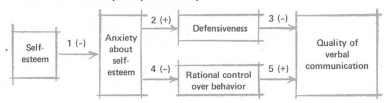

4. When the Control principle (changes in rational control influence
the quality of verbal communication) is also included in this figure,
as shown in arrow 5, this shows two ways that anxiety about self-
esteem tends to influence the quality of verbal communication. The
chapter also discussed a number of different skills that are involved
in using these principles, and several exercises were provided that
can be used to increase our ability to apply these ideas to our personal life situations.

SUGGESTIONS FOR FURTHER STUDY

Adler, Alfred   1930. "Individual Psychology," in C. Murchison (ed.),
    Psychologies of 1930's. Worcester, Mass.: Clark University Press.
Freud, Anna   1946. *The Ego and the Mechanisms of Defense.* New
    York: International Universities Press.
Fromm, Erich   1955. *The Sane Society.* New York: Rinehart.
Goffman, Erving   1959. *The Presentation of Self in Everyday Life.*
    New York: Doubleday Anchor Books.
Shibutani, Tomotsu   1961. *Society and Personality.* Englewood Cliffs,
    N.J.: Prentice-Hall, chap. 11–13.
Sullivan, Harry S.   1953. *The Interpersonal Theory of Psychiatry.* New
    York: Norton.

5

Communication skills

SCHOLARS who have studied communication have discovered very few general principles about it. However, in the process of trying to better understand the way people share information they have identified a number of different "skills" that can be used to help create effective communication. The difference between these skills and general principles is that general principles explain how various factors or variables influence one another, or, stated in slightly different words, they identify causes and effects that we can expect to occur most of the time. The skills, on the other hand, are techniques or behaviors that we can use whenever we think they will help us improve our communication. Since many of these skills can be useful in dating and marital relationships a chapter is included here that describes some of these communication skills and illustrates ways in which they can be used. The first section of the chapter identifies three skills that deal with nonverbal communication. The second section identifies six skills that deal with verbal communication. The third section identifies some skills that involve both nonverbal and verbal processes, and the final section identifies a number of factors that a communicator may want to take into account when trying to send or receive information. This chapter is less scientific than most of the chapters in this volume, but hopefully the concepts and skills that are discussed will be of some value.

NONVERBAL COMMUNICATION SKILLS

Most of us learn early in childhood that a large part of our communication with others is nonverbal. We learn that we need to pay

Touching

99

attention to the "way" people say things and that such behaviors as a sigh or a facial expression help us understand what others really mean. In addition we learn such an elaborate set of gestures with our own hands and faces that when we cannot see the person we are trying to communicate with or we cannot use our hands to help express ourselves we feel stifled and uncomfortable.

Touching is one method of communicating nonverbally. Even the relatively habitual process of shaking hands sends and receives messages, such as acceptance, friendship, and congeniality. There are in addition a large number of other ways that touch can be used as a medium of communication in dating and marital relationships. These methods include such relatively simple physical contacts as placing one's hand on the other person's forearm while saying something important to him or her. This type of physical contact can be used to add emphasis, to communicate personal closeness, to help communicate how intensely the verbal message is emotionally experienced, or to alleviate such feelings as rejection and aloneness. More complex forms of physical contact, such as kissing and embracing, communicate large amounts of information and feelings that are difficult to communicate verbally, and it may be that it is impossible to communicate some messages effectively when physical contact is absent.

Even though touch usually has meaning attached to it, much of the time this meaning is not universally understood, as it is unique to a particular subcultural group or a particular couple. We begin developing a language of touch early in our relationship with someone, and then as the relationship becomes more involved and we continue interacting with the other person we gradually acquire a consensus about what different forms of touch mean. A touch on the back of the hand in one situation may mean, "Good luck—I'm behind you and wish you well," and in another situation it may mean, "I love you—as a person you are very precious to me," while in still another situation it may mean, "I'm becoming sexually aroused and want to engage in more intimate sexual behavior."

Occasionally we might benefit from discussing our language of touch. This is especially true in situations in which certain types of physical touch seem to mean one thing to one member of the couple and something different to the other member, because in such situations a discussion of these differences in "meaning" might create understanding and agreement. Discussion of the language of touch

would be useful in a dating relationship in which one person interprets such behavior as necking and kissing to mean that he or she
likes the other person but does not want exclusivity or commitment
in the relationship while the other interprets the same touching experiences as connoting commitment and an exclusive relationship.
Another situation that illustrates the value of a verbal discussion of
what is communicated by touch is one in which one person interprets snuggling up in bed as a method of experiencing and showing
personal closeness while the other interprets it as an intrusion. The
following exercise creates a situation in which the meaning of several experiences is discussed.

INTERPRETING THE MEANING OF TOUCH

Goal: To identify the messages that are sent and received
through physical contact.

1. Identify a relationship that is fairly intimate, and ask the other
person to help you with this exercise.

2. List about five situations in which you have had some type of
physical contact with this other person or in which you wanted to
have a certain type of physical contact and didn't.

3. Discuss what was communicated in each of these situations by
identifying whether either person sent or received any messages
through the physical contact. If either did, identify (a) what the
person was trying to "say" and (b) what the other person "heard"
in the messages.

4. If you cannot identify any "messages" in the physical contact you
might benefit from asking others (such as members of a discussion group in class) to help you discover the nonverbal messages.
After you can identify these messages you might want to discuss
whether there are ways in which you can "improve" this type of
communication.

Body positions

One of the goals in the field of research known as proxemics is
to discover how differences in body position communicate information.[1] Among other things it has been discovered that when people
sit back in a chair they are usually less interested in what is occurring or being said than when they are leaning forward. This is,

---

[1] Research by Steinzor (1950), Sommer (1959, 1962, 1969), Little (1965),
Lyman and Scott (1967), Argyle and Dean (1965), and Dosey and Meisels
(1969), deals with the relationship between personal space and communication.

of course, not always the case, but the frequency with which it holds true has given use to the expression about people being "on the edge of their seats" when they are highly interested in something. In addition there is research showing that such behaviors as folding arms and crossing legs at the knees are more frequent when people are withdrawing from a conversation or trying to "close off" information coming to them. Most of us are also aware that our eyes frequently reveal how interested we are in what is being said. When a person's eyes are roving about a room, looking at the ceiling, or continually looking down, this usually indicates that the person is less interested in what is being said than if his or her eyes tend to focus on or near the person doing the talking.

There are a number of ways that knowledge about the role of body positions in communication can be used to promote effective communication. One way is to be aware that body positions can give us clues about such things as the level of defensiveness, amount of interest, and intensity of concentration that individuals have when we are trying to communicate with them. When we get clues that they are listening or not listening, open or closed to new ideas, interested or uninterested, we can check out our hunches verbally—or use nonverbal messages, such as silence, to check out our guesses—and then respond accordingly.

Another way we can use this information is to observe our own body movements and positions, as occasionally we may learn how we are responding to a communicating experience by noting that our attention is on the ceiling rather than on what is being said or that we are closing information off that someone is trying to give to us. When we learn these types of things about ourselves we can use that information to do a variety of things, depending on the situation. We can do such things as point out to the other person what we have learned about ourselves, change our behavior if we want to, or continue doing what we have been doing. Another way these insights about the role of body positions can be used in a marital relationship is to discuss them with one's spouse to see whether he or she is aware of them, because if the spouse were to learn the same things this might increase his or her ability to send and receive information more efficiently.

The following exercise is designed to help us increase our awareness of the information that can be gleaned from observing body positions.

> ## "HEARING" WHAT BODY POSITIONS SAY
>
> Goal: To increase the ability to receive accurately messages that are "sent" by body positions.
>
> 1. For one week try to be unusually alert to what body positions are "saying" to you. Keep a piece of paper with you so you can list ten instances in which you received information by observing different aspects of body positions.
>
> 2. When it is feasible, try to check the accuracy of these messages by doing such things as seeing whether others received the same "message" you did or seeing whether the individual sending the message intended to send the message you received.
>
> 3. Some body positions that *may* have information in them are:
>   a. Leaning forward or back in one's seat
>   b. Shading eyes with one's hand as if deep in thought
>   c. A set jaw
>   d. Turning one's back
>   e. No body movement at all—as if the whole body is intent on listening

A subjective view of right and wrong

Disagreements are inevitable in dating and marital relationships. The two individuals have, for one thing, been raised in different families, and they will have acquired a number of differences as a result of differences in the style of life in their families. Some of these differences are so irrelevant to the relationship that they can be ignored, but others are so important that they have to be resolved if the relationship is to continue. When couples encounter differences there is one aspect of those differences that is usually not verbalized, and it influences what happens when they try to resolve the differences. This is whether or not they appreciate the "subjective" aspects of right and wrong in marital disagreements.

It is possible to have a disagreement with someone and believe that our opinion or view of the situation is right in an absolute or objective sense and that the other individual is wrong in an equally absolute or objective sense. In marital relationships it is occasionally possible to determine in an absolute manner which person is right and which is wrong. Such a situation can occur, for example, when one person remembers that an event occurred on a certain date and the other thinks it occurred on a different date and the actual date can be determined. It is possible, however, for a person to be wrong in an absolute sense and right in a subjective sense. For example, an opinion may be incorrect in fact—that is, it would be indefensible if it were contested or unworkable if it were tried (and hence absolutely wrong)—but when a person believes that the opinion is correct the opinion is correct *to that person*. Or, in other words, the opinion is *subjectively* right even though in an objective or absolute sense it may be wrong.

It would be possible for married couples to try to resolve their differences by being highly concerned about the absolute correctness of their opinions and relatively unconcerned about the subjective correctness. Or it would be possible for them to be sensitive to the subjective correctness of their views while they try to resolve their differences or cope with problems. There are four reasons why the latter strategy may often be worth the effort.

First, many of the differences that occur in marital relationships are based on value judgments, or subjective interpretations, and in such instances it is impossible to determine which of two conflicting opinions is really, in an absolute sense, correct and which is incorrect. When differences of this type occur both individuals are right in a subjective sense even though they disagree, and a concern for the ultimate, objective, or absolute right and wrong frequently leads to frustration and confusion in the short run and difficulty in communicating and solving the problem in the long run. Here it may be wiser to recognize that subjectively both individuals are "right," and then to attempt to determine what to do given the fact that there are two different subjectively believed "right" opinions. This subjective view of right and wrong can lead to rather than interfere with finding a plan of action, a compromise or accommodation, that would be satisfactory to both individuals.

The second reason why it is frequently desirable to keep in mind the subjective aspects of right and wrong is that there seems to be something about human nature that often makes many people more defensive and closed-minded when someone views their ideas as objectively wrong rather than as, at that time, right to them. This allowance of at least subjective correctness, even though in an absolute sense the person may be wrong, seems to generate more open-mindedness and less defensiveness than does labeling an opinion as incorrect and saying that the person is in error for believing it. One way to approach this is to recognize that when the world is perceived from the "mind" of other persons, then, given the information they have, their values, and the way they perceive things, their opinions are correct to them. This gives the other persons a certain degree of integrity, respectability, and dignity that is subtly and almost imperceptibly taken away when the subjective rightness of their positions is not recognized.

It is likely that one reason why people react defensively when others don't appreciate the subjective rightness of their opinions is that their self-esteem is at least partly dependent on those beliefs and that differing with their opinion may threaten their self-esteem. This can occur because when self-esteem is intricately tied to a belief people tend to absolutize the belief and to hold to it rigidly, making it difficult for them to view the belief as an idea that in the last analysis is really only subjectively rather than objectively true. When this occurs it probably becomes difficult for them to modify the belief. If this were to occur in a marriage, one of the marital partners might find it impossible to change an opinion because of its emotional and unconscious ties to self-esteem. For example, a husband's view of his masculinity or his view of himself as an acceptable person might be jeopardized by certain behaviors that are very common in some subcultural groups. He might have grown up in a family situation in which the mark of the husband's manhood was that he handled the money, and this function is therefore of symbolic importance to him. Or, his opinion about the frequency of sexual intercourse may be intricately tied to his view of his manhood. The self-esteem of some women is linked to their ideas of how their children should be raised or to the importance of their role as mothers. In some segments of contemporary society women are socialized to believe that being a mother is their most valued role, and hence even discussing the possibility of not having children is threatening to such women. In other segments of contemporary society women are socialized to believe that they should have equality with males in every sense, and the self-esteem of these women may be threatened when this view is questioned.

A third advantage of the recognition of the subjective rightness of the other person's opinions is that it puts the person who is trying to change someone else's mind in a "helpful" role. This can facilitate communication and problem solving because many people respond much more openly to someone who seeks to play a helpful role than to someone who tries to establish an "I'm informed and you're not" or an "I'm right and you're wrong" kind of relationship.

A fourth reason why couples may find it useful to pay attention to the subjective aspect of right and wrong is that when all opinions are regarded as subjectively right the situation is not one in which one person will be considered right and the other wrong when a solution is found. Instead it is a situation in which both persons are right in their own eyes, and each is trying to get the other to understand how he or she views the situation and then to try to identify a solution that will be acceptable to both. Each spouse can try to communicate to the other that there might be new or different ways of looking at the situation rather than try to prove the other wrong.

Thus, when we adopt a subjective view of right and wrong by recognizing that others who disagree with us believe that their opinions are "right" (even though we may believe that in an objective or absolute sense our opinions are more correct), communication will probably be less *defensive* on both parts. We will also probably tend to be both more *adaptable* and *willing to listen* to the point of view of others, and to be more open to *suggestions.* Frequently the communication will be more *relaxed,* and the issues can be discussed in an atmosphere of respect for one another's opinions and respect for one another as people.

VERBAL SKILLS

Role reversal   Sometimes when we are communicating we are not sure that the messages we want to send are being correctly understood by the other person. Or, at other times we think that we correctly understand what someone else is trying to communicate to us, but the other person doesn't think that we understand him or her. The technique of *role reversal* can be used in such situations to determine how well the receiver of the message is understanding the sender. In role reversal the individuals agree to change positions temporarily so that the one who is trying to understand a message or a point of view becomes the one who is trying to communicate it and the one who is trying to communicate the information is the one who is listening. The person who is then assuming the role of the sender of the message tries to explain the information to the person who was previously trying to help him or her understand that same message.

At times we may understand the information others are trying to explain more correctly than the other persons think, and when we reverse roles the other persons are surprised to hear us accurately tell them what they have been trying to communicate. At other times, however, we may think we are accurately understanding, but we are not; and when this occurs role reversal can help the other persons explain their ideas because our attempt to communicate the information can give them some clues about which parts we do and do not understand. The opposite, of course, also works, as at some times we are better understood than we think we are, and at other times other individuals will not understand us as well as they thought they did. When they misunderstand us role reversal can help, as we can carefully observe which parts of our messages the other persons have not correctly understood and can then restate those parts.

There are several different ways that we can bring up the suggestion that role reversal might be useful. We can say such things as, "Let me explain to you what you have been saying . . . to show you that I do understand," or "Now I think I have it—let me make sure by seeing if I can explain it back to you," or "I still don't think you really understand my point of view—to see if you do, will you explain it to me?" Role reversal is a fairly time-consuming device, and it would be awkward to use it extensively. The device can, however, be useful in demonstrating that a person has "gotten through" or in demonstrating that a person hasn't been understood. It also frequently has a useful side effect because if a conversation is becoming heated or the individuals are becoming angry role reversal may be enough of a "break" in the exchange of points of view to disrupt the sequence of events. Also, what happens in role reversal is so unpredictable that it usually slows down the pace of the conversation and occasionally provides some useful humor. It takes time and patience, however, to use role reversal, and there are many situations in which it isn't appropriate and some people find it more trouble than it's worth.

The following exercise may be useful in increasing our ability to use role reversal.

ROLE REVERSAL

Goal: To increase the ability to use role reversal effectively by trying it.

1. The next time you are having a discussion in which either you or the other person has tried to explain something but believe that it has not been *really* understood, try role reversal.

   a. First, ask whether it is acceptable to the other person to reverse positions to determine how accurately the information is understood.

   b. When you reverse roles, do more than just use the other person's words. Try to actually "be" the other person by using the same tone of voice, inflections, gestures, and points of emphasis. Be fair rather than mimic or make fun of the other person.

2. After this experience, evaluate it to determine how valuable it has been in helping you to communicate effectively.

Reflecting

Another technique that can be useful in communicating is the process of reflecting. Here one person repeats to another person some of that person's ideas or feelings. Occasionally the other person's exact words can be used, but it is generally more helpful and appropriate to use different words. An example of reflection is the following sequence:

"I feel like mother is always watching me when she's here, and that inside she's shaking her head about how I do things. I've tried to not get stirred up inside, but there are times when I can just feel her eagle eye on me, and when she says something about how I ought to be doing things I just get all tied up inside."
"You resent it when she criticizes you."
"That's right, and it's more than just a little too. Sometimes . . ."

The reflective comment in this exchange is probably stated in such a way that it conveys such messages as "If I understand you correctly, you are really bothered, is that right?" or "I know what you mean," or "I see now what you're talking about." When such reflective comments are made they frequently encourage others to express more of their feelings, and this is especially useful when people have emotions that are bothering them and that they want to get out. The person who is reflecting can serve as a "listening post" while the other person gets his or her feelings into the open. Then, after the feelings are out, the couple can talk about other things, such as the causes of the situation or what to do about it, or it may be that expressing the feelings is all that is needed.

Many nonverbal messages are communicated when we reflect. If these messages have a connotation of condemnation or wrongness, the reflection will frequently tend to make the other person stop exploring his or her feelings, while if these nonverbalized messages convey an empathic understanding and concern the reflection tends to increase the exploration of feelings. As with all of the skills and techniques discussed in this chapter, reflection is not a cure-all for all communication problems. It does, however, seem to be a method of communicating that can be used at certain times to accomplish certain purposes. At other times it would appear awkward and inappropriate.

Gordon (1970) uses the concept "active listening" to refer to the process of reflecting back to a person the key parts of his or her message. His analysis of this process is helpful because he identifies several situations in which reflection is probably useful and several situations in which it is probably inappropriate. He suggests that it is maximally useful when persons have a problem (in Gordon's terms, *own a problem*), and it would be helpful for them to get the problem out in the open or talk about it in such a way that they can better define what the problem is, explore its implications, or search for ways to cope with it without having someone else actively make suggestions, propose solutions, or evaluate or judge them or the problem. He then suggests that reflection is useless and probably annoying at certain times. Reflection is inopportune, for example, when persons want to obtain information from someone else rather than to explore their own feelings, when there is too little time to "open up" feelings and work them out, when a situation is resolved, when persons are tired of exploring their own feelings, and when another person needs assistance or help. The following examples illustrate situations in which reflection is probably inappropriate in a marital relationship:

Husband: Can you give me a ride to the office this morning because my car is still in the garage?
Wife: You'd like a ride to the office.

Wife: How much would it cost us to re-cover the living room couch?
Husband: You're worried about the cost of re-covering it.

The following case example from Gordon's book (1970, pp. 54–55) illustrates an effective use of reflection. It is probably a situation in which more reflection is used than most people would be comfortable with, but it does illustrate how reflection helped someone redefine a problem and then tentatively develop some insights about herself and the problem.

Sally: I wish I could get a cold once in a while like Barbie. She's lucky.
Father: You feel you're sort of getting gypped.
Sally: Yes. She gets to stay out of school and I never do.
Father: You really would like to stay out of school more.
Sally: Yes. I don't like to go to school every day . . . day after day after day. I get sick of it.
Father: You really get tired of school.
Sally: Sometimes I just hate it.
Father: It's more than not liking it, sometimes you really hate school.
Sally: That's right. I hate the homework, I hate the classes, and I hate the teachers.
Father: You just hate everything about school.

Sally: I don't really hate all the teachers—just two of them. One of them I can't stand. She's the worst.

Father: You hate one in particular, huh?

Sally: Do I ever! It's that Mrs. Barnes, I hate the sight of her. I got her for the whole year, too.

Father: You're stuck with her for a long time.

Sally: Yes. I don't know how I'll ever stand it. You know what she does! Every day we get a long lecture—she stands up there smiling like this [demonstrates] and tells us how a responsible student is supposed to behave, and she reads off all these things that you have to do to get an A in her class. It's sickening.

Father: You sure hate to hear all that stuff.

Sally: Yeah. She makes it seem impossible to get an A—unless you're some kind of genius or a teacher's pet.

Father: You feel defeated before you even start, because you don't think you can possibly get an A.

Sally: Yeah. I'm not going to be one of those teacher's pets—the other kids hate them. I'm already not very popular with the kids. I just don't feel too many of the girls like me [tears].

Father: You don't feel popular and that upsets you.

Sally: Yeah, it sure does. There's this group of girls that are the top ones in school. They are the most popular girls. I wish I could get in their group. But I don't know how.

Father: You really would like to belong to this group, but you're stumped about how to do it.

Sally: That's right. I don't honestly know how girls get into this group. They're not the prettiest—not all of them. They're not always the ones with the best grades. Some in the group get high grades, but most of them get lower grades than I get. I just don't know.

Father: You're sort of puzzled about what it takes to get into this group.

Sally: Well, one thing is that they're all pretty friendly—they talk a lot and, you know, make friends. They say hello to you first and talk real easy. I can't do that. I'm just not good at that stuff.

Father: You think maybe that's what they have that you don't have.

Sally: I know I'm not good at talking. I can talk easily with one girl but not when there's a whole bunch of girls. I just keep quiet. It's hard for me to think of something to say.

Father: You feel okay with one girl but with a lot of girls you feel different.

Sally: I'm always afraid I'll say something that will be silly or wrong or something. So I just stand there and feel kind of left out. It's terrible.

Father: You sure hate that feeling.

Sally: I hate to be on the outside, but I'm afraid to try to get into the conversation.

Gordon's analysis of reflection (active listening) is also useful because he speculates that several beneficial consequences usually result when reflection is used early in a "problem identifying" conversation rather than such other types of responses such as offering a solution, judging, preaching, advising, or condemning. Gordon (1970, pp. 57–59) suggests that reflection tends to:

(1)   help individuals free themselves of troublesome feelings;
(2)   help individuals become less afraid of negative feelings;
(3)   promote a relationship of warmth between two individuals who are communicating;
(4)   facilitate problem solving by the individual to whom the reflection is directed;
(5)   create a greater tendency to be willing to listen to the reflector's thoughts and ideas;
(6)   leave the initiative in the conversation with the individual to whom the reflection is directed.

These speculations are useful because they come very close to being general principles about the effects of reflection. The terms need to be defined more clearly, to be stated more precisely, and to be subjected to some empirical testing before they can be viewed as full-fledged principles in which we can have confidence, but even if only some of them are true they can make a case for a selective use of reflection in marital communication. The following exercise is designed to help us try reflecting.

REFLECTING

Goal: To increase the ability to reflect by practicing it and evaluating its consequences.

1.   For a week be alert for a certain type of social situation. The situation you are looking for is one in which someone with whom you are fairly close (spouse, roommate, sibling, etc.) begins identifying a "problem" that she or he has that is important enough to create uncomfortable emotions.

2.   When this situation occurs, try to minimize as much as possible statements that (a) identify solutions to the problem (ordering, directing, commanding, advising, lecturing, warning, admonishing, threatening, exhorting, moralizing, preaching, suggesting, or giving logical arguments); (b) put the other person down (name-calling, shaming, ridiculing, judging, disagreeing, blaming, and especially criticizing); (c) are openly supportive of the other person (praising, agreeing, reassuring, sympathizing, consoling, or encouraging).

Try, whenever it is comfortable and appropriate, to repeat back to the other person IN YOUR OWN WORDS the meaning of the message that you think the other person is trying to communicate to you.

3. At the end of the week evaluate how those conversations tend to be different than they would probably have been if you had used more solution-proving, put-down, or supportive statements and fewer reflecting statements. How did these conversations make you feel? (This exercise will be doubly valuable if several try it and then later discuss and evaluate their experience.)

Issue versus personality

Another factor that a number of scholars (Magoun, 1948; Blood, 1969, chap. 17) believe is helpful in communication is to separate an issue that is being discussed from the personalities of the individuals in the discussion. It is not always possible to do this, but when issues can be depersonalized it is frequently easier to communicate effectively. This point can be illustrated with several different marital issues. One method ties the issue to a personality, and the other method tries to separate the issue from the person.

Separating issue from personality	*Mixing issue with personality*
I'd like to have a discussion about the things we have been having for dinner lately.	I think that your cooking is a problem.
I think we have a problem with some of the things we have been eating.	You're not buying the right food.
Our being late all of the time is frustrating to me.	You're always making us late.
Are you satisfied with that painting job?	You're a sloppy painter.
I'd like to get my way more.	I think you're too bossy.
I don't think my feelings and opinions are considered enough.	You're inconsiderate.

It is easier to separate issues from personalities when the problems that are being addressed are fairly impersonal, such as deciding which color to paint a living room, where to take a vacation, or whether to subscribe to a magazine. Many of the issues in marital relationships, however, are personal issues, and when such concerns are addressed it is more challenging and difficult to isolate the issue from the person as a whole. It is probably most difficult to depersonalize an issue when the problem is part of an individual's personality. Even when this is the case, however, the problem will seldom involve her or his total personality, and it may be wise in such instances to separate the one aspect that is being discussed from the individual as a whole. Such problems must be dealt with delicately and sensitively if they are to be coped with constructively. They are probably among the most difficult marital problems to solve, largely because of their personal nature.

The following exercise is designed to help us increase our ability to separate issues from personalities.

SEPARATING ISSUES FROM PERSONALITIES

Goal: To increase your ability to separate issues from personalities.

We all are able to separate issues from personalities somewhat. We can, however, increase our "repertoire" of phrases, sentences, or comments for separating issues from personalities and keeping them separate. To increase your repertoire, have a conversation with some-one such as a close friend or your spouse. The objective of this con-versation is to identify five *new* examples of ways to state problems so that the issues are separated from personalities as much as de-sirable. Review the examples that are mentioned above, and then think of the five new examples. State them in both the desirable (issues separated from personalities) and undesirable manners (issues mixed with personalities).

NONVERBAL AND VERBAL PROCESSES

Sometimes it is useful to spend some time creating a situation that is appropriate for a conversation before actually beginning to exchange information about the topic that will be discussed. This may involve a brief conversation that establishes an appropri-ate emotional climate, atmosphere, or "tone" before the discussion begins, or it may involve just a quick check to make sure that it is a good time to talk about a certain topic. This process of preparing for a conversation can be called establishing *rapport*. It can some-times be done very quickly, such as by asking "Could we talk about _____ now?" and getting a message in return that communicates that it is. The affirmation can be a nonverbal assent, such as a nod, shrug, or glance—as long as the meaning of the message is that it is agreeable to begin the conversation—because even a verbal yes may have a host of nonverbal messages that say no. At other times it's a difficult and time-consuming process to establish rapport. A

Establishing rapport

Coronet Films instructional film titled *Marriage Is a Partnership* has a sequence in which a couple trying to cope with a marital problem go through a fairly elaborate conversation before their defensiveness is overcome and they are both ready to talk about the problem. The rapport-establishing conversation is repeated below with some analytic comments about some of the history and nonverbal messages.

Dialogue from the film	*Comments*
Pete: Dotty, I . . . I got a surprise in today's mail, an offer of another job. A wonderful job, but it's way in Central City. Let's talk it over.	It is after dinner, and the couple are reading in front of a fire in a fireplace, so there seem to be few obstacles to having a conversation. This comment seems to communicate that the husband wants to talk.
It's time to get away . . . do something really decisive about the influence of your parents on our marriage.	He makes this statement cautiously rather than aggressively, but it is an emotionally packed statement, and it is put bluntly. His wife has been having problems with his mother and hasn't been aware of his problems with her parents, so she comes back with an understandably defensive comment . . . .
Dotty: My parents!!!	So far nothing has been said to establish rapport, and the wife's shocked, defensive reaction indicates that she is probably more inclined to retaliate, argue, and defend than to discuss.
Pete: Listen to me all the way, honey, before you get mad.	The husband could have chosen to pursue the discussion about the in-law problem, but instead he leaves the problem and actively tries to create rapport. The nonverbal messages in his comment are concern, pleading, caring, and not wanting to hurt his wife.
It's time we . . . well . . . we have got to talk this thing out. You don't know what it's like working in the same plant as your wife's father.	Again, he tries to bring up the problem, and indirectly communicates that part of his problem has to do with working with her father.

Dialogue from the film	*Comments*
Dotty: Dad likes you, Pete. He's done so much for you.	This remark communicates to the husband that his wife is still defending more than she is openly listening to his point of view.
Pete: Sure he has, dear. I know your dad's been swell. Try to understand me. It means so much to have you understand.	Rather than pursue the in-law problem he wants to get to, the husband again focuses on establishing an emotional climate in which they can share information. He goes over to his wife and puts both his hands on her arm and looks at her intently as he makes these comments, and these acts also communicate concern, love, patience, and his deeply felt emotions about what he is saying.
Dotty: Golly, if you feel that way, Pete, and you must, there must be reasons.	This statement communicates that the inclination to defend rather than listen is gone.
Pete: Only they might not seem very important to you.	This is a final rapport-establishing comment, and the husband seems to be ready to get to the problem.
Dotty: Tell me, Pete.	A second comment without defensiveness. The last two comments are both uttered with warmth and tenderness.
Pete: Things like, well, when I got that promotion in December, well, you said how grand it was of your dad to help. I mean, praising me to the boss and all. I felt as though I earned that raise myself, and stories of influence like that don't help any with the other fellows. And then you appreciated your dad's efforts. . . . [pause and awkwardness] I wanted you to appreciate mine.	This comment indicates a number of things. One is that the couple have enough of a sense of safety that they can talk about extremely delicate and sensitive feelings. Another is that the husband's feelings about himself are substantially influenced by his wife's feelings about him, and still another is that they have enough rapport to talk freely now.

There are numerous ways to establish rapport, and each couple has to discover which work best for them. Some couples seldom, if ever, need to consciously concern themselves with the rapport in their relationship. Others, if they are ever to have enough rapport to talk about serious problems or deeply felt emotions, have to spend more time getting ready to talk than they spend talking. Some couples seldom need to concern themselves about their rapport in a conversation after rapport has once been established, but others lose their rapport several times in most conversations and have to consciously reestablish it. Still other couples, however, aren't sensitive to the disappearance of rapport and try to keep talking about problems or decisions when they are defensive, angry, or frustrated . . . and then wonder why they have so much trouble communicating with each other. The following exercise is designed to help couples discuss the "rapport establishing" part of their relationship and to try to improve it if they think they should.

ESTABLISHING RAPPORT

Goal: To determine how adequate a couple is in establishing rapport and to improve this skill if they are less able to establish rapport than they want to be.

1. In a meaningful relationship, such as with a spouse, fiancé(e), or close friend, find 15 to 30 minutes when you can talk about how proficient you are at establishing rapport.

2. Identify several conversations that have occurred recently in which you tried to make a decision, solve a problem, arrive at a consensus about something, etc. Briefly labeling each of these conversations on a piece of paper may help you attain the goal of this exercise.

3. Evaluate how adequately you established and maintained a sense of rapport in each of these conversations, and try to determine whether having or not having rapport helped or hindered your ability to communicate effectively.

4. If you are satisfied with the "rapport establishing" aspect of your relationship, you have completed this exercise. However, if you would like to improve your ability to establish, maintain, or reestablish rapport, try to devise some strategies to improve that aspect of your relationship by talking with each other about it, discussing it in class, or talking with some friends about it.

A group of scholars doing research about factors that influence mental health[2] have identified one aspect of nonverbal communication that can be combined with a verbal process to produce very beneficial results in dating and marital relationships. The verbal process is referred to as metacommunication, but before this can be meaningfully discussed the nonverbal aspect needs to be discussed. The nonverbal phenomenon that is relevant here has to do with the difference between the *content* and the *relationship* messages that are exchanged whenever two people communicate.

Content messages are the information that is overtly and consciously exchanged in sentences, and relationship messages are the nonverbal communications that we all send and receive about how we interact or think we should interact with the other person. An illustration of the difference between the content and relationship aspects of communication can be seen in the simple sentence "Let's go." The content of this sentence is that a request is being made for an individual or a group to join with the sender of the message in "going" someplace, and this content is easily understood. This same sentence, however, could be uttered in a variety of relationships. If the statement were made, even casually, by a Marine sergeant to his recruits it would usually come across as a dominating statement that is virtually an order. Both Marine sergeants and their recruits assume that in their relationship the sergeant ought to act in a powerful, dominating manner, and the *sentence itself* would have nonverbal clues that convey the message that the sergeant is in command. However, if the same sentence were to be used on a date, different messages would undoubtedly be communicated by the nonverbal clues accompanying the verbal message. There would usually be a message of equality rather than of one person dominating the other, and other things, such as tender affection in the relationship, would probably also be communicated. If the same message were given by a small child to his parent, it is likely that the nonverbal messages would communicate deference and submission, and the sentence would be more a request than a command.

One of the phenomena that we communicate to others by the way we say things has to do with who has the power or control in a relationship. If we tell other persons what to do, this kind of statement communicates nonverbally that we think we have the right to tell them what they should do; and if we avoid telling them what to do, this probably means that we believe we do not have the right

---

[2] Gregory Bateson is usually credited with the initial distinction that is discussed here, and his ideas were further elaborated by others, such as Ruesch and Bateson (1951); Watzlawick, Beavin, and Jackson (1967); and Lederer and Jackson (1968).

to tell them what they should do, and that we think we should be either subservient to or equal to them. When we feel subservient to another person we tend to make cautious requests rather than imperative commands.

Several other aspects of relationships are structured and maintained largely through nonverbal aspects of our communication. One of these is the amount of privacy we have in our relationships. We gradually learn in childhood how to "tell" when we are becoming too private in our interaction with someone else, and when we can become more private. We learn that in close friendships there is less individual privacy than there is in fairly formal relationships, such as teacher-student relationships, but in our society this is very seldom discussed verbally. We usually rely on nonverbal messages to reach agreement on the amount of privacy we should have.

Another aspect of relationships that is usually communicated nonverbally is the right to question someone's opinions, motives, or instructions. We occasionally discuss this verbally, but usually we send and receive nonverbal messages to communicate how much it is appropriate to question each other. In many families, for example, young children do not really have the right to question their parents. Marital relationships tend to differ considerably in this because in some marriages the spouses assume that they can question each other while in others they develop relationships in which one member does not question the other or neither questions the other.

Most of the time an awareness of these nonverbal processes is probably irrelevant in marital relationships or any of our other relationships. This is because most of the time we develop *consensus* with others about such things as who has the power and how much privacy and independence we should have, and these nonverbal parts of our communication go unnoticed. The nonverbal messages are sent and received without anyone really being aware of them— partly because there is no need to be aware of them. This is done unconsciously, thus permitting us to focus our attention on other things. Occasionally, however, and this happens in marital relationships, there are conflicting views of what the relationship should be. When such differences occur in regard to events that we discuss overtly it is fairly easy to identify the problems and resolve them. We work out a compromise, one person changes his opinion or behavior, or something entirely new is done. However, when the differences occur in regard to the parts of our relationships that we usually take care of with our nonverbal messages (and hence not usually thought about) it is frequently difficult to identify the problems and it is usually harder to resolve the differences once the problems have been identified. Several examples of these processes would probably be useful at this point.

An example of nonverbal communication about relationships that is usually completely unconscious is our encounters with policemen directing traffic. Most of us usually assume that they have the right to give direct commands and that we as pedestrians or drivers, should obey those commands quickly and without a discussion about why the commands have been given and without making suggestions about better ways of doing things. Consequently when we are in such situations we watch for messages and then respond. The policemen are automatically, unquestioningly given the power in such situations, and we seldom, if ever, even think about the nonverbal aspects of the communication process.

The following case history illustrates a different situation in regard to nonverbal communication about a relationship. Here a married couple who disagree about the nature of their "relationship" are both struggling to get the upper hand in their interaction:

John: Darling, you're so fond of good meat, you really should try the rib-eye steak.

Mary: Thank you, darling, but I'd much prefer the filet mignon. It's a little more expensive than rib-eye, but I do think it has a better taste.

John: [Sensing that Mary has not accepted his superior knowledge of meat]. But people order filet mignon because of snob appeal; only connoisseurs really know about the rib-eye cut. You'll be missing an opportunity if you don't order it. Many restaurants don't even carry it.

Mary: I really appreciate your advice, John, but I do feel like having a filet mignon tonight.

John: I'm not giving you advice. I'm telling you the facts.

Mary: You are giving me advice, and I don't need it. If it's all right with you, I'd like filet mignon—or do I have to order fish?

John: Order what you damn-well please! (Lederer and Jackson, 1968, p. 165).

In these kinds of interchanges in dating situations or in marriage we usually do not understand what is really going on, and if we try to talk with each other about what has occurred we are likely to define the problem in fairly useless abstractions, such as that one or both of us have been inconsiderate, too rigid, impolite, ugly, ignorant, or insensitive. Few of us realize that one of the things that is occurring in such sessions is a difference of opinion about the nature of the relationship and that both parties are using nonverbal messages to try to create the type of relationship they want. In the example cited above both were trying to increase, demonstrate, or test their power or control.

Thus, problems concerning the nonverbalized aspects of relationships may occur in dating and marriage. When we are developing a relationship in a dating situation we encounter such problems fairly frequently. If the problems are not easily resolved the relationship is usually dropped and we start going out with someone else. If they are resolved in a satisfactory way we continue going out with each other, and the harmony in the interaction builds bonds and affection. After couples are married it is more difficult to terminate the relationship for a number of reasons (the legal ties are only one reason as there are usually other factors, such as interdependence, emotional ties, and interhabituation, that make it difficult to terminate a marital relationship), and it is more important for a couple to develop methods of coping with nonverbalized "relationship" problems. One method that has been suggested by the scholars who have done research in this area (Watzlawick et al., 1967; Lederer and Jackson, 1968) is to use what has come to be known in communication literature as *metacommunication*.

Metacommunication is the process of communicating about communication. It occurs when two or more individuals discuss what goes on when they are communicating, and this discussion can include nonverbal communication as well as verbal communication. The example of metacommunication given below follows up on the Mary and John case history mentioned earlier. Their statements are on the left and some interpretations of possible nonverbal messages are given on the right.

Statements	*Nonverbal messages in the statements*
John: I was awfully uncomfortable at dinner tonight.	John seems to be making a first attempt to bring up the earlier uncomfortable experience. This is a fairly "safe" statement in that if Mary is still too emotionally upset to talk about it John is not exposing his feelings so much that he is likely to be emotionally hurt. A safer but more indirect way to try to get into the conversation would be to say something like "The dinner was sort of a mess tonight, wasn't it?" The fact that John has taken the initiative indicates nonverbally that this is a relationship in which he can take leadership.
Mary: Yes, I was too. . . . What happened?	This indicates that Mary is probably over her anger and willing to talk about the experience. If a defensive statement like "Well, you should have been" had been made,

Statements	*Nonverbal messages in the statements*
	this would indicate that her emotions are still so intense that they would probably interfere with a calm conversation. Mary seems to be accepting nonverbally John's leadership in this conversation.
John: I'm not sure, but we really got into it.	An open, uncritical statement suggesting that John thinks both were involved, and suggesting that the problem was something about the couple rather than something external to the couple, such as the food, the waiter, or in-laws. The messages up to this point in this conversation are different from the messages in the earlier conversation because they do not include connotations that one is trying to dominate the other. Rather, they imply an acceptance of the other person as an equal. It is also nonverbally assumed that the relationship is sufficiently intimate for emotions to be discussed. These statements could have an underlying nonverbal message of warmth and caring for the other person, or they could be fairly neutral in affect. They do not have the competing, aggressive tone of the dinner conversation.
Mary: We seem to be having those kinds of . . . uh . . . fights quite a bit lately.	The fact that Mary has asked a question that made the conversation more involved and that she has now contributed a new idea indicates this is a relationship in which she too can take leadership and not be confined to reticent, submissive roles.
John: Yeah . . . I wonder why. We didn't used to . . .	The pauses indicated by the periods also communicate nonverbally. The pauses could indicate pensiveness, thoughtfulness, and an openness to ideas, and in this type of conversation they will

Statements	*Nonverbal messages in the statements*
	probably create an atmosphere in which more ideas will probably emerge.
Mary: You know, . . . one thing that might help us find out what's going on would be to think back about what we said to each other.	This is Mary's second initiating statement. Since John's opening comment he has been quite passive and she has had the more powerful, leading role.
John: You mean earlier tonight?	John seems to be very willing to let Mary continue to play the leading role. This could be because their relationship is always that way, or it could be because of something about this particular conversation or situation. It may be due simply to the fact that she has come up with a new idea that he doesn't fully understand and that he's asking for clarification.
Mary: Um hummmmmmmm.	A fairly passive response, but even this type of statement could have been made in such a way as to indicate leadership, power, and control.
John: You mean, talk about what we said?	The conversation does not seem to be a hectic, intense, or highly emotional experience. It is fairly low-keyed and open, and both individuals seem to have the opportunity to say what they want without being interrupted. This, unlike the earlier conversation, permits them to talk about their feelings.
Mary: Well, even more than that I get the feeling that . . . uh . . . some things were going on that weren't even said, and if we talk about what we said to each other we might be able to get a better picture of what happened.	Mary is now explaining what she wants to do without labeling it metacommunication, and she's explaining her reasons for wanting to do it. This is such an insightful comment that it is almost unbelievable that someone who has not learned what metacommunication and its value is would make it.

Statements	*Nonverbal messages in the statements*
John: Yeah, OK. . . .	John is still willing to let Mary take the initiative, but he seems to understand what she wants to do and seems willing to give it a try.
Mary: It seemed to start when we were talking about what to order.	Mary is nonverbally assuming that John knows what she means by "it," and his later comments indicate that she is justified in the assumption.
John: I remember talking about the different things on the menu . . . and you seemed to get all upset.	This is the most powerful statement John has made since the start of the conversation, and it is an initiative-taking comment. This could have been said in an aggressive manner, generating defensiveness in Mary, but judging from her response it wasn't.
Mary: Um hummm . . . Before that I don't think I was upset.	Mary indicates acceptance of John's comment in a passive way. She doesn't take a new initiative in the conversation.
John: Well, let's see what happened. . . . I thought you'd enjoy that rib-eye steak.	John is taking more initiative. He seemed to be trying to analyze what happened. One thing to note in this conversation is that the two are talking about thoughts (opinions or views) *and* emotions (feelings or sensations). John is not, at this point in the conversation, aware of the power struggle aspect of the earlier conversation or of what effect his "controlling" comments had on Mary.
Mary: And I probably would have, but . . . [pause]	Another confirming comment. Mary seems to be content to let John take the leadership role now, and nonverbally it is now apparent that in some situations in this relationship the two are flexible in letting each other be the more powerful, leading one. Pauses in conversations may have many nonverbal messages, and frequently

Statements	*Nonverbal messages in the statements*
	other nonverbal clues, such as taking a deep breath, a pensive glance, or holding up an index finger with an "I just thought of something else" look, can communicate complex messages.
John: I guess maybe I came on a little bit strong for some reason.	John is still taking the leadership and is apparently trying to figure out what went on in the earlier conversation by reconstructing it. Note that he is reconstructing more than just the "content" in the sentences, as he is talking about how he did something, and indicating that he's not sure why he did it—or perhaps he knows, but doesn't want to say why at this point.
Mary: Yes, and I resented that.	
John: You know, I'll bet that the reason I did was . . .	

This conversation illustrates metacommunication about the conversation the couple had had earlier. Metacommunication can also involve a discussion about the trends in a couple's communication that tend to reoccur in conversation after conversation. All relationships develop their own set of norms or rules about communication, and most of us never stop to identify or analyze our norms or rules. We are aware of many social norms that are characteristic of our larger culture or society. For example, we are aware that we "ought" to say please and thank you at certain times in our communication, and that it is more appropriate to use "proper" language in some situations than in other situations. Many of us tend to be unaware, however, of many of the norms or rules that gradually develop in our marital and family relationships. Examples of such norms are: "Don't talk about those subjects"; "The wife should not question the husband's judgment"; "The wife is the one who will always win in the end anyway"; "She can criticize him, but he can't criticize her"; "He has to think it's his suggestion or he won't go along with it"; "Children can't talk back to parents"; "She shouldn't get so sentimental"; and "Never make people feel guilty about something they've done." We may want to keep some of the rules in our relationships, but there are others that we would probably want to eliminate if we knew they were there.

Metacommunicating is not a cure-all for all communication problems, but it is a technique that can help get certain types of problems in the open where they can be faced and perhaps eliminated. It is also likely that few, if any, of us would want to spend a great deal of our time metacommunicating, but most of us would probably benefit from some metacommunication. The following exercise provides an experience in metacommunicating.

METACOMMUNICATION

Goal: To increase the ability to metacommunicate by practicing it.

1. In a relationship such as marriage, roommate, engagement, or a close friendship, set aside 15–30 minutes for this exercise.

2. Discuss how effectively you usually communicate in this relationship when you encounter a problem, difficulty, or issue or you need to make a decision. Some of the things you may want to discuss are:

    a. Does one person do certain things when communicating that the other person especially appreciates, such as being open-minded, considerate, or emphatic, or taking the time to listen rather than think of what to say next.

    b. Does one person do certain things when communicating that the other person doesn't like, such as clam up, not "listen," dominate the conversation, or ignore the other person.

    c. Sometimes norms or rules develop about "how" to communicate in a relationship, and couples are not even aware of them. You may want to think about whether you have any of these norms and then evaluate whether you like or dislike them. Examples of these norms are:

       (1) One person can criticize, but the other can't . . . or at least always seems to pay a psychological or emotional price for doing so.

       (2) Certain topics should never be discussed.

       (3) If the two people disagree, one of the two should have more say than the other one in deciding what to do.

       (4) It is acceptable for one individual, but not the other, to use covert techniques for controlling the situation (crying, getting a headache, withdrawing affection, whining, sweet-talking, etc.).

Feedback is another process that uses both verbal and nonverbal processes, and becoming skilled at giving and getting feedback can facilitate accurate communication.[3] Feedback is the process by which the sender of a message receives some information about the message he or she has communicated. Often seeking and getting feedback is a simple process, such as the sender asking whether the receiver understood what was said and the receiver responding with an affirmative glance or comment. At other times, however, the process of getting feedback is complicated and time-consuming, such as a discussion of the receiver's impressions about the sender's intentions or about other nonverbal aspects of the sender's message.

Feedback can include more than just verbal discussion about whether our messages are received accurately. People can get considerable "feedback" in a conversation by being alert to how others are responding to their messages. For example, if people are so intent on sending messages that they ignore our messages and keep trying to send messages about something else their behavior provides "feedback" about how they are responding to what we are trying to say, and the insights we get by observing how they are responding can be useful in knowing how to respond ourselves. We may, for example, want to deal with the issues they are trying to raise before attempting to further communicate our own ideas, or we may want to confront them with the fact that they are dealing with different issues than we want to. Other types of behavior that provide useful feedback are enthusiastically listening and responding to the issues being discussed, shaking the head either affirmatively or in disagreement, or becoming uninterested in a conversation. The nonverbal messages that others emit are among the most useful forms of feedback, and we are likely to be more effective communicators if we are alert to these forms of feedback than if we are insensitive to them. The process of role reversal discussed earlier can also be viewed as a feedback-providing situation since the payoff in role reversal is finding out what has and has not been understood.

Harper (1958) has suggested that the communication in most marriages would be better if couples were to develop the "art of asking," or of getting verbal feedback, rather than assume that they understand what the other person means or intends. He suggests that many couples develop misunderstandings when each assumes a great deal about what the other is, and that checking out their impressions by asking is frequently wise. He suggests that this is most important when a couple are having a difficult time with their relationship or when important or emotional issues are being

---

[3] Several more extensive discussions of feedback are in Nirenberg (1963, chap. 6) and Bauby (1972, pp. 153–57).

discussed. Apparently, during more routine periods of life couples can get by with more assumptions.

FACTORS TO CONSIDER WHEN COMMUNICATING

Many people are better communicators at some times of the day *Time of day* than at other times. For most people the time of day when it is apparently most difficult to be a pleasant, congenial communicator is just before the evening meal (Bossard and Boll, 1956). In the typical home, dinner time is a period of fairly hectic activity, as one or both parents are arriving home from the job, and not infrequently are hungry and tired. Also, after having to "perform" on the job all day it is not uncommon to want, but find it hard to get, some peace, quiet, and rest. This is also a time of fairly high home activity for children, and it is a time when the person or persons preparing the evening meal are hungry and usually very busy. The net effect is that for many families it is the most difficult time of the day to communicate about something that is problematic, irritating, or serious.

The time of day also influences communication because some people wake up more "slowly" than others. Some people are not really fully awake until 10 or 11 in the morning, and they find it difficult to communicate about serious or problematic situations before that. Others, however, wake up early and quickly, and the morning is the best time of day for them to "tackle their problems" and work things out. Some people are most proficient in discussing things after 10 or 11 at night, and others are so exhausted by that time that they are mediocre to poor communicators.

One conclusion that emerges from these differences is that each couple has to discover which time of day it is best for them to try to cope with problems, resolve issues, or make decisions and at which times of day it is wise for them to put off such discussions. This, of course, isn't arguing that couples should not talk to each other at certain times of day. A calm, humorous, or relaxed conversation just before dinner can be one of the best ways to make a day pleasant. This analysis does, however, suggest that if we paid attention to our unique daily cycles and rhythms we could talk about some things at certain times of day and about other things at different times of day, and that this might improve the communication in the relationship. The following exercise is provided to help couples discover the times of day that seem to be the best and worst times for serious conversation.

DAILY RHYTHMS EXERCISE

Goal: To identify which times of day are the best and worst for
serious conversation.

With somone who knows you quite well, try to identify whether there
are systematic differences in your ability to communicate effectively at
different times of day. If there are, try to determine which are the
most and least effective times. You may then want to try to change
your patterns, or you may decide that it would not be worth the effort.

External
pressures

All couples experience "outside" pressures that interfere with
the kind of communication that is necessary when major decisions
have to be made, differences have to be resolved, or problems have
to be coped with. Married couples who are still finishing their education will immediately recognize that things are more hectic and
pressured when "finals" roll around and that it is usually more
difficult to solve problems then. At later stages of life unusual and
substantial pressures that can interfere with communication are
brought into the home by such things as one spouse being ready
to "close a big deal," a company merger, a legal case that is coming
to a head, the architect needing the drawings in a hurry, or the
Christmas rush.

It may be that the wise way to deal with the impact external pressures have is to be sensitive to them when they occur and to try to
avoid facing issues that could be put off for a few days or a couple
of weeks. This suggestion is, of course, contrary to the advice heard
occasionally that married couples should "never let the sun set on
a problem," as it is proposed here that occasionally the most effective thing a couple can do is let a number of "suns" set on certain
problems—when there are other pressures that would make it difficult to cope with the problems that can be put off temporarily. This
is, of course, not arguing that couples should avoid facing problems
indefinitely—even though that too might be wise in some circumstances.

Physical
setting

Architects and designers have long recognized that the physical
setting influences the way people behave. Bright colors, such as
reds, oranges, and purples, excite and arouse people, while beiges,
greens, and blues relax people. Hard surfaces, such as tile, brick,
ceramic, and marble, create different moods than do soft surfaces,

such as carpeting, draperies, pillows, or coarse textures. These effects can be used in homes to create different types of moods in different places or situations. Soft light, low and calm music, and a fire in a fireplace are some commonplace ways to create an atmosphere of calmness and peace. In addition to these obvious examples, such other things as relaxing evening wear, slippers, a lighted pipe, reading material, and soft furniture also promote relaxation, calmness, and serenity. It is, of course, not always desirable to have a calm setting for discussions about important, sensitive, or problematic issues, but many times it is desirable to do what is feasible to create an appropriate setting for such a discussion. For many people, trying to resolve an important issue while driving in downtown traffic in a compact car would create obstacles to effective communication, and such situations can usually be avoided if we are sensitive to the role of physical factors.

Menstrual cycle

Most married couples eventually learn that the woman may experience systematic emotional and physical changes in the different stages of the monthly menstrual cycle. These changes can also systematically influence communication. Women differ considerably in the nature of these trends (Hartman, 1962; Pincus, 1965), but one common pattern is for women to be slightly more cheerful, patient, warm, and congenial during the second and third weeks after the start of the menstrual period and to experience the most physical discomfort and such resulting emotional responses as irritability, depression, and being easily frustrated just prior to the menstrual period. Many women, however, vary from this typical emotional cycle, and a large number of women experience no discernible emotional changes in the course of their menstrual cycle. If couples are aware that such systematic changes are occurring, this information can be valuable in marital communication because the couples will know that things do not go as well when they try to address problems or major decisions at "the wrong time of the month." Thus, couples would probably be wise to observe the woman for several months to determine whether she experiences systematic emotional changes. Then, if she does, they should take this information into account in determining when to face up to and when to temporarily avoid those problems that can be postponed.

Time involved

One of the many surprises that many newly married couples have is the amount of time it takes to solve some of the problems, issues, or difficulties that come up in a marital relationship. This is illustrated by the remarks of a newly married wife:

I thought that when things would come up we'd be able to sit down for a minute or so and decide what to do. That's what I've been able to do all my life, and that's the way most things were when we were going together. But we've had so many things come up that I never even thought about, and they get so involved and complicated that . . . we just take hours and hours talking about them. It's fun sometimes because we don't have that much else to do, and besides we don't have any money to go anyplace anyway, but I never had any idea that we'd spend as much of our time working things out as we do.

Different types of discussions take different amounts of time. When couples are initially discovering such things as how they like their eggs done, who is going to do what in the morning so they can get to work on time, and what type of entertainment they ought to have on a weekend, the discussions are usually neither complex nor time-consuming. However, when newly married couples talk about such things as how they feel when the other is gone or close, what they want out of life, the inadequacies that they do not let on about to others but that they want to share with each other, or sentimental events that are gradually building bonds between them, the conversations are very time-consuming. Also, after couples have been married for a number of years they may require vast amounts of time for conversations about new ambitions that are becoming important to them, personal frustrations they are experiencing in their careers, or ways their love has changed, and couples who do not allow adequate time for such conversations . . . don't have the same type of conversations that other couples have who do take the necessary time.

Psychic sets

Another factor to consider when communicating in a marital relationship is that both individuals have numerous preconceptions that influence communication. Such preconceptions have come to be known in the psychological literature as "sets." Some of these sets are systematically different for men and women, and this helps men communicate with men and women with women but makes it difficult for spouses to communicate with each other. The woman's comment as she looks into her bulging closet that "I don't have a thing to wear" makes sense within a female subculture, but sets in the minds of many males make such comments mystifying, if not inappropriate and aggravating. An example of the same type of situation reversed is the male's puzzled comment, "Do I have to *tell* her all the time how much I love her? She ought to be able to see that I do from the way I act. Why, I . . ." Many husbands feel that this is a fairly reasonable point of view, while many wives find it mystifying, if not inappropriate and aggravating.

The list of systematic differences between men and women that contribute to the difficulties of communication in marriage could be very long. Several examples of "traditional" differences are emotionality in many women and a comparative lack of emotionality in men, the higher importance many males attach to sports, the wife wanting her husband to help pick out fabric for sewing, the importance to a father that his son be successful in athletics, and the importance of new clothes to the wife. The changes in modern sex roles are eliminating some of these traditional differences, but new differences will also undoubtedly appear.

The following pictures illustrate that psychic sets can be created by our experiences. If one group of individuals is asked to study the picture below, and another group is asked to study the picture on page 132, they will get different "sets." Then if both groups look at the picture on page 133, the group that saw the picture below will see a young woman in the third picture, and the group that saw the picture on page 132 will see an old woman in the third picture. The two groups thus will see different things in the same picture, and one wonders how often a similar process occurs in marriage.

Part of a
relationship
Another factor that is sometimes useful to think about is that some problems in marital relationships deal with only small parts of the total relationship while others deal with the relationship as a whole. Frequently when couples are going together and just beginning a more permanent relationship, many of the issues they must cope with genuinely jeopardize the relationship. If an issue is resolved one way the relationship will be terminated, and if it is resolved another way the couple will continue to see each other. However, after couples have gone together for some time, their relationship is often so complex, important, and secure that most of the problems that confront them deal with only a small part of the total relationship and don't genuinely jeopardize the relationship. This is especially the case after a deeply felt love has developed and numerous "bonds" have been acquired.

An awareness of whether an issue concerns only a small part of a relationship or the entire relationship can be useful in facilitating communication, because if a person who is interested in maintaining a relationship erroneously believes that a problem jeopardizes the entire relationship, that person may experience such emotions as fear, anxiety, or depression—emotions that would not be experienced if it were realized that the issue does not jeopardize the entire relationship. Conversely, a person who fails to realize that a problem does jeopardize an entire relationship may not give that problem the attention and concern that he or she would otherwise give it. It doesn't seem useful to always identify the exact ramifications of every marital problem that arises, but on the other hand insufficient attention to the implications of problems may interfere with communication and problem solving.

Unconscious
motivation
Another factor that is probably useful to keep in mind is that at least some of the reasons humans do what they do are unconscious to them. Some schools of thought, such as psychoanalysis, argue that the human mind is like an iceberg, with only a small part of what goes on in it being "visible" to consciousness while the rest is unconscious. Other schools of thought, such as Rogers' self theory, argue that unless an individual is emotionally or mentally upset most of what goes on in the mind is conscious. However, even though differences of opinion exist on what proportion of our mental processes are unconscious, modern scholars are virtually

unanimious in believing that at least some of the reasons people behave the way they do are unconscious.

When couples are sensitive to the fact that some human motivation is unconscious this can influence what occurs in marital communication. For one thing, such couples will realize that searching for the "reasons" persons do something or the reasons they do not do something may be a futile exercise because the individuals themselves may not be and cannot become aware of the real reasons. Frequently this realization will lead couples to shift their concentration to what they can do about a situation rather than try to discover why the situation occurs, and this shift may very often be wise.

A final factor that is probably wise to keep in mind in marital communication is that each human being has a unique combination of traits, inclinations, needs, and tendencies. Many of these characteristics can be learned only through lengthy, intimate interaction with someone, but an awareness of what the person is and how this influences that person's interaction in a communicating situation can make a difference in the effectiveness of the communication. Some individuals love to argue and others will never argue. Some need to think they are always right, whether they are or not, and others always need to have someone around who they believe is strong and able. Some people can only get their true feelings off their chest in a stormy barrage, while others say things when they are upset that they and the people around them know they do not mean or believe. The illustrations of ways that we humans are unique could become a very long list, and each of us could add our own personal oddities to it. The point here, however, is not to elaborate on the nature of such idiosyncraises but to point out that an awareness of personal characteristics can help us to communicate more effectively in our marital relationships than we would be able to without these insights.

Personal idiosyncrasies

SUMMARY

Most of the chapters in this book are built around a group of general principles, but this chapter deviates from this pattern for several reasons. One reason is that at present there are very few known principles about human communication, but there is a great need to have effective communication in intimate human relationships, such as those that occur in marriage. Given this need but the lack of well thought-out, systematic knowledge, the best that can be done is to identify some of the concepts, processes, and skills that are discussed in the scholarly literature and to use these to try to enhance the quality of communication in marital interaction. Hopefully, future research will discover additional principles that can be clearly stated and empirically supported, but until that is accomplished we will have to continue to do the best we can with speculative ideas, such as the ones discussed in this chapter. A large number of different ideas were discussed in this chapter, and these ideas were grouped into four sections. The first section discussed several nonverbal skills and processes that can be used to enhance communication. The second identified several verbal skills, and the third discussed several processes in which both verbal and nonverbal skills are used. In the last part of the chapter a number of factors that influence the nature of communication in a marital relationship were identified. So many different topics were discussed in these four sections that they cannot be summarized effectively here, but Table 5–1 provides a list of them.

Table 5–1

Topics discussed in Chapter 5

1. Nonverbal communication skills

    Touching
    Body positions
    A subjective view of right and wrong

2. Verbal skills

    Role reversal
    Reflecting
    Issues versus personalities

3. Nonverbal and verbal skills

    Establishing rapport
    Metacommunication
    Feedback

4. Factors to take into account when communicating

    Time of day
    External pressures
    Physical setting
    Menstrual cycle
    Time involved
    Psychic sets
    Part of a relationship
    Unconscious motivation
    Personal idiosyncrasies

SUGGESTIONS FOR FURTHER STUDY

Anastasi, Thomas E.   1967. *Face-to-Face Communication*. Cambridge Mass.: Management Center of Cambridge.

Bauby, Cathrina   1972. *OK, Let's Talk about It*. New York: Van Nostrand, Reinhold.

Foote, Nelson and Cottrell, L. B.   1955. *Identity and Interpersonal Competence*. Chicago: University of Chicago Press.

Gordon, Thomas   1970. *Parent Effectiveness Training*. New York: Wyden.

Johnson, David W.   1972. *Reaching Out*. Englewood Cliffs, N.J.: Prentice-Hall.

Satir, Virginia   1972. *Peoplemaking*. Palo Alto, Calif.: Science and Behavior Books.

Watzlawick, Paul; Beavin, Janet Lemick; and Jackson, Don D.   1967. Pragmatics of Human Communication. New York: Norton, chaps. 1 and 2.

6

Effective and satisfying decision making[1]

D ATING and married couples are continually making decisions. Some are about such unimportant things as who is to take out the garbage and whether to have orange or grapefruit juice for breakfast. Others, however, are less routine and deal with important issues, such as whether to have a child, buy a house, or take a new job. Some couples learn how to make these decisions in a pleasant and efficient way, while others have nothing but problem after problem when trying to decide what to do. Note the differences between the following six couples:

She usually gets her way more than I do, but when something is really important to me and I let her know it she lets me have my way. One thing we have always been able to do is talk about our problems long enough that both of us usually feel good about what we decide to do.

Oh, we can talk to each other. That's not our problem. When we don't have something we disagree on we can just spend hours together talking, and those are some of the best times we ever have. We do that best in the late evening and sometimes we just sit up and listen to music and gab until three or four in the morning. Where we're having a problem is when we disagree on something. There's just something about us that clicks when we disagree. We both hate to lose or something when we've taken a stand we just don't give in. Then after we've had one of those sessions we both just avoid those situations and sometimes the problem just goes away. Sometimes though it doesn't and I wish we could find some ways to handle our differences. So far it hasn't hurt our marriage, but I'll bet it will if we don't do something about it.

[1] Appreciation is expressed to Margaret Jensen for her valuable assistance in developing this chapter. In many ways this chapter is coauthored.

I just wish things at home could be a little more like they are at the office. I'm used to a place where you decide what to do when you need to, and then you get things done. But he's so indecisive. He can't make his mind up about anything. It's always "Well, I don't know what to do" or "What will so and so think . . ." I liked the fact that he'd depend a lot on me when we were going together, but . . . we're not a couple of kids anymore. We have responsibilities, and he needs to carry his share of the load more.

My husband is a regular slavedriver. He believes everyone should work hard, but he is never satisfied and never appreciates what I do. Often I have a terrific urge to walk across the room and slap his face, but I don't dare. I don't really do anything to get even with him, except that I do unenthusiastically the things he asks me to do (Blood 1969, p. 362).

I took to Wayne because of his calmness. It seemed to be a good balance for my excitableness. I've discovered since we've been married, though, that this means he'll go into his shell and not talk to me for a week. I never can find out the reason for his sulkiness until he finally gets over it. It's pretty exasperating to know he's got something against me but not able to do anything about it since I don't know what it is (Blood, 1969, p. 362).

Both Sue and I had to learn to speak what was on our minds to each other. We had both been taught it was not right to inflict your problems on others, but we had to "unlearn" that principle so as not to shut the other partner out. We also found that by talking our problems out, we not only felt better, but sometimes the problems would sort of solve themselves when they were out in the open (Blood, 1969, p. 362).

Since couples differ so greatly in their ability to make decisions, and effective decision making is an important part of intimate relationships, this chapter is an attempt to provide some information that can be used to increase the effectiveness of couples in decision making. The first section of the chapter discusses the decision-making process by identifying the major components of decision making and then analyzing each of them. The subsequent sections identify nine principles that can be used by couples to increase the quality of their decision making and their satisfaction with their decisions.

THE DECISION-MAKING PROCESS

Decision making is defined here as the process of selecting a course of action or inaction when faced with a situation that has several alternatives.[2] The term *decision making* is used here because

[2] Decision making has been defined in a number of ways. Gould and Kolb describe it as "the dynamic process of interaction among all participants who determine a particular policy choice" (1964, p. 180), and Tallman defines it

it is widely used in the literature (Turner, 1970), even though there are several other terms that could be used, such as *problem solving* (Tallman, 1970; Aldous, 1971) or *conflict resolution* (Blood, 1969). The two latter terms are not used here because the words *problem* and *conflict* have negative connotations in that they imply that something has to be "wrong" or "inappropriate" if a decision has to be made. This would be an unfortunate connotation in the present context because decision making includes situations of choice between pleasant alternatives as well as those in which an undesired problem has to be faced. Decision making, of course, occurs in situations in which a couple are trying to resolve differences of opinion, but it also occurs in situations in which there is no conflict. For example, an offer of a new job produces a decision-making situation, but it may not involve a conflict or a difference of opinion.

Scholars have long recognized that individuals or groups usually go through a predictable, orderly sequence of events in making decisions. These scholars disagree about whether this sequence of events is best described as three stages that include a number of subevents or as eight or ten events,[3] but there is considerable similarity in the way most authors divide the decision-making process. The sequence that seems most useful here is:

Stages in decision making

1. Identifying an issue or problem on which a decision is needed.
2. Identifying alternative solutions to the issue or problem.
3. Evaluating the alternatives.
4. Making the decision by selecting one of the alternatives.
5. Implementing the decision.

Since these stages are important in the principles that are presented later in this chapter, each of the stages is discussed here in some detail.

---

as "those behaviors which individuals or groups choose and implement in order to achieve desired ends" (1970, p. 97). Turner describes it as "a process directed toward unambivalent group assent and commitment to a course of action or inaction" (1970, p. 97). These definitions are essentially the same, even though they use different terms and emphasize different parts of the decision-making process.

[3] Some examples of the stages that have been identified will illustrate the differences and similarities among the various ways of dividing decision making into stages. Bales and Strodbeck (1951) divided decision making into orientation, evaluation, and control stages. Blood (1968, p. 361) changed this slightly to orientation, evaluation, and execution. Aldous (1971, p. 266) referred to the five stages of identifying and defining of the problem, collecting information relevant to the problem, producing action alternatives, choosing a course of action, and evaluating the consequences of the action. Among the longer lists is the one used by Duvall (1957, p. 140), who identifies the nine stages: face the problem, look at the causes, set some goals, get more knowledge and understanding, be the other person, consider what to do, make a plan of action, check the plan with the goals, plan the follow-up.

Identifying the issue or problem. The first step that usually occurs in decision making is to discover that something needs attention and to identify what it is. What frequently occurs in marital interaction is that one person becomes aware of a problem or need and communicates her or his concern to the other. In a family one member usually senses the problem, and then others who are involved are told about it. The following statements are typical of this problem-defining stage:

> We need to talk about . . .
>
> What is *really* bothering you, dear?
>
> There have just got to be some changes made around here.
>
> As I see it, the problem is that . . .
>
> Well, apparently the issue is . . .
>
> I have a problem, and I'd like something done about it.

This stage is different in some important ways when a decision is being made by one person rather than by a couple or a family. When just one person is involved, as soon as that person is aware of the problem he or she can go on to the second stage. In the case of a couple, however, when only one member recognizes a problem it is still that individual's problem, not the couple's problem. Only when the individual communicates to the other person that there is a problem *and the other person recognizes the problem* does it become the couple's problem. And, as many married couples know, the process of convincing a spouse that there *really* is a problem is sometimes a very difficult task. In fact it is occasionally impossible, and the couple member who has recognized the problem then has to treat it as his or her problem rather than as the couple's problem. One of the useful observations made by Waller and Hill (1951, pp. 312–16) is what they termed Insightful Adjustment, namely, that the member of a couple who is sufficiently insightful to become aware of a problem may be at a disadvantage. If that member cannot convince the other member that there really is a problem he or she may also have to do all of the changing or adjusting.

Since some communication usually occurs in this stage of decision making, all the principles discussed in Chapters 3–5 can be used to help make the communication effective. Also, since defensiveness is one of the common reactions when a spouse tries to bring up a problem, the principles that deal with ways to decrease defensiveness are particularly relevant in this context. One scholar[4] has also suggested that an effective way to raise an issue is to make an "I" statement rather than a "you" statement. This is done by identifying how we respond, personally, to the problematic situation or by

---

[4] Gordon (1970, pp. 115–38).

identifying the effect that something has on ourselves rather than describing what someone else has done. Statements such as "I feel uneasy when I'm yelled at" or "I am very uncomfortable about . . ." are examples of "I" statements. The advantage of such statements is that they are not judgmental of the other person, as "you" statements about the same issues tend to be. "You" statements like "You yell too much" or "Your _____ makes me uncomfortable" tend to put the other person on the defensive. Also, "I" statements don't imply that the speaker alone knows what should be done, an impression that is sometimes communicated when we make "you" statements. An example of this is trying to identify a problem by saying, "If you would only quit yelling, everything would be better."

An effective way of making sure that there is consensus about the definition of a problem is for one person to make a "summary statement" as a couple move on to the second stage of decision making. This can be a very brief statement about what the problem or issue is, and the other person can then either assent or disagree. When the feelings, reactions, or behavior of one member of the couple is the problem, one way to summarize is to reverse roles and have that member describe the problem. Many couples have developed the ability to communicate nonverbally, and in such instances these statements would be unnatural if they were made very frequently.

Many times, previous events in a couple's relationship or in a parent-child relationship will permit them to move very quickly over this stage of decision making. Sometimes such things as the way a person acts, a gesture, or just a certain type of silence can communicate that a certain problem needs attention. At other times, however, we assume too much when we rely on gestures or other nonverbal methods of identifying problems and we later find out we did not really have consensus about whether a problem or issue existed or about what it was.

Identifying alternative solutions to the issue or problem. Once the problem has been defined, the next step is to identify several possible alternatives or solutions to the problem. During this step of the decision-making process, statements like this are called for:

One thing I've thought of is . . .

How about . . . ?

You know what _____ did about that?

Have you got any ideas about what we can do?

Now listen. As I see it, we've got two choices . . .

Let's write down all the possibilities here as they're mentioned.

I'm wondering what you'd like to see done about it.

Some researchers studying group decision making have been surprised at the small number of alternatives that are usually generated by a group.[5] People often have preconceived ideas of a solution, and when the preconceived ideas of several family members coincide, little effort may be devoted to exploring other, possibly better, solutions. Several writers[6] have suggested that it may be advantageous to complete generating alternatives before evaluating them. They suggest that identifying the disadvantages and advantages of alternatives or labeling them as good or bad may stifle the expression of other alternatives which might otherwise be forthcoming. This could occur because members may forget new ideas if the conversation remains focused around an idea already proposed. Or, the censoring atmosphere may make them hesitant about and critical of their own ideas, and they do not express them. This line of reasoning is tenable, and yet there is also evidence[7] that a brainstorming or completely evaluation-free listing of ideas can tend to produce many poor-quality ideas or ideas along only one thought train. Thus, it may be that *some* evaluation as ideas are proposed is desirable, but that too much or too conclusive an evaluation cuts off forthcoming ideas.

Evaluating the alternatives. After several alternatives have been proposed, it is possible to discuss the consequences of each alternative. These consequences can be cataloged as disadvantages or advantages, according to the couple's own value system, and each alternative can be weighed against the others. The following statements are characteristic of these evaluations of alternatives:

Well, if we stay home we'll at least have the benefit of air conditioning.

Hey, look, maybe we could do a little of each . . .

Grandma is apt to be too busy to visit with us if we go at the end of the month.

We *can* invite him to dinner, but it will make me miserably uncomfortable.

Yes, but it would be really hard to . . .

It seems to me that if we do that it will make it easier to . . .

Blood (1969, p. 367) argued that one pitfall of this particular stage of decision making is prematurely evaluating proposals as "right" or "wrong." He suggested that these labels are too simple and too abstract, and that calling a proposal "right" is another way of saying "This is the answer I choose," which immediately moves

---

[5] Blood (1962, p. 250); Maier (1963, pp. 177 ff.).

[6] Blood (1962); Hoffman (1956, pp. 114–16).

[7] See Hoffman's review (1965, pp. 114–16).

the decision making into the next stage. He suggested that it is more useful to identify the effects of the various alternatives in terms of advantages and disadvantages or feasibility and difficulty rather than just label them right or wrong. Frequently different alternatives have different advantages and disadvantages, and there is no way to get all the advantages and none of the disadvantages. When this happens a choice has to be made eventually, but more than one alternative has some "right" and some "wrong," or is good in some ways and bad in others. Kirkpatrick (1963, pp. 89–97) uses the term *dilemma* to describe such situations.

At this stage couples may find themselves moving on to the further stage of trying to implement a choice before they are aware of all the problems or complexities of a particular alternative, and they may thus find themselves moving back and forth between stages. If humans were highly efficient and completely rational this would probably be undesirable, because it is fairly disorganized to skip around from one stage of decision making to another. However, since emotional and interpersonal concerns are usually much more important in dating and marital decision making than in other types of decision making, this process of skipping around in a fairly disorganized manner is probably the way most couples prefer to interact. Sometimes, especially with complex or very important decisions, couples find it useful to list the advantages and disadvantages on a piece of paper.

Selecting one of the alternatives. This is the stage in the decision-making process at which a *decision* is made, because it is at this stage that one alternative or group of alternatives is selected and others are rejected. Some comments typical of this stage are:

OK, Rod, which do you think is best?

It looks to me like the best way to handle this is for us to have separate closets. What do you say about that?

Then let's do a little of both, but . . .

It sounds as though that last idea has the most agreement. What do you say we go ahead on it?

Sometimes a couple will define a problem and work with alternative solutions but never reach a final conclusion. Decision making is not, however, complete until a plan of action has been selected or inaction adopted through inability to agree on a decision. It is frequently helpful to state the final decision clearly and to see whether or not those involved agree that this is what was decided. This is useful because, as will be pointed out in a later principle, when people agree with decisions it is usually easier to carry them out. It is, of course, not always possible to get unanimity, and when unanimity is unobtainable another strategy is to see whether the disagreeing member or members of a group will go along with the decision without making too much fuss or having too much personal "cost."

Some couples find it very difficult to complete this stage. They are never able to make up their minds, or they do not really agree on what it is they have decided to do. All couples probably have some misunderstandings about their decisions and later find themselves making comments like "Oh, I thought that we decided to . . ." or "I understand that . . ." These misunderstandings occur more often with some couples than with others, and those who experience them frequently may then want to spend more time making sure they have the same opinion about what they have decided to do.

Implementing the decision. In many situations decision making cannot cope with a problem or issue unless the decision is actually carried out. Sometimes this involves detailed planning about what the couple or family is going to acquire or how things will have to be changed in order to carry out the decision. Several scholars who have analyzed decision making (Duvall, 1957, for example) suggest that this stage should also include some way of evaluating the plan of action later to make sure that the solution is really coping with the problem or meeting the need. Comments that are typical of this stage of decision making are:

Now that we've decided what to do, how are we going to do it?

Where are we going to get the money for . . .

For the next two weeks I'll . . .

Could you help me . . .

There isn't any way we can . . .

In summary. It is important to realize that the various stages of decision making usually occur in one form or another when decisions are made, but that many times in dating and marital interaction some stages are passed over quickly, some are given no conscious attention, some stages are dealt with simultaneously, and there is a great deal of skipping around among stages. Sometimes a gesture, such as a glance or a body movement, is enough to precipitate a decision, and not one word is said about what the issue is, the alternatives, the advantages and disadvantages of the alternatives, or the method of implementing the decision. The previous learning in the relationship can at times establish patterns of interaction that make it redundant to explicitly or consciously go through each of the stages. Much of what occurs happens quickly, nonverbally, and with no deliberate attention to the routine and habituated processes.

There are several different types of decisions. In one type, referred to as *consensus,* all the members of a group agree about the decision. In a second type, *accommodation* (Waller and Hill, 1951, pp. 306–7), there is disagreement about what ought to be done, but a decision is still made. The parties agree to disagree, but still decide what to do or not do. A third type consists of defacto decisions (Turner, 1970, pp. 99–100), which are made by what happens rather than by what is specifically decided. As Turner comments:

Many discussions finish inconclusively and are then decided by events. An argument about which motion picture to attend may be decided by the failure to reach agreement until it is too late to attend any. Indecision about what to have for dinner leaves a decision that effects the whole family in the hands of the wife when she goes shopping. Such decisions sometimes follow ineffectual discussions and sometimes occur in the absence of any group consideration of the question at all. What all such events have in common is that agreement is by the absence of dissent rather than by active assent, and, more important, commitment is by the course of events rather than by acceptance. Such decisions are made in fact rather than in words but in a context of events such that members of the group find themselves committed (1970, pp. 99–100).

FACTORS INFLUENCING THE QUALITY OF DECISIONS

One of the main objectives in this chapter is to identify several principles that can be used to improve two aspects of decision making. These aspects are the *quality* of decisions and the *satisfaction* of individuals in a couple or family with the decisions that are made. Since these two dimensions of decision making are fundamental factors in this chapter, it seems useful to describe in some detail just what they are and how they differ from each other.

Maier (1963, p. 253)[8] was one of the first to differentiate between the quality and the satisfactoriness of decisions, and he described the satisfaction dimension as the way the members of a group feel about the decision that is made. The satisfaction dimension can be defined as the degree to which individual members feel contented or happy about or accepting of a decision that has been reached, and it is a continuous variable as shown below. The differ-

---

[8] Several others have identified the same dimensions even though they have used slightly different labels. Hoffman (1965, pp. 120–22), for example, differentiated between them, and Cartwright and Zander (1968, p. 406) described two dimensions that they termed "fairness to individuals" and "group effectiveness."

Satisfaction with decisions

Very low   Low   Medium   High   Very high

ence between the satisfaction dimension and the more objective
efficiency or quality dimension is illustrated by the following incident.

Mom called all of us together for a family council. We all sat down
facing each other across the big round kitchen table. The subject of the
council was deciding how to get all the "Saturday's work" done. After
about 15 minutes the council was over and a decision had been reached.
Hand that final decision over to any efficiency expert, and it would rate
high. Every detail was taken care of, and it was a good workable plan.
Yet my sister and I got up from that table and went to our rooms with
resentful, unhappy feelings; and I was vaguely aware that Mom seemed
to feel discouraged about our lack of enthusiasm.

In some situations satisfaction is the most important dimension
of decision making. These are the situations in which the correctness or wisdom of the decision is not of overriding importance, and
what matters most is that both members of the couple be happy
about what has been decided and the way in which it has been
decided. An example is a decision concerning which guests to invite
to dinner. There may be no objective way to evaluate whether the
"right" or "best" guests are invited, and what matters most is that
both the husband and wife be pleased with the selection of guests.
In contrast, there are other times when the wisdom or adequacy
of the decision is the major issue. This may occur, for example,
when many alternatives are pleasing but not all are wise. Perhaps
the couple would be satisfied with many different menus for the
dinner party, but the main concerns are that the menu be consistent with their budget and not too spicy for Harry's ulcer. It
would be foolish to suppose that in each decision-making situation
only one of these dimensions will be salient as it is frequently difficult to separate the dimensions. However, at a given point in time
it may be more crucial to work on one than on the other.
Diagramed in the following way, the *quality* dimension is also
a continuous variable. It can be defined as the degree to which

Quality of decisions

Very low   Low   Medium   High   Very high

a decision is an efficient, wise method of attaining the goal that is sought when the various circumstances in a situation are taken into account. The principles discussed in this section of the chapter deal with factors that influence the quality of decisions in courtship and marital situations, and the principles discussed in the last section of the chapter identify factors that influence satisfaction with decisions.

One factor that frequently influences the quality of decisions is the number of alternative solutions that are identified. This principle can be illustrated with the following situation.

The Alternatives principle

Phil and Jennifer, an engaged couple on a tight budget, were deciding where to look for housing. "Basement apartments are usually most inexpensive," said Jennifer. Phil agreed, and they looked in the newspaper listing, jotting down the addresses of basement apartments. They found one they liked pretty well, and decided to take it although they didn't like the neighborhood.

It may be that this couple found an apartment that filled their needs well, but the small number of options they considered may have excluded other possibilities that would have been wiser choices. For example, they might have found a mobile home, an upstairs apartment, or a duplex that would have given them a better combination of their desires in housing; but these possibilities were excluded by their narrow range of alternatives. The independent variable here is the number of alternatives that are identified in decision making; and it can be diagramed as follows:

Number of alternatives

Very small   Small   Large   Very large

The principle that relates the number of alternatives and the quality of decisions is:

THE ALTERNATIVES PRINCIPLE: The number of alternatives considered in decision making influences the quality of the decision making, and this is a curvilinear relationship.[9]

Figure 6–1 diagrams the type of relationship that is thought to exist in this generalization. It shows that the quality of decisions is usually lower when very few alternatives are identified, and that the quality tends to improve when more alternatives are identified.

---

[9] See Turner (1970, pp. 112–13) for a discussion of this principle and evaluation of related research.

Figure 6–1

The relationship between the number of alternatives
considered and the quality of decisions

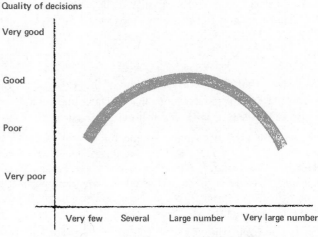

Apparently, however, after an optimum number of alternatives
have been identified, attempts to find additional alternatives tend to
interfere with decision making. This may be because couples tend
to become bogged down considering the alternatives when they
have too many. The findings of research that has tested this principle have been conflicting, but the reason may be that some of the
researchers have not viewed the relationship as curvilinear. One
study (Springborn, 1963) found a negative relationship between
the number of alternatives and the quality of decisions, but this
study dealt with variation between a rather sizable number of alternatives and an extremely high number; and, as Figure 6–1 suggests, there is a negative relationship when the number of alternatives is relatively high. Other researchers (Hoffman, Harberg, and
Maier, 1962; Hoffman, 1965) have found a positive relationship
between the number of alternatives and quality, and this is probably because they have only studied variation between very few
and a moderate number of alternatives.

One other important aspect of this relationship is the categories
or values used to denote the "number of alternatives." It would be
possible to use definite numbers rather than such qualitative distinctions as "very few" and "a very large number." However, the
number of alternatives that would be considered "very large" is
different in different types of decisions. For example, it would be

relatively easy for many couples to list 10 or 20 different possibilities for an annual vacation, and it may be that an optimum number
would be about 5 or 6. It would be relatively difficult, however, to
identify that many alternatives when trying to decide whether or
not to have another child. There are several alternatives, such as
beginning a pregnancy immediately versus waiting a year or two
versus adopting a child, but a large number of alternatives for that
type of decision is probably 4 or 5 rather than 10 or 20.

This principle has a number of practical implications. One is that
in many instances the natural tendency is to generate too few ideas
for a wise, creative choice. Since generating alternatives takes
time, thought, energy, creativity, and stick-to-itiveness, it may occasionally be desirable for couples to seek alternatives from someone
else. We could use several different sources, such as friends, teachers, counselors, or the mass media, and try to find sources of ideas
that would give several different kinds of ideas.

On the other hand, it is apparently detrimental to decision making to spend too much time and energy proposing and evaluating
diverse alternatives. For example, if Jennifer and Phil had generated
a list of 42 apartments to look at, they might have become so frustrated with the combinations of advantages and disadvantages that
their judgment would have been adversely affected.

At least two skills are involved in using this principle. One is the
ability to discern how many alternatives we usually identify in decision-making situations: some of us may usually only seek one, a
few, or a large number, and we may not have an accurate understanding of how many we tend to seek. Research about problem
solving in organizations has shown that people usually have a very
narrow range of alternatives when they are faced with decision
making, as they tend to think of frequently encountered similar situations in the past and only suggest the things that were done before or very slight variations from these customary solutions (Feldman and Kantor, 1965, pp. 620–23). It has been this author's
experience in marriage courses that when students complete the
"Number of Alternatives" exercise (below), many are surprised to
learn how few alternatives they usually consider when making decisions. Most discover that their usual pattern of decision making
is to identify one possible solution and then decide whether or not
to do it. Only when that alternative is undesirable do they usually
try to find a second. The following exercise is thus included to help
discover what our usual patterns are.

NUMBER OF ALTERNATIVES

Goal: To determine how many alternatives we usually think about in decision-making situations.

1. Think about the way you usually make decisions in a relationship with someone such as your spouse, dates, or roommates and identify what you think is the *average* number of alternatives you usually consider in making fairly unroutine decisions. (Exclude such routine decisions as deciding whether it is time for lunch or deciding how to get to work or school.) Write that number down.

2. At the end of each day for the next week take a few minutes and identify two or three decision-making situations that have occurred during the day. Identify decisions that were made with someone else rather than decisions you made alone, and try to identify fairly *unroutine* decisions. Count the number of alternative solutions that were identified in each decision-making situation and record the average number of alternatives per decision.

3. At the end of the week compare your predicted average number and the actual number. If the actual number is lower than the predicted one or the actual number is higher than the predicted one you are among the majority. If the numbers are the same you are among the insightful minority.

The second skill that is involved in using this principle is to be able to increase or decrease the number of alternatives we usually consider in decision making—depending on whether we usually have too few or too many to be optimally efficient. The following exercise is designed to help those who are interested in increasing the number of alternatives they usually consider. Those who want to try additional ways to help them change their usual behavior can use class discussion groups, instructors, or friends to help them devise other strategies for changing their behavior.

INCREASING ALTERNATIVES

Goal: To increase the number of alternatives that are usually considered in decision making.

1. Usually when we are making decisions we get to a point where we are ready to *decide* what to do. At this point we make comments like "So let's . . ." or "I think we ought to . . ." or "Then we'll . . ." For the next week at least once during each day STOP the decision-making process and quit working at the

process of deciding what to do. Hold up your hand. Stand up and turn around if you need to get things stopped, but stop the decision making.

2. Once the decision-making process is stopped, do two things:

   a. Itemize and count the alternatives that have been identified. Count them on your fingers or write them on paper, but explicitly identify each alternative and note how many have already been brought into the open.

   b. Have the attention of the group or couple focus briefly on the following question: "Are there any other possible solutions we ought to consider?" Try to think up at least one or two more, and add them to the list. Then resume the normal process of coming to a decision.

3. At the end of the week think about several times you have been in other group decision-making situations and note whether you have found yourself "interrupting" or "stopping" yourself at that certain place in the decision-making process to see whether there are other alternatives you might want to consider. If you have changed your usual behavior so you interrupt yourself in decision making, you have accomplished the goal of this exercise. You are sensitized to the process of identifying alternatives, and you probably will be identifying more alternatives than you were before. You might want to try the "Number of Alternatives" exercise again to see just how much you have changed.

The Rationality principle

Holly and Ted had just become engaged the night before. It had been an exciting day, telling friends at work of their marriage plans and then phoning some relatives in the evening. To add to the excitement Ted's parents had just given the couple their first wedding gift, which was extra money for their honeymoon. Holly and Ted sat down and decided to drive to Yosemite National Park for their honeymoon. Weeks later they had to change their decision when with some thoughtful planning they realized that the drive would be much too far and too exhausting. Holly and Ted were so excited that the decision made under those circumstances was not as wise as the one that was made later in a more thoughtful situation.

This experience illustrates a generalization that can help improve the qualities of decisions. The principle is:

THE RATIONALITY PRINCIPLE: The greater the rational control over behavior the better the quality of decisions, and vice versa.[10]

---

[10] Blood (1962, pp. 256–61) has explicated and illustrated this principle, but no systematic research has been found that has empirically tested this hypothesis.

Here, as in Chapter 3, rationality is defined as the amount of intellectual control over behavior. It is a continuous variable ranging from high to low, as diagramed below.

Amount of
rational control over behavior

None   Low   Medium   High   Complete

The Rationality principle asserts that decisions made when people feel hurried, are tired, are not sober, are paying attention to other things, or feel their self-esteem threatened tend to be of poorer quality than those made under opposite conditions. A few specific examples of conditions under which low rationality may exist are:

It is dinnertime. The parents want to have the family make a decision about scheduling the use of the car. The teenage daughter is chewing her food as quickly as possible in order to leave for a play rehearsal.

A girl and her boyfriend are deciding how much time they can spend together this week. The girl says, "But it takes you so long to do your homework—why do you take so long on it for such mediocre grades?"

It is 5:30 P.M. A wife is dividing her attention between frying pork chops, a baby banging his spoon on the high chair, the table setting, and the boiling pudding. Her husband comes into the kitchen saying, "What should we do about this offer to sell the house?"

The newlywed husband has just come in the door with his arms full of groceries. He went $7.00 over the weekly budget and is feeling very disappointed in himself and pretty low about his ability to manage money. His wife says, "OK, let's sit right down and decide how to handle this budget business."

One of the important skills in using this principle is being able to recognize when our lack of rational control over our behavior is interfering with the decision-making process. A second skill is being able to do something about it when we realize our relative irrationality. Both of these skills were discussed in Chapter 3, and the exercises identified there are helpful in the present context. In addition we can do many other things to increase our rationality in decision-making situations. One type of activity is to change the conditions that impair our rational control, such as eliminating distractions like loud music or fatigue, postponing an appointment we might have been hurrying to get to, taking the time to establish rapport, counting to ten, or just exerting more effort to remain rational when it is difficult to do so.

RECOGNIZING SELF-CONTROL

Goal: To increase the ability to recognize when your self-control tends to be high or low.

1. Get someone who knows you well to help you recognize when you are high or low in "self-control." This will take 10–15 minutes daily for one week.

2. At the end of each day, do two things with the other person:

   a. Identify (and list on a piece of paper) three situations in which you had discernibly *less* control.

   b. Identify the "clues" that helped either of you to tell whether the control was high or low, and list these clues each day on the piece of paper. Discuss these clues enough so that both individuals understand what they were.

3. At the end of the week, evaluate the effects of the week's activities have had on your ability to understand your self-control.

Tallman's (1970) review of previous research led him to postulate that "effective family problem solving requires open channels of communication for all family members competent to contribute to a problem solution" (1970, p. 96). The independent variable in this principle is the *openness* of the communication in a group. This is very similar to the variable described in Chapter 2 that was labeled the "willingness to communicate about deeply felt emotions." However, Tallman's variable is not restricted to deeply experienced emotions. He includes openness of communication about other things, such as opinions, ideas, goals, and emotions. As diagramed below, this is a continuous variable, of which one extreme is having very closed communication. At that extreme some persons in a relationship (especially those with low status) are not willing or able to share their ideas. High openness exists when the individuals in a group are willing and able to share their views. An

The Openness of Communication principle

Openness of communication

| Very closed | Quite closed | Quite open | Very open |

example of this variable is found in Straus's (1968) research with problem solving in three societies. He found that women and children in the San Juan and Bombay samples did not share their insights with the husband-father nearly as freely as in the Minneapolis sample. This principle is:

THE OPENNESS OF COMMUNICATION PRINCIPLE: The more open the communication in a group the better the quality of the decision making, and vice versa.

No information is available about the nature of this relationship other than that it is positive. However, enough empirical evidence[11] supports it to justify considerable confidence in it as a fairly well-substantiated principle.

There are many ways we can use this principle in our personal lives. For example, we can do a number of things to increase the amount that various members of a group share their ideas. We can reward individuals with such reinforcers as attention and praise when they do communicate, slow down the decision-making process whenever possible to make sure that everyone's opinions are heard, and specifically ask others what they think at various stages of decision making. Intently listening to others' opinions and treating their opinions with respect also probably increases the amount that people communicate in most groups.

INCREASING OPENNESS

Goal: To determine how open people tend to be in one important relationship, and (assuming that we wish to increase the openness) to increase the openness in the decision making in that relationship.

1. Identify a relationship you have in which there is considerable interaction (marriage, engagement, family, roommates, etc.).

2. For one week, be alert for situations where "decision making" or "problem solving" is occurring, and *whenever it is,* observe which individuals are the least open (don't suggest alternatives, don't

---

[11] Maier (1960); Hoffman et al. (1962); Bass (1963); Hoffman (1965); Bower (1965); Straus (1968).

get involved, sit quietly, leave the group, avoid taking initiative, etc.). Also identify which individuals are the most open. Do not make any attempts to change these patterns during the first week.

3. Evaluate the amount of openness in the decision making in this relationship and what effect it would probably have on the effectiveness of the decision making if there were more or less openness. If you think the relationship has an optimum level of openness, you have completed this exercise. If, however, you think the decision making would improve if there were more openness, complete steps 4 and 5.

4. During the next week, continue to be alert to when decision making is occurring. However, whenever possible try to do what you can to create a situation that will increase the openness of the individuals who tend to be the least open. Some possible ways to do this are:

   a. Before selecting one of the alternatives in the decision making, *ask* others whether they can think of any other possibilities or what they think about the options.

   b. Point out to the "leader" that some individuals seem to be highly involved and some don't, and suggest that more should be done to involve others.

   c. Realize that the individuals who are less "open" may have insights others don't, and treat them as though they have important information to contribute.

5. At the end of the second week, evaluate the level of openness to see whether it has changed. If it has not changed you may find it useful to indicate to the others that the lack of openness in the decision making is a problem and then create a "problem solving" situation about the level of openness to see whether the group can change the situation.

Another principle that Tallman (1970) gleaned from previous research has to do with the leadership role in a couple, group, or family when they are making decisions. Apparently the more agreement that individuals in a group have about who the leader is, the more efficient they tend to be in making decisions. The independent variable is the amount of *consensus about leadership*. This variable is diagramed below. At the low end of the diagram there is dis-

The Leadership principle

Consensus about leadership

Disagreement about
who leader is

Some
agreement

Consensus about
who leader is

agreement about who the leader is, or no one is a leader. At the high end one person is clearly the leader, and the other members of the group are willing to give him or her the authority to lead in decision making. There is no evidence that this person has to be the leader in other aspects of the couple's or family's interaction, but she or he does need to "get things done" in decision-making situations. The principle that summarizes this idea asserts that if the members of the couple or family agree that a certain individual is the leader in a decision-making situation, and that person then coordinates the problem-solving efforts of the various members of the group, the group will usually be more efficient in making a decision than if there were no clear-cut leader. Or, more formally:

THE LEADERSHIP PRINCIPLE: The greater the degree of consensus among the members of a group about the leader in decision-making situations the better the quality of the decision making, and vice versa.

There is considerable research (Tallman, 1970) that supports this principle. Thus, it is one in which we can have confidence.

In using this principle in our personal lives, it is probably useful to realize that nothing in the research literature suggests that one person has to be the leader all of the time in a certain relationship or group. Thus, it may be possible to have different individuals lead in different situations. For example, the wife could be the leader in making decisions about certain issues, and the husband could be the leader in other areas; or they could probably change the leadership roles other ways. There also doesn't seem to be any reason why fairly mature children couldn't also assume the leadership position for certain types of decisions.

We should probably also realize that high consensus about leadership in decision making is sometimes a mixed blessing. It seems to help couples or families increase their efficiency in decision making, but there is evidence that it also occasionally makes the individuals in the group less satisfied and happy with the decision making than when they are in a less structured group. This has practical consequences for decision-making families because high morale is also usually a fairly important family goal. The result is that families may want to identify a leader, but they may want also to have the leader be conscious of ways he or she can act to avoid the dissatisfaction that frequently accompanies having a leader in a decision-making group. The two principles in the "Satisfaction" section at the end of this chapter can be used to help accomplish this, and the following exercise can help couples or families better understand who usually assumes the leadership role.

LEADERSHIP

Goal: To gain a better understanding of who assumes and who does not assume leadership roles in decision making, and to determine how much consensus there is about this leadership.

1.   In an ongoing group or in a relationship such as marriage or engagement, set aside 15–30 minutes to complete this exercise.

2.   Have each individual (without discussing or letting the others know his conclusion) determine where each person in the relationship usually is on the continuum below:

Person in relationship

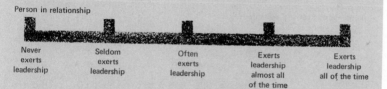

| Never exerts leadership | Seldom exerts leadership | Often exerts leadership | Exerts leadership almost all of the time | Exerts leadership all of the time |

Some behaviors that suggest leadership are:

a.   Suggests new and novel alternatives.

b.   Suggests that the group come back to the central issue when the group wanders.

c.   Asks others for their suggestions or ideas.

d.   Summarizes where the group is or asks someone else to summarize.

e.   Moves the group from one stage of decision making to another with such statements as "OK, now we're ready to . . ."

f.   Decides when a problem should or should not be talked out.

g.   Is usually the "central" one in the communication, and is often the one who talks the most.

h.   Is expected to take the initiative in decision making.

3.   Compare the "individual" estimates of leadership, and try to arrive at a "group" definition of where each person is on the above continuum. In the process you will probably find yourself talking about the differences in individual perceptions, and you will be able to determine how much consensus you have had in the past.

4.   Evaluate how much consensus there is about the group definition you acquired in step 3, and try to determine what implications this probably has for your decision-making ability.

*The Quality
of Attention
principle*

Turner (1970) has identified two other factors that seem to influence the quality of decision making in marital and family situations. One is what he terms the quality of the attention that is given to the suggestions made by various members of a group. As he points out:

Suggestions made by a child are often received with a friendly pat on the head and given no serious thought. . . . thus if the father is viewed or views himself as omnipotent relative to other family members, he is less likely to take their suggestions seriously, and the quality of family solutions will be poorer (1970, p. 113).

The same type of depreciation may be applied to the opinions of a date or spouse, and it will apparently have the same effect. As diagramed below, the quality of attention given to others' opinions is a continuous variable, and the relevant principle is:

Quality of
attention given to others' opinions

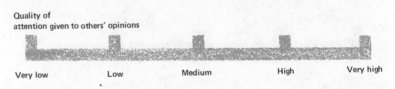

Very low   Low   Medium   High   Very high

THE QUALITY OF ATTENTION PRINCIPLE: The higher the quality of attention that is given to opinions of others in the group the better the quality of the decision making, and vice versa.

Turner has suggested that this principle is correct, and it does seem reasonable. Turner does not, however, cite any empirical data that test this generalization, and the author is not aware of any systematic research about it. Thus, the confidence we can place in this principle rests on Turner's analysis, its inherent plausibility, and its consistency with our everyday experience.

We are probably familiar with situations in which attention is given to opinions and with situations in which it is not given. Some of the comments that occur at these times are:

"Hmmm, let's consider that. What do the rest of you think about it?"

"Tell us what you mean. Let's hear a little more about that."

"Fine, son" (and the conversation goes on essentially uninterrupted without dealing with the son's ideas).

"But I think that we ought to . . . ." (which changes the topic right after someone suggests a new idea).

Quality of attention involves more than just turning one's head and passively listening to what someone is saying. It includes an alertness to subtleties of tone, posture, gestures, and facial expressions, and an interest in the other person's contributions. Also, it frequently has ramifications beyond the quality of a particular decision because whether people's ideas are ignored or viewed as important can influence how they will feel about themselves. If people are ignored they get feelings of inadequacy or unimportance and often withdraw from a situation. If others treat their ideas with respect and attention they are more likely to feel respected and hence respectable and to feel that they have important contributions to make. Good listening basically entails focusing one's attention on understanding what the other person means. Some skills that can be used to give high-quality attention are: (1) keeping the focus on the speaker; (2) using invitations to speak; (3) checking for understanding; (4) attending to feelings; (5) sticking to the issue being discussed; and (6) attending to nonverbal cues.

Several qualifications probably should be made in applying this principle in our personal lives. It is wise to take into account the maturity of the individual who is giving opinions, as a suggestion of the three-year-old that the family go to Africa for their vacation may not be a very reasonable alternative. Serious attention to such opinions would interfere with the quality of decision making—especially when time is precious. On the other hand the spontaneity and the creativity of children frequently provide alternatives that older individuals wouldn't think of. Also, it seems reasonable that paying attention to children's views may pave the way for their more serious participation later.

The other relevant principle that Turner (1970, pp. 113–14) has suggested is that the willingness of couples or families to "take risks" is also related to the quality of their decision making. As he points out, this is probably a curvilinear relationship. Too little or too much risk hinders the quality of decisions, and there is a certain optimal level of risk taking. It may be that it is impossible to identify in general how much risk taking is desirable, because we can be more risky in some situations than in others, but his idea is nonetheless thought provoking.

The Risk principle

THE RISK PRINCIPLE: The amount of risk taking in decision making influences the quality of the decision making, and this is a curvilinear relationship.

This author is not aware of empirical research that provides support for this hypothesis, but it too has an inherent plausibility. The curvilinear relationship that Turner suggests is diagramed in Figure 6–2.

Figure 6–2

The curvilinear relationship between risk taking and the quality of decisions

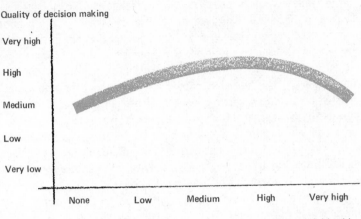

Each couple, of course, needs to decide just how to implement this principle. Some of us may be more risky than is wise, while others may be so afraid of breaking traditional patterns that we make much less wise decisions than we could. The following exercise is designed to help determine how optimal our usual patterns of risk taking are.

RISKINESS

Goal: To gain a better understanding of how risky we tend to be in decision making and to evaluate the effect this has on our decision making.

1. One way to gain more insight into how risky we usually are is to get feedback from others about what they think we do. To do this, ask three people who know you fairly well how they would evaluate you on the following question (try to not bias their opinions before they commit themselves): "When I'm in a problem-solving or decision-making situation, which of these statements best describes my usual behavior?"

a. eager to take chances or gamble with new and novel solutions —even if they involve some risk

b. more willing than most to take chances

c. somewhat willing to take chances

d. usually quite reluctant to agree to risky solutions

e. very unwilling to take chances

2. Use this feedback and your own perceptions to assess how risky you tend to be, and what implications this has for your decision-making ability.

One essential ingredient in quality decision making is coming to a conclusion about what to do or not do. Some of us raise issues and problems and talk about the relative advantages and costs of various alternatives, but we find it difficult to come to a conclusion about which course of action or inaction we want to adopt. This is illustrated by the following situation: *The Decisiveness principle*

Fran and Roger were upset about some of the behavior of their three-year-old son. They had discussed the matter and had come to the conclusion that a large part of the problem was that each of them responded to him differently—they sensed that they were defeating each other's goals. A few suggestions that they might try were made, but no plan that they both agreed upon was reached. Time went on, and their son's troublesome behavior continued.

It is easy to see that Fran and Roger did not really come to a conclusive decision, and it is this "decisiveness" that is the important variable in this principle. Decisiveness can be viewed as a continuum, as shown below, and low decisiveness occurs when an issue

Decisiveness

Low   Medium   High

is still "up in the air" after the decision making is over. High decisiveness exists when a decision is made that is very clear. At intermediate levels of decisiveness some members may think a decision had been reached while others are vague and uncertain about what it is. The principle involved here is:

THE DECISIVENESS PRINCIPLE: The decisiveness in decision making affects the quality of decisions, and this is a positive relationship.

No research is known that has tested this principle. The bases for suggesting that it is valid are its rationality and the fact that a rather large number of couples in the author's Marriage courses have indicated that indecisiveness is one of the major obstacles in their own decision making.

As with so many other instances, the first step in applying this principle in our personal lives is an introspective analysis to determine where we are as a couple or a family. Are any or all of us excessively indecisive, or it this an area that is not a problem in our relationship? It is, of course, also possible that one member of a couple moves to the deciding stage of decision making too quickly, and one way to improve the decision making might then be to have that person find ways to delay closure.

The following exercise is designed to help us develop our own plan of action for increasing or decreasing our decisiveness. This same exercise can also be used in many other contexts, such as helping us improve some of our communication skills or helping us develop decision-making skills, such as openness of communication and attentiveness. We may, of course, want to alter the format of these "Action Plans" to suit our own needs, personalities, or situations.[12]

AN ACTION PLAN

1. What do you want to change?

    . . . Is it to *stop* doing something?
    . . . Is it to *start* doing something?
    . . . Is it to do something *more often?*
    . . . Is it to do something *less often?*

    State what it is you want to do. _____

    _____

2. How much commitment do you have to make the change?

    . . . Will you be honest about your actions in regard to the action plan?

---

[12] The format for these "Action Plans" is from Scoresby et al. (1974), and appreciation is expressed to Duane Laws for calling it to my attention. Readers may find it useful to refer back to this outline as they try to develop ways to use principles discussed in later chapters.

. . . Will you be responsible for what you do? (no shifting of the responsibility to another person or to situational circumstances)

. . . Do you really want to make the change?

. . . What will be the reward for changing?

State how committed you are to change. _____

_____

3. What exactly is your action plan?

. . . Is it a small unit of observable behavior? (This may be part of a larger unit you are interested in changing, but keep it small and manageable.)

. . . How often do you plan to do it?

. . . When do you plan to do it?

. . . State it in behavioral terms; include *who* will do *what* for *whom* and *when* you will finish it.

4. Follow-up.

Keep a record of the results of your action plan. Remember that approximations are successes, not failures. Perseverance may bring total success.

Describe the results of your action plan after completing it. _____

_____

_____

_____

SATISFACTION WITH DECISION MAKING

Considerable research indicates that when people are left out of the decision-making process, and the decision substantially influences them, they are usually less satisfied with the decision that is made; and, conversely, when they are included they tend to be more satisfied. The independent variable is the amount or extent of participation in the decision-making process. Participation is more than just the amount a person says in the discussion. As Tallman points out, "It is the sense that one has played an important role in contributing to the problem's solution" (1970, p. 96). The low end of this continuum can be seen in the following situation.

The Amount of Participation principle

Frank's wife-to-be came over to his apartment two weeks before the wedding with a notebook under her arm. "It's budget-discussing time," she announced, and she explained to him the categories she had laid out and noted the monthly amounts of money she had allotted to each category. "Well, that's it," she concluded. "Now are you ready for our date?" He was not happy about the amount of money in the recreation and food categories, and anticipated living within the budget with reservations.

The extent of a person's participation in the decision-making process has to do with the degree to which that person expresses his or her views and feelings about the issues at hand—gets his or her word in. Such participation ranges from low to high, as shown below. The low end would be characterized by complete exclusion

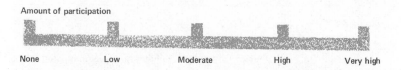

Amount of participation

None   Low   Moderate   High   Very high

from the decision-making process, as in the example given above. Fairly low on the participation scale is the case in which a person says very little of what is on his mind and mildly assents while others carry the conversation and make the decision. High on the participation scale is the case in which a person says what he thinks, suggests alternatives, and comments about the family's interaction while the decision is being made. Frank's fiancée in the above example could have increased the likelihood of his satisfaction with the decision if she had included him in the planning of the budget and listened to his preferences and ideas about it. This principle is:

THE AMOUNT OF PARTICIPATION PRINCIPLE: When people have an interest in the outcome of a decision, the more they participate in the decision-making process, the more satisfied they usually are with the decision, and vice versa.

There is considerable empirical support for this proposition, as a number of studies have found this relationship to occur.[13] This is thus one of the principles in which we can have considerable confidence. There are also several additional reasons why this principle seems credible. One is that most of us have experienced the negative feelings brought about by not being able to participate in the making of a decision concerning ourselves. A sense of injustice often results, somewhat akin to the American colonists' indignation over "taxation without representation." Apart from our resentment over the fact of not being included, there is also the likelihood that our views were not really considered and were not incorporated into the decision, and this can contribute to dissatisfaction. Then, too, persons not present when a decision was made may be indignant

---

[13] See Cartwright and Zander (1968, pp. 406–11) and Hoffman (1965) for reviews of much of this research. See also Maier and Hoffman (1960, 1962) and Tallman (1970).

over a decision other than their preferred alternative because they did not hear and become aware of all the demands of the situation and points of view that were considered.

This principle has a number of very practical implications. There may be many times when family members are tempted to exclude someone from the decision-making process. If a wife knows that her husband disagrees with her on some issue she could save time, get her own way, and avoid having to lay out all her reasoning (to be vulnerable to change by confrontation with *his* reasoning) if she made the decision without him. This is especially so if the decision gets at least partly carried out so that it is somewhat irreversible by the time he finds out about it. One trouble with that strategy, however, is that the decision is less likely to be satisfying to and accepted by him. His grumbling, his lack of commitment and follow-through, his feeling of being slighted—all these outcomes suggest that leaving him out may backfire and that in the long run it might be simpler and easier to make the decision with him.

A family member may also be left out of decisions in ways other than physical absence. For example, he may be reticent or afraid or may not care to participate, or he may think that his ideas will probably not be understood or considered. Also, an idea may not be developed well enough for a person to be willing to venture into a discussion, or his self-esteem may be so precarious that he does not dare to risk rejection. He may feel so inferior to others that he preevaluates his ideas and censors them as not being worthwhile. Then, too, a person may not care enough about the decision being made to contribute, or he may not have done enough thinking to have many relevant ideas to express. Here are some other times when participation is likely to be lower than optimum:

- when partners don't allow enough time to discuss decisions;
- when one partner is overly certain that his own views are best;
- when one person thinks that the other doesn't care what his opinion is;
- when a person articulates his ideas poorly (in which case others tend to "tune him out" and behave in ways that reflect to him a lack of interest in hearing more);
- when listening skills are not well-developed;
- when one person's self-esteem is low, and he reacts by trying to be controlling.

The following exercise is designed to help us determine how much each of the individuals in one of our ongoing relationships is involved in decision making.

AMOUNT OF PARTICIPATION

Goal: To determine how much individuals usually tend to be involved or uninvolved in decision making in one of our ongoing relationships.

1. Identify one of your relationships such as your relationship with your parent's family, with your spouse, or with a roommate.

2. Observe the decision making in this relationship for one week without letting the others know you are observing the interaction.

3. Try to determine which individuals are highly involved in the decision-making process, and whether anyone is excluded or left out of the decision making. Do not try to change what seems to be "naturally" happening until the week is over. Even if you are unhappy about the situation, it has undoubtedly existed for some time and a few more days will make little difference. You ought to take the entire week to be sure that the patterns that disturb you are repetitious enough to be a problem.

4. Evaluate what effect participation or lack of participation has on the satisfaction of the individuals with their decision making. You may or may not then want to intervene in the situation to try to change the amount people participate.

The Consensus principle

Another factor affecting satisfaction with decisions is the amount of consensus that is reached in making them. Consensus refers to the degree to which the members of a group agree that the alternative chosen is the best one. On the high end of this continuum all members of the group feel that the alternative chosen is, all things

Amount of consensus

None   Low   Moderate   High   Total

considered, the best. Intermediate degrees are found in situations in which some members accept an alternative only in order to reach agreement, or disagree with the decision but are forced into submission. At the low end of the continuum are decisions made by coercion, in which most members of a group agree to a proposal because they have no other choice or because they cannot accept what would happen if they did not agree. The following hypothetical example illustrates a range from high to low consensus.

Ross likes dinners to be served punctually. Marie values leisurely spending time with the children, and helping them when they need it, more than she values punctuality. Ross is upset by Marie's tardiness; Marie is upset by Ross's impatience. The problem has been defined, and two alternatives identified: (*a*) Marie can continue to serve dinner at irregular times, continuing to talk and play with the children during dinner preparation (Marie's proposal). (*b*) Marie can stop interacting with the children during dinner preparation and serve dinner promptly (Ross's proposal).

Suppose they make a highly consensual agreement:

During the discussion of alternatives Ross perceives that Marie's main concern is that the children not be shut out from parental attention in early evening. He offers to spend time with them while Marie prepares dinner by herself. This achieves the major end that Marie wanted, and Ross will get dinner on time. Both feel that the new alternative is best.

Suppose they make a less consensual agreement:

Marie and Ross favor their own proposals. Both are interested in reaching an agreement, though. Ross suggests that dinner be served sometime between 6:00 and 6:30 P.M. He would rather have it at one specific time, and Marie would rather not have time limits, but in order to reach a decision they agree this new proposal will be adopted.

Suppose they do their decision making with very low consensus:

Marie says, "Do you want me to prepare dinner, or don't you?" Ross says, "Of course, I want you to fix it." Marie replies, "Then quit grumbling, OK?" "Oh, all right," says Ross.

The principle that describes the relationship between consensus and satisfaction is:

THE CONSENSUS PRINCIPLE: The more consensus there is about a decision the greater the satisfaction with the decision, and vice versa.

Not all decisions can be highly consensual, even in "ideal" relationships. Couples *can*, however, increase the degree of consensus in their decisions by working at it, and this will usually increase their satisfaction with the decisions they make. Even though the partners' initial choices of alternatives are different, consensus can be reached by such things as: (1) creating new alternatives consistent with the values and desires of each partner; (2) changing one's evaluation of a particular alternative in light of a different value whose relevance has been suggested; (3) perceiving a particular alternative differently than one did before (for example, "My original idea doesn't seem as good now that I've thought it over" or "That idea looks better to me now that we've discussed it"); or (4) learning how strongly others feel about an issue.

Sometimes it takes more time and effort to keep working at consensus than it does to settle for an accommodating or coercive decision, but the resulting increase in satisfaction may be worth it. At other times couples or families may find that achieving consensus is too costly and that they would be better off with lower satisfaction and an accommodating or coercive decision. Each situation has to be assessed on its individual merits, but knowing that getting consensus creates greater satisfaction can be useful in practical situations.

SUMMARY

The first part of this chapter described the sequence of events that usually occurs in decision making. The decision-making process was divided into the five stages of: (1) identifying an issue or problem on which a decision is needed, (2) identifying alternative solutions to the problem or issue, (3) evaluating those alternatives, (4) making the decision by selecting one of the alternatives, and (5) implementing the decision. There are, of course, other ways that decision making could be divided into stages, and some scholars have used a three-stage division while others have divided the decision-making process into eight or nine stages. In real life couples frequently do not go through these stages systematically. They often jump around from one stage to another and skip from early stages to later stages without finishing the first ones. In addition, with some decisions, couples who have been around each other a great deal can sometimes accomplish the whole process through a few gestures, without a word being spoken.

The last part of the chapter identified seven factors that are thought to influence the quality of decision making and satisfaction with decisions. The causal variables in these principles are (1) the number of alternatives considered, (2) rationality, (3) openness of communication, (4) the amount of consensus about who occupies the leadership role, (5) the quality of attention given to opinions, (6) riskiness, and (7) decisiveness. All of these variables are thought to influence the quality of decisions, and these seven prin-

Figure 6–3

Causal model of general principles in Chapter 6

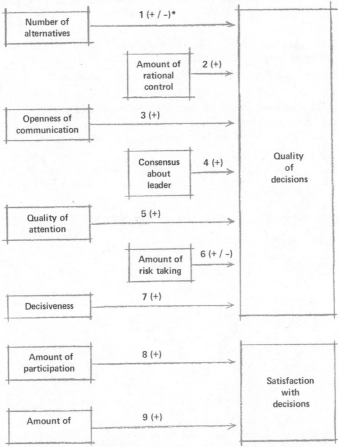

*The "(+/−)" symbol stands for a curvilinear relationship like the one drawn in Figure 6–1. The independent variable has a positive relationship with the dependent variable up to a point, and above that point the relationship is negative.

ciples are summarized in Figure 6–3. With some of these variables the more of the variable the better the quality of decisions, and with others there is an optimum amount, and too little or too much of the variable worsens the quality of the decisions. Two other variables, (8) the amount of participation in decision making and (9) consensus about the decision, tend to influence the satisfaction with decisions, and these two principles are summarized at the bottom of Figure 6–3. Various ways to apply these principles in real life situations were discussed.

SUGGESTIONS FOR FURTHER STUDY

Aldous, Joan, ed. *Family Problem Solving*. Chicago: Dryden Press.

Blood, Robert O., Jr. 1969. *Marriage*. Rev. ed. Glencoe, Ill.: Free Press, chap. 17.

Deutsch, Morton 1973. *The Resolution of Conflict: Constructive and Destructive Processes*. New Haven: Yale University Press.

Hoffman, Lois W. 1961. "Effects of the Employment of Mothers on Parental Power Relations and the Division of Household Tasks." *Marriage and Family Living* 22:27–35 (no. 1).

Kieren, Dianne; Henton, June; and Marotz, Ramona 1975. *Hers and His: A Problem Solving Approach to Marriage*. Hinsdale, Ill.: Dryden Press.

Tallman, Irving 1970. "The Family as a Small Problem Solving Group," *Journal of Marriage and the Family* 32:94–104 (February).

Turner, Ralph H. 1970. *Family Interaction*. New York: Wiley.

Premarital relationships

There are many important issues, turning points, and developmental tasks in premarital interaction where general principles of human behavior can be useful, and this section addresses several of these. Chapter 7 deals with the process of assessing before a marriage how compatible two people will be after they are married. Most of us are convinced at the time we marry that we are and will be fairly compatible with the person we marry, but the fact that there have been about 40 divorces for every 100 marriages in recent years is an indication that many of us later find ourselves more incompatible than we thought. It is, of course, impossible for all of us to be 100 percent accurate in determining our compatibility, but hopefully the principles identified in Chapter 7 will help us to be more accurate than we would be without them.

Chapter 8 deals with several ways that individuals can create or diminish their love feelings for each other. Most of us use these principles fairly effectively before we are married to develop deeply felt and rewarding feelings of love for each other, and many of us tell ourselves that we want to maintain those feelings after we are married. Mostly, however, we find that our love feelings tend to fade and become less intense after a few years of marriage. Some of us discover that when all things are considered we prefer life that way, but others would rather have a marriage in which we maintain very intense love feelings for our spouse. The principles in Chapter 8 can help us to create and maintain whatever intensity of feelings we want to have.

Chapter 9 identifies several factors that we may want to evaluate before we decide that we are ready for marriage, and Chapter 10 evaluates some of the causes and effects of various premarital sexual attitudes and behaviors. The principles identified in Chapter 10 can be used to change several attitudes about sexuality and ways of behaving. Chapter 11 identifies a number of generalizations that can be used to minimize some of the frustrations that couples experience as they marry and to maximize some of the joys and pleasures of marriage.

7

Appraising compatibility

W HEN two individuals are considering whether to marry, they are faced with the question of how compatible they will be after they are married. If their later marital relationship were to be a continuation of courtship it would probably be fairly easy to make this appraisal, as it is likely that their compatibility in their court-ship would be a good indicator of their compatibility in marriage. Whether we like it or not, however, marital interaction is usually quite different from premarital interaction, and many couples who are highly compatible in their dating find themselves fairly incom-patible in a marital relationship. This is illustrated by the two fol-lowing case histories.

When we were going together before we were married we got along really great. She was so agreeable about things like what to do on dates and agreed with me on so many things that I figured I'd found a perfect wife. It wasn't long after we were married though that things started to break down between us. . . . She lost a lot of interest in some of the things I like to do and she wanted to go out like we did before we were married. Heck, you can't keep running around like you did when you weren't married and didn't have a lot of responsibilities, but she never seemed to understand that. She spends a lot of time now gadding around with the gals in this club she belongs to and I guess that sort of takes care of her social life. Me, I watch a lot of TV and spend a lot of time down at the track. . . . I guess to answer your question, we don't really get along the way I thought we would when we first decided to get married.

Tom, my husband, has a terrible temper. He will explode over the smallest trifle. One time before our marriage I thought it over and decided I could not endure a married life of quarrels and recriminations. I wrote him that everything was off between us and returned the ring. That night I lay awake and found I loved him too much to break with him. I resolved to go into marriage with my eyes wide open and make all the necessary adjustments. It has not been easy, I assure you, but I regard my marriage as very happy. I try to do nothing to irritate him, but he still explodes on the slightest provocation. I never realized until after marriage how a man can swear. I never make any suggestions unless he asks for them. If they work, I never remind him that I made them (Burgess and Wallin, 1953, p. 532).

The first couple were more compatible in their dating than in their marriage, and they weren't able to predict very accurately how compatible they would be. In the second situation the couple seemed to work out a fairly satisfactory arrangement because the wife realized certain characteristics of the relationship and gauged her behavior by them. As these cases show, however, marital compatibility can be elusive, difficult to predict, and hard to come by. Since this is the case, it seems useful to identify several general principles that couples can use to increase their insight into how compatible they will probably be after they are married, and then to identify several ways that these principles can actually be applied in dating situations to provide clues about compatibility. This chapter attempts to do this by identifying eight principles and discussing ways to use them.

PRINCIPLES ABOUT COMPATIBILITY

Socializing agents of prospective spouse

The social sciences have identified a number of factors that influence how much we copy (model, identify with, imitate) other people or groups of people. The factors that have been found to be most important are the amount we interact with the other persons, the warmth of the other persons, the amount the other persons control our rewards and punishments, the social status of the other persons, and our feelings of like or dislike for the other persons.[1] The conditions that lead to the greatest copying are large amounts of interaction with a warm person who has high control over our rewards and punishments when this person has high status and is liked.

When people try to identify the individual or individuals who best fit this description they also usually identify the person or group of persons they have copied most in their style of life. For most people, the two persons who are usually at the top of this list are their parents. There are, of course, exceptions. For example,

[1] Bandura and Walters (1963, chap. 3) is an excellent review of this research. Numerous studies have been conducted in this area, and two widely quoted examples that deal with family situations are Brim (1958) and Elder (1963).

when people have parents who are deviant in one way or another, there is usually another individual or a group of individuals who have become parent surrogates, and these serve as the social parents in place of the biological parents. The individuals who are usually next in line to the parents are siblings—especially older siblings. The next most important groups usually include such individuals as other kin, friends, church leaders, and teachers. The two most important conclusions that emerge from this analysis are that most of us *tend to be more like our parents than anyone else,* and that *we tend to repeat in our own marital situation many of the patterns we observed in our parents' marriage.* These conclusions provide the basis for a general principle that is useful in testing marital compatibility. This principle is:

THE MODELING PRINCIPLE: The closer an individual's prospective spouse's parents' marital relationships are to the individual's ideal marital relationships the greater the chances that the individual will be satisfied with the marriage, and vice versa.

This principle thus suggests that usually a careful analysis of the marital relationship of the parents of the person we are thinking about marrying will provide some valuable clues about our compatibility with that person. There are a number of limitations to this general rule. One is that science has not yet discovered at what ages the parents' relationship has the greatest impact on children. There is some evidence that children are greatly influenced in regard to such things as a basic sense of trust in the first few years of their lives (Erikson, 1951), but there is no evidence that this period is the most important in influencing the kinds of things that matter most in marital relationships. It may be that the adolescent years are the time when children observe and internalize the beliefs, attitudes, and behaviors they will exhibit years later in their own marriages. This means that if parents radically change their lifestyle during the children's youth it is now impossible to tell how this will influence the relevance of this principle for the children.

Another caution about this principle is that children will not be exactly like their parents. It is certainly possible to systematically not copy parents and to model other people. One way this is done is to be in a situation in which the parent-child relationship does not have the characteristics conducive to copying—interaction, warmth, control, status, and affection. When this occurs, however, these individuals will usually have relationships with other individuals they will have copied, and the Modeling principle can be applied to these other relationships.

Before discussing ways to use this principle, it is probably also useful to discuss the dependent variable in some detail. The dependent variable in this principle is the *chances for marital satisfaction*. This is a continuous variable that ranges from zero to 100 percent certainty of success, as shown below. Most married couples

Chances of
being satisfied in marriage

0   50   100%

have a better than fifty-fifty chance of being happily married, but probably only slightly better. Since there were over 20 million weddings and about 6½ million divorces and annulments in the United States during the 1964–73 decade, the ratio of divorces to marriages was about one to three for that decade.[2] If that ratio remains fairly constant over the next few years, then, when it is combined with the rather repetitious research finding that around 70–80 percent of couples who are not divorced indicate that they are either "satisfied" or "very satisfied" with their marriage[3] the

---

[2] The most easily available source for these statistics is the annual edition of the *Statistical Abstract,* and the most current source is United States Department of Health, Education and Welfare, National Center for Health Statistics, Monthly Vital Statistics Report.

[3] Various methods are used to measure how "happy" or "satisfied" people are with their marriages, but the most frequent method is to use a questionnaire that is filled out anonymously. Such questions usually include questions like the following:

1. Check a dot on the scale line below which best describes the present degree of happiness, everything considered, of your marriage. The middle point, "happy," represents the degree of happiness which most people get from marriage, and the scale gradually ranges on one side to those few who are very unhappy in marriage, and on the other to those few who experience joy or felicity in marriage.

Present degree of
happiness of marriage

Perfectly   Happy   Unhappy
happy

2. Do you consider your marriage a *success* in accomplishing the goals which you want your marriage to achieve?
   ( )   very definitely
   ( )   mostly
   ( )   somewhat
   ( )   in many ways, no
   ( )   quite unsuccessful

This method of quantifying marital satisfaction has several problems, and not the least of these are that people can quickly detect what the researcher wants to know and can then distort the answers if they want to. It is, however, the best method thus far developed to measure this variable. Numerous

result is that the average couple now has a slightly over 50 percent chance of being satisfied or happy with their marriage. Some couples' chances are, of course, higher and some lower than the average. Also, the chances of being satisfied in our marriages can undoubtedly be increased or decreased substantially by using the principles identified in this book.

The Modeling principle can be applied in a number of ways. One is to try to become acquainted with the parents of a prospective spouse and to evaluate their marital relationship. If their marriage tends to be fairly similar to the type of relationship that we want, this provides some evidence that we will be compatible with the prospective spouse . . . particularly if the prospective spouse is not interested in being dramatically different from her or his parents. If, however, the relationship is very different from the type of marriage that we desire, this provides an indication that our chances of compatibility may not turn out to be as high as we might have thought previously.

Probably one of the most beneficial results of a careful analysis of the parents' marriages is that it may help identify some issues we can then discuss to determine how relevant they are for our own situation. This type of discussion can provide new insights into a relationship that some of us would probably never be able to acquire in any other way until after we are married. Occasionally we, or our fiancé(e), may observe something in one of the parents' marriages that we would really like in our own marriage, and we can then discuss it to determine whether both of us want that particular characteristic. We may also find some things we don't want to repeat in our own marriage, and once these are identified it is then possible to determine whether both of us want to avoid the pattern and whether we have the skills to avoid it. This latter point about the ability to attain or avoid something in marital relationships is important because, on occasion, everyone wants to "not do" something in our marriage but the behavior is so deeply ingrained that we aren't able to avoid it. A thoughtful analysis of the parents' marriages can facilitate a discussion of these possibilities

Another aspect of these issues is that some of the things that we

---

studies, beginning with several large studies in the 1930s—Burgess and Cottrell (1939); Terman et al. (1938); Kelley (1955); Burgess and Wallin (1953)—and continuing up to the present, have found that between 65 percent and 85 percent of people indicate that they are happy or satisfied with their marriages.

copy from our parents are vague and subtle, and it is hence difficult to see them in premarital behavior. Also, many times the behaviors or beliefs we may observe in our parents may not be apparent in us until we have been married for a number of years. The following case history illustrates this process:

My mother was a very dominating person who also had a short temper. When we children used to get out of line we were disciplined very quickly and usually with more than gentle firmness. When I reached an age where I started thinking about how I wanted to act as a mother I repeatedly said to myself that I would be much more patient and less punishing with my children. It was really a revelation, though, when my own children started to grow up. Whenever I would respond in a natural, uncontrolled manner I would act just like my mother did—even though I didn't want to. And it has been one of the biggest struggles of my entire life for me to try to become more patient, permissive and relaxed.

The fact that we tend to copy our parents even against our own will is also illustrated by the following story:

There is an oft-told tale about a French peasant and his son, who did not get along together well. While the boy was young, his father abused him, and the son looked forward to the day when he would be stronger than his father. The son reached maturity and one day a disagreement arose. The young man knocked his father down and dragged him into the orchard. As they passed the third row of trees, the father cried out, "Stop! Stop! I dragged my father only to the second row." (Waller and Hill, 1959.)

The two following exercises are designed to help implement this general principle. The first is designed for individuals who are not married to help them evaluate some characteristics of their parents' marriages, and to help them to determine how the things they find will influence the probability of their being compatible. The second exercise is designed for married couples, and it is an attempt to go through the same type of analysis and then evaluate what impact their parents' marriages have had or are having on their own marriages. The married couple exercise is not very useful in making predictions about compatibility, but it is frequently useful in getting new insights into why certain things occur in a marriage.

PARTNER'S FAMILY

Goal: To test compatibility by getting to know a prospective spouse's family. (Where there are special circumstances, such as one parent not living in the family, this exercise can be modified to accomplish this goal.)

1. Get to know the prospective spouse's family fairly well. If you live close this can be done through a series of contacts. If you

live a great distance from the parents a visit of a week or two is one effective way to accomplish this.

2. Observe such things as the relationships, mannerisms, and traits of all members of the family, but especially observe the parents. Some things you may want to notice are:

    a. How affectionate are they?

    b. How are they on a boisterous-serene continuum?

    c. How formal versus informal is the family?

    d. How do wife and husband treat each other? Do they do such things as boss, ignore, act tenderly, defer, tease, joke with, praise, help, insult, and support.

    e. Is the family active or passive?

    f. How mannerly are they in the home?

    g. How quickly do they lose their tempers, and how do they act when they do?

    h. What do they do to each other's self-esteem—build it up or cut it down?

    i. Are they loners or group oriented?

    j. How are decisions made?

3. Observe how your prospective spouse may be different in the home where she or he grew up than he or she is on campus or at work. Sometimes we try to be our "best" selves so much while we are courting that some of our "real" traits aren't visible. When we are at home, however, we usually act more naturally—if for no other reason than a little sister or brother teasingly commenting, "Why don't you act the way you always do. . ." or "How come you're so nice when he's around?"

4. Talk with your prospective spouse about your impressions. You will probably find some things you want in your marriage and some things you don't want, and your prospective spouse probably feels the same way about his or her family. Talk about both the good and bad parts, and hopefully the new information will help you know more about your chances of being compatible as spouses.

ASSESSING HOW COPYING PARENTS
INFLUENCES A MARRIAGE

Goal: To identify ways that spouses copy and do not copy their parents, and to determine how this influences their marriage.

1.   Get two pieces of paper—one for the husband and one for the wife.

2.   Make four lists on each of the sheets of paper. The lists are:

   a.   Traits copied from the parents that the person is glad were copied.

   b.   Traits copied from the parents that the person wishes hadn't been copied.

   c.   Traits not copied from the parents that the person wishes had been copied.

   d.   Traits not copied from the parents that the person is glad were not copied.

   The types of traits you may find useful in getting started are such things as: impatient, affectionate, domineering, won't listen to others' opinions, always has to be "right," considerate, understanding, compassionate, aggressive, timid, religious, cynical, insulting, pessimistic, etc.

3.   Discuss with each other your reactions to these lists. Does this analysis of the origins of such traits provide new insight into why some parts of your marital relationship are the way they are? Does the analysis help you to be more patient with yourself and others?

The Modeling principle is highly relevant for those of us who want a "style" of marriage that is fairly similar to the style of our parents' marriage. However, it is also relevant for those of us who want a style of marriage that is either more or less conventional than our parents' marriage. One reason it is relevant is that it is extremely difficult to completely eliminate our parents' influence on us. If we were raised in fairly conventional homes and want to have a radically different style of marriage, such as a Temporary or Two-Step marriage, or if we have experienced a religious conversion and want to have a more religiously orthodox style of marriage than did our parents, we will probably find that an analysis of our parents' marriage will still be of value because some of our attitudes, styles of relating to people, values, methods of reacting to situations, and mannerisms will probably not be altered by our new style of life. Another way this principle is relevant for those of us who want to be highly different from our parents is that we have undoubtedly acquired new interpersonal relationships that we use as the "anchor points" or "reference groups" in our new style of life. Since the Modeling principle deals with the point that *we become like those with whom we interact intimately,* we would probably be wise to observe the marital or marriagelike patterns in our new reference groups and the new reference groups of our fiancé(e) to determine how acceptable they are.

There is a third way that the Modeling principle is relevant for those of us who wish to have a style of marriage quite different from that of our parents. This is that sometimes young couples want a radically different life-style (and marriage) when they are in their late teens and early twenties, but change their views and decide to adopt a more conventional style of marriage after they get into their late twenties or their thirties and have a child or two. We may want to try to determine how likely this will be in our own situation, as this type of change not only has implications for our compatibility but also means that the Modeling principle may be more relevant than it may seem to be when we are getting married.

It is likely that this principle is much more relevant for some couples than for others. There is no scientific basis for making this differentiation, but the principle is probably irrelevant for those of us who do not plan to have a long-term marital relationship. Hence, those of us who want a Temporary or Two-Step style of marriage or who do not value permanence in a marital relationship would probably experience little benefit from a careful evaluation of the nature of our parents' marriages.

There is some research[4] that indicates that the reactions of certain other people can provide valuable information about our probable compatibility with a prospective spouse. All of the major marriage prediction studies have found that the amount that parents and friends approve of a prospective spouse is related to the probability that the marriage will succeed. If the parents or friends, or both, approve of the prospective spouse the chances that the couple will be successful are higher than if the parents or friends disapprove. At the present time research has not discovered why this occurs, but the fact that it does occur is information that can be useful in evaluating the probable compatibility of a couple. These research findings can be summarized in the following generalization.

Approval by intimate associates

> **THE APPROVAL PRINCIPLE: The more that intimate acquaintances approve of a prospective spouse the greater the chances that a couple will be satisfied with the marriage, and vice versa.**

---

[4] The relationship discussed here was found in all of the following studies, and no studies that have tested for it and have failed to find it: Burgess and Cottrell (1939, p. 408); Burgess and Wallin, (1953, pp. 560–64); Locke and Karlsson (1952); DeBurger (1961, p. 76); Schnepp and Johnson (1952); King (1951); Terman and Oden (1947); and Locke (1951). The principle is thus fairly well established.

Thus, we can use the evaluations of our intimate acquaintances as one piece of data in assessing our chances of being satisfied with a prospective spouse. It would be unwise to give this one factor an undue amount of importance, but research suggests that it would probably also be unwise to ignore it. It also seems reasonable to believe that this principle can be used in another way. There is no research to base this on, but it seems reasonable to believe that discussions with our intimate acquaintances about their *reasons* for approving or disapproving of a prospective spouse might provide some useful insights into our relationship that we might not otherwise have. It is also possible that different types of insights might be gathered from parents and from friends since we have different types of relationships with these two groups, and the two groups are probably sensitive to different characteristics of our relationships. The following exercise is designed to help us acquire and evaluate the opinions of these intimate acquaintances.

INTIMATE ACQUAINTANCES

Goal: To acquire and evaluate the opinions of some intimate acquaintances about a prospective spouse.

1.   Select a person who is very important to you—such as a parent or a very close friend, and find a time when the two of you can talk privately and without interruption for a while.

2.   Talk with the other person about how he feels about your chances of success if you marry the person you are thinking of marrying. The discussion will probably be most useful if you discuss his reaction in some depth by examining such things as his reasons for believing and feeling the way he does, hunches he has, and feelings that are hard for him to put his finger on.

3.   After the discussion think about how you responded to what you learned from the other person. How open were you to new ideas, and did you give his opinions some credence. If you did not view his opinions as valuable you might profit from repeating the exercise with other intimate acquaintances.

Length of courtship

Research has found that the shorter a courtship the greater the probability that a marriage will be unhappy or end in an unpleasant manner, and that the longer a courtship the greater the chances that the ensuing marriage will be satisfying and pleasant. The research does not explain why this relationship exists, but the fact that its existence is well documented[5] suggests that it may be wise to take the relationship into account. The principle that summarizes this relationship is:

THE LENGTH OF COURTSHIP PRINCIPLE: The length of the courtship that precedes a marriage is positively related to the chances of being satisfied with the marriage.

This principle has obvious practical implications for courtship, but it is also important to identify several limitations. As a statistical tendency, a relatively long courtship is associated with success in marriage. However, nearly anyone knows couples who married after a very short courtship and have had very pleasant and satisfying relationships. The author, too, has a number of acquaintances who married, quite successfully, after only a few days or weeks of courtship. These exceptions to the general rule do not invalidate the general principle because all the principle states is that couples with very short courtships have lower *chances* of success. Couples who marry when they know very little about each other undoubtedly have little assurance that they will be compatible in their marriage, and they probably do a great deal of learning about each other during the first months of their marriage. If they turn out to be compatible they are part of a lucky minority, because research indicates that most such couples find themselves disappointed and disillusioned and fail in their marriages. Couples who spend considerable time testing their compatibility before they marry have less to learn after the marriage, and their chances of being compatible are higher. Undoubtedly one of the main reasons this occurs is because individuals who find that they are not compatible with their partner tend to terminate their relationship before they marry and to seek other partners.

One interesting aspect of this principle is that time itself is probably not the crucial *causal* variable. If time were the important factor, it would be possible for an engaged couple of whom one member was away at school or in the military for a number of months to be as informed about their compatibility as an engaged

---

[5] Burgess and Cottrell (1939, p. 406); Locke (1947, p. 190); Terman et al. (1938, p. 197); Locke (1951, p. 90); DeBurger (1961, p. 59); Locke and Karlsson (1952, p. 13) and King (1952, p. 285).

couple who interacted regularly and intensely during the same period. If all other things were equal, the couple who interacted regularly would undoubtedly be more aware of how compatible they would be as spouses. The important causal factor is probably whether the individuals take the time to really get to know each other and to know how they respond to each other in a variety of everyday life situations. If this is the case, what the principle says is that most couples don't get very well acquainted in short courtships, and that there is an advantage in interacting for a longer period of time so that they will be better able to accurately assess their compatibility.

No doubt, this principle is more useful for certain marital styles than it is for other styles. It is probably useful for the styles of marriage in which couples want a lifelong commitment, but it may be virtually irrelevant when couples want such styles of marriage as the Two-Step or Temporary forms. Hopefully, future research will discover just how principles like this one operate in the various styles of marriage.

PRINCIPLES ABOUT SIMILARITY

When we ask ourselves whether we should or should not marry another person, we usually find that a number of other questions also become very important. One of these questions deals with whether differences or similarities between us and the person we are thinking of marrying will influence the later happiness of our marriage. The following case study illustrates this issue.

Jane and Harry have been dating seriously for seven months. Jane is sure she loves Harry and has wanted to become engaged for several weeks. Harry is still not sure they can make a go of it. They have a lot of things in common, but he is seven years older than she is, and he isn't very religious, while she comes from a highly religious home. He also doesn't want to finish college, but she already has. He is worried because he is a real sports fan and she just can't get interested in sports. Harry sometimes thinks they have enough in common, but he sometimes wonders whether their differences will be a problem in their later life. Still, at other times he wonders whether these things are worth worrying about.

Such researchers as Newcomb (1961) and Stouffer (1948) have demonstrated that individuals have to be fairly *similar* to each other to maintain even a close friendship, and it seems reasonable to infer that they would have to be even more similar if they are to have a pleasant marital relationship. If this is true it is not even necessary to ask whether being fairly different from each other influences marital happiness. Unless two individuals are quite similar it would probably be impossible for them to have a successful marriage. The key question is thus: *"How different can we be before this will seriously interfere with our marriage?"* Or, since some differences undoubtedly have more effect than others, *"How can we tell which differences will influence our marriage and which will have no effect?"* Or, finally, *"How much should differences and similarities influence my decision about whether to marry this person?"*

The overall objective of this section is to provide information that will help answer these questions, and to provide help in acquiring or enhancing the skills that are needed in using this information. First, four fairly general principles are introduced. These are fairly simple ideas, yet they integrate the findings from a vast amount of research, and they summarize most of what the social sciences know about the effects of similarity versus dissimilarity on marital satisfaction. These propositions are the *Similarity, Importance, Relevance,* and *Relative Status* principles. After these four generalizations are identified, their practical implications are discussed and several exercises are provided to help apply them in dating situations.

The Similarity principle deals with two variables: the *amount of similarity* and *the chances for marital satisfaction.* The first factor refers to how alike two individuals are in an area of life, such as social class, education, ethnicity, role expectations, interests, race, hobbies, or religion. This is not a variable that varies continuously, as shown below:

The Similarity principle

Amount of similarity
in an area

None   Small   Large   Total

If two individuals have nothing in common in an area, this is the extreme of no similarity. If they are virtually identical in the area, this is the opposite extreme of total similarity. The dependent variable in this principle was defined earlier, and the general hypothesis is:

THE SIMILARITY PRINCIPLE: The more similar two individuals are in any one area of life the greater their chances of being satisfied with their marriage, and, conversely, the more dissimilar they are the lower the chances that they will be satisfied with their marriage.

The Similarity principle is undoubtedly not true with regard to all aspects of life. For example, having eyes that are the same in color versus having eyes that are different in color is probably unrelated to marital happiness. Also, if this hypothesis were true in all cases men and women would tend to be more happily married to someone of the same sex, and for most people that is also probably not true. The principle only holds for some characteristics and only in certain kinds of situations or circumstances. The next three generalizations to be discussed identify some of the circumstances and situations which determine when the similarity principle operates and when it does not operate. First, however, it seems useful to describe briefly the research findings related to the Similarity principle.

There is a vast amount of evidence that this principle is *generally* true. Research has been conducted on similarity in age, income, social class, ethnicity, religion, role definitions, values, background characteristics, intelligence, and education,[6] and the evidence is overwhelming that the greater the similarity the greater the likelihood of marital success. There are, however, two areas in which the data are so conflicting that they do not support the generalization. The contradictory findings in these two areas do not demonstrate that the principle is untrue, but rather that it is premature to conclude that it is valid in these two areas. The areas are interracial marriages and similarity of personality "needs." Some research suggests that interracial marriages have more difficulty than same-race marriages (Baber, 1939; Golden, 1954), while other research suggests that the net effect of racial intermarriage might actually be that it is irrelevant or even helpful (Smith, 1966; Cheng and Yamamura, 1957; Kimura, 1947; and Monahan, 1970). Winch et al., (1954) suggested that it may be that it is being complementary rather than being similar that is important in regard to personality "needs," but the conceptualization and the research that has been undertaken to test this idea is so fraught with measurement problems, inconsistencies, contradictions, and irrelevancies that we still have no clear idea whether or not the similarity principle operates in regard to personality needs.

The evidence does not yet establish the shape of the relationship, but there are some grounds for expecting that it is similar to the curve shown in Figure 7–1. If this figure does correctly diagram the relationship, then changes in the similarity variable make the

---

[6] There are dozens of studies about whether similarity in regard to these variables is related to marital satisfaction. Those interested in further reading in this area will find Kirkpatrick (1963, chaps. 15–18), Burgess et al. (1963, chap. 15); Bernard (1964), and Burr (1973, pp. 105ff.) useful beginning places.

Figure 7–1

The relationship between amount of similarity in an area of life and the chances for marital happiness

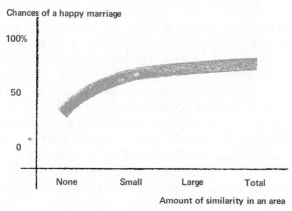

Amount of similarity in an area

most difference when similarity is fairly low. It will be noted that the slope of the line is very flat. This is because the amount of similarity in any one area probably makes very little difference in the probability of a marriage being pleasant and satisfying. It is only when the net effect of a number of areas is considered that the powerful role of this principle can be seen.

The Similarity principle has a number of practical implications for courtship and marriage. However, since the three other principles discussed in this section qualify and refine the similarity principle, these principles will be identified before we discuss the practical implications of the Similarity principle.

The importance of similarity

It is unthinkable that similarity versus dissimilarity in some areas of life will make as much difference in marital satisfaction as similarity versus dissimilarity in other areas. It is probably ridiculous, for example, for a left-handed person to concern himself about whether he is marrying a left-handed person or for someone who drives a compact car to look for someone who also drives a compact car. On the other hand, a Greek Catholic who wants an Intrinsic marriage would probably be wise to marry someone with a similar philosophy of life. The Importance principle helps resolve this problem because it points out that the differences and similarities that are viewed as most important in a culture have the greatest impact on a marriage and that the less important the differences or similarities the less influence they have on the chances for marital satisfaction.

The Importance principle involves two variables: the *importance of similarity* and *the amount of influence that variation in similarity has on the chances for marital satisfaction*. This principle is sufficiently complex and abstract that it is essential to define these variables clearly. The importance variable refers to the amount that a certain type of similarity or dissimilarity is defined by an individual (and by the individuals with whom he interacts intimately) as salient, significant, or valuable. Certain factors, such as similarity in height or color of hair, are usually defined as irrelevant in marriage, but all cultures or subcultures believe that it is important to be similar in some areas. For example, conservative religious groups usually believe that religious similarity is important, and those segments of societies that view themselves as socially "proper" define similarity in social affiliation as important. This variable thus ranges between the extremes of being unimportant and being extremely important, and it is diagramed below.

Importance of similarity
in marriage

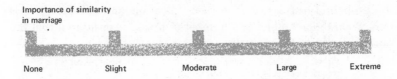

None   Slight   Moderate   Large   Extreme

The dependent variable in this principle is *the amount of influence that variation in similarity has*. This is a very abstract and complex idea, but it is an essential one. This dependent variable refers to the amount that a particular similarity or dissimilarity affects or influences (causes or determines) marital satisfaction. Some dissimilarities are unimportant, and they have little detrimental influence on later marital happiness. Other dissimilarities are more important, and they have a proportionately greater detrimental effect. Also, when couples are similar in unimportant areas, these similarities contribute little, if anything, to the happiness of the marriage, and when couples are similar in a very important area, this similarity tends to have a substantial positive impact on satisfaction with the marriage. Thus, the "amount of influence" can

Amount of influence that variation in similarity
has on chances for marital satisfaction

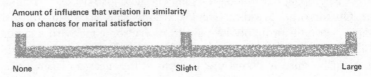

None   Slight   Large

vary from none to a great deal, as shown below. The principle that identifies the relationship between these two variables is:

THE IMPORTANCE PRINCIPLE: The more important a particular similarity or dissimilarity is (personally or in a culture) the greater the influence it has on marital satisfaction, and vice versa.[7]

This principle is so abstract and complex that it is diagramed in two ways to help communicate the idea. Figure 7–2 shows how the relationship in the Similarity principle is changed by the importance variable. When similarity in a certain area of life is low in importance, variation in similarity has virtually no effect on the

Figure 7–2

Changes in the relationship between similarity and chances of marital success when the importance variable is controlled

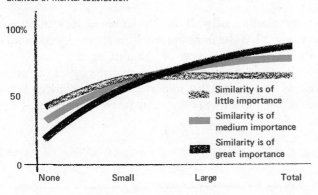

Chances of marital satisfaction

chances for marital satisfaction, as shown by the solid line. However, as the importance of similarity increases, variation in the amount of similarity has progressively greater influence on the

----

[7] This principle exists in several different schools of thought in sociology and social psychology. It is fundamental to Newcomb's (1961, chaps. 1, 2) balance theory of attraction, as is the relevance principle discussed later in this chapter. See Burr (1973, pp. 62–69 and 95–98) for a more technical discussion of Newcomb's idea. The more general idea that social values determine the social consequences of things is central to Mead's (1934) thinking, even though the idea was not very explicit until Rose (1963, chap. 1) analyzed it theoretically and Burr (1967, 1971) tested it empirically in another context. This idea has not been well researched with quantified data, but these theoretical essays, the qualitative data upon which they are based, and the inherent rationality of the principle provide considerable basis for believing it to be valid.

Figure 7–3

The relationship between marital satisfaction and the importance of a particular similarity

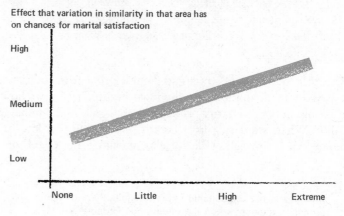

Effect that variation in similarity in that area has
on chances for marital satisfaction

High

Medium

Low

None   Little   High   Extreme

Importance of similarity in a particular area of life

chances for marital satisfaction. Variation in similarity in highly important areas has the most influence, as shown by the dotted line.

Figure 7–3 is another way of diagraming the idea in the Importance principle. This figure shows that the *effect* of variation in similarity is related to the importance of similarity. When importance is low the effect is low, and when importance is high the effect is high.

One of the practical consequences of the importance principle is that couples can profit from being sensitive to those aspects of life that are highly valued by the subcultural groups to which they belong. Some individuals believe that they are not influenced by their social groups, but this point of view is not shared by most social scientists. Most modern social scientists believe that virtually every important belief a person has is shared by the individuals with whom that person interacts intimately. A vast amount of scientific evidence shows that individuals are continually checking themselves against the views of the figures who are "significant" to them (Mead, 1934)— and this can include parents, friends, co-workers, groups of peers, a divine being, church officials, members of a club, or a spouse. Many individuals in groups as diverse as the jet set, the New Left, religious sects, and back-to-nature groups, argue that they are

asserting their individuality by breaking away from traditional society. *In actual fact, what they are doing is changing the groups that
are significant to them.* They change their models from parents and
school officials to a select group of peers or other associates. Their
patterns of dress and grooming are ultra-conforming to the standards
of the new group, and so are a whole host of values, beliefs, and
ways of interacting with other people. The main point here is that if
individuals can be sensitive to which things are important in their
social groups they can identify which areas of smilarity are probably important for them in selecting a spouse. An exercise is described on page 201 which helps to accomplish this.

A school of thought in social psychology that has come to be
known as "balance theory" (Heider, 1958; Newcomb, 1961) has
developed another principle that seems to be helpful in understanding when similarities or differences influence marital satisfaction. This principle is called the Relevance principle here, and the
independent variable is *relevance for marital interaction.* Newcomb
(1961, p. 13) defined this variable as the amount that the members
of a couple are jointly dependent on something. In other words it is
the amount that something has a consequence for, pertinence to,
bearing on, or germaneness for a couple. It is a continuous variable
as diagramed below.

*The relevance
of similarity*

Relevance of similarity
for marital interaction

None   Slight   High

The dependent variable is the same one as that in the Importance
principle, namely, the amount of influence that variation in similarity has on chances for marital success. This principle is:

**THE RELEVANCE PRINCIPLE: The more a similarity or dis-
similarity is relevant for marital interaction the greater the
influence it has on marital satisfaction, and vice versa.**

The main idea in this general hypothesis is that the more something is "relevant" for marital interaction the more influence similarity or dissimilarity in that area has on the chances for marital
satisfaction. When dissimilarities occur in areas that are unrelated
to marital interaction they have little effect on the marriage, and
when they occur in areas that are central to marital interaction
they have proportionately more effect. It is thus probably more im-

portant to be similar in even unimportant marital role expectations than it is to be similar in such irrelevancies as the type of fishing bait one prefers or political beliefs.

This principle is theoretically plausible because it is a part of balance theory, and that theory is well formulated and widely accepted. It should be recognized, however, that no empirical data have been found that test the validity of this particular principle. It thus seems that this generalization has enough basis to justify its use, but that we should remain tentative in accepting it as valid.

This principle also has a number of practical implications for courtship and marriage, but these will not be discussed until the fourth principle is identified. The fourth principle deals with the relative status differences in a couple.

Relative status

Many times there are status or prestige implications when individuals are dissimilar to each other, and these status differences also help us understand why some dissimilarities influence marital satisfaction and some do not. Thus, research on social class differences and marital happiness (Roth and Peck, 1951) shows that when the members of a couple are different in their "social class" this is less disruptive in the marriage if the husband is the one who has the higher social status. The same tendency also seems to occur with age (Burgess and Cottrell, 1939; Locke, 1951, p. 343; Karlsson, 1951, pp. 52–53) and intelligence (Terman, 1938; Terman and Oden, 1947; and Locke, 1951, pp. 255–351). The greatest likelihood of marital happiness occurs when the members of the couple are similar, but when they are dissimilar, the difference tends to be less disruptive if the husband rather than the wife is older or more intelligent—at least in contemporary society. These findings seem to justify the formulation of the following generalization.

THE RELATIVE STATUS PRINCIPLE: When a couple are dissimilar in an area, and this difference has status implications, the dissimilarity tends to be more disruptive if the husband is inferior than if the wife is inferior.

Scholars on the family have recognized for some time that there are more problems when the husband is in a lower social stratum than when the wife's social stratum is lower (Blood, 1969, pp. 93–95; Udry, 1971, pp. 290–96), and this idea was later generalized to other differences and similarities by Burr (1973, pp. 111–12). Considerable empirical research corroborates this principle, so we should apparently have considerable confidence in it. However, one qualification should undoubtedly be placed on this generalization, namely, that it probably only operates in a society dominated by males. If this is the case, the generalization will probably be less relevant in the United States society when greater equality of the sexes is attained, and it is probably not relevant now among those segments of the society in which most of the differences between the sexes have already been eliminated. Conversely, however, if a society were to become dominated by females this principle would probably be relevant if the general idea in it were reversed.

The Relative Status principle has a number of implications for dating, some of which are widely known. For example, it has been common knowledge in the dating subculture for decades that if a woman is more intelligent than the man she is dating and shows it, this will frequently cause problems in the relationship. Accordingly, many women act less intelligent and competent on dates than they actually are in order to increase their dating popularity (Shulman, 1972). Because more far-reaching consequences may appear in marriage, couples would apparently be wise to examine their dissimilarities carefully when these have status implications. Some of us detest the traditional sexist discriminations (male domination) so intensely that we have rejected any of the traditional differences between the sexes, and for us this principle is probably irrelevant. However, those of us who retain more conventional views about masculinity and femininity and those who live in female-dominated cultures may find it useful to pay attention to this principle.

One of the implications of these principles is that it is impossible to make hard-and-fast rules about the areas in which couples should be similar and the areas in which similarity does not matter. In one situation a particular difference, such as ethnicity, will have a lot of influence, and in another situation it will have no effect. It is, however, possible to use these four principles to determine which similarities and differences will probably have an impact on marital happiness *in our personal situation*. This point can be illustrated by describing how that situation determines the effects of educational differences. In one social situation the intimate people in a couple's lives may view educational similarity as extremely important, and in another social situation the same similarity may be virtually irrelevant. When this is the case, the Importance principle leads us to

Implications of these four principles for courtship

expect that educational differences will have considerable influence in the first situation and less influence in the second. Thus, it is not possible to conclude anything about the overall impact of educational differences. It is only possible to know something about the probable impact these differences will have in a specific social situation.

In the research done during the mid-20th century in the United States culture, several factors seem to be relatively important for most couples. Similarity in age (Bernard, 1934; Terman and Oden, 1947; Locke, 1951, p. 343; Karlsson, 1952, pp. 52–53), role expectations (Luckey, 1961), socioeconomic status (Roth and Peck, 1951), education (Davis, 1929; Terman and Oden, 1947), and general intelligence (Terman, 1938) seems to help most people. Similarity in religious denomination is important for some segments of the population and unimportant for other segments (Burchinal, 1964; Christensen and Barber, 1967). Apparently similarity in interests (Benson, 1955) does not make much difference for most people. *These research findings about differences in the proportion of people who find these things important is not, however, very useful information* because it merely describes what tends to happen to most people in society, and it is indefensible to try to apply such findings to our individual lives. Just because similarity in social class is important for 80 percent of the people in a society does not mean that it will be important for you or for me. We may be among the 20 percent who would do well to ignore social differences and similarities. If this is the case, and if we then pay attention to social class because it is important to 80 percent of the people, we are behaving quite indefensibly, as we are giving undue attention to something that is irrelevant for us and probably at the same time giving too little attention to factors that are important to us. This then leads to the question . . . WHAT SHOULD WE DO ABOUT SIMILARITIES AND DIFFERENCES? The best answer is to apply the general principles and ignore the research that deals with the proportion of people who find different things important or relevant. We are only interested in whether the similarities or differences are important or relevant in *our* particular situation.

It seems to this author that five different processes are involved in using the four principles in this chapter, and that there is an orderly sequence in those processes. *First,* we should carefully analyze our own relationship to identify the areas in which we are similar and the areas in which we are different. *Second,* we should determine how great our differences are because the greater the differences the greater the likelihood that these differences will have a detrimental effect on our relationship. *Third,* we should try to determine which areas of similarity or dissimilarity are really "important" to us and the people we intimately interact with—and which are unimportant. If we are either similar or dissimilar in a dispropor-tionate number of highly important areas, the Importance principle suggests that this will probably make for a considerable difference in the effect these similarities and dissimilarities will have on our chances for marital satisfaction. If the important areas are areas in which there is similarity this increases our chances for success, and if they are areas in which there is dissimilarity this decreases our chances for success. *Fourth,* we should attempt to determine how relevant these areas are in the particular style of life we plan to live. Again, if similarities tend to occur in the areas of life that are relevant for marital interaction this increases our chances of marital success, and if the dissimilarities tend to occur in the relevant areas this decreases our chances for success. *Fifth,* we should determine whether we will live in a social situation in which there will be an equality of the sexes or whether we will live in a social situation in which one sex will tend to have more "say" than the other. If we will be in the latter situation, we ought to examine our dissimilarities to determine whether they have "status" implications. If they do, we should try to determine what effect this will probably have in our relationship.

The application of these principles requires rather complex in-tellectual processes, as it consists of analyzing our relationship with some person and then using the insights we get from this analysis as *part* of the basis for making a decision about whether or not to marry that person. The following two exercises will help couples through these steps, and hopefully couples will be able to design other experiences on their own that will also be useful in applying the principles. The following exercises are probably the most useful for couples who are in the process of deciding whether or not to marry. They are, however, also useful for couples who are not seriously considering marriage and for married couples. Couples not considering marriage can use the exercises to increase their ability to use the principles, and married couples can use the exercises to gain an increased understanding of the effects of some of their similarities and dissimilarities on their marital relationship.

IDENTIFYING SIMILARITIES AND DISSIMILARITIES

Goal: To increase your ability to use the similarity principle by identifying similarities and dissimilarities in a relationship.

1. Do this exercise with a member of the opposite sex with whom you have a relationship, preferably a spouse, fiancé(e), or dating partner, but if that is not possible, do it with a friend or a fellow class member.

2. Make a very long list of aspects of life (variables) on which you could be similar or dissimilar. The following items will get you started, and then you can add other aspects that are relevant for the type of marriage you want:

    age
    education
    ethnic background
    socioeconomic status
    religion
    race
    height
    beliefs about equality of the sexes
    desire for children
    desire to travel
    "themes" you want to center your life on, such as:

        outdoorish—camping, fishing, hiking, etc.
        intellectual—reading, attending lectures, graduate education, etc.
        religious—meditative, prayerful, church activity, etc.
        service oriented—helping others, joining
        cultural—opera, symphonies, theater, etc.
        sports—spectator or participating in auto racing, football, golf, etc.
        leisure oriented—visiting, relaxing, vacations, diversions, etc.
        improving social conditions—activist movements, community action, etc.

    hobbies
    emphasis on stylish clothes
    amount you like music
    amount of freedom you think spouses should have
    strictness of discipline you think children should have
    amount you want innovation versus stability in your life

You may find it useful to go ahead to the "Role Expectations" exercise on page 205 because it is designed to help you discover what you expect from your spouse, and similarities and dissimilarities in these expectations are relevant here.

3. Assign a number to the amount you are similar or dissimilar in each of the above aspects. Use the following scale:

Similarity and
dissimilarity in aspect of life

0	1	2	3
Very different	Quite different	Very similar	Identical

4. Evaluate whether you are more or less similar than you thought you were, and try to determine what effect this would have on your marriage if you were to be married. The next exercise will help you make this evaluation.

EVALUATING THE IMPORTANCE AND RELEVANCE OF SIMILARITIES AND DISSIMILARITIES

Goal: To increase your ability to use the importance and relevance principles by practicing the evaluation of similarities and dissimilarities.

1. First, complete the prior "Identifying Similarities and Dissimilarities" exercise.

2. Complete steps 3 and 4 as individuals rather than as a couple. Then, complete step 5 as a couple.

3. Go through the entire list of "aspects of life" you identified in the prior exercise and make two evaluations of how "important" each item is to *you* personally in your life. Rate it first according to how important it is to you now to be similar to your spouse, and second time according to how important it will probably be to you in 15 years. Use the following scale to evaluate each item's importance.

Importance of aspect of life

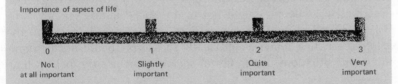

0	1	2	3
Not at all important	Slightly important	Quite important	Very important

4. Some aspects of life are relevant in marriage and some are not, and some aspects that are relevant in one style of marriage are not relevant in other marital styles. For example, similarity in leisure interests might be relevant in an Intrinsic marriage but not in a Utilitarian or a Temporary marriage. Determine which of the items in the prior exercise will probably be (or are, if you are married) relevant and which are irrelevant. You may find it useful to mark them with an "R" for relevant, and an "I" for irrelevant. Do this for your life situation now and for your perception of what your life situation will probably be in 15 years.

> 5. As a couple, discuss the evaluations you made about the importance and relevance of the similarities and dissimilarities. You will want to pay particular attention to two types of situations: (a) those in which you are similar and the aspect of life is important and relevant, and (b) those in which you are dissimilar and the aspect of life is important and relevant. The former will say something about areas which will probably help the marriage, and the latter will say something about areas which will probably create problems.
>
> 6. Again, try to determine what effect your similarities and dissimilarities would have (will have) on your marriage.

Consensus about role expectations

One school of thought in social psychology has discovered a number of principles that are useful in understanding and controlling many aspects of marital relationships. This school has several labels, but the one used in this volume is symbolic interaction.[8] Most of the discussion of this theory or school of thought will be in later chapters, but one of its principles is discussed here because (a) it is particularly useful in helping couples determine how compatible they are, and (b) it is a more specific instance of the Similarity principle discussed earlier. The principle involves several terms that must be clearly defined, and these terms are *social norms*, *role expectations*, and *consensus about role expectations*.

Social norms[9] are beliefs or opinions about what people "should" or "ought" to do or not do. One type of norm, proscriptive norms, describes what people ought not to do. Social norms seldom state that a behavior is either appropriate or inappropriate in an absolute sense, but define what usually should or should not be done in various situations. Examples of social norms are the beliefs that

---

[8] There are several names for this school of thought. It is known as interactionism, symbolic interaction (Stryker, 1964, 1972), role theory (Sarbin, 1968; Biddle and Thomas, 1966), self theory (Rogers, 1951; Hall and Lindzey, 1957), and social behaviorism (Martindale, 1960). Whatever label is used, it is the branch of social psychology that emerged from the writings of William James, C. H. Cooley, and George Herbert Mead. Technical readers will recognize that there are slight differences in emphasis in some of the different traditions in this theoretical orientation. For example, the dramaturgical approach used by Goffman (1959) differs from the more formal approach used by Biddle and Thomas (1966); and the more quantified methodology used by some is different from the more qualitative approach suggested by the older University of Chicago approach typified by the work of Strauss and Blumer. These subtle differences can be ignored for the purposes of a text that focuses on the application of the basic ideas of this school of thought rather than the discovery and justification of new ideas.

[9] Biddle and Thomas (1966, pp. 26–27).

people ought to wear clothes in public, ought to have an appropriate amount of loyalty to their friends, ought to express appreciation by saying "thank you" when others do them favors. Some norms are legally codified while others are very informal and subtle. Some norms, such as beliefs about murder and incest, are very important, while others, such as beliefs about jaywalking and hair length, are less important. If people are asked to list the social norms that govern their lives they usually have difficulty thinking them up (Bott, 1957). However, when they are asked about specific acts or behaviors they usually know what they think should occur, and these are some of their social norms.

Role expectations are normative beliefs that deal with a particular role in society. They are the beliefs that describe what individuals are supposed to do or not do when they occupy a certain social position or social role. Examples of such expectations are the beliefs that medical personnel ought to be extremely cautious about infection when they perform operations and that drivers ought to drive safely. There are many role expectations about courtship and marital roles. For example, there are beliefs about how much independence husbands and wives should have, how permissible it is to engage in premarital or extramarital sexual intercourse, and how people ought to relate to their in-laws.

Consensus about role expectations[10] refers to the amount that two people agree or disagree in what they expect or want someone to do in a particular role. In this context it refers to the amount that two people agree about their marital role expectations. This can vary from total consensus, in which two people have identical role expectations, to very low consensus, or high role conflict, in which they have very different views about what each spouse ought to do. This can be diagramed as follows. The principle relevant here is

Consensus about
role expectations

Low   Medium   High   Total
agreement

that the greater the consensus the fewer the interpersonal problems in the relationship and the more likely the couple are to have a satisfying marital relationship. Stated more formally:

---

[10] The term *role conflict* is frequently used to refer to this phenomenon. The term has several other meanings, however (Gross et al., 1957; Biddle and Thomas, 1966, Chaps. 1, 2; Burr, 1973, pp. 128–33), so the more descriptive term *consensus about role expectations* is used here.

THE CONSENSUS ABOUT EXPECTATIONS PRINCIPLE: The greater the consensus about marital role expectations the greater the chances of marital satisfaction, and vice versa.

There is a considerable amount of evidence that this principle is valid,[11] and this evidence also suggests that the relationship is linear. It may be that subsequent research will demonstrate that when consensus is extremely high or low the relationship is not linear, but at present the existence of this relationship and its linearity are two of the most thoroughly substantiated ideas in this book.

This principle is highly relevant for premarital interaction for several reasons. It is a more specific instance of the Similarity principle since it deals with the amount of similarity in a particular part of a relationship, and it is an *important* aspect of the relationships of most couples. Also, it is a principle that can be easily applied. It is immediately apparent, for example, that the dating period is a time when we can discuss our marital role expectations and get an idea of how much consensus we are likely to have if we were to marry. Most of us are aware of many things that we want to do and not do in our marriages, and of many things that we want our spouse to do and not do. It would, of course, be impossible to discuss all of these in one lengthy session about role expectations, but the topics can come up a number of times during a courtship, and gradually we can get a feeling for the level of compatibility of our role expectations.

One advantage of becoming well acquainted with the intimate acquaintances (parents, siblings, friends) of our prospective spouse is that this gives us an opportunity to learn more about the role expectations these acquaintances have. Once these role expectations are identified we can discuss, as a couple, whether they are expectations that we are likely to adopt or whether they are expectations we very strongly want to avoid.

If it were possible to identify all the role expectations that both members of a couple have or will have, there would probably be fewer marital failures because people would then be able to select spouses with whom they were compatible. However, a number of

---

[11] Jacobson (1952); Kotlar (1961); Luckey (1960); Stryker (1964); and Sarbin (1968).

factors make it impossible to know many of our marital role expectations before marriage. For one thing, we develop expectations in
so many different aspects of marital relationships that it is impossible to isolate and discuss all of them. When we are occupied with
the complex and challenging issues that face us in adolescence and
early adulthood we do not have the time or the perspective to think
about all of the various kinds of things that we will encounter in
marriage. In addition our later life situation will be influenced by
so many events that are impossible to predict beforehand that the
most perceptive and insightful persons can identify only a fraction
of the role expectations that they will find important in their marriages. Furthermore, many of our role expectations are not yet
formed in the courtship stage of life and won't be formed until we
actually get into different situations later in life and work through
our beliefs and feelings.

What this means is that we should not expect to get a thorough
or completely accurate estimate of the compatibility of our role
expectations while we are still unmarried. We can get some idea,
and the more insightful and mature we are the more accurate our
estimate will be, but we all discover many new ways in which our
role expectations are compatible and incompatible after we are
married.

These qualifications do not imply that the Consensus about Expectations principle is useless in helping couples determine how
compatible they are. Knowing that it is impossible to get a *thorough*
understanding of the amount of role conflict that will exist in a
marriage should only cause us to recognize that this principle does
not give us a final or complete determination of compatibility.
However, even though the principle isn't a cure-all, it can provide
some insights, and these insights may frequently make the difference between selecting someone with whom we will later be
compatible and someone with whom we will be incompatible. The
following exercise is designed to help couples to identify role
conflicts and compatibilities and to evaluate their effects.

ROLE EXPECTATIONS

Goal: To gain an increased understanding of role expectations.

1.   Have a discussion with two or three other individuals, such as
     roommates, siblings, or friends. Spend at least 20–30 minutes,
     and try to describe a large number of your expectations about
     (a) your own role as a married person and (b) your spouse's role.

2. There are three steps in fully understanding these role expectations. These steps are:

a. Making a relatively long list of "behaviors" that you think you or your spouse should *do* or *not do.* These behaviors are ways of acting or behaving in a marriage, and the following examples will get you started on your own list. Being: romantic, outdoorish, interested in "high" culture, companionate, close to friends outside the marriage, considerate, closed to new ideas, intellectually stimulating, impatient, affectionate, nagging, good at fixing things around the house, emotional, leisure oriented, orderly at home, sports-minded, interested in sex, spiritual, open to differences of opinion, interested in spending time with children, etc.

Average hours each
week watching sports

| 0 | 10 | 20 | 30 | 40 | 50 |

b. The behaviors you identify can all vary in either *quantity* or *quality* or both. Nagging, for example, varies in quantity, as a person can never nag, or can nag occasionally, frequently, or all the time. Emotionality, on the other hand can vary in quality, as a person can be very unemotional. YOU WILL NEED TO IDENTIFY WHAT *FOR YOU* IS A LOW, MEDIUM, AND VERY HIGH QUANTITY OR QUALITY OF EACH OF THE BEHAVIORS ON YOUR LIST. Don't worry about how others would define low and high amounts of qualities of these behaviors because it is your opinions that are important. One good way to do this is to list each behavior on a sheet of paper and then draw a continuum alongside each behavior and describe how it varies. The following examples illustrate how this can be done for "time spent watching sporting events" and "amount of affectionateness."

Amount of affectionateness

| None | Little | Quite a bit | Large amount | Very, very affectionate |

c. Next you will need to decide what you think of the desirability or undesirability of the various ways of behaving in marriage. A good way to do this is to think of different responses and give them numbers. Some examples are: (1) very undesirable, (2) slightly undesirable, (3) irrelevant (it just doesn't matter), (4) slightly desirable, and (5) very desirable. You can then put numbers next to various places on the continuum, and what you then have is a fairly precise description of your role expectations.

3. You'll find it useful to make two lists. Make one for role expectations for yourself and the other for expectations for your spouse. To determine the desirability of the behavior for your spouse, ask yourself: "What would I think *if* he (or she) were to behave that way?" and to determine the desirability of the behavior for yourself, ask yourself: "What would I think *if* I were to act that way?"

4. This exercise should have two benefits. One is that it will give you a greater understanding of your own marital role expectations. The second is that when you are considering marrying someone (or are married) discussing the lists can give you both some insights into where you agree and disagree on role expectations. You can then evaluate the importance of these agreements and disagreements, and that evaluation may help you determine how your agreements and disagreements will help or hinder attaining a successful marriage.

One of the exercises in a later chapter is also somewhat relevant in this context. An exercise in Chapter 12 is designed to help couples turn some disagreements about role expectations into consensus about expectations. This is the "Increasing Consensus about Role Expectations" exercise on page 308. Some may find it useful to complete that exercise now.

SUMMARY

This chapter has identified eight principles that may help couples judge how compatible they are likely to be in marriage. In the first part of the chapter three principles were identified. (1) The *Modeling* principle states that the more similar a prospective spouse's parents' marriage is to the person's ideal style of marriage the greater the likelihood of compatibility, and several practical ways of using this principle were discussed. (2) The *Approval* principle states that the more that intimate acquaintances, such as parents or close friends, approve of a prospective spouse the greater the chances that a couple will be satisfied with their marriage. (3) The

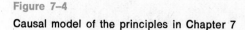

Figure 7–4

Causal model of the principles in Chapter 7

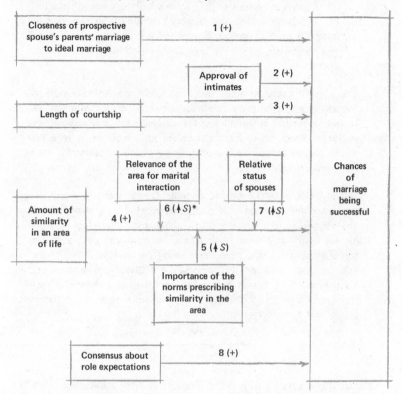

* The symbol (↑ S) refers to a relationship in which increases in the contingent variable strengthen the relationship between the independent variable and the dependent
variable, and decreases in the contingent variable weaken the relationship between the
independent variable and the dependent variable. In this situation the relevance of the
area for marital satisfaction is a contingent variable, the similarity in an area of life is the
independent variable, and the chances of marriage being successful is the dependent
variable.

Length of Courtship principle states that the length of courtship is
positively related to the probability of marital satisfaction. Research
has not yet shown whether length of courtship is itself important, or
whether the important variables are things related to length of
courtship, such as the amount of opportunity couples have to interact and test their relationship, but there is considerable empirical
evidence supporting the principle. These three principles are shown
in the top part of the causal model in Figure 7–4.

The last section of the chapter focused on the question of how
much similarities and dissimilarities influence our chances of being
satisfied and happy in marriage. The main principle identified as-

serts that generally speaking the greater the *similarity* between two people the greater the likelihood that they will be satisfied in their marital relationship. This principle was then qualified by three additional principles, which pointed out that the *importance* and the *relevance* of the similarities and dissimilarities determine how much effect these will have in the marital relationship. Similarities and dissimilarities that are viewed as important and relevant by the subcultural groups with whom we interact intimately will have considerable effect on our chances for satisfaction in marriage. Conversely, similarities and dissimilarities that are viewed as unimportant and irrelevant can be expected to have less effect on the marital situation. A fourth principle asserted that in societies in which males tend to have more power dissimilarities where the husband has lower status or prestige will usually have a greater effect on marital satisfaction than dissimilarities in which the husband has higher status or prestige. The last principle discussed was the *Consensus about Expectations* principle. This is a specific case of the Similarity principle since it deals with a particular type of similarity.

The general theme of this chapter was that similarity tends to promote compatibility in marital relationships, and a vast amount of scientific research argues that this generalization is probably true. This generalization should not, however, lead to the conclusion that conflict, dissension, and dissimilarity are always to be avoided and never constructive. Disagreements are inevitable in intimate human relationships, and they can have many positive effects. Encountering and then managing or resolving differences can produce growth, creativity, intimacy, and fulfillment. It is only when encountered dissimilarities are not managed so that they can be lived with or resolved that they become problems.

SUGGESTIONS FOR FURTHER STUDY

Blood, Robert O., Jr. 1962. *Marriage*. Glencoe, Ill.: Free Press.

Burgess, Ernest W., and Wallin, Paul 1953. *Engagement and Marriage*. Philadelphia: Lippincott, chaps. 6, 16, and 17.

Heiss, Jerold S. 1960. "Premarital Characteristics of the Religiously Intermarried in an Urban Area." *American Sociological Review* 25: 47–55.

Landis, Judson T. 1956. "The Pattern of Divorce in Three Generations." *Social Forces* 34 (no. 3): 201–7.

Landis, Judson, and Landis, Mary G. 1946. "Length of Time Required to Achieve Adjustment in Marriage." *American Sociological Review* 11 (December):666–677.

Locke, Harvey J. 1951. *Predicting Adjustment in Marriage: A Comparison of a Divorced and a Happily Married Group.* New York: Henry Holt and Company.

Terman, Lewis M., et al. 1938. *Psychological Factors in Marital Happiness,* New York: McGraw-Hill.

Udry, J. Richard 1966. Revised edition in 1971. *The Social Context of Marriage.* Philadelphia: Lippincott, chap. 12.

8

Developing and nurturing love in relationships [1]

L OVE is probably the most important aspect of marriage to most
people in our society. Most of us decide whether or not to get
married more on the basis of our feelings of "love" than of any
other aspect of our relationship, and we evaluate the success of our
marriage more on the basis of those feelings than of any other
aspect of the marriage. And one surprising feature of this aspect of
marriage is that even in these times of rapid social change and
innovative life-styles it is an aspect that most people do not seem
to want to change. Many people in contemporary society want to
eliminate phony and superficial adjuncts of love, such as exploita-
tion, infatuation, and over romanticization, from their own marriages, but with the exception of participants in Utilitarian marriages everyone seems to want love to be an important part of the
marital relationship.

This very important part of marriage is, however, difficult to
study because love means very different things to different people,
and because it is an extremely difficult experience to define. Poets,
artists, theologians, and, in the past few years, social scientists
have tried to find definitions of love that are clear and fairly
universally acceptable, but none of them have been very successful.
Because of the ambiguity in the meaning of the term *love* an attempt is made at the beginning of this chapter to describe how the
term is and is not used in the chapter. This is done in the first
section. Then, in the last section, an attempt is made to identify one

[1] Appreciation is expressed to D. Eugene Mead for his insights and assistance during the time when this chapter was being organized.

very general principle and five less general principles that can be used to increase or decrease the love feelings in a relationship. In addition the last section discusses ways to apply these principles in marriage.

DEFINING LOVE

It seems useful to begin by identifying some of the ways that the term *love* has been defined. The ancient Greeks used two different words to describe two different types of love. *Agape* was the term for an unselfish, brotherly, or spiritual type of love which did not include sexual implications. *Eros* was the term for a more sensuous, sexually desiring love. Some scholars have described love as a desire for a certain type of relationship. For example, Magoun's (1948) analysis of love and marriage states that

love is the passionate and abiding desire on the part of two or more people to produce together the conditions under which each can be able to spontaneously express his real self; to produce together an intellectual soil and an emotional climate in which each can flourish, far superior to what either could achieve alone.

Several scholars have defined love as an emotion that results when our personal needs are met. Saxton, for example, states that "love is a vital and profound emotion which is experienced as a result of a need satisfaction" (1972, p. 30), and Bell states that love is "a strong emotion between two individuals which involves and satisfies the need of giving and receiving. This implies either the reality or the expectation of emotional, physical, and intellectual exchange" (1963, p. 113).

The term *love* is used in this book to refer to a particular type of emotional feeling that one person has about another person. This feeling can be best understood by first visualizing the "liking" continuum diagramed below. At one extreme is the condition of "liking" another person. Here we have kindly, favorable, or friendly feelings toward the other person, or what psychologists call positive *affect*. The midpoint on the continuum is a condition of not having feelings of like or dislike for the other person. It is neutrality, as there is neither positive nor negative affective response to the other person. At the other extreme is a condition of disliking the other

Feeling about another person

Dislike   No feeling of   Like
                                 like or dislike
                                 (neutral)

person. In the view used here, love is a more intense positive affective experience than just liking another person, and there is no other word in the English language to describe that experience than the word *love*.

When love is defined in this way it does not include any behaviors or acts. It is an emotional experience that is felt rather than something that is done. Of course, when we experience intense love feelings we are highly motivated, and this active arousal leads us to do all kinds of things. Sometimes we do things that we are later glad we did, and other times we do things we later feel embarrassed or sorry about, but these behaviors are *effects* of love and not the emotion itself. The emotion of love, as it is defined here, also usually leads to having a number of other emotional and intellectual experiences, such as caring very much about other persons, being concerned about their welfare, trying to do things for them that they appreciate, and wanting to be around them, but these too are effects of love—when it is defined the way it is defined here.

There is, of course, the opposite emotional experience of disliking a person more intensely than the mere term *dislike* implies, and *hate* is probably the best term in the English language to describe this emotional experience. Thus, it is possible to identify a continuum like the one diagramed below that has love at one ex-

Feeling about another person

Hate   Dislike   Neutral   Like   Love

treme and hate at the other. Since this chapter is concerned with variation between intense love and the absence of loving feelings, this will be called the love variable. It may be that it should be labeled the "sentiment" or "attraction"[2] variable, as is done in some of the social psychological literature, but the more common term *love* seems the most useful.

An issue that is very important to most scholars of courtship and marriage is the difference between infatuation and the less fragile love feelings that most couples want to acquire and maintain in their courtship and marriage. This author's view is that we cannot make such distinctions in love feelings. If we experience feelings of intense liking or love for someone because of sudden infatuating experiences, our love feelings are just as genuine as is

---

[2] Homans (1950, 1961), Newcomb (1961), and Byrne and Rhamey (1965) have used these other labels.

the love that has been built up over a long period of time. What is different is the *basis* of the feelings. We may not be very wise to marry as a result of love feelings that arise very quickly (love at first sight or infatuation), as these feelings are also usually lost with equal speed and with relatively short-lived pain. However, the feelings are not illusory, and are not qualitatively different from feelings that are based on a more durable relationship—at least in this author's opinion. The more quickly arising and departing feelings of love are just as real as the more "mature" type of love, and this author thinks that it is a distortion of reality to discredit these types of love by labeling them as misconceptions or as false types of love.[3] The difference between more enduring love feelings and the highly intense love feelings that are based on idealism, romance, and exotic expectations is that realism, responsibility, and a less exotic life-style take over. And love feelings fade if individuals do not acquire other bases for love than idealism, romance, and exotic expectations. On the other hand, love feelings are more durable if they are based on such things as mutual respect, common goals, support during crises, concern for each other's welfare, a common philosophy of life, and a sense of trust. Such love feelings are not more durable because they are more real, less phony, or more genuine than the more fragile love feelings. They are more durable because they are based on more enduring aspects of a relationship.

Hopefully, this discussion of the way the term love is defined in this chapter provides a reasonably clear meaning for the term. The definition used here is narrower than the definitions many people would prefer. It does, however, make it possible to identify some general principles about love that can be used in dating and marital relationships.

A VERY GENERAL PRINCIPLE ABOUT LOVE

Love is so elusive a phenomenon that the social sciences have thus far discovered relatively few principles about it. There is, however, one relatively simple principle about love that is a part of several different schools of thought in the social sciences. The main idea of this principle can be stated in fairly untechnical language. It is simply that the more a person provides pleasurable

---

[3] Most texts for courtship and marriage courses differentiate between true love and mistaken or misconceived forms of love, such as romantic love and infatuation (Landis and Landis, 1968, chap. 9; Bowman, 1970, p. 78; Fullerton, 1972, chap. 15, Blood, 1969, pp. 110–13). When love is defined as it is in this text this distinction is not defensible, and the attention in these issues should turn from a true-false dichotomy to the bases of love. The definition of love used here is, of course, only one of many, so there are undoubtedly others who would disagree with our point of view.

or rewarding experiences for us the more intense our "love" feelings will be toward that person.

Since a number of different terms have been used to describe the independent variable in this principle, it is important to define this variable very carefully. Homans (1961, pp. 61–62) used the term *profit* to label this variable, and he defined profit as the particular balance of rewards and costs that an individual experiences from something. These rewards and costs are not limited to monetary rewards and costs. The monetary rewards and costs in marital relationships are usually a minor part of the total rewards and costs. In marital relationships contentment, pride, being needed, and being cared for are usually very important rewards, and hurt pride, deflated self-esteem, rejection, loneliness, and frustration are usually important costs. The following continuum illustrates this variable.

Rewards and
costs in a relationship

| Highly costly | Slightly more costly | Equal costs and rewards | Slightly more rewarding | Highly rewarding |

Thibaut and Kelley (1959) have essentially the same definition of this variable as Homans, but they use the term *outcome* rather than the term *profit* to label it. They state:

For some purposes it is desirable to treat rewards and costs separately; for other purposes it is assumed that they can be combined into a single scale of "goodness" of outcome, with states of high reward and low cost being given high-scale values and states of low reward and high cost, low-scale values. . . . The cost is high when great physical or mental effort is required, when embarrassment or anxiety accompany the action, or when there are conflicting forces or competing response tendencies of any sort. Costs derived from these different factors are also assumed to be measurable on a common psychological scale, and costs of different sorts, to be additive in their effect (1959, p. 13).

Another term that is also used to describe this variable is the amount of *reinforcement* (Skinner, 1953) a person receives. Reinforcing events are usually defined in terms of their effects—as stimuli that change the probability that a preceding behavior will recur. This definition, however, seems circular and tautologous rather than meaningful, and thus Homans' label and definition are used here. A formal statement of the principle is:

THE PROFIT PRINCIPLE: The greater the profit a person experiences in a relationship the greater the love for the other person, and vice versa.

There is a vast amount of empirical evidence for this principle, and this evidence has been accumulated in both psychological research (Bachrach et al., 1961–62; Brewer and Brewer, 1968) and sociological research (Homans, 1961; Newcomb, 1961). In addition this principle has been viewed as sufficiently documented to be used as the basis for treatment programs in marriage counseling, and empirical evidence has been acquired that demonstrates its utility (Stuart, 1969). It is one of the most thoroughly documented principles that is discussed in this volume, and hence it is one that we can apply with considerable confidence in its validity.

The Profit principle is so encompassing and abstract that when it is stated as it has been stated above it is difficult to identify specific ways to apply it. Because of this, several less general principles are deduced from this highly general principle in the next section of this chapter, and then an attempt is made to apply these less general principles. The Profit principle is such an abstract idea that it is made the basis for intermediate ideas that are more usable than the Profit principle itself.

IMPLEMENTING THE PROFIT PRINCIPLE

The Interaction principle

Homans (1950) identified a more specific instance of the Profit principle which can be called the Interaction principle. It asserts:

THE INTERACTION PRINCIPLE: When the interaction between two individuals is profitable, the more they interact the stronger will be their love for each other, and, conversely, the less they interact the less intense their love.

Those familiar with Homans' initial writing will recognize that he used the term *sentiment* rather than the term *love* in his statement of this principle. He defined sentiment, however, in much the same way that love is defined in this chapter, referring to it as the affective feelings one person has toward another, and he (Homans, 1961) pointed out that sentiment varies between the two extremes of strong positive sentiment and strong negative sentiment, with a neutral point in the middle. Thus, the slight change in terminology made here seems to be warranted.

The other variable in this principle is the amount of interaction. This variable refers to how much two individuals do things together. If they do nothing together there is obviously no interaction, and if they spend great amounts of time doing things together the amount of interaction is high. This variable is a continuous variable in that the amount of interaction is a continuum that has no inter-action at one extreme and a very high amount of interaction at the other extreme, and the interaction of two individuals could be any-place between these two extremes. This variable is diagramed below.

| No | Intermediate | High |
| interaction | amount | amount |

The main idea in this principle is that if two individuals increase the amount they interact, then, if nothing else changes in the relationship, they will probably feel more intense love for each other. Conversely, if they interact less, then, again assuming that nothing else changes, they will probably feel less love for each other. This is a more specific case of the profit principle insomuch as the amount of profit is dependent on the amount of interaction. If a couple were to interact very little they would have little profit, and if they interacted more, when the interaction is profitable, the interaction would increase the profit—and hence the love.

The Interaction principle can be applied in a number of situations. For example, during courtship and early marriage most couples are interested in increasing the intensity of their love for each other, and the principle suggests that one thing they can do is spend a lot of time doing pleasant things together. Actually the things most couples seem to do naturally during the courtship period are the very types of things that the principle suggests are useful. Couples usually spend great amounts of time in dating activities in which they are dressed up, away from their work roles, and in pleasant surroundings. In addition most couples spend vast amounts of time in expressing their affection for each other in casual and serious conversation. The very large volume of messages that communicate such things as endearment, tenderness, importance, caring, and the like increase profit in the interaction and undoubtedly increase the love feelings in the relationship. In fact, it is likely that love is usually felt so intensely during the courtship and early married stages of life in large part because couples find it very natural to implement this principle. And, if this is the case, it also suggests some things couples might want to do throughout their marriage to maintain and enhance their love feelings—assuming that this is one of their marital goals.

The Interaction principle can also be useful in several less obvious and natural situations. For example, when couples are separated during their courtship or even after their marriage, the principle suggests that if they want to maintain intense love feelings they will find it useful to continue to have positive interaction. Modern technology makes it possible to interact at such times by making long-distance telephone calls, exchanging cassette tapes, or even sending movies or videotapes to each other.

This principle also has practical implications in situations in which individuals or couples are trying to reduce their love for other persons. The principle suggests that if they continue to interact with those other persons and if the interaction is rewarding, they will find it more difficult to extinguish their feelings than if they reduce or terminate the interaction. The Profit principle also suggests, however, that if the interaction is costly rather than rewarding continued interaction will probably help to extinguish their positive affect for the other persons and to replace it with negative affect.

At least four different things can be done to use the Interaction principle to increase love feelings. The most elementary is knowing a variety of things that a couple can do together. If we don't have a fairly sizable repertoire of things that *can* be done the chances are very slim that we will have much interaction. A second way to implement the Interaction principle is to increase the amount of rewarding interaction. A third way is to decrease costly interaction, and a fourth way is to increase the amount of profit a couple has in the interaction. The following exercise is designed to help us increase our repertoire of ways to interact.

DISCOVERING NEW WAYS TO INTERACT

Goal: To increase awareness of the activities married couples can do together.

Get together with a small group of friends and make a list of specific activities that husbands and wives can do together without children. In each of the following categories try to come up with at least five or six activities that you think are pleasant in addition to the examples given to get you started.

a. Recreational interaction (take a quiet walk together; have dinner at home alone—by candlelight; join a dancing club; get season tickets to the symphony)

b. Learning activities (learn a language through records; take an adult education class together; learn a new sport together)

c. Communicating (look at partner while speaking and listening; put little notes in partner's pocket; write a poem for partner)

d. Doing diferent things while near each other (one shine shoes in the kitchen while other does dishes)

e. Working together (wash car or dishes together; work in yard together; redecorate a room together)

f. Expressing affection (seat wife at a dinner table; turn down blankets and lay out slippers and robe for spouse; hold hands while window-shopping; touch seated spouse when passing him or her)

When we want to increase our love feelings toward someone and we know more things we *can* do than we *are* doing, one obvious way to implement the Interaction principle is to increase the amount of interaction that occurs. The following exercise is designed to help a couple increase their interaction.

INCREASING INTERACTION

Goal: To increase the amount of rewarding interaction in a relationship.

1. Identify a relationship. (This exercise will be most efficient if you select an ongoing relationship that you have had for months.)

2. Identify three feasible ways to increase your interaction in this relationship. (Do more of something you've already been doing, or do something you haven't done yet.) You will probably be ahead to discuss these with the other person in the relationship.

3. With the other person, select one of these possibilities and try to implement it for a reasonable period of time.

4. Identify any changes in your feelings in the relationship that you think are a result of the change in interaction. (Sometimes the effects of increasing or decreasing interaction cannot be seen for weeks and months, so take as long as you need before assessing the effects of the change.)

The third way to implement this principle is to decrease costly interaction. The following exercise is designed to help accomplish this.

DECREASING COSTLY INTERACTION

Goal: To increase love feelings for someone by decreasing some costly interaction in the relationship.

1. Get in mind a relationship you are active and interested in. Preferably use a spouse, a girlfriend, or a boyfriend. Otherwise, focus on your relationship with a roommate, a family member, or a close friend.

2. List all the things you do regularly with this person that are costly to you—things which you think aren't worthwhile. (If you can't think of any, you obviously won't be able to change your feelings by eliminating an activity.)

3. Try to eliminate *one* of these activities. Discussing the change with your partner might be a help, but it might not. You be the judge. It might be best to just quit the activity altogether, making whatever other arrangements are necessary.

4. Later, evaluate the effect the elimination of the activity had on your feelings toward the other person. If you did not experience an increase in satisfaction with your relationship due to the change, try to find some reasons why the general rule did not work in this situation.

A fourth way of implementing the Interaction principle is to increase the amount of profit in the interaction in a relationship. This is probably the strategy that is most useful in marital relationships that are a few years old because it is so common to gradually quit doing the things that keep profit high. Many times a little effort (and note that often a little cost is required) will have very large payoffs. It is like investing money in something and then getting many times the value of the money in something else (love feelings). There are many little things that we can do to increase the profit in our interaction. For example, many of us forget that little words of affection and appreciation have great meaning to most of us, and, since they take little effort the payoff is usually considerably greater than the initial cost. Most of us also find that attractiveness in a spouse is highly rewarding, and spending a few minutes sprucing ourselves up can have a very large impact on our spouse's profit. Being trustworthy, consistent, supportive, open-minded, and fair are other ways to increase profit. The following exercise is an attempt to help us practice this process of increasing profit.

INCREASING THE PROFIT IN INTERACTION

Goal: To change a regularly occurring interaction so that it has more profit (to decrease the cost or increase the reward). The aim is to change the *quality* of the interaction. It is against the rules here to quit the interaction altogether or to add another positive interaction to compensate for it.

1. Identify a relationship, such as a spouse, fiancé(e), date, friend, family member.

2. List three regularly occurring interactions in this relationship in which you might be able to increase the profit. Using a piece of paper in the following manner is often useful:

a. Eating dinner	By the time I have prepared the meal and sit down I am too tired and flustered to be responsive company.
b. Saying good morning	I'm slow to wake up and grouchy.
c. Visiting in-laws	No particular cost or reward.

3. Choose any of the items you listed, and think of some way to reduce or eliminate its costly aspects or to increase its rewards. This planning may be done most fruitfully by planning with your partner, using problem-solving skills you practiced in Chapter 6.

4. Implement your plan.

5. After a reasonable time, determine whether you actually increased the profit. If so, describe any effects this had on your feelings in the relationship. If not, what probably hindered you?

One central theme in several different bodies of literature is the idea that people want and strive for a feeling that they "belong" and are important to at least a small group of other people. Fromm's writings about freedom (1941, 1947) and love (1956) emphasize the significance of the sense of belonging. Relatedness is also a main idea in Adler's (1930) theory of personality and the writings of Carl Rogers (1951, 1972). The idea is relevant here because if it is correct, then individuals find it extremely rewarding (highly profitable) to feel that they are very important to other

A sense of importance

persons and that those other persons "care" a great deal about them—not for what they can do but for what they are as persons. On the assumption that the idea is valid it is possible to state:

THE SENSE OF IMPORTANCE PRINCIPLE: The more important an individual feels he or she is to someone else the stronger the love feelings will be toward the other person, and, conversely, the less important he or she feels the less intense the love feelings toward the other person.

The independent variable in this principle is not defined very precisely in most of the literature that discusses it, and there is a very understandable reason for this. A sense of importance is an emotional experience, and in many ways it is more meaningful to communicate about emotions through a poetic, literary, or figurative style than through the more precise, technical terminology used in the social sciences. There is, however, also something to be gained from terminological precision, and because of this an attempt is made here to define this variable fairly clearly. It can be defined as an emotional feeling that others care, that they are concerned, and that they have an investment in you. It also involves a feeling that their caring is appropriate or good, and hence that there is a rightness about their concern. This is, of course, a variable in that others can care for us and we can care for them a little or a great deal, and the variable can be diagramed as follows:

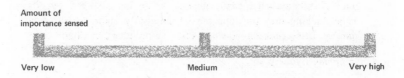

Amount of
importance sensed

Very low   Medium   Very high

There are many ways to tell how much caring exists in a relationship, and there are some ways to increase or decrease caring. One thing that provides clues about how important one person is to another is the amount of attention paid to the person. When people are of little importance little attention is paid to such things as their opinions, concerns, wishes, or feelings. When they are more important they get more attention. It is, of course, possible for us to pay attention out of fear or anxiety, but when we do this the important thing is what the other persons may *do* to or about us rather than the persons themselves. It seems hard, however, to imagine a situation in which a person highly important to us is given little attention.

One trap many of us fall into is telling ourselves that someone is extremely important to us, *but* . . . that we aren't able to show this as much as we want. We have to do such and such at the office, or there are such and such demands around the house. In actual fact what we are frequently doing is telling ourselves that the other things are really more important because the way we *act* is probably a more accurate indicator of how important they really are than the self-deceiving things we tell ourselves. Hence, we can implement the Sense of Importance principle by examining how we actually treat others and using that as the measure of how important they really are. We may or may not want to change our view of how important they are and the way this view of importance leads us to behave.

EVALUATING THE "IMPORTANCE" OF SOMEONE AS A PERSON

Goal: To gain a better understanding of how "important" some-one else *really* is.

1. Determine how frequently you think the following ten events oc-cur. Rate their frequency in this way: N—never occurs; O—oc-casionally occurs; F—frequently occurs; A—always occurs.

N O F A   (1)   We attentively listen to the other person.

N O F A   (2)   We express appreciation or approval for some-thing the other person has done.

N O F A   (3)   We go out of our way to greet the other person when we meet or to say good-bye when we sepa-rate.

N O F A   (4)   We plan to *really* "take into account" the other person's suggestions.

N O F A   (5)   We are concerned about the other person's "feelings."

N O F A   (6)   The other person expresses a wish or desire, and we ignore it.

N O F A   (7)   The other person states an opinion, and we treat it as unimportant.

N O F A   (8)   We are in a situation in which the other person deserves an apology, but we don't give it.

N O F A   (9)   The other person wants help, but we are "too busy."

N O F A (10)   We keep the other person waiting.

2. Get the other person to rate how frequently these ten events occur, and compare your evaluations.

(If your first five answers tend toward the "A" side and your second five tend toward the "N" side, this indicates a sense of importance. If the other person perceives you as showing less importance than you perceive, this may indicate that his or her actual importance to you is less than you think.)

Emotional help

There seems to be a reciprocal relationship between the intensity of love feelings and the amount people help us cope with our emotional distresses. The more strongly persons are loved the more people turn to them for help with such emotional problems as discouragement, frustration, depression, confusion, emptiness, and loneliness; and the more they receive help with such problems the stronger their feelings of love for the other persons become. In the present context the important part of this reciprocal process is the fact that love feelings seem to be influenced by help with emotional problems. If this process is stated in terms of the Profit principle, then what apparently occurs is that people find it very satisfying and rewarding (profitable) to receive support and assistance when they are coping with undesirable emotions, and if this is the case it is possible to state:

THE EMOTIONAL HELP PRINCIPLE: The more help a person provides in times of emotional distress the greater the intensity of the love feelings toward this person, and, conversely, the less help a person provides the less intense the love feelings.

This principle is probably more relevant for marital relationships in the modern society than it was in earlier historical periods. In the past several centuries the institution of marriage has changed in a number of systematic ways, and one way is that marital and family institutions have stopped performing a number of "functions" for society (Ogburn and Nimkoff, 1955; Parsons, 1955). For example, the production and distribution of goods have stopped being primarily family functions, and are now functions of elaborate industrial and commercial institutions. Educating children for their occupations is no longer primarily the responsibility of parents, and the protective function is no longer organized on a family basis, as it is now the responsibility of the military, the police, and fire-fighting institutions. The fact that the family institution has lost several functions, however, should not lead to the conclusion that it no longer performs vital functions for the family. As Parsons has suggested, this loss of certain functions

. . . resulted in the transfer of a variety of functions from the nuclear family to other structures of the society, notably the occupationally organized sectors of it. This means that the family has become *a more specialized* agency than before, probably more specialized than it has been in any previously known society. This represents a decline of certain features which traditionally have been associated with families; but whether it represents a "decline of the family" in a more general sense is another matter; we think not. We think the trend of the evidence points to the beginning of the relative stabili-zation of a *new* type of family structure in a new relation to a gen-eral social structure, one in which the family is more specialized than before, but not in any general sense less important, because the society is dependent *more* exclusively on it for the performance of *certain* of its vital functions (1955, pp. 9–10).

Parsons' point that those of us who live in modern society are more exclusively dependent on marital and family relationships for *certain* functions explains why the Emotional Help principle is more relevant in modern marital relationships than in the marital relation-ships of earlier historical periods. In earlier times more extensive kinship interaction and the more personalized nature of inter-personal relationships probably provided alternative sources of emo-tional support, and the marital relationship was apparently less in-tensely personal, less companionate, and less emotional. However, in modern "mass" society many nonmarital sources of emotional support have disappeared and most people are more exclusively dependent on their marital relationship—or have to turn to such professionals as psychiatrists or counselors.

It is not possible for all couples to develop a type of relationship in which there is a great deal of emotional support, and some couples do not want to have that type of relationship. Thus, the main point here is that the amount of emotional support or help can be used to either decrease or increase the intensity of love feelings in a relationship. If couples increase their mutual helpfulness they will probably increase their affective feelings toward each other, and if they turn to other sources for emotional help their affective feel-ings will tend to shift. The following exercise is designed to help couples determine how much emotional support they receive from their marital relationship and to decide whether it is an optimal amount or an amount they would like to change.

SOURCES OF EMOTIONAL HELP

Goal: To determine your sources of emotional help and how satisfactory they are.

1. Have a relaxed, uninterrrupted conversation with someone with whom you have a close relationship. This conversation may take considerable time, so select a time when you do not have other obligations.

2. Most (and perhaps all) people occasionally experience different combinations of sadness, discouragement, loneliness, and depression. Discuss what you do when you experience these emotions. Whom do you find helpful? Determine whether it is friends, parents, children, spouse, roommates, or someone else. Try to determine how different people help in different ways—if they do.

3. Emotional help is usually also needed in a time of crisis, such as a severe illness, a serious accident, or death. Talk about what you do at such times. To whom can you turn for encouragement and support. Again, try to determine how different individuals help in different ways.

4. Evaluate how you feel about your interpersonal resources for these types of emotional help. Are you satisfied with these relationships, or are there ways they could be improved? Is your spouse of too little help or does he or she try to help too much?

5. If you would like to make changes in your sources of emotional help, try to identify specific things that could be done to effect such changes.

Similarity

Another principle that can be viewed as a more specific instance of the Profit principle was discovered in the marriage research in the 1930s (Burgess and Cottrell, 1939; Terman, 1938), and it is also a main idea in balance theory (Heider, 1945; Newcomb, 1961). This is:

THE SIMILARITY-LOVE PRINCIPLE: When two individuals have an enduring relationship, the more similar they are to each other the stronger will be their love, and, conversely, the more different they are the less intense will be their love.

A large body of empirical research supports this principle. The research stimulated by balance theory[4] has investigated the relation-

---

[4] Examples of this research are Newcomb (1961), Tagiuri (1958), Backman and Secord (1959, 1962), Broxton (1963), Byrne and Nelson (1965), Byrne and Clore (1966), Byrne and Griffitt (1966), and Byrne, Griffitt, Hudgins, and Reeves (1969).

ship between attraction and similarity of attitudes, and research about marital dynamics has found that various types of similarity in a wide variety of different areas, such as age, education, role expectations, values, and status (Pineo, 1961; Blood and Wolfe, chap. 8), are related to the intensity of love feelings.

This principle has several practical implications. One of them is that, as Foote (1956) and Brim (1963) have pointed out, husbands and wives gradually change throughout their adult life, and they change in a number of different ways. Occupations that seem attractive at one stage of life are less attractive years later. Leisure-time interests that take physical stamina are extensively sought in the early years of adult life, but they are gradually forsaken for more passive activities, and even religious views and values (Kelley, 1955, 1961) change. Foote (1956), Waller and Hill (1951), and the O'Neills (1972) have suggested that marriage can be profitably viewed as an opportunity to enhance individual development—and many of the ways in which this can be done can promote similarity. If couples want to maintain intense love feelings over a lifetime they can discuss ways to learn new things together, read the same types of literature, and associate with the same types of groups so that in these ways they will promote similarity in their views. This principle probably shouldn't be pushed to the extreme of advocating that spouses lose their individuality in order to maintain their love feelings, but it does argue that maintaining similarity may prove very useful in maintaining love—and that promoting dissimilarity may be useful in decreasing it. The two exercises on pages 199–201 are useful here, as they help one determine how similar she or he is to someone else.

Bondedness

It is very likely that another factor that influences love feelings is the "bondedness" two individuals experience in their marriage. When few things provide "glue" in a couple's relationship it seems reasonable to believe that their love feelings will usually be fairly low. On the other hand, when many different bonds tie them together, and these bonds are fairly strong, this probably adds to their love feelings. The author has not found this idea that bondedness influences love feelings in the existing scientific literature, but the idea is mentioned here for three reasons. One reason is that the idea can be viewed as a more specific instance of the Profit principle. When the bonds in a relationship are rewarding or pleasurable, then it is possible to deduce from the Profit principle a less general principle:

THE BONDEDNESS PRINCIPLE: The stronger the bonds in a marital relationship the greater the intensity of the love feelings, and, conversely, the weaker the bonds the less intense the love.

The second reason this idea is mentioned here is that it seems to be consistent with the author's observations of married couples. The third reason it is suggested is that Chapter 13 deals with factors that influence bondedness, and if bonds do influence love feelings the principle provides a useful link between the two chapters. The various factors that influence the strength of the bonds in a marriage can then be viewed as indirectly influencing the love feelings in the relationship. These reasons are the author's only bases for this principle. Thus, the principle should be accepted only very tentatively, though it does suggest a way to use the Profit principle and a way to relate the ideas in Chapter 13 to the issues dealt with in this chapter.

SUMMARY

This chapter has attempted to identify several general principles that can be used to increase or decrease feelings of love. The term *love* has so many meanings that the first part of the chapter attempted to describe how the term is and is not used in this chapter. Love was defined as emotional or affective feelings of attraction toward another person. It is a variable because such feelings can vary in intensity. Intense love feelings are at one extreme of a continuum that has intense hate at the opposite extreme and indifference in the middle. Liking and disliking are feelings intermediate between the midpoint and the two extremes. This definition of love excludes many connotations that the term *love* has to many people, but it has the advantage of providing enough clarity and precision to permit a discussion of love which excludes private definitions of the term.

After the meaning of the term *love* was discussed a very general and abstract principle was identified. This was the *Profit* principle, (1) which asserts that the more "profit" (reward or reinforcement) an individual experiences in a relationship the more loving feelings that individual experiences toward the other person. Then five less general, more specific instances of the Profit principle were identified. These more specific principles suggested that: (2) the greater the interaction the greater the love; (3) the more a person feels that he or she is, as a person, important to someone else the greater the love feelings toward that other person; (4) the greater the help a person provides in times of emotional distress the greater the

Figure 8–1

Causal models of principles in Chapter 8

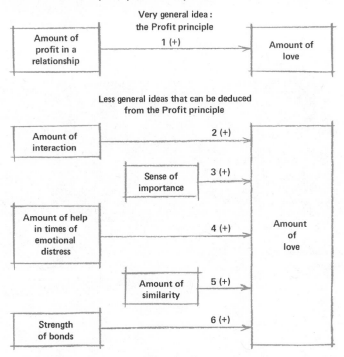

intensity of the love feelings toward that person; (5) the more similar two individuals are to each other the greater the intensity of their love; and (6) the stronger the bonds between two individuals the more intense their love. These principles are summarized in Figure 8–1.

SUGGESTIONS FOR FURTHER STUDY

Fromm, Erich   1956. *The Art of Loving.* New York: Harper.

Fullerton, Gail Putney   1972. *Survival in Marriage.* New York: Holt, Rinehart and Winston, chap. 15.

Homans, George C.   1961. *Social Behavior: Its Elementary Forms.* New York: Harcourt, Brace and World, chaps. 1 and 2.

Landis, Judson, and Landis, Mary G.   1968. *Building a Successful Marriage.* 5th ed. Englewood Cliffs, N.J.: Prentice-Hall, chap. 8.

Magoun, F. Alexander   1948. *Love and Marriage.* New York: Harper.

Martinson, Floyd M.   1960. *Marriage and the American Ideal.* New York: Dodd, Mead, chaps. 7–9.

Newcomb, Theodore M.   1961. *The Acquaintance Process.* New York: Holt, Rinehart and Winston.

9

Personal readiness for marriage

AN UNAVOIDABLE and important question that is faced when considering marriage is, "When is a person ready for marriage?" Few would agree that a child of 10 or 12 is mature enough to marry in the contemporary United States, but it is undoubtedly also true that some individuals who are 20, 25, or older are not yet ready to assume the personal and social obligations of marriage. The issue of readiness for marriage is extremely complex because so many factors enter into it, including biological development, mental and emotional maturity, financial adequacy, emancipation from parental control, and the ability to perform the many roles that come with marriage. This chapter is an attempt to deal with this complex issue by discussing: (1) some of the factors involved in readiness for marriage; (2) five principles about the impact these factors have on a person's chances for happiness in marriage; and (3) ways to take those principles into account in making decisions about when and whom to marry.

Unfortunately the research that produced the principles discussed in this chapter was all done with couples who had very conventional styles of marriage, and because of this the social sciences know very little about whether those principles apply to the newly emerging styles of marriage. Some or all of the principles discussed in this chapter may be applicable in such innovative styles of life as Temporary, Group, and Swinging marriages, but until additional research is undertaken in this area we cannot be sure, and it may be that the principles are quite irrelevant for such innovative styles of marriage. The best that can be done at the present time is to identify the principles that have been discovered and then to make educated guesses about the styles of life for which they are relevant and the styles for which they are not relevant. And, as will become evident in this chapter, some of this guessing is done here.

A VERY GENERAL PRINCIPLE ABOUT READINESS

A married person is obligated to perform a large number of tasks. Individuals have to be fed, clothed, and housed, and this usually involves a complex array of skills, such as knowing how to prepare a balanced diet; being able to secure the necessary money; knowing how to wash, mend, and take care of clothes; being able to acquire living facilities; being adequately but not overly insured; and knowing what to do when illnesses occur. In addition a large number of socioemotional demands are usually placed on spouses. It is inevitable that people will be discouraged, depressed, and angry; and it is virtually inevitable that there will be disruptive disagreements between spouses on issues that are important in their relationship. Such socioemotional situations demand a complex set of interactional skills that are neither easily nor automatically learned. The main point here is that all the forms of marriage are very involved, complex interpersonal arrangements and that married persons need a large number of *skills* if they are to create a pleasant relationship. When the individuals are relatively adequate in the necessary skills this facilitates marital success, but when they do not have those skills this proves to be an obstacle to marital success.

The key variable in this context is related to the *social norms* that were defined in Chapter 7. As will be recalled from that discussion, social norms are beliefs that individuals have about what a person ought to do and not do in a social role, and in the present context they are beliefs about what a spouse ought to do and not do in a marriage. These norms prescribe that individuals should do certain things and not do other things, and if individuals have the ability to accomplish what is normatively prescribed this makes a substantial contribution to their readiness for marriage. The general principle that summarizes this idea is:

> THE SKILL PRINCIPLE: The amount of skill a person has to behave in the ways normatively prescribed for a marital role influences the chances of marital satisfaction, and this is a positive, curvilinear relationship.

Figure 9–1 is an attempt to diagram the author's speculation about the shape of this relationship. As can be seen in that figure, what is proposed is that variation in the amount of skill, when the

Figure 9–1

The relationship between the skills for behaving in ways
normatively prescribed for marital roles and the
chances of marital satisfaction

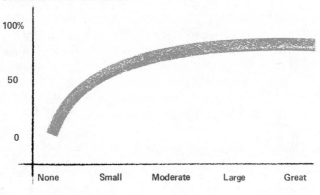

Chances of marital satisfaction

amount is fairly low, probably makes the most difference in marriage. When persons have a moderate or a high level of skill any
variation up or down in the skill probably has relatively less impact
on the probability of satisfactory marriage. This principle is an important part of role theory (Sarbin, 1968), and the basic idea has
been discussed extensively in the family literature.[1] In addition,
there has been considerable research that supports this idea. Some
of this research is cited in the following pages where several deductions from this principle are discussed.

This principle is really a very commonsense idea, since what
it says is that ability to function in a particular situation says something about whether a person is ready to enter that situation. The
fact that the idea is simple and easily understood should not, however, lead to dismissing it as irrelevant or unimportant. Most
scientific laws tend to become "common sense" after they are
formulated and known, and laws about gravity, evaporation, and
genetic processes are simple enough to be understood by school-age
children. The question of whether the Skill principle is relevant or
important should be determined by how useful it is in helping us
recognize when we are ready for marriage, and this principle is of
considerable value if it is viewed as a very general principle that can
be used to identify several less general principles. Four of these less
general deductions are discussed in the following pages.

---

[1] Several examples of discussions of these issues are in Blood (1969, pp.
8–9) and Landis and Landis (1968, chap. 8).

In trying to apply the Skill principle or the more specific generalizations that are deduced from it, we should keep in mind that some of the skills needed may be unique to the particular style of marriage we select. In an Open style of marriage one needed skill will be the ability to be flexible, and in an Intrinsic marriage one expected skill will be the ability to develop and maintain a long-term, intimate relationship. The skills that are prescribed for marriage thus include some of the traditionally expected norms, but they also include norms that are unique to each relationship.

LESS GENERAL PRINCIPLES ABOUT "SKILLS"

Age

There has been considerable research investigating the relationship between age at marriage and the probability of success in marriage, and the findings have been remarkably consistent. Studies conducted as early as the 1930s and as late as the 1960s have discovered the same curvilinear relationship.[2] The line in Figure 9–2 summarizes these findings, showing that the older people are

Figure 9–2

The relationship between age and the probability of a satisfying marriage

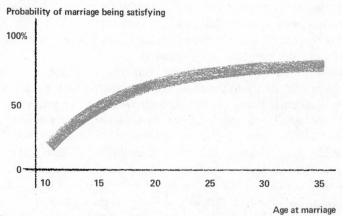

Probability of marriage being satisfying

Age at marriage

---

[2] Among the studies that have found a relationship between age at marriage and marital success are Burgess and Cottrell (1939, pp. 122, 271); Burgess and Wallin (1953, p. 521); Locke (1951, pp. 102, 343); Terman et al. (1938, p. 181); Karlsson (1963, p. 56); and Landis and Landis (1946; 1968, pp. 122–23). The fact that no research study that has investigated this relationship has failed to find it adds weight to this evidence that the relationship exists. The principle is thus one of the most highly proven ideas in this book.

when they marry the greater their chances for a satisfying marriage. Age seems to make the most difference in the teenage years, as the line has a very steep slope during that period. Apparently a year or two during late adolescence makes considerable difference in the chances for a successful marriage. During the low twenties age still seems to make a substantial difference, but after the middle twenties age differences seem to have relatively little impact. One aspect of this research that surprises many individuals when they first learn about it is that the chances for having a successful marriage are actually greatest for individuals who have reached their late twenties or early thirties. This research justifies:

THE AGE AT MARRIAGE PRINCIPLE: Age at the time of a person's first marriage is related to the probability of the marriage being satisfying, and this is a positive, curvilinear relationship.

The Age at Marriage principle can be viewed as a more specific case of the Skill principle if it is assumed that individuals who marry young have fewer of the skills they will need and that individuals who marry at older ages have acquired more of those skills. At present research has not documented which skills vary according to age, and it may be that some do while others don't. For example, the ability to communicate effectively may not increase between ages 16 and 26, but the ability to secure an adequate income may. Hopefully, future research will discover more about these differences.

There is little basis for speculating about whether this principle is more relevant for some of the alternative styles of marriage than for others. It may be that the emphasis on permanence in the Judaic-Christian and Eternal styles and the complexity of the relationships in the Intrinsic, Group, and Open styles of marriage argue that the principle is highly relevant for those forms of marriage. If this is the case, the de-emphasis on stability and relative simplicity of the relationships in the Temporary marriage and the first stage of the Two-Step marriage probably argue that this principle is least important for them. These speculations, however, are no more than reasonable guesses, and this issue is certainly subject to other interpretations.

There are two different ways to look at the Age at Marriage generalization when applying it in our personal lives. One way is to conclude that something about age itself makes a difference, and then to conclude that if everything else is the same, individuals will have greater chances of being happy if they marry at an older age. The other way to look at this rule is to conclude that age itself is not really a causal factor, and that it has such a clear relationship to marital happiness because a number of other things associated with age influence a person's chances for marital success.[3] It is suggested here that there is some validity to both of these points of view, and hence both of them will be elaborated on.

The point of view that will be dealt with first is that age in itself is really not very important, but that a number of factors associated with age make a difference. One problem with this point of view is that the other factors haven't yet been identified and measured with enough precision to be studied scientifically. This means that we are not yet sure what to pay attention to if we don't pay attention to age. Some scholars have suggested these factors may include mental and emotional maturity, adaptability, the perspective that comes with experience, and the fact that people marry for different reasons when they are older.[4] At present this type of speculative analysis is the only basis for the point of view that age itself is not the important factor. Nevertheless, it may be the most defensible position. On the assumption that it is the maturity exercise below has been developed, and this exercise is an attempt to apply the Age at Marriage principle.

MATURITY EXERCISE

Goal: To determine ways that we are more *and* less mature than most individuals our age and the implications of these differences for our readiness for marriage.

1. We are all more "mature" in some areas than in other areas, and the purpose of the first part of this exercise is to identify those areas. Make two lists—one identifying facets in which you are *less* mature than most and the other identifying facets in which you are *more* mature. (This could be done in a discussion with some individuals who know you well or through introspection.) Some areas to get you started are:

   ability to be responsible for own behavior?

   ability to be independent from parents?

   meaningful philosophy of life?

   ability to control expression of emotion?

---

[3] Udry (1971, pp. 282–83) suggests that this is the correct interpretation.

[4] Burgess and Wallin (1953, chap. 19 and p. 521); Landis and Landis (1968, pp. 122–24); and Blood (1969, pp. 162–66).

> ability to support self?
>
> ability to get along with others?
>
> ability to accept the consequences of choices?
>
> 2.   Use these two lists to evaluate your maturity and the implications of this maturity for your readiness to marry. If you wish to try to alter some of these behaviors, use the "Action Plan" outline on pages 164–65 to develop a program.

Next, looking at the point of view that age itself is an important factor, it is not very intellectually satisfying to many people when they are told that age really makes a difference in a person's chances in marriage. There is, however, some evidence that this is the case. It may be, for example, that marrying at a young age interferes with educational or other types of preparation for marital responsibilities, and if this is the case age is an indirect causal factor. Coombs et al. (1970) found some evidence that this is the case, and hence they suggested that there may be something about the age factor that in some manner does make a difference. When this point of view is taken at least two things can be done to apply this principle in our personal lives. These are (1) to avoid marrying at very young ages (assuming that we want to maximize our chances for marital happiness), and (2) if we do decide to marry at a young age, to be aware that at least one factor is probably working against the marriage's success and then to be sure we can identify a number of other factors that can counterbalance this negative factor, such as level of maturity, similarity of basic values, and approval from family and friends.

Education

Several studies have found that a person's educational level is related to the probability of having a happy marriage.[5] Less education has been associated with lower probabilities of marital success, and higher education has been associated with higher chances of marital success. This idea can be summarized:

---

[5] A large number of studies have found a relationship between education and such variables as marital adjustment and divorce, and no studies are known that tested for this relationship and failed to find it. The studies reporting the relationship include: Burgess and Cottrell (1939, p. 271); Burgess and Wallin (1953, p. 516); Terman et al. (1938, p. 189); Weeks (1943); Hollingshead (1949); Kephart (1954); Goode (1956); and Udry (1958). Glick (1957) and Hillman (1962) found a curvilinear relationship, but Udry (1967) demonstrated that that appeared because they were really dealing with a different variable than the marital happiness, adjustment, or marital stability type of variable.

THE EDUCATION PRINCIPLE: The greater the amount of education the greater the chances of marital satisfaction, and vice versa.

This principle can be viewed as a specific instance of the Skill principle if those with less education have fewer of the abilities they will need in marriage and those with more education have more of those abilities. This seems reasonable, but, as with age at marriage, no research has been undertaken which shows which maritally relevant skills are acquired in the process of getting an education. Again, hopefully, future research will shed additional light on this question.

It seems reasonable to speculate that the Education principle is much more relevant for some styles of marriage than for others. It is probably least relevant for Temporary marriage and the first phase of the Two-Step style of marriage. It is also likely that the marital forms demanding very complex interpersonal relationships would be the ones for which this principle is most relevant because more education would probably increase skills in dealing with abstractions and complexities. If this is the case this principle may be most relevant for the Open, Intrinsic, and Group styles of marriage. These are, of course, only speculations, but, hopefully, future research will provide a basis for more definitive conclusions.

One way to apply this principle in our personal lives would be to get as much formal education as possible if we want to maximize our chances for marital happiness. Another application would be to marry a relatively well-educated person or to encourage a prospective spouse to increase his or her education. Still another way would be to try to attain the qualities of the well educated even though we don't have the opportunity to get a formal education. This effort could include such things as extensive reading; learning to think analytically, objectively, and clearly; learning to express one's thoughts and ideas on paper; and becoming aware of the history of man's thought.

Desire for children

Some research suggests that an individual's attitudes toward having children are related to the probability of being happily married.[6] The independent variable apparently is the desire for

---

[6] Several studies have tested this relationship (Williams, 1938; Burgess and Cottrell, 1939, p. 414; Reed, 1948, p. 324; and Locke, 1951). All of them

children, and this is a continuous variable that ranges from the extreme of not wanting children to a strong desire for children. The principle that summarizes this research finding is:

> **THE DESIRE FOR CHILDREN PRINCIPLE:** The amount an individual desires children is related to the chances of marital satisfaction, and this is a positive relationship.

The research findings about this generalization do not provide enough information to tell whether the relationship is linear or curvilinear; but there is evidence from the studies referred to earlier that the relationship is positive. It is probably also important to point out that the "desire for children" variable in this principle has nothing to do with the number of children wanted or how soon after the marriage they are wanted. The issue is just whether or not the individuals want children.

The social sciences have not yet discovered anything about the relevance of this relationship for the various alternative forms of marriage. The research has all been conducted with fairly traditional types of marriages. Therefore, the relationship probably occurs in Intrinsic, Judaic-Christian, Eternal, and, of course, Traditional marriages. It seems unrealistic, however, to expect that the relationship exists for Temporary marriages or the first phase of Two-Step marriages. Additional research is needed so we will know how and where the principle applies.

The application of this principle in our personal lives is fairly straightforward. If we want to maximize our chances of happiness in marriage (and we are opting for one of the more traditional styles of marriage), we could defer marriage until we want children. Or, if we want to marry while not wanting children we could weigh carefully this negative factor against the other factors that are predictive of success or failure. If a number of other factors argue for success they may easily counterbalance the effects of this factor.

One factor involved in using this principle is to discover just what one's attitudes are toward having children, and the "Attitudes toward Parenthood" exercise below is designed to help in this process.

---

found a positive relationship between the two variables, and they even controlled other variables, such as the actual presence of children.

ATTITUDES TOWARD PARENTHOOD

Goal: To discover more about your attitudes toward having and rearing children.

1. Take some time to think about your opinions about being a parent, and then write a paragraph on a sheet of paper that summarizes your opinions about the following three things:

   a. In your life scheme, do you want to be a parent or not?

   b. If your answer to a is yes, then describe what satisfactions and personal sacrifices you will probably make as a result of this choice. If your answer to a is no, then describe what other aspects of your life will provide the sense of purpose and the satisfactions that most people in contemporary society expect (though they may not wind up getting them) from parenthood.

   c. Identify how "strongly" you feel about these opinions. For example, are they opinions you could easily change, or are they opinions of central importance to you as a person?

2. Identify a person whose opinions you respect, and ask that person to read what you have written. Discuss her or his reactions to your views and how you respond to those reactions.

3. Later, evaluate how you now "feel" about what you wrote, and revise it if any of your opinions have changed.

Conventionality

One final aspect of readiness for marriage has to do with conventionality. Many scholars of the family argue that marriage is usually a fairly "conventional" institution (Locke et al., 1963, p. 320; Udry, 1971, p. 429; Burr, 1973, pp. 112–14) and that the types of people who usually fit most easily into this institution are fairly conventional people. Individuals who tend to be radically innovative or who want to make major changes in the established customs of a society or subculture tend to have more difficulty fitting into the marital institution; and if they do fit in they frequently have a marital situation that most people in the society view as odd or bizarre. Thus, in assessing readiness for marriage (at least readiness for one of the relatively typical or socially normal types of marriage) prospective spouses would probably profit from examining their own and their prospective spouse's conventionality. The general principle that seems to operate in this context is:

THE CONVENTIONALITY PRINCIPLE: The amount of an individual's conventionality is related to the chances of marital satisfaction, and this is a positive relationship.

A great deal of scientific data indicates that this principle is valid—*for fairly conventional marriages,*[7] and no research is known that has tested the principle in any of the innovative life-styles that have appeared in recent years. Most of the supporting evidence comes from research that tried to determine whether certain personality traits or behaviors are related to marital success; and the most defensible conclusion that emerges from this research is that if the traits or behaviors are conventional *in the societal culture or subculture in which they occur* they are related to marital success —regardless of what the behaviors are. This conclusion is supported by research as varied as Mead's (1935) analysis of life in three New Guinea cultures and Christensen's (1969) analysis of premarital sexual attitudes. In addition, as Locke et al. (1963, p. 320) have pointed out, a great deal of the research conducted in the United States also supports the conclusion.

It should also be mentioned that this generalization does not in any way rule out the possibility that an unconventional person can have a happy, pleasant, and satisfying marital relationship—even in one of the more conventional styles of marriage. The principle just says that an unconventional person's chances of being satisfied and happy with his or her marriage are lower than those of a conventional person. Also, as is the case for any of the factors involved in marital success, the effects of this factor can be counterbalanced by the effects of other factors.

It is very likely that conventionality is not something that can be easily changed because the amount of conventionality we have seems to be a basic aspect of our style of life. If that is the case this principle is probably more useful in determining our chances of marital satisfaction than in increasing or decreasing our chances of satisfaction. Because of this the only exercise that has been developed to help use this principle is an exercise to help determine conventionality. It is:

IDENTIFYING CONVENTIONALITY

Goal: To determine the extent to which individuals have the type of conventionality that seems to be associated with happiness in fairly traditional forms of marriage.

---

[7] This research is summarized and evaluated in Burgess et al. (1963, pp. 319ff.), Udry (1974, pp. 370–84), and Burr (1973, pp. 112–14).

Previous studies have found that certain personal characteristics tend to occur in "happy" marriages and that others tend to occur in "unhappy" marriages. The following list is selected from these research findings. Determine which characteristics are or are not typical of the other person and/or yourself. The more things that are typical of a person the greater the likelihood that that person will be satisfied with her or his marriage.

Both men and women

a. Are you cooperative with others.

b. Tend to be fairly but not overly conservative in religion, morals, and politics.

c. Have a fairly even and stable emotional tone.

d. Are not overly reactive to social opinion.

e. Are usually optimistic.

f. Are careful and saving with money.

g. Are fairly methodical and painstaking in work.

h. Have benevolent attitude toward inferiors and underprivileged.

i. Are not highly self-conscious.

j. Are comfortable in subordinate roles.

Women only

a. Do not look upon social relationships as rivalry situations.

b. Are not annoyed by advice from others.

c. Enjoy helping others.

d. Are more concerned with being liked than with being important.

e. Are not excessively romantic.

Men only

a. Tend to take responsibility.

b. Give close attention to detail.

c. Show attitude toward women that reflects equalitarian ideals.

d. Are self-confident.

e. Take pleasure in leading others.

SUMMARY

Folklore suggests that many factors are involved in determining when a person is ready for marriage. These factors include such things as whether the person has cut the apron strings, is able to be financially independent, is emotionally mature, is objective, has a realistic conception of marriage, has a reasonable self-evaluation, and is willing to accept the responsibility for mistakes. The scientific study of such factors, however, has so far turned up only a few general principles that can be viewed as tentatively valid. In addition all the research that has been done has been confined to traditional styles of marriage, and it is doubtful that many of these factors are important in some of the innovative styles of marriage, such as the Temporary, Two-Step, and Group forms. Five principles were discussed in this chapter, and there is considerable evidence that these principles are important in the fairly typical styles of married living. The most general idea was (1) the *Skill* principle, which asserts that the amount of skill a person has to behave in the ways normatively prescribed for a marital role influences her or his chances for marital satisfaction. Four less abstract principles were then deduced from this generalization, and these were (2) the *Age at Marriage* principle, which states that age at marriage is positively and curvilinearly related to a person's chances for a happy marriage; (3) the *Education* principle, which states that education is positively related to chances for marital satisfaction; (4) the *Desire*

Figure 9–3

Causal model of the principles in Chapter 9

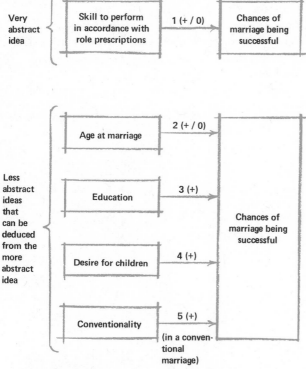

* The (+/0) symbol signifies that there is a positive relationship when variation occurs at low levels of the independent variable and no relationship when variation occurs at the higher levels of the independent variable.

for Children principle, which states that the degree to which people want children is positively associated with chances for marital satisfaction; and (5) the *Conventionality* principle, which states that the more conventional people are the greater their likelihood of finding marriage a pleasant experience. These five principles are diagramed in a causal model in Figure 9–3. The implications of each of these principles were discussed, and several exercises were provided which can be used to help apply the principles in our personal lives. It was suggested that some of the five principles are undoubtedly more relevant for some styles of marriage than for others, but that at present our only bases for assessing these differences are intuition and reason.

SUGGESTIONS FOR FURTHER STUDY

Blood, Robert O., Jr.   1969. *Marriage.* Rev. ed. Glencoe: Free Press, chap. 6.

Bowman, Henry A.   1970. *Marriage for Moderns.* 6th ed. New York: McGraw-Hill, chap. 5.

Fullerton, Gail Putney   1972. *Survival in Marriage.* New York: Holt, Rinehart and Winston, chaps. 1–3.

Landis, Judson, and Landis, Mary G.   1968. *Building a Successful Marriage.* 5th ed. Englewood Cliffs, N.J.: Prentice-Hall, chap. 8.

Mace, David R.   1972. *Getting Ready for Marriage.* New York: Abingdon Press.

10

Premarital sexual attitudes and behavior

THAT sexual attitudes and behavior are important in dating and marriage seems self-evident, if only because of the diversity and intensity of the sexual feelings we all have. Also, according to common report, the gratification of sexual desires is one of the most satisfying and pleasurable experiences known to human beings. In addition, sexual activity is essential for the physical continuation of the human race, and all societies have developed elaborate sets of moral beliefs about sexual behavior.[1] And last, but certainly not least, for many people sexually related behaviors are a means of developing, expressing, and fostering delicate and intimate love feelings as well as being a form of fun and recreation (Foote, 1954). Sexual attitudes and behaviors are now uniquely important in dating relationships because changes in social norms are creating uncertainty. Consequently many persons are unsure about what is being done, what should be done, and the consequences of participating or not participating in the many different aspects of sexuality. This chapter is designed to provide some information about this important part of life. The first section is an analysis of changes that seem to be occurring in contemporary sexual attitudes and behaviors, and this is followed by an analysis of what is currently known about the consequences of various premarital sexual behaviors. The last section of the chapter identifies several

---

[1] Discussions of reasons why it is essential for all societies to have some control over sexuality appear in Goode (1959) and Kirkendall (1961).

principles that can be used to help change attitudes about pre-marital sexuality.

TRENDS IN SEXUAL ATTITUDES AND BEHAVIOR

It is very difficult to determine what the trends are in sexual attitudes and behaviors in the contemporary American society. Dozens of research studies have tried to investigate these trends, but they have used different methods of gathering data, have asked different questions, and have sampled very different populations. And, to complicate the issues still further, premarital sexual behavior is closely related to several other variables, such as age and how close a person is to getting married, and this makes it still more difficult to determine what the trends are. The older a single person is the greater the likelihood that the person will have engaged in premarital coitus, and the closer people are to being married the greater the likelihood that they will have engaged in coitus. These complications mean that the conclusions drawn here or elsewhere about sexual trends should be viewed as tentative estimates that are only partially documented.

Reiss (1960, 1967), Bell (1966), and others have persuasively argued that there have been substantial changes in *attitudes* toward sex and in willingness to talk about sexual issues. They contend that the major attitudinal change has been a decrease in the proportion of individuals who subscribe to a "double standard" of sexual morality and an increase in the proportion who subscribe to a "permissiveness with affection" standard. The double standard is the belief that it is acceptable for men to be permissive, but not for women, and the permissiveness with affection standard is the belief that premarital sexual intercourse is acceptable for both men and women, provided that there is a meaningful affectional tie between the two individuals. It is difficult to identify a particular time when these attitudinal changes have or have not occurred, but it is likely that the changes took place gradually during the first six decades of the 20th century and that there have been substantial changes in recent years. Tables 10–1 and 10–2 document some of the recent changes.

The best available evidence indicates that changes in sexual *behavior* occurred during two different periods in the 20th century. The first period was the first two decades of the century, and the second period was the late 60s and early 70s. The evidence generally used to document that a change took place in the early 1900s is presented in Table 10–3. These data were gathered from a sample of 792 individuals in California in the middle 1930s, and they show that persons who were born after 1900 experienced substantially

Table 10–1

Percentage of white men and women in the United States who believe that premarital relations are not wrong, 1969 and 1972

	1969		1972	
Age	Men	Women	Men	Women
Under 30............ ..	48	27	65	42
30–44..................	26	13	45	29
45 and over...........	12	10	21	12
Total.................	23	14	37	23

Source: Udry (1974, p. 108).

more premarital sexual coitus than persons born earlier. The table provides some evidence of a change in sexual behavior, but there are several reasons why we should be tentative about viewing it as conclusive proof of a change. It may be that the subjects who were born before 1900 were more reluctant to admit their sexual activity. The fairly repressive attitudes about sex that existed until very recently, and the fact that the older subjects were in the process of raising children, could have had the effect of creating more distortion in their answers than in the answers of the younger subjects.

Table 10–2

Percentage of students at four different points of time checking each of four statements representing attitudes on premarital sex standards

Approved standard	Cornell 1940	11 colleges 1952	18 colleges 1967	2 colleges 1971
		Men		
	(N = 73)	(N = 1,056)	(N = 1,005)	(N = 63)
Sexual relations:				
For both...............	15%	20%	47%	70%
None for either..........	49	52	24	13
For men only...........	23	12	8	1
For engaged				
persons only........	11	16	22	16
		Women		
	(N = 100)	(N = 1,944)	(N = 2,184)	(N = 135)
Sexual relations:				
For both...............	6%	5%	21%	59%
None for either..........	76	65	39	15
For men only...........	11	23	17	7
For engaged				
persons only........	6	7	23	19

Source: Landis and Landis (1973, p. 148).

Table 10–3

Premarital sex experience in relation to date of birth (Terman subjects)

Premarital sex experience	Before 1890 (N = 174)	1890–99 (N = 291)	1900–1909 (N = 273)	1910 or later (N = 22)
Husbands				
None	50.6%	41.9%	32.6%	13.6%
Spouse only	4.6	7.6	17.2	31.9
Spouse and others	9.2	23.0	33.7	40.9
Others only	35.6	27.5	16.5	13.6
Total	100.0%	100.0%	100.0%	100.0%
Wives				
None	86.5%	74.0%	51.2%	31.7%
Spouse only	8.7	17.7	32.7	45.0
Spouse and others	2.9	5.8	14.0	20.0
Others only	1.9	2.5	2.1	3.3
Total	100.0%	100.0%	100.0%	100.0%

Source: Reproduced from Burgess and Wallin (1953, p. 324). They adapted the table from Terman (1938).

Table 10–4 summarizes the findings from a number of studies that appeared between 1910 and 1972. The table shows that there was considerable variety from study to study during the middle part of the 20th century, but that there was no pattern of change from the 1920s to the late 1960s. Two longitudinal studies (Bell and Chaskes, 1970; Christensen and Gregg, 1970) that investigated similar samples in the 1950s and 1960s, however, found a pattern of change among women, namely, that women were participating in premarital sexual intercourse more extensively. Bell and Chaskes conclude that "the commitment of engagement has become a less important condition for many coeds engaging in premarital coitus" (1970, p. 84). Also, studies appearing in the 70s (Bauman and Wilson, 1973) seem to show that the late 60s and 70s were a period in which a larger percentage of women were participating in premarital sexual intercourse.

In attempting to assess trends it is important to realize that when changes do occur they occur at different rates in different parts of society, and that even when a substantial part of society is involved in a change some segments are not involved and some segments may actually be experiencing a change in the opposite direction (Goode, 1963, chap. 3). During the mid-20th century the predominant segments of American society apparently experienced a decrease in taboos about sex and an increase in the freedom to talk about sex openly. In addition, the sexual behavior of women has apparently been liberalized among most groups in the contemporary society. It is likely, however, that in some subcultural groups both women and men were very permissive before the general liberalization be-

Table 10-4

Percentage of college-age subjects in United States who reported they had ever participated in premarital sexual intercourse

Author	Date of publication	Males	Females
Eastman................................	1972	55	49
Fujital...................................	1971	46	31
Christensen and Gregg.................	1970	50	34
Robinson...............................	1970	65	37
Luckey and Nass......................	1969	58	43
Peretti.................................	1969	48	21
Katz....................................	1968	36	23
Packard................................	1968	57	43
Burr, Lewis...........................	1967	54	27
Elias...................................	1967	72	53
Freedman.............................	1967		22
Kaats and Davis.......................	1967	60	41
Robinson..............................	1965	65	29
Ehrmann...............................	1959	65	13
Christensen and Gregg.................	1958	51	21
Reevy..................................	1954		7
Burgess and Wallin....................	1953	68	47
Landis and Landis.....................	1953	41	9
Gilbert.................................	1951	56	25
Ross....................................	1950	51	
Finger..................................	1947	45	
Hohman and Schaffner.................	1947	68	
Porterfield and Salley..................	1946	32	9
Landis.................................	1940		23
Bromley and Britten...................	1938	52	25
Peterson...............................	1938	55	
Terman................................	1938	61	37
Dickinson and Beam...................	1934		12
Davis..................................	1929		11
Hamilton...............................	1929	54	35
Peck and Wells........................	1925	35	
Peck and Wells........................	1923	35	
Exner..................................	1915	36	

gan and that, on the other hand, in other subcultural groups there has been little, if any, change in sexual attitudes and behavior.

THE EFFECTS OF PREMARITAL SEXUAL BEHAVIOR

"Trends" in sexual attitudes and behavior are of historical interest, but the consequences of participating or not participating in various premarital sexual behaviors are a more weighty issue for most readers of this book. This issue includes not only the consequences of sexual coitus but also the consequences of less intimate sexual behavior, such as necking and petting, and the consequences of not engaging in any premarital erotic behavior. Unfortunately the social sciences have not yet discovered a large number of general principles that can be applied to these matters, but one generalization is fairly well documented, and it can be applied here. The generalization deals with the amount sexual behavior is congruent or incongruent with the social norms in a culture and with the personal norms of individuals.

Deviation
from norms

The best current research evidence (Christensen, 1969) indicates that the effects of premarital sexual behaviors, such as petting or sexual intercourse, are at least partly dependent on how much these behaviors are consistent with or deviate from social "norms." Norms were defined in Chapter 4 as beliefs about what people should do or not do in various social situations. In the context of the present discussion, norms are beliefs about whether people should or should not engage in sexual behaviors such as kissing, necking, or coitus prior to marriage. The conclusion that emerges from the research indicates that when individuals live in a culture in which it is believed that it is permissible or desirable for unmarried persons to participate in sexual behaviors prior to marriage these experiences seem to have positive effects, such as helping young couples learn how to relate to and interact with each other. However, when individuals live in cultures in which the accepted beliefs are that such behaviors should be avoided, the same behaviors have different consequences. They tend to produce guilt, frustration, and anxiety, and they seem to interfere with meaningful interpersonal relationships.

Some of the scientific evidence supporting this generalization comes from anthropologists who have described isolated island cultures, such as those of Samoa and New Guinea (Mead, 1935). These anthropologists have documented that where the predominant social norms encourage such premarital sexual activity as petting and coitus, the individuals who do not participate tend to experience greater guilt, frustration, and social isolation.

The most convincing evidence for this generalization, however, is provided by a series of studies in which Christensen (1963, 1969) and his colleagues investigated the correlates of sexual behaviors in three different cultures. They gathered data from samples in three societies that differed markedly in their norms about premarital sexual behavior. One of the societies was fairly permissive in that the vast majority of individuals believed that premarital coitus was permissible. The second society was fairly restrictive in that the predominant belief was that moderately intimate sexual behaviors, such as petting, should be avoided before marriage and that coitus prior to marriage was a serious moral impropriety. The third society was intermediate between the other two in sexual permissiveness. It was found that behavior tended to conform to the normative expectations in that the behavior of the sample in the permissive society was the most permissive and that of the sample in the restrictive society was the least permissive. However, the finding that is most relevant in the present context is that the same sexual behaviors seemed to have different effects in the three cultures. When premarital coitus occurred there was the least guilt and disruption of the courtship relationship in the permissive culture and the most in the restrictive culture, and when pregnancy was discovered the tendency to hurry weddings was greatest in the restrictive culture and least in the permissive culture. Also, the association between premarital pregnancy and later divorce was highest in the restrictive culture and lowest in the permissive culture. These studies thus seem to justify Christensen's conclusion that the "negative consequences of premarital coitus adhere, not so much to the act itself, but to how the act lines up or fails to line up with the standards held" (1969, p. 218). This idea can be stated in the way most of the principles are stated in this volume:

> THE SEXUAL NORMS PRINCIPLE: The more that social or personal norms proscribe premarital sexual behaviors the greater the negative consequences when these behaviors occur, and vice versa.

It is possible and it is probably useful to identify how this hypothesis is a specific case of a more abstract and inclusive generalization. The more general hypothesis is the idea from symbolic interaction theory (Rose, 1962; Stryker, 1964) that the meaning given to something influences the effect that "something" has on other things. This very general hypothesis can be tied to the Sexual Norms principle by pointing out that the Sexual Norms principle deals with the *meaning* of sexual behavior rather than with the sexual behavior itself because it asserts that the meaning of the behavior, in terms of how congruent it is with normative beliefs, has a systematic effect on the consequences of the behavior. It may be that the behavior itself *also* has certain systematic effects, and one of them will be discussed later in this chapter, but the point here is that the meaning given to a behavior has some influence on the effects of the behavior.

The Sexual Norms principle has a number of practical implications. One of them is that, if this idea is valid, a number of individuals in the contemporary American society will experience negative consequences, such as guilt, anxiety and perhaps some disruption in their later marital relationship, if they participate in highly intimate sexual activities before marriage. Others, however, will not experience adverse negative effects from exactly the same behaviors. To complicate matters even more, however, there are many who are involved in more than one subcultural group, and the norms are different in the different groups. For example, some college students grow up in a restrictive setting in which they learn to believe that such premarital intimacies as petting and coitus are wrong, but then they leave their parental home to enter a different subcultural group that defines the same behaviors as desirable. These individuals undoubtedly experience some conflict in their beliefs and experience some frustration and some satisfaction no matter what they decide to do—unless they reject the values and norms of one of the groups. People also experience conflict when they change from one to another subcultural group several times. For example, it is not unusual for college students to start out in a restrictive culture, then become involved in a permissive university culture, and then move back to a restrictive culture after leaving college. These individuals may experience different consequences at different times. For example, they may experience positive consequences from sexual behaviors while at college and negative consequences from the same sexual behaviors later when they define the behaviors differently.

Two things can be done to decrease the undesirable consequences of premarital sexual behaviors when an individual participates in sexual activities proscribed by his or her culture. One alternative is to change one's behavior so that it conforms to the norms, and the other is to change personal norms so that they conform to the behavior. Considerable research indicates that when individuals are in this type of situation they do one of these two things to resolve their guilt (Heider, 1958). There are several complications however, with both alternatives. One problem when trying to change one's behavior to conform to the restrictive norms is that sexual activity is so pleasurable that once an individual begins experiencing the pleasures of the more intimate forms of sexual activity it is extremely difficult to forgo them. It would take rather drastic changes in setting and rather high amounts of self-discipline to pursue this alternative.

A problem with the other alternative is that frequently personal norms are not easily changed. Often these norms are intricately tied to other beliefs or values, and it is not possible to change the sexual beliefs independently of those other beliefs. This is especially the case where the sexual norms are based on a philosophy of life that considers sexual proscriptions to be of divine origin. In the Judaic-Christian tradition there is a clearly defined proscriptive philosophy, but the reasons for it are obscure. The best that most people can do when they are asked why their religion or God wants them to be sexually restrictive is to observe that it is a "commandment." Occasionally people think up "reasons" for the commandment, but these are only guesses. When an individual adopts an orthodox view of Christian ethics it is extremely difficult to superimpose a permissive sexual ethic on that view, and the person is left with such alternatives as being internally inconsistent, accepting part but not all of the Christian ethic, or changing his or her sexual beliefs. If a person rejects traditional Christianity it is then possible to adopt a different philosophy of life and correspondingly different beliefs about sexual behavior, and very large segments of the American population seem to be choosing this alternative.

Numerous studies have attempted to determine whether relationships exist between coital experience before marriage and various socially important variables in the American culture. Unfortunately these studies have not differentiated between the normative differences in the subcultural groups that were studied, so the findings must be interpreted very cautiously. There has, however, been enough research to permit a few generalizations about the relationship premarital coital experience currently has with (1) marital satisfaction, (2) the probability of divorce, (3) the proportion of time the wife experiences orgasm, and (4) sexual adjustment in at least some segments of the American culture.

Marital satisfaction.   Several research studies have investigated the relationship between premarital coitus and marital satisfaction. It should be noted, however, that the measure of marital satisfaction that was used was designed to measure satisfaction with a "traditional" form of marriage, and hence the findings from this research can only be safely generalized to very conventional styles of marriage. It is thus very unlikely that the conclusions that emerge from this research are valid in such innovative styles of marriage as Swinging and Open marriage. All of the research studies that have tested this relationship (Terman, 1938; Burgess and Cottrell, 1939; Burgess and Wallin, 1953; King, 1951, 1952) have found that a slightly larger proportion of virginal individuals were satisfied with their marriages and a slightly larger proportion of nonvirginal individuals were dissatisfied with their marriages. These findings must, however, be interpreted with two cautions. One is that the differences were very small, indicating that if virginality actually does make any difference it is a very minor factor. The second caution is that the data in all but one of these studies were gathered by having

The effects of premarital coitus in the American society

the subjects indicate whether they had participated in premarital coitus and how satisfied they were with their marriages. Thus, it may be that the "halo effect" operated and that some people tended to give the most socially desirable answers and indicated that they did not participate in premarital coitus and were, of course, happy in their marriages. Nevertheless, the available research has found a weak but positive relationship between premarital virginity and marital satisfaction—in Traditional forms of marriage.

Marital stability. Only one study is known that has investigated the relationship between premarital sexual coitus and the probability of divorce, and this was Locke's (1951) comparison of a divorced sample with a happily married sample. Locke found slightly higher rates of premarital coitus among the divorced group, suggesting that there is a weak but inverse relationship between virginity and the probability of divorce. He, too, did not take into account any differences in preferred styles of life, and his finding may not occur in contemporary society.

Proportion of time wife experiences orgasm. Kinsey (1948, p. 385) discovered that nonvirginal wives experience sexual orgasm (a climax) a higher proportion of the time than virginal wives. It is not possible, however, to determine from Kinsey's data why this relationship appears. Some scholars have suggested that women with high sex drive tend to participate in coitus premaritally and that their higher sex drive also tends to create higher frequencies of marital orgasm. On the other hand, it may be that premarital sexual experience somehow influences marital sexual experience, with the premarital experience providing skills or knowledge that influence the marital orgasm rate. Whatever the reason, the available data suggest that there is an inverse relationship between virginity and the frequency of orgasm in marriage.

Sex adjustment. It is possible to differentiate between the frequency of orgasm and overall satisfaction with the sexual aspect of marriage. It is useful to make this distinction because some women experience orgasm frequently but are not satisfied with their marital sex life while other women experience orgasm rarely, if ever, but are satisfied with the sexual aspect of their marriage. Researchers who have made this distinction have tried to determine whether premarital coital experience is related to sexual adjustment in marriage, and the findings differ according to how long the couple have been married. There is some evidence that during the first weeks of marriage premaritally experienced women are more satisfied with their sex life than are inexperienced women. Kanin and Howard's (1958) data—reproduced in Table 10–5—provide the best evidence of this relationship. As can be seen in that table, virginal wives evaluated their experience less favorably than did nonvirginal wives.

Table 10–5

Wedding night and honeymoon sexual satisfaction of virgin and experienced brides

Evaluation of intercourse	Virgin brides		Experienced brides	
	Wedding night	After two weeks	Wedding night	After two weeks
Very satisfying......................	18%	34%	33%	56%
Satisfying...........................	29	42	39	36
Not satisfying.......................	49	24	23	8
Very unsatisfying...................	4	0	5	0
Total...........................	100%	100%	100%	100%
Number of cases..................	100	100	77	77

Source: Adapted from Kanin and Howard (1958).

However, after the initial transition into marriage the difference between virginal and nonvirginal wives tends to disappear. The two studies that provide data about this (Kinsey, 1948; Terman, 1939) found no relationship between virginity and overall sexual adjustment. The conclusions that thus seem to emerge are that virginity is inversely related to sexual adjustment during the initial weeks and perhaps months of marriage, but that after a period of time the virginal group tends to become as well adjusted sexually as the nonvirginal group.

CHANGING ATTITUDES ABOUT PREMARITAL SEXUAL BEHAVIOR

Occasionally people want to change their attitudes or feelings about premarital sex, and there are three situations in which this occurs fairly frequently. These are: (1) when individuals want to have more permissive attitudes; (2) when individuals want to become less permissive; and (3) when individuals have conflicting or ambivalent feelings about sexual permissiveness and want to eliminate the incongruence. These three situations are illustrated by the following comments of college students.

I'm beginning to believe that the ideas I've been taught about sex and . . . were just as wrong as what I was taught about our so-called democratic processes, the military, and the business world. And it's not as though the old ideas were good for an earlier generation and inappropriate now. They were as bad then as they are now. . . .

Now that I've found Christ, I want to live the way He wants me to. I've always tried to do what seemed right at the time, but I realize now that a lot of the things I was doing like . . . sex with a lot of different girls and . . . were really wrong. I'm trying to repent in every way and live every day for my Savior. It's hard in some ways to change overnight, and I still have lots to do, but . . .

I grew up in a strict Catholic home, and I grew up with the feeling that sex outside of marriage was bad. My folks never even said the word *sex*—not once, but I knew how they felt about it and we heard plenty about it at school. . . . There's more to it than that, though. Most of my friends have, uh, gone all the way, and some of them stay weekends with boys all the time. We've talked about it at the dorm, and I'm the most old-fashioned one there. . . . I guess what this all means is that I'm still not sure what I believe about sex before marriage. I don't have any arguments against what most of the kids at school say, but there is something inside me that keeps holding me back.

The modern social sciences are only beginning to unravel the very complex business of changing sexual attitudes and behaviors, but several principles have been discovered that seem to be useful. Three of these will be discussed here, and they are called the *Salience, Responsibility,* and *Profit from Sex* principles.

Salience of reference groups

Social psychologists discovered in the 1920s and 1930s that the beliefs people have are highly influenced by the individuals and groups with whom they interact. One scholar (Mead, 1934) used the terms *significant other* and *generalized other* to refer to the individuals who influence us the most. Later Hyman (1942) coined the term *reference group,* and since then that term has been used to describe the groups we use as frames of reference or comparison points in forming and changing our attitudes or beliefs. Gradually a large body of research and theory has emerged, and this has come to be known as *reference group theory.* Most of the research and most of the ideas in this theory are not relevant for the issues discussed in this chapter, but one highly relevant generalization is:

THE SALIENCE PRINCIPLE: The greater the salience of a group to an individual the more the norms of that group are internalized by that individual, and vice versa.

The two variables in this generalization are the salience of a group and the amount that norms are internalized. The salience of a group refers to how important, significant, or valuable a group is, or how much the group tends to be relevant, noticeable, conspicuous, or prominent relative to other groups. We all belong to many different groups, and these range in salience from groups that are transient and unimportant (such as a group waiting to board a bus) to groups that are intimate, important, and long-term relationship (such as a group of very close friends). This is a continuous variable, as shown below. Reference groups are usually groups

Salience of a group

Very low   Low   Moderate   High   Very high

whose acceptance and approval is desired, but in some circumstances we are influenced by groups we dislike or oppose. When this occurs we are usually motivated to adopt attitudes opposite to those of the group, and the group is called a negative reference group (Secord and Backman, 1974, p. 144). The present discussion focuses only on ways that positive reference groups influence us.

The internalization of norms refers to the amount we personally adopt the norms of a group. Norms, it will be recalled from earlier chapters, are beliefs about how we ought to act or not act in various social situations. This too is a continuous variable, as shown below. A variety of other terms have been used to describe this same process, and these include *absorbing, modeling, interiorizing,* and *identifying.*

Amount norms
of a group are internalized

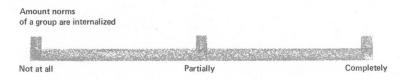

Not at all   Partially   Completely

A large body of research supports the Salience principle, as illustrated with studies by Festinger (1954), Kelley (1955), and Charters and Newcomb (1958). Sherif and his colleagues (1965, 1967) have provided excellent reviews of this research, and it can be concluded from these reviews that the Salience principle deserves considerable confidence. It should also be pointed out that there is some research evidence that the Salience principle operates whether or not we are aware of the influence of the group we associate with (Siegel and Siegel, 1957).

The Salience principle can be used in many dating and marital situations. For example, it could be used when two spouses differ in their role expectations, and they want one or both to change those expectations. The principle suggests that *if* they could find ways to change the salience of the reference groups that support some of their views they would probably change those views. In the present context, however, the central concern is how to use this principle to change beliefs about premarital sexual permissiveness, and the principle is used here by making two logical deductions from it. One deduction is that, if the Salience principle is valid, and if reference groups differ in their norms about sexual permissiveness, it follows that changes in the salience of reference groups which have high premarital sexual permissiveness are positively related to the permissiveness of an individual's premarital sexual norms. Since the term *premarital sexual permissiveness* (Reiss, 1967, 1974) has been widely used to refer to the permissiveness of these norms, that term is used here. It should be kept in mind, however, that it is normative *beliefs* rather than *behaviors* that are denoted by this term. The second deduction is that, if the same two assumptions hold, it can be concluded that changes in the salience of reference groups that have low premarital sexual permissiveness are positively related to an individual's premarital sexual permissiveness. These two deductions from the Salience principle could be called less general principles, but no label is provided for them here. The dotted lines in Figure 10–1 show the connection between the salience principle and the two deductions, and the arrows in that figure show how the three causal processes operate.

Figure 10–1

Two deductions from the Salience principle

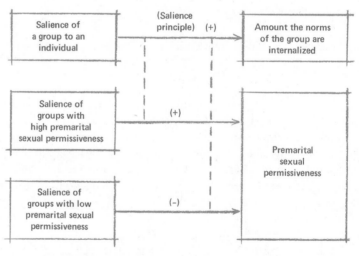

These two deductions are very similar to principles 17 and 18 in Reiss and Miller's (1974) autonomy theory of sexual permissiveness. The only differences are that the ideas are integrated here with reference theory and that they are stated here in a slightly more abstract or general form than Reiss and Miller state them. Thus, the research on which Reiss and Miller (1974, pp. 83–84) base their generalizations should be regarded as additional evidence that the ideas discussed here are valid.

We would want to use these ideas only when we want to change some of our beliefs, and we need to first determine how we would like our attitudes or beliefs to be different. Do we want to become more or less permissive than we have been, or do we want to increase or decrease the conflict or ambivalence we have about premarital sexuality? Second, after determining what kinds of changes we want to make, we need to identify what effects different reference groups are currently having on us and what effects these groups would probably have on us if they were to be more or less salient. Then, finally, we need to determine how we could actually do something about the salience of various groups. Since these three processes are fairly abstract, it is probably useful to be more specific. This can be done by applying the processes to one of the situations identified earlier in the chapter. One situation was:

I'm beginning to believe that the ideas I've been taught about sex and . . . were just as wrong as what I was taught about our so-called democratic processes, the military, and the business world. And it's not as though the old ideas were good for an earlier generation and inappropriate now. They were as bad then as they are now. . . .

This comment was made by a male student in one of the author's classes who seemed to be struggling with his identity in a number of ways.[2] He was reared in a small town in Oregon, and apparently his family had been fairly conservative in many ways. He had come to an urban university during the late 1960s during the height of the campus unrest of that period and was being exposed to a radically different view of the world. He was experiencing a new sexual freedom and a variety of other new freedoms, and was trying very hard to think through what he ought to believe about sexual interaction. It seemed to the author that he was gradually becoming convinced that sexual intercourse before and outside of marriage was morally appropriate. If this was what he was actually coming to believe he was completing the first of the three steps identified in the previous paragraph because he was trying to decide what changes he wanted to make in his beliefs about sexuality. The second step would be for him to try to identify how a variety of reference groups were influencing him. He was being financially supported by his parents,

---

[2] The student gave the author permission to discuss this if his anonymity were protected.

and the frequency with which he talked about them indicated that his parents were a salient reference group for him. He was also studying in a department in which several of the "opinion leaders" were members of the New Left who were actively attempting to liberalize campus life. His involvement with that student group indicated that they were also a salient reference group, and that their sexual norms were different from the norms the student's parents seemed to have. These two observations indicate something about how he was being influenced by reference groups. He was experiencing conflicting pressures about his premarital sexual attitudes, and, if the Salience principle is valid, if he were to increase the amount he used his peers as references he would undoubtedly become more permissive, while, on the other hand, if he were to increase the salience of his parental family he would become more restrictive.

This student implemented the Salience principle in this situation, even though he probably did not do it consciously. During the year the writer knew him his visits to his parents dropped from weekly to every several months, and he seldom wrote or telephoned them during the last part of the year. His clothing and hairstyle became more like those of the other students, and he spent an increasing amount of time with fellow students. Thus, this student proceeded through at least two of the three processes involved in using the Salience principle. He went through the first step of trying to determine what he wanted to believe when he became aware of ambivalence and conflict in his attitudes. It was not possible to determine whether he used the second step of evaluating what the effects of his reference groups were and how these effects would be different if his relationships were different. He did, however, use the third process of changing the salience of at least two of his reference groups—his parents and his fellow students. It should probably also be pointed out that if this same student had decided that he wished to retain a restrictive sexual ethic he probably could have also used the Salience principle to help him accomplish that goal. He could have increased his interaction with and involvement with social groups such as conservative religious groups on campus or his parental family.

It is likely that the most difficult and challenging process in using the Salience principle is finding ways to change the importance of various reference groups, but unfortunately the social sciences have little to suggest at the present time. Some of the writer's students, however, have tried a variety of strategies, and listing some of these would at least provide some suggestions. Thus, several specific ways of behaving are identified in the following exercise, and, hopefully, readers can find additional strategies that are useful for them.

CHANGING THE SALIENCE OF GROUPS

Goal: To find new ways to change the influence that reference groups have on your premarital sexual attitudes.

1. First, write down on a piece of paper how you would like your attitudes or beliefs about premarital sexual permissiveness to change in the near future. Be as specific as possible in your descriptions of these changes. (If you do not wish to change any of your beliefs about premarital sexuality, this exercise is not relevant for you.)

2. Identify the groups of individuals who are most important to you. Two ways to do this are: (1) to identify the people you turn to when you are upset, troubled, or trying to figure something out, and (2) to identify the people whose opinions you tend to respect highly.

3. Describe how each of these groups influences your attitudes toward premarital sexuality. If none of these groups influence you toward the goals you identified in step 1, try to identify several groups you could interact with who would.

4. Identify and implement several specific things you could do either to decrease the importance of groups who would not exert an influence toward your goals or to increase the importance of groups who would exert an influence toward your goals. Some of the following alternatives may be possible, and you can probably think of others that would also be useful.

Increasing salience

a. Change residence so it is close to group.
b. Increase the amount of time you spend in informal social contact.
c. Find new books that are written "for" a group and read them.
d. Spend considerable time talking with people about "why" they believe the things they do.
e. Change such items of appearance as clothes, makeup, and patterns of grooming to conform to the group you wish to emulate.

Decreasing salience

a. Move away from a person or a group.
b. Read literature that is written against the point of view represented by the group.
c. Decrease interaction with the group whenever possible.

(You will note that attitudes toward sexuality do not exist in a social vacuum, and you will probably also find that other attitudes, beliefs, and values also change as you change your reference relationships.)

Responsibil-
ity for family
members

A number of other principles in the Reiss (1967) and Reiss and Miller (1974) autonomy theory of sexual permissiveness are very useful in understanding the antecedents of variation in sexual permissiveness. Most of the ideas in that theory, however, are not relevant in the present context because they do not identify factors that individuals can manipulate or change in their own life situations. There is, however, one principle that seems to have relevance for readers of this book, and that is:

THE RESPONSIBILITY PRINCIPLE: The greater the responsibility one has for other family members the less one's premarital sexual permissiveness, and vice versa.

The independent variable in this generalization refers to how much a person is expected to take care of or be accountable for someone else in a family. Parents of small children have high levels of responsibility, and single adults who live alone usually have little responsibility. This is apparently a continuous variable ranging from no responsibility to a high amount, as shown below.

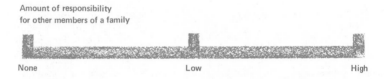

Amount of responsibility
for other members of a family

None   Low   High

Only a small amount of research has been conducted that is relevant for this principle, and Reiss and Miller's review of this research states that the evidence is not conclusive (1974, p. 47). Hatch's (1973) later study, however, provided additional evidence that the principle is valid. Thus, there is some reason to believe that this principle is valid, but the level of proof is low.

The Responsibility principle could be applied by college students in several ways. Those of us who wish to increase our permissiveness can take steps to minimize our responsibility for other members of our parents' family and avoid taking on new responsibilities. This could be done by moving away from home while at college and decreasing our interaction with younger siblings, or at least decreasing our sense of being responsible for them. Such changes are frequently acceptable to the other members of families, and this may be because they can be a part of the process of getting out on one's own and becoming independent. Those of us who wish to decrease our permissiveness could make the opposite changes by doing such things as doing more to help younger siblings cope with the many problems they encounter, providing more companionship for aging members of a family, and "helping" members of our family in various other ways.

The Profit from Sex principle is slightly different from the two previous principles because it deals with a different dependent variable. It deals with a method of increasing or decreasing the intensity of an individual's sexual motivation, stimulation, or drive. This principle is included because there is a great deal of evidence that it is valid, and because a number of students in the author's marriage classes have been genuinely interested in what they could do to become either more or less interested in sex. The generalization is:

Profit from sexual stimuli

THE PROFIT FROM SEX PRINCIPLE: The greater the profit from sexual stimulation the greater the intensity of sexual motivation, and vice versa.

The independent variable in this generalization is the amount of profit that is received from sexual stimulation. The "profit" factor was discussed in detail on page 217, where it was defined as the balance of rewards and costs that an individual experiences from something. In the present context it is the profit received from sexual stimulation, and this could involve such rewards as excitement and thrill, sensual pleasure, feelings of closeness and love, and an enhancement of interpersonal relationships. The costs that could be incurred from sexual stimulation include feelings of guilt, embarrassment, anxiety, lowered self-esteem, and, in some situations, interference with interpersonal relationships. The profits and costs are undoubtedly different for people who have been reared in different circumstances, and they are probably different from one situation to another. This reward/cost ratio can be put on a continuum in the following way:

Profit from sexual stimulation

| Highly costly | Slightly more costly than rewarding | Equal costs and rewards | Slightly more rewarding than costly | Highly rewarding |

The dependent variable in the Profit from Sex principle is the intensity of sexual motivation, and this refers to the overall strength of a person's sexual drive or interest rather than to the person's level of erotic arousal at a particular time. Some people are highly interested in sexual stimulation, and others are much less interested. This too can be diagramed as a continuous variable.

Intensity of sexual motivation

Very low   Low   Moderate   High   Very high

The Profit from Sex principle can be deduced from several theories in the social sciences, and a vast amount of research supports these theories. Exchange theory (Homans, 1961; Simpson, 1968) is one perspective that can be used to derive this principle, since a basic postulate in exchange theory is the idea that rewards and costs (profit) influence the amount people are motivated to do anything. Another theoretical perspective from which this principle can be deduced is behaviorism (Skinner, 1953), since this idea is also a basic postulate in that school of thought. Behaviorists usually prefer the term *reinforcement* rather than the term *reward,* and they are less interested in the person's perception of the situation and more interested in overt behavior, but the idea is almost identical. Hardy's (1964) appetitional theory of sexual motivation is another theoretical perspective which includes the Profit from Sex principle. Thus, the Profit from Sex principle is highly substantiated by theory and research, and it is therefore a principle in which we can have great confidence.

The Profit from Sex principle can probably be used in many premarital and marital situations, and the four following situations illustrate the variety of circumstances in which it is applicable. First, some of us may be more reluctant to become sexually aroused or to participate in even moderately erotic activities than we would like to be, and we may wish to free ourselves from these inhibitions. Second, others of us may be fairly free and uninhibited about sexuality, but wish to increase our sexual motivation still further. Third, some of us may be very highly motivated to participate in intimate erotic activities, but also believe that it would be morally inappropriate to do so in our present situations and think that the best way to cope with this dilemma would be to decrease our sexual drive. And, finally, others of us may be in marital situations or other relationships in which we believe that we should participate in coitus, and realize that we would have a more satisfying total relationship if slight changes could be made in one or both individuals' desire to participate or not participate in intimate sexual interaction. Most of us in these or similar situations could probably use the Profit from Sex principle to help us attain our goals. We must realize, however, that the profit we receive from sexual stimulation is only one of many factors that influence our sexual motivation, and in many situations it may have little effect on sexual motivation.

Those of us who wish to increase the intensity of our sexual motivation will want to find ways to increase the reward or pleasure that accompanies our sexual stimulation and to decrease the costs or punishments that result from or accompany sexual excitement. Since each of us is uniquely different from anyone else it is not possible to describe behaviors, situations, or activities which would accomplish this for everyone. We would each need to learn which sexual activities give us pleasure or displeasure and then participate in the activities which give us pleasure while avoiding the activities which give us displeasure. Hopefully, we will be able to gradually increase the number of things that give us pleasure. Those of us who wish to decrease the intensity of our sexual motivation need to do just the opposite. We need to participate less in the sexual activities we find highly pleasurable.

There are a variety of forms of sexual participation that can be either increased or decreased—depending on what we want to accomplish. We can see more or fewer highly erotic films or read more or less erotic literature. We can increase or decrease the amount of time we spend enjoying sensual pleasures with our own bodies through caressing, holding, fondling, or stimulating erogenous parts of our bodies, such as our genitals, the inside of our thighs, or our breasts. We can increase or decrease the amount of time we spend in interpersonal lovemaking, such as holding hands, caressing, embracing, necking, and petting. We can alter the decor of part or all of our living quarters to make them more or less erotic. We can increase or decrease the emphasis we give to nonerotic aspects of life and the pleasure we receive from them. For example, intellectual, athletic, artistic, or economic activities can be immensely rewarding, and they can occupy our concerns too little or too much—again, depending on our goals. The following exercise is designed to help us think through whether we would like to change our sexual motivation, and then, if we want to make any changes, to devise a strategy for making those changes.

SEXUAL MOTIVATION

Goal: To determine whether you wish to change your sexual motivation and, if changes are desired, to make them.

1. Evaluate how satisfied you are with the current level of your sexual motivation. Is your sexual motivation too high, about right, or too low? If you are satisfied with your current sexual motivation you have finished this exercise. If you are not satisfied, go to the other steps.

2. Write a description of (a) your current sexual motivation and (b) what you would like your sexual motivation to be if you could change it.

3. Review very carefully the paragraph preceding this exercise to identify several parts of your life that could be altered to change the "profit from sexual stimulation." Then spend some time trying to identify other parts of your life which you could change which might influence your profit. List these on a piece of paper, and then use the "Action Plan" outline on pages 164–65 to develop and carry out a program of gradually changing your profit from sexual stimulation.

SUMMARY

The first section of this chapter discussed the changes regarding premarital sexual attitudes and behavior that are occurring in the contemporary American society. The second section discussed the consequences of participating or not participating in erotic activities before marriage. The *Sexual Norms* principle was identified, and it is diagramed as the top arrow (1) in Figure 10–2. The last section of the chapter discussed several principles that deal with changing attitudes about premarital sexuality. The relatively abstract *Salience* principle (2) was discussed. That principle is also shown in Figure 10–2, with two deductions from it which show its relevance for premarital sexual attitudes. The *Responsibility* principle (3) identified another factor which influences the permissiveness of the individual's norms, and the *Profit from Sex* principle (4) identified one factor that influences the intensity of sexual motivation. Several ways to apply these principles were discussed.

Figure 10–2

Causal models of the principles in Chapter 10

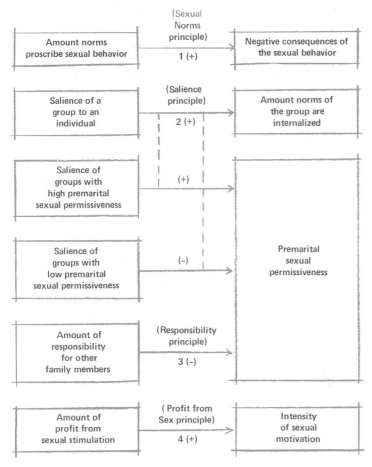

SUGGESTIONS FOR FURTHER STUDY

Bell, Robert R.   1966. *Premarital Sex in a Changing Society*. Englewood Cliffs, N.J.: Prentice-Hall.

Cannon, Kenneth and Long, Richard   1971. "Premarital Sexual Behavior in the Sixties." *Journal of Marriage and the Family* 33:36–49 (February).

Cox, Frank D.   1968. *Youth, Marriage, and the Seducing Society*. Dubuque, Iowa: Brown.

Crawley, Lawrence Q.; Malfetti, James L.; Stewart, Ernest I.; and Vas Dias, Nini   1964. *Reproduction, Sex, and Preparation for Marriage*. Englewood Cliffs, N.J.: Prentice-Hall.

Kirkendall, Lester A.   1961. *Premarital Intercourse and Interpersonal Relations*. New York: Julian Press.

Reiss, Ira C.   1960. *Premarital Sexual Standards in America*. New York: Free Press.

Stokes, Walter R.   1962. "Our Changing Sexual Ethics." *Marriage and Family Living*, 24:269–71 (August).

Vincent, Clark   1961. *Unmarried Mothers*. New York: Free Press.

11

Easing the transition into marriage

THERE ARE a number of times in life when we make large changes in our roles. For example, when we begin and graduate from school, begin to date, marry, become parents, and retire, we make major shifts in roles. Some of these transitions are fairly simple changes that are easily made. The transition, for example, into the role of automobile driver is usually an uncomplicated process of learning how to control a car, learning the laws that govern driving, and passing a driving test. It can be accomplished in a short period of time, and most of us accomplish it easily. Many of our role transitions, however, are more complex and involved and are difficult to make.

The transition into marriage is without question one of the more complex transitions people ever make. It is probably not as large a transition as the process of becoming a parent, but it is still sufficiently involved to be a challenge for all of us and an awesome ordeal for some of us. This chapter deals with the transition into marriage by applying a number of general principles about role transitions to the process of changing from a single to a married status. Most of these generalizations were developed initially in research about other role changes, such as becoming a student, adjusting to the birth of the first child, and retiring. The principles are sufficiently general to be relevant for the transition into marriage. The specific goals in the chapter are:

1. To describe four principles that identify factors that influence how easy or difficult it is to make role transitions.
2. To apply these principles to the transition from an unmarried to a married state.

3. To describe some learning experiences that can be used to increase the ability to use these principles.

ROLE TRANSITION PRINCIPLES

Prior learning

THE LEARNING ABOUT THE SPOUSE ROLE PRINCIPLE: The amount of prior learning about the spouse role influences the ease of making the transition into this role, and this is a positive, curvilinear relationship.[1]

The main idea in this generalization is that the ease of adjusting to a new role is partly determined by the amount an individual has previously learned about that role. This is a relatively simple and obvious idea, but it seems to make a great deal of difference when we actually start a new social position. The point can be illustrated by a person becoming a driver of an automobile. If we have not previously learned such things as how to signal, what to do to stop the car, or which way to watch when the car is moving, we will have more than a little difficulty if we are suddenly put in a situation where we have to drive a car. If, on the other hand, we have experienced such prior learning as being able to observe other drivers for some time, occasionally sitting in the driver's seat and imagining that we are driving, or reading books on driving, we will probably make the transition more easily.

Simple as it seems, this principle contains several complex ideas, so it is important to define the variables clearly. The *amount of prior learning* is a variable that can vary from having no learning at all to having very large amounts of prior learning, as illustrated below.

Amount of prior learning

| None | Very little | Small | Moderate | Large | Very large |

More abstract and difficult to specify is the variable that is of major interest of this chapter. That variable is the *ease of making the transition into marriage,* and it can be defined as the degree to

---

[1] This theoretical idea was first described by Cottrell (1942), and more abstract, general versions of it have been further refined by Merton (1968, pp. 316 ff.) and Burr (1973, pp. 124–27). A number of studies (Davis, 1940, 1947; Dyer, 1963; Deutscher, 1962; Ellis and Lane, 1967) have empirically tested the relationship between prior learning and the ease of making other role transitions, but no empirical tests are known that specifically test the relationship between prior learning and the ease of making the transition into marriage. The evidence in all of the other areas, however, is so convincing that it seems to this author that there is virtually no risk in generalizing the findings to the transition into marriage.

which there is freedom from difficulty and the presence of easily available resources to make the change from being single to being married (Burr, 1973, p. 124). In this situation the change involves more than just going through a wedding ceremony, as it refers to how easily we can become a spouse in the full sense of the term. If persons have difficulty in making the transition into marriage this is low ease, and if they are able to make the transition with relatively little difficulty this is high ease. This variable can also be diagramed.

Ease of making the
transition into marriage

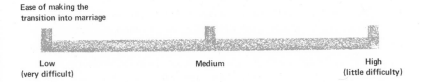

| Low | Medium | High |
| (very difficult) | | (little difficulty) |

This relationship is diagramed in Figure 11–1, and the line describes the curvilinearity that is presently thought to exist in this relationship (Cottrell, 1942; Burr, 1973, p. 125). Without prior learning virtually everyone attempting to make the transition would have low ease. A little bit of learning, however, seems to go a long way because relatively small increments of learning cause rapid increases in the ease of the transition. Then, after moderate amounts of learning have occurred, there seems to be a point of diminishing returns because additional learning has less effect on the ease of making the transition.

Figure 11–1

The effect of prior learning on the ease of making the transition into marriage

Ease of making the transition into marriage

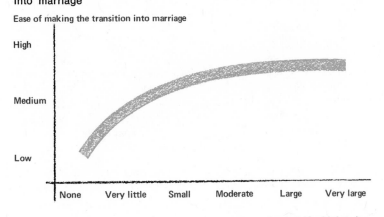

Amount of prior learning

Probably the most obvious practical implication of the Learning about the Spouse Role principle is that couples who want to make the transition easily will want to learn as much as possible about what their marital situation will be like before they marry. This learning can occur in many ways. The ordinary experience of observing one's parents may help, but this type of learning is frequently not enough. For one thing we can't observe our parents' marriage at its beginning. What we observe is a marriage that is 10 to 30 years old, and many of the things our parents might have done early in their marriage could have been unique to that particular stage of life. We can also learn from observing newlyweds—if we are lucky enough to be around them enough. However, even if we are around them a great deal we will not be able to observe many aspects of their relationship. Additional learning can also be done through courses on courtship and marriage and through reading *accurate* literature about marriage.

Another source of knowledge is learning from friends who have preceded us into marriage, and this may be one of the more valuable methods of acquiring useful information. This method is limited by the fact that friendships between individuals who marry and their unmarried friends tend to wane, as married couples tend to associate more and more with their married acquaintances, but this is still a viable alternative for some of us. The following exercise is an attempt to use this particular method of prior role learning.

PRIOR LEARNING ABOUT MARITAL ROLES

Goal: To acquire new information about what it is like to be married.

1. Locate a married couple who have been married less than two or three years and ask them whether you can visit with them for about 30 minutes as part of an assignment for your class. There are certain advantages to doing this with a couple you already know, as you can establish rapport with them easily, but this can also be done with a couple you haven't known previously.

2. Tell the couple that what you want to learn are the things that are not usually known about what it is like to be married. You can have them respond to such questions as:

>   a. What were some of the surprises they had after they were married . . . things they hadn't anticipated?
>
>   b. What advice would they give a couple now that is different from the advice they would have given before they were married?
>
>   c. What parts of marriage were they or their friends least prepared for?
>
>   d. If they had any distorted or unrealistic expectations, or if they had to "unlearn" some things, what were they?
>
> 3. Summarize in writing (a) the new things you learned in this exercise, and (b) the things you didn't really learn for the first time, but concerning which your insight or understanding was increased.

Another practical implication of the learning about the Spouse Role principle is also important. This is that (even though we may not want it to occur) much of the prior learning about marriage that most of us have is excessively romantic, or distorted, or unrealistic and inaccurate in other ways. Most of us experience marriage very differently from the way it is presented in television or the movies or from the glimpses we get into marital relationships in novels, advertising, or newscasts. Hollywood, TV, and advertising distort reality so thoroughly by overromanticizing and glamorizing it that watching these media probably does more to create unrealistic expectations than to provide useful insights about marriage and family living. Then, to make matters worse, contemporary newscasts, novels, and soap operas distort in the opposite direction by sensationalizing the unusual, tragic, and difficult parts of life. Most of us, of course, realize this, and we are able to view much of this information for what it really is; but . . . on the other hand . . . how many unrealistic and overly romanticized expectations do we acquire from these media when we have such a steady diet of them year after year? There is evidence (Pineo, 1961; LeMasters, 1957; Luckey, 1967) that most of us have many unrealistic expectations about marriage and parenthood, and that we eventually experience some disillusionment and eye-opening realism . . . after we are married. *The main point here is* that the prior learning needed to help make the transition into marriage easier is useful if it is accurate, realistic learning, and it is probably problematic if it is not. The unrealistic information will have to be corrected later, and often this unlearning process is fairly painful. The following exercise is designed to help us in this unlearning. Question *d* in the previous exercise is also designed to help uncover some of these distortions, and you may want to devise other methods to further determine whether you have inappropriate expectations.

MARITAL EXPECTATIONS

Goal: To use a class discussion to identify unrealistic expectations about marriage.

1. Have the single students in a courtship and marriage class list 8 or 10 distorted or unrealistic expectations that they think "many" single students have. Be specific rather than just writing down such general things as "overromanticize." DO NOT CONSULT MARRIED STUDENTS YET.

2. Have the married students in the class list 8 or 10 distorted or unrealistic expectations that they think "many" of the single students in the class have.

3. Put both lists on a chalkboard or overhead projector, and compare the two lists to see whether being married provides a different perspective on the invalid expectations.

Transition procedures

THE TRANSITION PROCEDURES PRINCIPLE: The importance and definiteness of the transition procedures for becoming married influence the ease of making the transition into marriage, and this is a positive relationship.

This second principle about role transitions has to do with the procedures for actually making a transition. Cottrell (1942) has theorized that the more definite and clear-cut the process of making a transition the easier the transition is, and that the more obscure and vaguely defined the procedures the more difficult it is to make the transition. The main variable here is the *importance and definiteness* of the transition process, and this can be diagramed as follows:

Importance and definiteness
of transition procedure

| Unimportant and indefinite | Moderately important and definite | Very important and definite |

This principle is one of the least substantiated generalizations in this book, so it should only be tentatively accepted as valid. Cottrell

(1942) was the first to formally state it as a hypothesis, but he did not describe the data he used as the basis of his assertion, and no empirical tests of its validity have been found. The proposition is included here primarily because of its reasonableness and its practical implications for some of the emerging forms of marriage rather than because it is a well-tested theoretical idea.

In most societies the procedure for making the transition from single to married is a highly visible, clear-cut, and ceremonious occasion, which, if this principle is valid, facilitates the transition. In some of the newly emerging forms of marriage, however, the process of becoming married is only vaguely defined, and in some of these forms people aren't really sure just when the marriage starts. The Transition Procedures principle suggests that the vagueness of the transition process probably makes it unneccessarily difficult to adjust to these forms of marriage. It may be that in some of these new marital life-styles we would find it useful to develop a more clear-cut procedure for entering and leaving the marriage than has been devised thus far.

In some role transitions only a few social norms change, but in other transitions a large number of norms change. For example, when a couple become engaged relatively few norms change as compared to the number of norms that change when they become parents. Engaged couples are usually expected to be more exclusive and to seriously plan on marrying each other, but literally hundreds of new normative obligations are assumed when a person becomes a parent. The following principle deals with these variations:

Amount of normative change

THE NORMATIVE CHANGE WITH MARRIAGE PRINCIPLE:
The amount of normative change that occurs as one assumes the role of spouse influences the ease of making this transition, and this is an inverse, curvilinear relationship.

Burr (1973, p. 140) has speculated that this relationship is an inverse, curvilinear relationship like the one diagramed in Figure 11–2. According to this figure, variation in the number of normative changes does not have an adverse effect on role transitions until there is a rather substantial amount of change, and then additional changes very rapidly make the transition more difficult. This generalization was initially developed by Cottrell (1942), and it was further elaborated by Burr (1973, pp. 139–40). The

Figure 11–2

The relationship between normative change and the ease
of transition into marriage

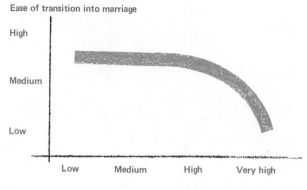

Amount of normative change

principle seems eminently reasonable and has several practical
applications, but no systematic research has been found that empirically tests it. It should thus be viewed as only tentatively
acceptable.

This generalization can be applied in several ways. One way has
to do with the timing of a wedding. If a wedding occurred at about
the same time as several other role transitions, this would make the
transition into marriage more difficult. A rather extreme example
illustrates this point. If, for example, a couple were to marry at about
the same time that they left their parents' home, graduated from
college, took a new job in a different city, and decided to set up a
small business . . . there would be numerous changes in the social
norms relevant for them, and the couple would very likely have some
difficulty making that many changes at once. It may be that some
couples want to time their marriage close to some of these other
transitions, but the Normative Change with Marriage principle permits us to predict that they will find their transitions more difficult
than if they were to spread them out some.

Another way this principle can be applied in our personal lives is
to systematically make some changes before the wedding that are
usually made simultaneously with the wedding. For example, couples can decide well before their marriage how they will do their

shopping and begin shopping that way in advance of their marriage. If, for example, the wife-to-be is a seamstress, and she wants her future husband to go with her while she picks out patterns and fabric, they could start shopping this way long before their marriage. If both members of the couple want to do the grocery shopping or if they want one of them to be the primary grocery shopper the desired pattern could frequently be established before the couple actually marries.

Another aspect of marital relationships in which changes can be made before a wedding is the economic area. There is considerable evidence that money and the various issues associated with it, such as deciding how it is to be spent, getting the bills paid, keeping track of where it went, etc., are usually the number one problem areas in American marriages (Goode, 1956, chaps. 4–5; Landis and Landis, 1968, p. 368). It is also usually true that couples don't really combine their finances until after they are married. The author's informal studies of students in marriage classes indicate that before the marriage about 10 to 20 percent of the couples either pool some money to purchase such things as furniture or have a joint savings account, but that it is a rare couple who combine their finances in other ways. There do not, however, seem to be any reasons why couples cannot make premaritally at least *some* of the many economic changes that they will make when they marry, and there are several potentially valuable consequences of such premarital changes. Before discussing these consequences it seems useful to examine some of the alternatives that are available to couples.

Probably the most extreme form of becoming "married" economically would be for a couple to combine their finances before their marriage in the same way that they will after the marriage. This is impossible if the individuals live in widely separated areas, but it is possible when couples live only a few blocks apart. They could have a joint checking account or use any of the other methods that newlyweds use, such as separating their money in bottles or envelopes. They could keep most of the money at one of their houses and do such things as make decisions about how to spend it, actually spend it, and keep their financial records in the same way they plan to after the wedding. A more conservative approach would be to have a joint checking account, and put only the money in it that will be spent for such things as rent, joint recreational activities, car payments, etc. There are all sorts of varieties of this process of combining money, and a system that will work for one couple will be different from one that will work for another. In some marriages one individual handles all of the money except for a daily or weekly allowance that the other individual has, and this too would be workable premaritally for some couples.

This process of becoming married "economically" before the actual wedding has several potential advantages and disadvantages. On the positive side handling money as a couple is quite different from handling money as individuals, and each couple must adopt or invent their own set of norms or rules about how they are going to do it. If they can make these changes before the wedding they will not have to cope with this area after the wedding. In addition, sharing money is an area of interaction that many couples find difficult, and observing their ability to make adjustments in this area might give a couple some insight into how they will do when married. Some couples might find some basic incompatibilities and temperamental quirks that they would not have found otherwise until after the marriage, and if these are sufficiently problematic to justify terminating the relationship it is usually much easier to do this before the wedding than after. Other couples will discover qualities that make them even more attractive to each other and more confident in their relationship. A third potential advantage of this type of premarital collaboration is that couples can observe *how* they make decisions in important areas of their lives. What they learn may make them want to develop new ways of making decisions, or it may provide additional confidence in their likelihood of success as a married couple.

There are several potential disadvantages of combining money before marriage. The first one that is usually brought up in class discussions is that "if things don't work out we may lose some money." It doesn't take long in these discussions, however, for the idea to also come out that this may actually be a less serious loss than the economic losses of a divorce and the emotional losses that are usually involved when a marriage is broken. In fact it may be that the premarital loss should actually be viewed as a good investment. A more genuine disadvantage is that when individuals combine their money, problems occasionally arise in premarital situation that would not occur after a couple are married. This is probably most likely if the couple live some distance from each other or are so involved with work and/or school roles that they don't have as much time to discuss their finances as they will have after they are married. This potential disadvantage speaks well for wisdom and caution in making these changes before a wedding.

Sexual interaction is an area in which there is great variation in the amount of normative change couples experience when they marry. In some societies and in some of the subcultures in the American society there are no normative proscriptions against couples living together and experiencing sexual intercourse before their wedding. In these cultural situations there may be very minor changes or no normative changes when a couple marry. In other situations, however, such as the traditional American pattern, the situation is entirely different. Couples are taught that before marriage any highly erotic sexual interaction, such as petting or coitus, is evil and taboo, but that after the wedding there is a moral and legal obligation to participate in sexual intercourse. This may not seem to be a problematic distinction to some, but when the premarital definition of sexuality includes a complex set of negative attitudes and feelings toward sexual interaction a massive discontinuity is created. When women, for example, are taught from their preschool years on that they are to conceal their bodies, be modest, "stop" the men they date when sexual advances are made, and view intimate sexual interaction as evil, dirty, sinful, and debasing, this creates attitudes that are very difficult to change. It is one of the classic absurdities of all time to believe that a short, ceremonious wedding will change these deeply ingrained attitudes and emotions. The result is that the initial weeks and months of many marriages are an extremely difficult period of change.

Most individuals in the contemporary American society probably lie someplace between these two extremes of having no normative changes in regard to sexuality when they marry and having the monumental changes described in the previous paragraph. In addition there is such diversity among the different segments of the American society that the ways that some of us can use the Normative Change with Marriage principle are *very* different from the ways that others of us can use it. Nonetheless it seems useful to identify several different ways that this principle can be applied in regard to sexual interaction. Those of us who have few or no restrictive norms about premarital sexual interaction could initiate our sexual interaction before we marry. Those of us who believe that virginity at marriage is important but have no aversion to engaging in highly erotic sexual activities, such as petting to a sexual climax, could begin these noncoital sexual activities before marriage if we wished to spread out the changes that are required in marriage. For others among us it may be important to refrain from any highly erotic sexual activity, but it may not be essential that sexuality, as such, be viewed as evil or taboo. Such people could try to determine what their attitudes are toward sex, and if they find that they have attitudes they would not want to have after they are married, they could work at changing those attitudes. Thus, each of us needs to determine what type of premarital sexual interaction is desirable and feasible for us in our unique sociocultural situations.

There are several other areas in which couples can make premarital changes that will decrease the changes they will have to make after they are married. These areas include such things as relationships with in-laws, attending churches or social organizations, developing a style of making decisions, deciding whether contraceptives will be used, and, if so, which of the various types will be used. Thus, each couple must determine which parts of the transition into marriage it would be wise to make before their wedding, and the following exercise can help couples make this decision.

MAKING CHANGES BEFORE A MARRIAGE

Goals: The three goals in this activity are (1) to identify several changes that are usually made when couples marry; (2) to determine how desirable it would be to make some of these changes before your marriage; and (3) to decide how to make the desirable changes.

1.   Identify a large number of new or different obligations or ways of doing things that couples usually acquire when they are married. Then evaluate each of these changes to determine which of them are desirable and feasible for you and which of them are not desirable and feasible. The following list will get you started. You can probably add other changes that you will be making. (Some of the changes in the following list may not be appropriate for everyone.)

   a.   Combine savings accounts.

   b.   Begin making decisions together when purchasing major items, such as furniture, insurance policies, or a car.

   c.   Begin doing routine shopping, such as shopping for groceries, the way you will after marriage.

   d.   Attend social activities, such as clubs or church, the way you will after marriage.

   e.   Begin interacting sexually the way you will after marriage.

   f.   Make any changes in residence that would ordinarily be made when you marry.

   g.   Begin the patterns of relating to and interacting with in-laws that will exist after the wedding.

   h.   Leave your parents' home and "set up house" on your own or with someone else.

   i.   Change your name.

   j.   Buy additional insurance.

   k.   Begin "decision making" and "problem solving" the way you will after marriage.

2.   Decide how, when, and where to make those changes you think are desirable. You may find the "Action Plan" outline on pages 164–65 useful in making these plans.

THE CONSENSUS ABOUT MARITAL EXPECTATIONS PRIN-CIPLE: The greater the consensus about expectations for the spouse role the greater the ease of the transition into marriage, and vice versa.

Consensus about expectations

The independent variable in this generalization, the amount of consensus about marital role expectations, was discussed in Chapter 7 when the Consensus about Expectations principle was introduced. This variable was defined in Chapter 7 as the amount that two people agree or disagree in what they expect or want someone to do as a spouse. The idea in the *Consensus about Marital Expectations* principle introduced here is similar to the Consensus about Expectations principle that was introduced in Chapter 7, and these two principles are easily confused. There is, however, an important difference between these two ideas. The consensus about expecta-

Figure 11–3

The effects variation in consensus about role expectations has on two different variables

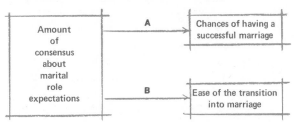

tions generalization introduced in Chapter 7 asserts that the consensus influences the probability of a successful marriage, and this idea is summarized with arrow *A* in Figure 11–3. The generalization introduced here, however, states that consensus influences the ease of making the transition into marriage, and this idea is diagramed as arrow *B* in Figure 11–3. Thus, these two principles describe two different effects or consequences of variation in consensus about role expectations.

The differences between the Consensus about Marital Expectations principle and the Transition Procedures principle is important for two reasons. *First,* the "chances of marital satisfaction" and "ease in making the transition into marriage" are two different factors. It would be very possible for a couple to have a difficult time making the initial adjustment to marriage but then to have a very successful marriage. And, conversely, it would be very possible for a couple to have a very easy time making the initial transition into marriage but then to find themselves in a miserable marital situation. *Second,* several variables discussed in Chapter 7 influence the chances of having a successful marriage, but there is no scientific basis for speculating that these variables also influence the ease of making the transition into marriage. For example, two factors that seem to influence the probability of having a successful marriage are the approval of intimates and how close the marriage of a fiancé(e)'s parents is to what one wants in marriage. There is, however, no evidence that either of these variables influences the ease of making the initial transition into marriage. There is, however, reason to believe that consensus about marital role expectations influences the ease of this transition.[2]

The Consensus about Marital Expectations generalization has considerable practical relevance because it is possible to determine how much consensus a couple has and, in many cases, to change the quantity of consensus. The two skills involved in using this principle are being able (a) to recognize how much consensus or lack of consensus exists in a relationship, and (b) to change the amount of consensus. Two exercises in other chapters are designed to help us increase these two skills. The "Role Expectations" exercise on pages 205–6 helps us discover more about our own expectations, and if both individuals complete that exercise the two lists of expectations can be compared to determine where there are agreements and disagreements. The "Role Consensus" exercise on page 308 is then designed to help the couple acquire consensus about some of the areas of disagreement. Hopefully, working with one or both of these exercises will help us move into marriage more easily than we would have without them.

Other relevant   It also seems useful to point out that several of the principles
principles   that have been discussed in earlier chapters seem to be relevant in the present context. It is likely, for example, that the principles that dealt with communication and problem solving can all be applied to the transition into marriage. Couples who are able to use their emotions to facilitate rather than interfere with communication,

---

[2] Cottrell (1942) was the first to state the idea that consensus about expectations influences the ease of making role transitions. The generalization was later refined by Burr (1973, pp. 128–31). No empirical research is known that specifically tests the idea in regard to the transition into marriage, but there is research that tests the idea in other contexts, such as becoming a minister (Campbell and Pettigrew, 1959) or a school superintendent (Gross et al., 1957).

who have developed a type of relationship in which they are willing and able to communicate about important feelings, and who have developed the capacity to make decisions in an effective and satisfying manner will undoubtedly find the transition into marriage easier than couples who are less able to act in these ways.

SUMMARY

This chapter has identified four principles that can be used to help maximize the ease and minimize the difficulty of making the transition into marriage. The *Learning about the Spouse Role* principle was discussed first, and it states that the more that is learned about what the marital status will be like before that status is entered into, the easier the transition will be. This principle is shown as the top arrow in the causal model in Figure 11–4. The second generalization discussed was the *Transition Procedures* principle, which suggests that the more definite and important the process of making a transition the easier it tends to be. The third generalization analyzed was the *Normative Change with Marriage* principle, which asserts that when we are married, or, for that matter, when we make any major role transition, the greater the

Figure 11–4

Causal model of the principles in Chapter 11

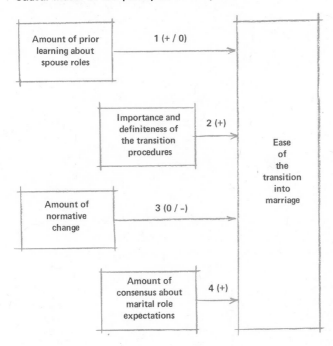

change in the social norms that are incumbent upon us the more difficult the transition is. The last generalization was the *Consensus about Marital Expectations* principle, which asserts that the more two people agree on how they ought to act as spouses the easier the transition into marriage. These last principles are also summarized in Figure 11–4. A number of the practical implications of these principles and ways to implement them were also discussed.

SUGGESTIONS FOR FURTHER STUDY

Blood, Robert O., Jr.   1969. *Marriage*. Rev. ed. Glencoe: Free Press, chaps. 7–9.

Burgess, Ernest W., and Wallin, Paul   1953. *Engagement and Marriage*. Philadelphia: Lippincott, chap. 13.

Burr, Wesley R.   1973. *Theory Construction and the Sociology of the Family*. New York: Wiley, chap. 6.

Foote, Nelson N.   1956. "Matching of Husband and Wife in Phases of Development." *Transactions of the Third World Congress of Sociology, International Sociological Association* 4:24–34.

Landis, Judson, and Landis, Mary G.   1968. *Building a Successful Marriage*. 5th ed. Englewood Cliffs, N.J.: Prentice-Hall, chaps. 10 and 15.

Saxton, Lloyd   1972.   *The Individual, Marriage, and the Family*. 2d ed. Belmont, Calif.: Wadsworth, chap. 8.

Marital relationships

The last section of this volume is an attempt to analyze several processes that occur in marital interaction, and to identify a number of principles that can be used by couples to better attain their marital goals. Chapter 12 analyzes ways couples can reach agreement about how they ought to behave and how they actually behave in their marital roles. This process is not one that is resolved for all time at the beginning of a marriage. Because developmental changes and idiosyncratic changes occur throughout our lives the generalizations in this chapter are continually relevant in marital interaction.

Chapter 13 identifies a number of factors that couples can manipulate to increase or decrease the bonds in their relationship, and Chapter 14 analyzes the combined effects of companionate interaction with friends and with one's spouse on the satisfaction we have with our marital relationship. Chapter 15 differs slightly from most of the chapters in that it contains considerable descriptive information about human sexuality, but in addition it presents several principles that can be used to help attain pleasant, rewarding sexual interaction. Chapter 16 addresses the fact that all marriages and families encounter difficulties and also identifies six generalizations that can help prevent potentially stressful events from being excessively disrupting and six other principles that can be used to recover from disruptions we are unable to avoid. Chapter 17 discusses several issues couples are faced with in deciding whether to be *parents, explains the techniques that are available to control conception, and discusses several factors that couples can manipulate to minimize the difficulties of the coming of children and maximize the joys of parenthood. The last chapter analyzes some of the events and concerns that couples experience as the years of marriage pass, and discusses several principles that can be used to enrich a marital relationship.*

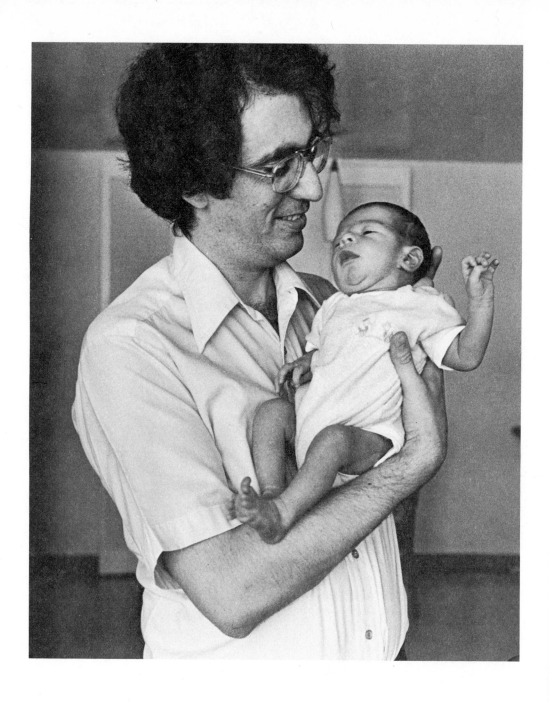

12

Achieving satisfaction in marital roles

WHENEVER people participate in enduring interpersonal relationships many parts of those relationships become regular and repetitious. For example, in marriages that conform to the traditional styles in society and even in the variant forms that have been emerging, such as Group and Two-Step marriages, the spouses gradually develop routine ways of responding to each other in such things as the way they talk, the way they decide to get tasks accomplished, who tends to do what tasks, and how they respond when the other person has various emotional experiences, such as discouragement, excitement, or frustration. Eventually the individuals in these relationships come to view the stabilized interaction patterns as the ways that they and the other person "should" act, and they are uncomfortable when one of them breaks these "rules" or "norms."[1]

Much of the time this process of gradually acquiring consensus about the norms that each of us wants to live under is a natural process that occurs without our even being aware of what is happening. At other times, however, couples find that they need to deal consciously with disagreements or problems in the ways they act in their spouse roles. For example, couples find it necessary to

---

[1] The term *norm* has long been used in sociology and anthropology to describe such beliefs. Widely used references of this definition appear in Linton (1936), Bates (1956), and Bott (1957). The writings that have emerged from scholars working at the Mental Research Institute at Palo Alto, however, have introduced the term *rule* to describe exactly the same phenomenon (Satir, 1964; Watzlawick et al., 1967). These two labels thus mean the same thing, and the redundancy in the literature is unfortunate. The term *norm* is used in this text because of its priority and more extensive use.

address this type of problem when they interpret something in two different ways. This is illustrated by the following actual situation.

I grew up in a family where we always gave each other nicely wrapped presents on special occasions, such as birthdays and anniversaries. We didn't have lots of money, so often the presents were very inexpensive and small, but the thought of concern and love was always shown through giving something. My husband grew up in a family where they gave each other money rather than presents. I have since learned that this is very meaningful to them, but in our family we viewed giving money as being worse than not giving anything at all, because the only time we gave money was done when someone forgot to get a present, and that communicated that they were not as concerned as they should be. For the first several years of our marriage this created a problem because I would give my husband presents and he would give me money. Both of us thought we were doing what the other would want, but neither of us was very comfortable. He would make little comments about how what I had given him didn't fit or how he wished he could get something else with the money, and I felt that he wasn't very thoughtful and considerate to give me money. I used to wish that he would use the money to give me something that he'd selected. Eventually we talked about how we both felt and worked it out, but that was after we had been married for over two years.

This chapter identifies eight principles that couples can use to help them work out satisfactory role arrangements in their marital relationships. These principles are sufficiently general to be applied in various role problems, such as deciding how to handle finances, relate to in-laws, adjust sexually, or cope with religious behavior; and this chapter has several illustrations of ways to apply each of the principles in specific marital situations.

CONGRUENCE OF ROLE EXPECTATIONS AND BEHAVIOR

Eventually in every marital relationship the spouses become aware that the other person is doing some things that they don't want him or her to do or that they are doing things themselves that they don't want to do. If these were all minor issues, such as the wife wanting the husband to clean his whiskers out of the wash basin or the husband wanting his wife to hang her nylons someplace other than on the tub, and if there were only a few issues, they wouldn't make much difference in marriage. Each spouse could make a few changes, and all would be well. That isn't the way life usually is, however, and it is likely that every couple finds that some of these problems are important and disruptive to the one who isn't getting his or her way. This kind of marital problem is illustrated by the three following case histories.

We have three children, and they are all gone, but I thought growing older together was going to be different. I need more attention from him now because when the boys left home I suddenly felt deserted and very alone. I turned to him for some of the companionship we had when we were first married, but he doesn't seem to want to be bothered with me now. We only go someplace when I force him. He doesn't really fight with me about it; sometimes I wish he would. He just gets that resigned, hangdog look on his face.

Tony's a good husband and father in almost every respect. He works hard and he's getting ahead, but he gives in to his mother all the time. What good is there in having a man if he won't stand up for you? My father shouted and hollered a lot, and I hated it. I was very glad when I got a man like Tony, who was gentle and quiet. But now I see that my father yelled just as much when he was for you as when he was against you. I guess I want a man like that too.

I got sick of asking her to go out on Sundays. She was always very sweet and self-sacrificing about just having too much to do, and she would urge me to nap or amuse myself. So I got in the habit of watching television and snoozing. Mind you, she encouraged me to do it! Then she began to complain bitterly to the neighbors about what a bum I was and how I abused her. I tell you, I couldn't believe it the first time I heard her say it, but now she says it to me, too. She seems to get a lot of satisfaction out of feeling abused. Sure, it makes me feel like a heel, but what can I do about it? She still won't go out, even if I ask her.

Since every married couple encounters these discrepancies between desired and actual behavior, and since considerable research has found that *some of these discrepancies have a very disruptive effect* on marriages (Ort, 1950; Kotlar, 1961; Hawkins and Johnson, 1969; Burr, 1967, 1971), the two principles identified in this section are extremely valuable in marital interaction. The first generalization is the *Congruence* principle, and the causal variable in it is the amount of congruence between role expectations and role behavior (Mangus, 1957). Since this variable includes two fairly technical terms, it is important to define them. *Role expectations,* which were discussed in Chapter 7, are the normative beliefs or rules we have about what people ought to do or not do in a particular role. These expectations are intellectual opinions, such as believing that a husband or wife should call his or her spouse on the phone when staying at work later than usual or believing that one should avoid flirting with others at parties. *Role behavior* refers to the way a person really acts or behaves in a role. If one spouse expects the other to call when working late, and she or he calls, the call is the role behavior. The congruence of the expectations and behavior is a variable because the number of areas in a relationship in which

there can be congruence or a lack of it can vary from none to a
large number. The relevant generalization is:

THE CONGRUENCE PRINCIPLE: The more congruence between role expectations and role behavior the more satisfied individuals tend to be with their marriage and, conversely, the less congruence the less satisfied they tend
to be.[2]

This principle was first made explicit by Ort (1950), and since
that time it has been empirically tested with several different meth-

Figure 12–1

The effect congruence between role expectations and role behavior
has on marital satisfaction when the importance of the expectations
is taken into account

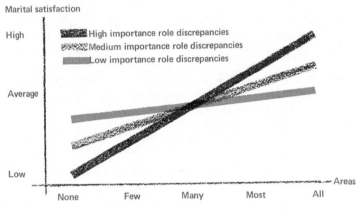

Amount of congruence between role expectations and role behavior

ods of measuring the variables (Mangus, 1957; Kotlar, 1961;
Hawkins and Johnson, 1969; Burr, 1967, 1971). The principle is also
a fundamental idea in symbolic interaction theory, so theoretical
reasoning and empirical evidence suggest that it is valid. It should
not, however, be concluded that all discrepancies between expectations and behavior have an equally disruptive effect on marriages.
Some discrepancies probably have little impact, and some are probably extremely disruptive.

One factor that seems to influence how much disruptive effect an
incongruence will have on marriage is the *importance of the role*

[2] More technically, the research has shown the independent variable to account for 40 to 50 percent of the variance in marital satisfaction. None of the
research, however, has used test variables to test for spuriousness. This means
that the relationship may be very important in understanding marital relationships but that more research is needed to determine just how important.

expectations. If a person believes that it is relatively unimportant whether his or her spouse conforms to a particular role expectation, then a lack of congruence in that area will have little adverse effect on their relationship. If, however, either spouse believes that it is highly important that a behavior conform to an expectation, then an incongruence in that area will be more disruptive. This difference in the effects of congruence is shown in Figure 12–1, and the principle is:

> **THE IMPORTANCE PRINCIPLE: The more important the role expectations the greater the effect that variation in the congruence of expectations and behavior has on marital satisfaction, and the less important the less effect.**[3]

Applying these two principles

These two principles have several practical implications for marital relationships. One implication is that when discrepancies between expectations and behavior occur in our marriages they frequently have a very disruptive effect in our relationship, and if we ignore them or cannot eliminate them we will probably have a less satisfying marriage than if we are able to eliminate them.

A second implication is that at least some of the time it is possible to tell which discrepancies are disruptive and which are not because the more important we believe it is to have conformity to a role expectation the more detrimental a discrepancy in that area will be. This means that when we feel strongly about role expectations we would probably be wise to clarify to ourselves and to our spouse what our expectations are. Some of this can be done before marriage, but surprisingly much of it cannot be done then. We have many role expectations that are very important to us of which we are not even aware until long after we are married. This is illustrated by the facts that thousands of situations arise in marriage that cannot be foreseen while dating, and that preferences about such things as how independent the two spouses should be from each other change at different stages of the family life cycle. This means that we will all encounter new role discrepancies as a routine part of

---

[3] This principle is implicit in sociological theory from Sumner (1906) on, but it was first empirically tested by Burr (1967, 1971), and the evidence in that study supports the idea. In addition the principle has an intuitive rationality to it. Thus, theoretical, empirical, and intuitive bases for this principle provide considerable support for its validity.

marriage, and it is therefore important that we learn ways to resolve them so that our behavior can be congruent with our expectations.

Another implication of these principles is that incongruences in expectations have intellectual, behavioral, *and* emotional aspects. If they had only intellectual and behavioral aspects they would probably not be highly disruptive in marriages, and it would be relatively easy to resolve them. The fact, however, that feelings are intricately tied to role expectations, to role behavior, and to the discrepancies themselves frequently makes our reactions to the discrepancies explosive, intense, delicate, and much more complex than may appear to be the case at first. This point can be illustrated with a role discrepancy that at first glance seems to be relatively minor, unimportant, and easy to resolve. If a wife grew up in a family in which the mother handled the finances and the husband grew up in a family in which the father handled the finances, it is common for both the husband and the wife to expect to have the responsibility of handling the finances. This seems like a relatively simple discrepancy that could easily be resolved—until it is also realized that in most cases they both have more than just casual and unimportant expectations that they should handle this responsibility. They frequently have strong emotional reactions if they do not get to behave in the way that is consistent with their expectations. For example, the husband's belief that he should handle the money may be tied up with his view of himself as an adequate "man," and if he does not handle the money his manhood may be threatened. Or, the wife may feel that if she doesn't handle the money this indicates that she is in some way inferior or inadequate. These conflicting views make the total situation very disruptive.

When emotional reactions such as these are tied to role discrepancies, the discrepancies become extremely involved, important, delicate issues, and this means that couples have to take their *emotional responses* into account as they try to resolve the discrepancies. It also means, however, that when a resolution of the discrepancies is made so that the behavior is congruent with the expectations, the solution and the subsequent congruent daily interaction provide deeply satisfying feelings, such as closeness, importance, caring, and love, and these feelings add infinitely to the joys of marriage. The main point here is that eliminating discrepancies does more than just eliminate undesirable aspects of marriages. Congruence between expectations and behavior is important in *adding* to the desirable aspects of marriage. On the other hand, when discrepancies are not resolved, the individual who experiences the discrepancy usually carries around a certain amount of negative emotion, such as resentment, anger, or frustration. When such feelings build up in a person, then, at moments when the person least expects it, the feelings will frequently be vented in a destructive manner—and, as will be recalled from the section on "The Nature of Emotions," in Chapter 3, the individual may not even be aware of the fact that his negative emotions have led him to do what he did.

There is another aspect of these incongruences that has relevance for marriage. This is that sometimes individuals' role expectations or role behavior or both become so deeply intertwined with other aspects of their belief system or their habits that they find it extremely difficult or even impossible to change them. Most couples find that they are able to resolve most of the discrepancies they encounter relatively easily and quickly, but that some discrepancies are very difficult to eliminate and that they have to work at resolving them for months and years before they are finally eliminated. In addition it is probably impossible to be married very long and not encounter at least a few discrepancies that just cannot be eliminated.

Skills to help cope with discrepancies between expectations and behavior.   It thus seems to be the case that role discrepancies are inevitable in any relationship that lasts for very long, and that these discrepancies are especially inescapable in a marital relationship since it is a highly intimate, long-term relationship that involves many aspects of our lives. Thus, it seems important to identify some skills that can help us cope with role discrepancies. When we encounter role discrepancies it is possible to turn them into events that actually strengthen rather than disrupt a marriage, but there are very few courses of action that will do this. Four options that can bring this about are: (1) change the role expectations; (2) change the behavior; (3) change the amount of importance that is attributed to the discrepancy; or (4) change the compensatory aspects in the relationship that counterbalance the negative effects of the discrepancies. It is, of course, possible to use more than one of these options at the same time, such as changing both the expectation and the behavior a little in order to reduce or eliminate the disruptive effects of a discrepancy. There is no best way to go about the process of using these options, and probably the most helpful observation about how to resolve them is that *the techniques that are useful in resolving any of the other interpersonal problems we encounter are the techniques we will find useful in resolving role discrepancies. The information in the communication and problem-solving section of this volume (Chapters 3–6) is therefore very relevant in this context.*

It is possible to identify four skills that can help us implement one or more of the options mentioned in the last paragraph. The easiest of the four skills is the ability to recognize a role discrepancy when it occurs. Although this skill is the easiest of the four mentioned here, some of us have a very difficult time recognizing *any* role discrepancies, and even those of us who are able to detect role discrepancies some of the time are not able to recognize them *all* the time. In addition, even those of us who have considerable skill in recognizing role discrepancies may occasionally experience one for some time, become irritated at the situation, and respond in an unpleasant, inappropriate manner before we recognize the role discrepancy. Because of this, all of us can *improve* our ability to recognize discrepancies, and the following exercise provides practice in this skill.

RECOGNIZING DISCREPANCIES BETWEEN EXPECTATIONS AND BEHAVIOR

Goal: To improve ability to recognize role discrepancies.

1. Focus your thinking on a role you play in a relationship with someone else. (It is usually best to use your spouse if you are married or your fiancé(e) or a person you have recently dated if you are not married.)

2. Think of something in the relationship that is probably a role discrepancy.

3. Write down the role expectation.

4. Write down the role behavior.

5. Check yourself by seeing whether (a) the statement in step 3 identified some behavior or action that one of you thinks *ought* to be done or not done; (b) the statement in step 4 identified some action or behavior that is actually done; and (c) the behavior described in step 4 is different from the expectation described in step 3. If these all occur you have probably correctly identified a role discrepancy.

6. Try this again with several other role discrepancies.

Appreciation is expressed to Margaret Jensen for her creative ideas in helping develop and test the effectiveness of the exercises in this chapter.

A second skill that is useful in resolving role discrepancies is being able to recognize the effect that a role discrepancy has on a relationship. Sometimes it is difficult to know what our role expectations are or to know how important we think it is for our spouse or ourselves to conform to a particular role expectation, and the only way we become aware of a role discrepancy is to first recognize that something has changed in the relationship and to then realize that the change has occurred because of a role discrepancy. Thus, it is important to be able to recognize the effects of role discrepancies. The next two exercises are designed to help acquire or improve the ability to do this.

RECOGNIZING THE EFFECTS OF DISCREPANCIES—1

Goal: To increase skill in understanding the effects that role discrepancies have on relationships.

1. Focus your thinking on a relationship with someone else, such as a spouse, fiancé(e), daughter, boyfriend, or girlfriend.

2. Choose one expectation that you imagine the person in the relationship has for your behavior. It should be an expectation you can violate in some way (e.g., the expectation that you should make your bed, that you should take only your share of food at the dinner table, that you should contribute to mealtime conversation).

3. Violate the expectation for a short time. (You will want to select a person who can take it and use good judgment and discretion.)

4. Afterward, ask the other person how he or she felt about and was influenced by your new behavior and explain the purpose of your experiment to the other person.

5. How did your behavior affect the other person's satisfaction with your relationship or other feelings?

RECOGNIZING THE EFFECTS OF DISCREPANCIES—2

Goal: To increase ability to understand the effects that role discrepancies have on relationships.

1. Focus your thinking on a role you play in a relationship with someone else—roommate, spouse, daughter, boyfriend, girlfriend, or fiancé(e).

2. Identify two role discrepancies you are aware of in this relationship—two ways in which the other person does not meet your expectations.

3. Think about how each of these discrepancies affects your feelings of pleasure in the relationship.

4. Is one discrepancy more important than the other? If so, does the more important discrepancy have a greater impact? If it doesn't, can you figure out why it is an exception to the general rule?

A third skill that is useful in coping with role discrepancies is being able to change a relationship so that a discrepancy will not be disruptive in the relationship when the discrepancy cannot be eliminated. This usually involves such things as: (1) changing the importance that is attributed to the discrepancy; (2) changing the expectation or behavior slightly so the discrepancy is not so large that it is disruptive; (3) periodically venting the anger or resentment that is created by the discrepancy; or (4) changing the awareness of the discrepancy by putting it out of one's thoughts through such techniques as suppression or repression. The old adage of having one's eyes wide open before marriage and half-shut after marriage is an example of this last process, and most couples find it helpful advice at one time or another. The following exercise is designed to help either acquire or improve the ability to decrease the undesirable consequences of a role discrepancy.

IMPORTANCE

Goal: To decrease the importance of a role expectation.

1. Think about a relationship. (Preferably your marriage, engagement, or a steady dating relationship. If you don't have one of these, then think of a relationship with someone who is very close to you, such as a member of your family or a close friend of the opposite sex.)

2. Identify a role discrepancy that *you* have in this relationship— a discrepancy in which *your* expectation is violated. Think of a role discrepancy that is fairly important to you.

3. Do one of the three following things to try to convince yourself that it is not *really* as important for the other person to conform to your expectation as you have previously thought it was.

   a. Talk to the person about the discrepancy, with the goal of the conversation being to see whether you can change your belief of how important it is that the other person meet your expectation. Try to change your view of importance rather than your expectation, and if you do wind up changing your expectation, go back and identify a new discrepancy.

    b. Talk to a close friend about the discrepancy, following the instructions given in *a*.

    c. Set aside 10–15 minutes to think about the discrepancy, and try to think up several new reasons why it is not all that important that the other person conform to this particular expectation. Again, if you change your expectation, find a new discrepancy.

4. Were you able to change your opinions about how important the expectation is? If the answer is yes, describe any changes that have also occurred in the disruptive effects of the discrepancy. If the answer is no . . . well, some exercises don't help much, do they?

The fourth skill, probably the most useful means of coping with role discrepancies, is being able to do something that will eliminate them. This is frequently done by having one member of the couple communicate to the other that a discrepancy exists and then having the couple identify things they could do either to change the expectation or to change the behavior. This is not, however, the only way to eliminate role discrepancies. Frequently the person who experiences the role discrepancy cannot convince the other person that a discrepancy exists or that it is sufficiently important that they need to talk about it. When this occurs the individual who has become aware of the discrepancy has the options of (1) changing his or her expectation, (2) living with the discrepancy, (3) eliminating the undesirable consequences of the discrepancy, or (4) coming up with ways to change the other individual's behavior even though the other person isn't involved in deciding what it is that needs to be changed. The next exercise is designed to help acquire or enhance skills in eliminating role discrepancies.

ROLE DISCREPANCY

Goal: To eliminate a role discrepancy.

1. Think about a relationship with someone close to you, such as a member of your family or a close friend of the opposite sex.

2. Identify a role discrepancy that either you or the other person has. Try to identify one that is fairly important, but choose one that is probably solvable (avoid those you have been trying to solve for years).

3. Set aside a time when you can talk with the other person about the role discrepancy. It is preferable to have an open-ended time, such as a free evening, but if that is not possible have at least 15 to 30 minutes available.

4. Select a pleasant physical setting.

5. As you begin the conversation, make sure you have a pleasant emotional climate by first "venting" negative emotions sufficiently so that they will not interfere with having a pleasant conversation, and if either person gets very upset during the conversation, focus your attention on reestablishing a pleasant emotional climate before proceeding with the discussion of the discrepancy.

6. Next, one of you state the role discrepancy, and make sure you both agree on what it is.

7. Then try to identify two or three ways that it *might* be possible to resolve the discrepancy.

8. Evaluate each alternative and select the one that seems to be the best bet for eliminating the discrepancy.

9. Identify some reward, tangible or intangible, for the individual who will be changing his or her expectation or behavior.

10. Try to implement the change for several days.

11. What has happened to the discrepancy after several days have passed?

CONSENSUS ABOUT ROLE EXPECTATIONS

Another principle in symbolic interaction theory that is relevant in this chapter was discussed in Chapter 7. This generalization is:

THE CONSENSUS ABOUT EXPECTATIONS PRINCIPLE: The greater the consensus about marital role expectations the greater the chances of marital satisfaction, and vice versa.

Consensus about role expectations was defined in Chapter 7 as the amount of similarity versus dissimilarity of the beliefs or desires two individuals have about what should or should not be done in a particular role, and it ranges between no consensus and a great amount of consensus. There are theoretical reasons to believe this principle is true since it is a major idea in symbolic interaction theory (Stryker, 1964). Also, considerable research has tested this idea.[4] Thus, this is a generalization in which we can have considerable confidence.

<hr>

The reason this principle is relevant in the present context is that /after couples begin living together they will learn much more about each other's role expectations than they did when they were in a dating situation, and some of these expectations will undoubtedly be different. When individuals learn about differences in expectations before a marriage this is useful in helping them decide whether or not to marry, and at that time it is relatively easy to break off the relationship—if too many serious role conflicts are discovered. However, after the relationship has developed to a point at which the individuals have made the personal commitments of a non-legal marital relationship or the legal and personal commitments of a more conventional form of marriage, they have considerably more invested in the relationship and are usually more interested in solving their role conflicts so that they can continue to enjoy the relationship. This is even the case in a Temporary marriage though usually this type of relationship is more quickly and easily terminated than the other forms of marriage.

There are two ways that dissensus about expectations can be changed so it is not disruptive. The most obvious method is for one or both of the spouses to change their role expectations so that the couple can agree rather than disagree. This easy-sounding solution is frequently, however, difficult to implement because some of our role expectations are highly valued, and some are so ingrained that we can't change them—even when we want to. Other expectations are such an intricate part of a highly valued style of life that it would be very disruptive and costly to change them. Frequently, however, it is possible for one spouse to change his or her expectations so that they are compatible with those of the other spouse, or for both spouses to make slight changes so that there is a mutually agreeable compromise arrangement. Some of us would undoubtedly benefit if we increased our skill at doing this, and the following exercise is designed to help us determine how skillful we are and to enhance our skill.

<hr>

[4] Jacobson (1952); Luckey (1960, 1961); Pineo (1961); Kotlar (1961); and Komarovsky (1962).

INCREASING CONSENSUS ABOUT ROLE EXPECTATIONS

Goal: To increase the ability to eliminate conflicts about role expectations.

1. Select someone who is fairly close such as a spouse, parent, fiancé(e), or friend, and ask that person to help you do something to improve your relationship.

2. Find one or two conflicting expectations in your relationship that you would like to eliminate. If you already know of some, use them. If you don't know of any, use the list of role expectations (adapted from Dunn, 1960) given below. The way to use this list is for each of you to go through it and mark on a sheet of paper whether you agree or disagree with each statement. Then compare your sheets to find areas in which you disagree.

A list of role expectations

a. If there is a difference of opinion the husband should decide where to live.

b. Husbands and wives should share housework equally.

c. A wife should be as well informed as the husband concerning the family's financial status and business affairs.

d. Wives should combine career and motherhood.

e. A husband should leave the care of the children entirely up to the wife when they are babies.

f. It is more important for the wife to be a good cook and housekeeper than to be an attractive, interesting companion.

g. Unless there are very unusual circumstances, each spouse should agree to participate in sexual intercourse when the other is interested.

h. Keeping the yard, making repairs, and doing outside chores should be the responsibility of whoever wishes and has the time to do them.

i. The husband and wife should have equal privileges in such things as going out at night.

j. The husband and wife should have an equal voice in decisions affecting the family as a whole.

k. After marriage a woman should forget an education and become primarily a homemaker.

l. It is more important that a husband be congenial and loving than that he earn a good living.

m. Husbands should spend most of their energies in getting ahead and becoming a success.

    n. Being married should cause little or no change in either the husband's or the wife's social or recreational activities.

    o. The wife should fit her life to her husband's more than the husband should fit his life to hers.

    p. Husbands and wives should feel equally responsible for the children.

    q. Traditional views on which jobs men and women should do around the house should be completely ignored, and interests and abilities should determine who does what.

    r. As children grow up, the boys should become more the responsibility of the father and the girls the responsibility of the mother.

    s. Add to the list by writing down your own expectations.

3. Check the disagreement so that each of you understands how the other feels. You may want to try role reversal (pages 106–8) to make sure you understand each other's views.

4. Next, use the steps in decision making (pages 141–46) to try to create consensus. Try to do this by talking about the disagreement to see whether you can find a solution, such as one of you changing his or her opinion, both changing a little, or deciding that the area of disagreement is unimportant or irrelevant. If you are able to arrive at a satisfactory solution to the problem, you have finished this exercise. However, if you cannot solve the problem alone, go on to step 5.

5. Talk with an acquaintance or a group you can trust, and see whether they can help you arrive at a satisfactory solution. You could use friends, class discussion groups, or other associates who would probably be useful resources. If this discussion creates a satisfactory solution, you have finished. However, if you cannot resolve the disagreement in this way, go on to step 6.

6. Talk with a professional person, such as the instructor of a marriage course, a counselor in a student counseling center, a minister, or a clinical psychologist, to see whether that person can (a) help you resolve the difference you have identified, and (b) help you increase your ability to resolve other differences.

A second way to cope with dissensus about role expectations is to eliminate the undesirable consequences when the dissensus cannot be eliminated. This can occasionally be done by changing the relevance of the role expectations, compartmentalizing the expectations so that certain things will be done only when they are most acceptable, bargaining so that there is some sort of acceptable equality in the role conflicts, trying to suppress the conflicts so that they do not emerge into consciousness, or having periodic sessions to cope with the frustrations that are caused by unalterable role conflicts. No exercises to practice these alternatives have been developed, but readers may find it useful to devise situations in which they can practice these alternatives.

COMPATIBILITY OF ROLES

Another principle in symbolic interaction theory that is useful in working out satisfactory marital role arrangements deals with the compatibility versus incompatibility of the roles in our lives. At one time or another most married individuals find themselves in situations in which two or more of the many roles they occupy interfere with one another. Some examples of this are found in the following situations.

After the baby came, I wanted to keep my job, but I just couldn't keep up with it all. It was so much more work than I thought it would be that I just about died. . . . I only worked for about three more weeks, and then I just had to quit.

Boy, I thought everything would come apart the other night. Betty and I were at this party, and the gal I was out with last week was there. She kept looking over at us, and I knew she caught on we were married. . . . Once she looked like she was coming over where we were so, boy, did we get up fast and dance. . . . I'm gonna just hafta be more careful.

I know he's lonely and wants me around more, and I'd really like to spend more time with him, but with the demands of my job and school there just doesn't seem to be any way I can.

The main variable in these situations is the compatibility of roles. Roles are compatible when they do not interfere with each other, or when the expectations for some roles do not conflict with the expectations for other roles. They are incompatible when some of our roles make it difficult to carry out others or when the expectations for one role interfere with other roles. Role compatibility is a continuous variable that ranges between low and high amounts, as shown here, and the principle that ties role compatibility and marital satisfaction together is:

Role Compatibility

Low   Medium   High

THE ROLE COMPATIBILITY PRINCIPLE: The greater the role compatibility in marriage the greater the marital satisfaction, and vice versa.[5]

This principle can be applied to dating and marital situations in several ways. One way is to be sensitive to the presence of incompatible roles and to try to determine whether they are having an adverse effect on the relationship. If they are, several things can be done either (a) to eliminate the incompatibilities or (b) to eliminate the adverse effects of the incompatibilities. One way to eliminate incompatibilities is to terminate one of the roles, and another way is to change one's behavior in one of the roles so that the role is more compatible with the rest of the roles in one's life. This latter procedure is routinely followed by couples when the occupational roles of either the husband or the wife become incompatible with the rest of his or her obligations. For example, at certain times the wife or husband may put in less overtime or may work only part-time. Another example of eliminating a role would be for a couple to stop going out with others upon becoming engaged.

In addition to resolving role incompatibilities by terminating or changing roles, it is also possible to do several things that eliminate or at least reduce the harmful effects of incompatibilities. One strategy for doing this that Goode (1960) has suggested is to compartmentalize incompatible roles. This can be done by playing one role in one physical and social setting and playing roles that tend to be incompatible with that role in other physical and social settings. This process can be illustrated by the fact that many occupational roles are fairly incompatible with family roles and that the strain on individuals would increase if they had to work and live in the same place. Certain role combinations are highly incompatible, and unless such roles are compartmentalized they will seriously disrupt an individual's life situation. Examples of these are having an affair, being a mistress, or engaging in illegal activities while trying to retain a socially "respectable" position in society.

The application of this principle in our personal lives seems to

---

[5] This principle is a slight modification and extension of a group of propositions developed by Cottrell (1942) and Goode (1960) and later refined by Burr (1973). No empirical studies are known that specifically test this principle in marital relationships, but Cottrell and Goode were both using large bodies of sociological literature as the bases of their ideas. Thus, confidence in the validity of this principle rests on their informal analysis of the literature and on the plausibility of the principle.

be a very straightforward process and does not seem to involve complex or unique skills. It is merely a process of recognizing various incompatibilities and then finding ways to change them when necessary.

UNDERSTANDING AND MARITAL SATISFACTION

Several schools of thought in the social sciences argue that the ability to accurately perceive such subtle aspects of others as their role expectations, attitudes, values, and emotional responses is a major factor in determining the quality of interpersonal relationships.[6] In addition it is so widely believed in the American society that the ability to accurately understand one's spouse is an important asset in marital relationships that this is viewed as almost a law of human behavior (Klemer, 1970, p. 4). However, a number of empirical studies have attempted to determine whether variation in the ability to understand one's spouse affects marital satisfaction, and these studies suggest that the relationship between understanding and marital satisfaction is more complex than it first appears. Because the complexities of this idea are not widely known, it seems useful to identify the general principle that relates understanding and marital satisfaction and then to identify some of the factors that seem to complicate this relationship. This develops into a fairly complex group of principles, but after they have all been identified it will be possible to identify several ways that some of us can use these principles in our dating and marital relationships.

The main independent variable in this idea is the accuracy with which spouses understand each other. This fairly commonplace phenomenon is labeled here the *accuracy of understanding*,[7] and it can vary from very low to extremely high understanding, as diagramed below:

Accuracy of understanding

| Very low | Low | Medium | High | Extremely high |

----

[6] Foote and Cottrell (1955), Mead (1934), and Roberts (1940, 1972) illustrate the schools of thought that hold this view.

[7] Several other labels could be used. In symbolic interaction theory, for example, the term *role taking* is used to describe this phenomenon, and in most of the empirical research about this process (Dymond, 1949, 1953; Hobart, 1956; Hobart and Clausner, 1959; Hastorf and Bender, 1954; Locke, 1956; Vernon and Stewart, 1957) *empathy* has been the most widely used term.

Most of the previous literature that has speculated about the relationship between accuracy of understanding and marital satisfaction suggests that:

THE UNDERSTANDING PRINCIPLE: The more accurately spouses understand each other the greater their marital satisfaction, and vice versa.

The studies that have investigated this relationship have measured the level of understanding by asking one spouse to identify such things as her or his values, attitudes, or interests, and then asking the other spouse to indicate what she or he thinks was identified. The spouses who made the most errors were then judged as having the least understanding and the ones who made the least errors were classified as having the most understanding. When these scores have been compared to the level of marital satisfaction the findings have been so conflicting that they are almost inconclusive if only these two variables are taken into account. Dymond (1953), Wallen (1957), and Karlsson (1963) found a positive relationship between accuracy of understanding and marital satisfaction; Corsini (1956) found no relationship; and Clements (1967) found that accuracy of understanding such things as personality and personal characteristics was related to marital satisfaction while accuracy of understanding such things as role beliefs was not. The only finding that has appeared consistently in the research is that there is a sex difference in the effects of understanding. Both Luckey (1960, 1961) and Stuckert (1963) controlled for sex, and both found that the accuracy of the wife's understanding of her husband was related to her marital satisfaction while the accuracy of the husband's understanding was not related to his marital satisfaction.

Thus, the empirical studies that have investigated this relationship do not provide conclusive evidence either for or against the Understanding principle. One attempt to explain why these conflicting findings have occurred is the suggestion that the relationship in the understanding principle may be curvilinear, as diagramed in Figure 12–2 (Burr, 1973, p. 63). This figure suggests that having a very low understanding of one's spouse interferes with marital satisfaction, but that after a moderate level of accuracy has been achieved additional increases in accuracy are not related to marital satisfaction. If the relationship does have this shape it is not too surprising that some studies have found no relationship while other studies have found a positive relationship. Studies that used samples in which there were very few individuals who were inaccurate in their understanding or in which the analysis of the data failed to separate out those individuals, would find no relationship,

Figure 12–2

A suggested shape of the relationship between accuracy of understanding
and marital satisfaction

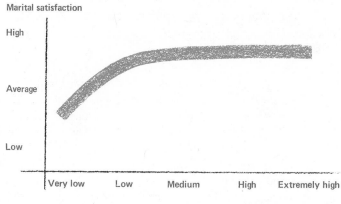

while studies that separated out relatively inaccurate understanders
would find a relationship.

If this resolution of the conflicting research is correct, and if
most people are moderately accurate in their understanding of their
spouse, this means that it is relatively useless for most people to
try to increase their understanding of their spouse as a means of
increasing their marital satisfaction. Increases in accuracy of understanding would only make a difference for the few individuals who
are very low in their ability to accurately understand their spouse.

*The effects
of power*

Another complexity in the relationship between accuracy of
understanding and marital satisfaction has to do with the fact that
several studies have found that the relationship existed for wives
but not for husbands. It is, of course, possible that nothing should
be read into this finding, but such scholars as Luckey (1960),
Stuckert (1963), and Udry (1974, p. 216) have speculated that this
difference is probably not due to biological differences between the
sexes. Instead, they have suggested that in contemporary society the
male tends to have greater power than the female and that the wife
therefore usually has to make more adaptations in the relationship
than the husband. They therefore suggest that the *power* a person
has in a relationship influences whether or not accuracy of under-

standing will make a difference in that person's satisfaction with the relationship. It is probably useful to state this idea as a principle at this point because several additional ideas that are introduced later make the entire formulation more complex. This idea is:

THE POWER-UNDERSTANDING PRINCIPLE: The more power either spouse has the less likely that that spouse's accuracy of understanding is positively related to his or her marital satisfaction, and vice versa.

Figure 12–3 is an attempt to diagram this very complex idea. The solid line shows the relationship between accuracy of understanding

Figure 12–3

The relationship between accuracy of understanding one's spouse and marital satisfaction when power in the relationship is controlled

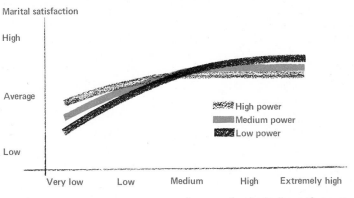

and marital satisfaction when one spouse has higher power than the other. The dotted line shows the relationship between accuracy of understanding and marital satisfaction when one spouse has less power than the other. The dashed line shows the relationship when the power of both spouses tends to be equal. As can be seen from these lines, the relationship between accuracy of understanding and marital satisfaction is systematically influenced by the distribution of power in the marital relationship.

Another way of stating this idea is that marital satisfaction is influenced by variation in understanding—under certain conditions. However, under other conditions variation in understanding has no impact on satisfaction with the marital relationship—and one of those conditions is the distribution of power in the relationship. When unequal power exists, the ability of the person with high power to understand the person with low power seems to make less difference to the person with high power, and the ability of the person with low power to understand the person with high power seems to have more influence on the satisfaction of the person with low power.

The Power-Understanding principle has several important implications for marital relationships. One of these is that, if the generalization is true, women in some of the more "traditional" types of marriages will find their marriages more satisfying if they cultivate their ability to accurately understand their husbands, but that the men in such marriages will probably not increase their marital satisfaction by cultivating this skill. And in the more "modern" marriages in which couples want to have a more equal distribution of the power in their relationships, the principle implies that it is no more crucial for the woman to be understanding than it is for the man, and that a moderate level of ability to understand the other will probably facilitate satisfaction for both sexes, but that increases in understanding beyond that level will have progressively less impact on satisfaction.

It seems to this author that we could use these principles in three ways. First, we could try to determine what the actual power distribution is in our relationship. Second, we could try to determine how proficient we are in understanding each other. Third, we could determine whether our marriage would be improved by making one or more of several changes. If, for example, one of us has believed that we should be highly proficient in understanding the spouse and has been devoting considerable time and energy to becoming more accurately insightful, that person might find it useful to spend this time and energy in other aspects of the relationship or in other aspects of his or her individual life. This would apparently be especially true if the one who has been trying to increase his or her understanding is clearly dominant in the relationship. We might also want to make changes if we determined that one spouse is very inaccurate in his or her understanding of the other. If this turned out to be the case we would probably benefit from actively attempting to increase the accuracy of that person's understanding. In such instances, use the "Action Plan" outline on pages 164–65 to develop a strategy for improving the accuracy of understanding.

The effects of similarity

Stuckert (1963) introduced two other variables that seem to help explain when and how variation in the accuracy of understanding one's spouse influences marital satisfaction. One of his variables is the amount of *similarity* between the spouses. He suggested that understanding may have different effects when people are similar to each other than when they are different. If they are similar to each other an accurate understanding may enhance their satisfaction with the relationship, but if they are different from each other they may be better off with an inaccurate understanding than with an accurate understanding. This is an application of such old adages as "Ignorance is bliss" and "What you don't know won't hurt you," in the sense that accurately perceiving differences may create a less satisfying situation than inaccurately believing that one's spouse is more like oneself than he or she really is. It may also be the basis for such sayings as the one attributed to Benjamin Franklin: "Keep your eyes wide open before marriage and half-shut afterwards."

Stuckert's idea that the similarity of spouses influences the effects understanding has on marital satisfaction has only been tested on one sample (Stuckert, 1963), but the findings in that sample are consistent with his thesis. This idea, thus, seems to justify a speculation that the more unlike couples are, the greater the likelihood that accuracy of understanding will have a detrimental effect on satisfaction with the relationship. This principle is:

THE SIMILARITY-UNDERSTANDING PRINCIPLE: When two spouses are similar, accuracy of understanding tends to be positively related to marital satisfaction, but when they are dissimilar the relationship tends to be inverse.

The following example illustrates this principle. A couple known to the author had developed a style of married life that was fairly satisfying to both of them until the wife became aware of some of the husband's previously hidden thoughts and experiences. The husband engaged in several forms of sexual fantasy when they were engaging in precoital lovemaking and in sexual intercourse, and this included thinking about sexual experiences with other women in his life and recalling erotically stimulating pictures he had seen. This had occurred regularly throughout their marriage, but the wife was not aware of it until they had been married for several years. When she accidentally learned about his fantasies she was extremely resentful and felt that not only was she inadequate sexually but that she had been exploited by her husband. Her reactions led to problems in other aspects of their relationship, and they later sought professional help in coping with their problems. They were partly successful in maintaining a pleasant relationship, but her satisfaction with the marriage was substantially altered. A number of factors other than her unwelcomed insights undoubtedly contributed to their problems, but it seemed to those involved in the

situation, including their counselor, that their marriage would probably have been better off if she had never learned of his fantasies.

The Similarity-Understanding principle can be used in several
ways. One way is for couples to realize that a thorough and complete understanding may not always be desirable in marital relationships. It may be that on occasion the wisest course for couples
would be to assess their level of understanding of each other and
then decide that, for them, increased understanding would probably
not be desirable. In fact, in some relationships couples might be
best off if they were to increase their independence from each other
in order to insulate each other from certain aspects of their life
situations.

REFERENCE GROUPS AND MARITAL SATISFACTION

Another major idea in symbolic interaction theory that is useful
in influencing marital satisfaction has a long history in sociology
and social psychology. In fact rudiments of the idea can be found
in writings that date back to the 19th century,[8] even though the
idea was not well developed until Hyman (1942) coined the term
reference group and an examination was made of American soldiers
in World War II in a series of volumes entitled *The American
Soldier* (Stouffer et al., 1949; Merton and Kitt, 1950). The idea is
that people's evaluation of how satisfied they are with something is
partly a function of how they view their situation relative to
"reference groups," "comparison points," or "significant others."
Applied to the marital situation the theory predicts that if people
think that their marriage is about the same as most marriages they
will tend to be satisfied with the marriage, while if they think that
their marriage is either better or worse than most marriages they
will tend to be more or less satisfied with their marriage than is the
person with an average marriage.

The literature in sociology discusses how reference relationships
influence people's evaluation of their own situation, and it includes
long discussions of several aspects of this principle. This author has
not, however, found a precise definition of the variables or a brief
statement of the principle. Because of this, an attempt is made here
to synthesize the principle out of the prior literature and then to

---

[8] Durkheim (1893); James (1890).

state it in a concise, clear manner. The main independent variable seems to be the differences in a person's situation *relative to* or *in comparison with* that of other individuals who form a reference point for that person. If a person's situation is fairly undesirable in an objective or absolute sense, but the other individuals with whom he compares himself are worse off than he is, the person will probably be quite satisfied with his own lot. If, on the other hand, the same person—in exactly the same social circumstances—were to be worse off than most of the individuals whom he uses as his comparison points or reference points, that person is probably much less satisfied with his situation.

The term that has been coined to label this variable has some unfortunate connotations, but it has been so widely used that it would probably be less confusing to use it here than it would be to invent a new term. The term is *relative deprivation,* and it is a continuous variable that can range from being much less well off to being much better off than one's reference group. At its midpoint an individual is about as well off as the significant others in his or her life situation. Having low deprivation denotes a condition of being much better off than one's reference group, and having high deprivation denotes being much more deprived. This can be diagramed as follows:

Relative deprivation

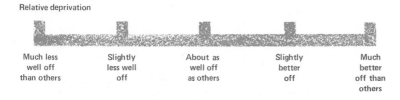

| Much less well off than others | Slightly less well off | About as well off as others | Slightly better off | Much better off than others |

The main idea in the principle[9] is that the more deprived a person is relative to his reference group, the less satisfied she or he will be. The principle is:

THE DEPRIVATION-SATISFACTION PRINCIPLE: The relative deprivation of one's marriage as a whole influences marital satisfaction, and this is an inverse relationship.

The author knows of only one empirical study that has tested this idea in a marital situation, and this was not really an adequate test because it was applied to only part of a sample of 50 couples (Stuckert, 1963). However, a vast amount of evidence has been amassed to test the more abstract idea that satisfaction in a given situation is partly a function of the relative deprivation in that

[9] This is a specific instance of more general principles in Festinger (1954) and Davis (1959).

situation. The idea has been tested for example, in regard to such diverse phenomena as military life (Stouffer et al., 1949), social movements (Jahoda, 1942; Runciman, 1966), and industrial relations (Roethlisberger, 1945; Patchen, 1961). The idea of relative deprivation is also such an essential part of very complex and widely accepted sociological theories that the deprivation-satisfaction principle should be viewed as having enough scientific support to be virtually a social law.[10]

The application of this principle to courtship and marital situations is fairly straightforward. If couples want to become more satisfied with their own situation they can focus their attention on couples around them who are as well off or worse off than they are; if they want to decrease their satisfaction with their own situation they can focus their attention on couples who are discernibly better off than they are. Both of these options are realistic, as the two following case histories illustrate.

I grew up in a family where the parents never had a cross word in front of the children. I now think that they did have differences and arguments, but I was unaware of them all while I grew up, and just assumed that that was the way marriage was. After Jane and I were married we used to have differences, and, as you know, she's a fairly verbal and strong-willed gal, so some of those sessions got heated. We'd work things through, but for the first eight years of our marriage I really felt bad about the way we handled our problems. I remember wondering why we couldn't solve our problems like most people did. Eventually, though, I learned that most of our friends had differences and frustrations that were very much like ours, and that my view of what a marriage ought to be was what was out of step. After that it became sort of a curiosity for me for some time, and I'd observe others and talk about this with them. I learned Jane and I were pretty typical.

I always assumed [stated a marriage counselor] that my first marriage was all right. Then, after I'd been in practice for several years, I finally realized that I had more problems and less satisfaction in my own marriage than most of the people I was seeing at the clinic. We talked about it for a while, and both of us talked to some of our friends about the situation. Finally we decided that we'd probably both be better off if we got a divorce. Before we called it quits we both wondered if we were doing the right thing, but now I'm sure we did.

The Deprivation-Satisfaction principle can be applied to satisfaction with a marriage as a whole or to specific parts of the relationship. For example, if a couple are experiencing something problematic they can broaden their perspective by reading books,

---

[10] Homans (1961); Blau (1964); Merton (1968); Hyman (1968).

talking to other people, attending divorce courts, doing volunteer work in agencies designed to help people with serious problems, etc.

It should also be remembered that this principle can be used to either increase or decrease satisfaction. If one person in a relationship is satisfied with something that is not satisfactory to the other person, and the dissatisfied person wants to create some dissatisfaction in or reduce the complacency of her or his partner, this principle can be used to help accomplish that too. This is illustrated by the following situation.

. . . but he just doesn't seem to understand what's going on. He doesn't even think there's a problem. I've tried to tell him how upset I am, but he just says I worry too much and am making a big fuss about nothing. If things go on like this for much longer, though, I just can't take it. We've just got to do something about it. It might be OK for some people to live like this, but I just won't do it. . . . It's gotten to a point where we hardly say anything to each other. He's over at that track all the time, and when he's home he just sits in front of that TV or reads.

In situations such as this a change in the reference groups *for either spouse* might change their satisfaction with their situation. The following exercise is an attempt to change satisfaction with some aspect of a relationship by getting different reference relationships.

REFERENCE GROUP CHANGES

Goal: To change satisfaction with something by changing reference relationships.

1. Find some aspect of your life in which you want to either increase or decrease your satisfaction.

2. If you want to increase your satisfaction, find some people who are as well off as you are or worse off than you are, and visit with them. As you visit with them, compare your situation to theirs. There are many places where it is possible to interact with individuals who are in less or more advantageous situations than one's own. For example, visiting with neighbors or friends, and visiting institutions that care for the disadvantaged, the retarded, or the elderly can be of service to them *and* helpful in realizing how well off one is.

3. Later, evaluate your own situation and determine whether you feel differently than you did before.

COMPENSATIONS IN MARRIAGE

Probably every marriage has some problems that cannot be eliminated or viewed as irrelevant. These are undoubtedly different in different relationships, but it is still likely that every couple has some unresolvable problems. An example of such problems is the inability of spouses to change deeply ingrained traits, such as a quick temper, excessive jealousy, or indecisiveness. Unresolvable role discrepancies, conflicts in expectations, or incompatibilities of roles don't, however, doom a marital relationship for a number of reasons, and one of these reasons is that other aspects of a relationship or life situation can *compensate* for them. This process of compensation occurs when desirable aspects of a relationship balance out the negative effects of undesirable aspects of the relationship (Wallin and Clark, 1964; Burr, 1973, pp. 51–52). The process of compensation is extremely valuable in marriages because when the negative effects of some things can be neutralized by a compensatory part of the relationship, the net result is at least a neutral, if not a pleasant, situation. The process of compensation is illustrated by a tale about a man who was having difficulty deciding which of two women to marry. One of the women, so the story goes, was extremely beautiful and charming, and he loved her deeply. The other woman sang exceptionally well, and he was also deeply in love with her. He finally decided to marry the woman who sang because he reasoned that the physical beauty would not last while the musical talent would become even more pleasant as the years passed. Upon waking up and turning over the first morning after the marriage, he looked at his new wife, covered his eyes, and said pleadingly, "Sing! Sing!"

The compensation process has several practical implications. First, it helps us understand why it is possible to have deeply rewarding and pleasant marital relationships even though there are some aspects of a marital relationship that are not exactly as we would prefer them . . . and all married couples eventually learn that their marriage too has such aspects. Second, it is possible to manipulate the pleasant aspects of marital relationships and to focus attention on them so that they compensate more effectively for the negative aspects. If, for example, a couple were to find that certain experiences, such as dancing together, outdoor recreational activities, or collecting antiques, were highly pleasurable aspects of their relationship they could cultivate those parts of their life so that they would become more salient and dominating *themes* (Hess and Handel, 1967) in their interaction. As those parts of the couple's life become more salient and highly valued they would then tend to be more effective in compensating for the negative aspects of their relationship.

SUMMARY

This chapter has identified several principles that can be used to create compatibility in the roles that two individuals have in marriage. The first generalization discussed was called the *Congruence* principle, and it is diagramed with line 1 in Figure 12–4. It suggests that variation in the amount of congruence between role expecta-

Figure 12–4

Causal model of principles in Chapter 12.

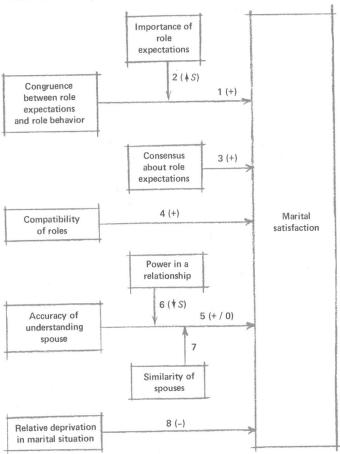

tions and role behavior influences marital satisfaction. The next principle was the *Importance* principle, and it is diagramed with line 2 in the causal model. It asserts that the more individuals view role discrepancies as important the more disruptive the role discrepancies tend to be. The *Role Consensus* principle states that the amount that spouses disagree about their role expectations usually influences their satisfaction with their relationship, and the *Role Compatibility* hypothesis suggests that the more various roles tend to interfere with one another the more disrupted the marital relationship. These two principles are diagramed in Figure 12–4 with lines 3 and 4.

Several generalizations were then discussed that deal with how variation in how well spouses understand each other influences their marital relationship. It was suggested in the *Understanding* principle (line 5) that there is a curvilinear relationship between the accuracy of understanding one's spouse and marital satisfaction. The *Power-Understanding* principle asserts, however, that understanding makes more difference for individuals with low power than for individuals with high power, and the *Similarity-Understanding* generalization suggests that when individuals are quite different from each other the relationship between accuracy of understanding and satisfaction may even be inverse. These last two hypotheses are shown with arrows 6 and 7 in the causal model. The final principle discussed was the *Deprivation-Satisfaction* principle, which asserts that satisfaction is partly a function of how well off we are relative to others who are significant to us. Various ways of applying these principles were also discussed.

SUGGESTIONS FOR FURTHER STUDY

Blood, Robert O., Jr., and Wolfe, Donald M. 1960. *Husbands and Wives: The Dynamics of Married Living.* Glencoe, Ill.: Free Press.

Burgess, Ernest W., and Cottrell, Leonard S., Jr. 1939. *Predicting Success or Failure in Marriage.* Englewood Cliffs, N.J.: Prentice-Hall.

Burgess, Ernest W., and Wallin, Paul 1953. *Engagement and Marriage.* Philadelphia: Lippincott.

Burr, Wesley R. 1973. *Theory Construction and the Sociology of the Family.* New York: Wiley, chap. 3.

Cottrell, L. S., Jr. 1933. "Roles in Marital Adjustment." Publications of the *American Sociological Society* 27:108–15 (May).

Davis, James A. 1959. "A Formal Interpretation of the Theory of Relative Deprivation." *Sociometry* 22:280–96 (December).

Goode, William J. 1960. "A Theory of Role Strain." *American Sociological Review* 25:488–96 (August).

Hyman, Herbert H.   1968. "Reference Groups." *International Encyclopedia of the Social Sciences,* vol. 13.

Jackson, Jay M.   1966. "Structural Characteristics of Norms," in B. J. Biddle and E. J. Thomas (eds.), *Role Theory: Concepts and Research.* New York: Wiley.

Leslie, Gerald R.   1967. *The Family in Social Context.* New York: Oxford University Press, chap. 15.

Mangus, A. R.   1957. "Role Theory and Marriage Counseling." *Social Forces* 35:209–20 (March).

13

Controlling bonds in marriage [1]

THE TERM *bond* refers to the ties that keep two or more people together in a relationship. A number of other concepts in the social sciences have virtually the same meaning, and some of them are: *cohesion, attachment, connectedness, solidarity, interdependence,* and *attraction.* The word *bond* rather than one of these other terms is used here because it has been the most widely used in recent literature (Turner, 1970) and has fewer other connotations than most of the similar terms. In a more common-sense terminology, the bonds in a relationship are the glue or magnetism that keeps a couple together.

There are two reasons why bonds are important enough to have an entire chapter devoted to them. First, most couples in contemporary society want to have relatively strong ties to each other in their marriage, and having these ties is more than just a passing matter. It is something that most couples feel strongly about. This does not mean that all couples want to have intense bonds or that all couples want the same degree of bondedness. Some couples want extremely intense bonds while others, such as the O'Neills (1970), want weaker ties. These differences are illustrated by the two following comments:

Jay and I find most of our satisfaction in life in the things we do as individuals rather than as a couple. We want to stay married, but pretty much to have our separate lives—I think it is our own individual interests that really keep us lively and enthusiastic about life.

[1] Appreciation is expressed to Margaret Jensen for her assistance in writing this chapter. Readers familiar with Turner's (1970, chaps. 3, 4) analysis of bonds will recognize our dependence on his ideas throughout this chapter.

We want to be a close-knit couple—to be very much involved with each other—to feel like a team instead of just two people who are married.

The first couple want their marriage to have a certain degree of interconnectedness, but they don't want the extremely strong bonds that the second couple seem to want.

Second, bonds are important in marriage because people sometimes want to *change* the strength of the bonds they have with their partner. During courtship, for example, most people want to increase their ties to the other person, and they use such things as songs, promises, pins, rings, and affection to strengthen those ties. At other stages of the family life cycle people want to decrease their ties to others. An example of this is that all marital relationships are eventually broken by death or divorce, and when this occurs most people want to decrease their interdependence with the other person. In fact, some research evidence suggests that recovery from the disruptive effects of death or divorce is influenced by how well people are able to break their bonds with the other person (Goode, 1956). There may also be times when couples want to become "closer" to each other or want to feel slightly less "tied" to each other, and at such times it is important to know how to increase or decrease bonds. The main goal in this chapter is thus to discuss principles that can be used to increase or decrease the bonds in a marital relationship. Before these principles can be discussed, however, it is important to define the term *bond* more clearly.

THE MEANING OF THE TERM *BOND*

Bondedness was briefly defined earlier as the ties that keep two or more people together, and several synonyms were identified. More needs to be said about the term's meaning, however, or it may be easily confused with several closely related terms, such as *love, harmony,* and *marital satisfaction.*

Bonds, as the term is used here, differ from love. Love frequently arises from or accompanies bonds, but love is not bondedness itself. One author has clarified the difference between love and bonds by stating that "love is a feeling or experience that reflects the presence of bonds between people more than it is a bond in itself" (Turner, 1970, p. 47). Another way of looking at this difference is that love is a sentiment or emotion that an individual experiences while bonds are a characteristic of a relationship.

Bondedness in marriage is also different from satisfaction with the marital relationship. Marital satisfaction is a subjective evaluation of the quality of a marriage, and bonds are the interpersonal ties or interconnectedness of the relationship. When we are think-

ing about a couple's bonds we are thinking about how interdependent they are or how tied they are to each other, not how
satisfied they are with their marriage. It would be possible for a
couple to have very intense bondedness and not be satisfied with
their marriage at all, or to have very low bondedness and be very
satisfied with their marital situation. If a couple were to want a
certain amount of cohesion in their marriage, their marital satisfaction would undoubtedly be *affected* by whether or not they were as
cohesive as they wanted to be, but the cohesion and the satisfaction
are two different phenomena.

Harmony or consensus is another concept that is mistakenly
equated with cohesion. Turner (1970) defines harmony as lack of
conflict. It is the degree to which people agree or disagree, or the
amount they support rather than detract from one another's identities. High bondedness can exist when there is high harmony, but it
is also possible to have high harmony and low bondedness. It is also
possible to have low harmony and either high or low bondedness.
The distinction between bondedness and consensus was also made
by Durkheim (1893) when he pointed out that bonds can be created
by either consensus or a division of labor.

It is also important to understand that bondedness is a variable.
The lowest point on the variable is no bonds, and this occurs when
there is indifference or a lack of attachment. It is a condition in

Bonds in a relationship

None   Few   Some   Many strong

which there is no involvement between the persons, no interdependence, no indication that the other person matters. This low
point of bondedness is not the same as having negative feelings
about the other person because sentiment is a different phenomenon than bondedness. It is also not true that a divorce implies an
absence of bonds. As the following comment illustrates, many kinds
of ties can remain after a marriage is dissolved.

I see now that there's not much of me that isn't Joe's wife. Even though
I've been eager to have this divorce finalized and to begin a different
life, there are so many ways I'm still connected to him—even silly
things like counting on him to tease me back when I start to tease him
about his weight. I miss that, in spite of myself.

Brown has described the experience of high bondedness as "a
feeling of union with someone else, a feeling that the self has grown
beyond its skin" (1965, p. 82). High bondedness is also illustrated
by the husband who tells a friend, "We're pregnant!" or the wife

who says, "We got a new job." Low bondedness is illustrated by the following account, "He did ask me out three weeks ago, but he doesn't stop and talk when we meet on campus, and he hasn't called me again. I guess he's just not interested."

PRINCIPLES ABOUT BONDS

Each of the following six principles identifies a factor or variable that usually influences the bonds in a relationship. Hopefully, a knowledge of these principles, when coupled with the skills to implement them, will increase our ability to create the degree of cohesion we want in our marriage, dating, or other interpersonal relationships. This should not be interpreted as an argument that very strong bonds are necessarily an optimum goal. The amount of cohesion that is optimal in some relationships may be fairly low, while the amount that is optimal in other relationships may be high. It is our value system, with its ideas about the importance and functions and style of marriage, that will determine the strength of the bonds we want in a marriage, and the principles are vehicles we can use to help us attain our goals.

Shared experience

Turner (1970, pp. 81–83) has suggested that the amount of shared experience influences bonds. Shared experience refers to the amount that two individuals have common experiences, either by doing something together or by talking about something in enough detail to genuinely share it. One kind of shared experience occurs when people interact with each other, as in dating or in working together. Another kind of shared experience occurs when people learn that they have had a similar experience, even though no interaction between them was involved (for example, both saw the same TV show; both worked in the same political campaign; both were raised in large families). An experience of one person alone can become a shared experience when two people discuss it with each other. The amount of shared experience is a continuous variable ranging from none (between a girl and the boy who "doesn't know she's alive") to a very high amount. The principle that ties shared experiences and bondedness together is:

THE SHARED EXPERIENCE PRINCIPLE: The amount of shared experience a couple has influences the strength of their bonds, and this is a positive, linear relationship.[2]

---

[2] Turner (1970, pp. 81–83) has extracted this principle from the symbolic interaction literature. As with most ideas in symbolic interaction, the idea is an integrated part of a very complex description of human interaction, but empirical tests of the ideas have not yet been made. Turner ties the idea to other analytic essays, such as Halbwachs (1950, pp. 1–34) and Berger and Kellner (1964), and this makes the idea fairly plausible. This principle is

Probably one reason there is a relationship between shared experience and bondedness is that when two individuals experience the same things and discuss what has happened and how each feels about the experience, they begin to have similar conceptions of reality and similar attitudes. This provides a validator for each person, and gives him confidence in his ideas, since another person thinks the same way. Sharing thus provides a more stable basis for action than one person alone would have. Sharing also provides a basis for interaction, and as shared experiences accumulate over time both members of the couple become more interdependent. Another reason that shared experiences probably foster cohesion is that when a couple interact "alone together" outsiders consider them to be a unit and treat them as such, and this tends to make the couple think of themselves as connected with each other (Bolton, 1961).

The implications of this principle are many. Suppose, for example, we wanted to increase the cohesion between ourself and a person we are dating. The principle suggests that we should increase shared experiences. One way we could do this is to continue dating, as a backlog of shared experience will gradually build up in this way. We could also deliberately spend time talking about each other's past and present experiences, thus making nonshared experiences into shared ones. In addition, the more we explain our own attitudes, perceptions, and feelings as we talk with the other person the more shared experience we are acquiring.

This principle can also be used after a couple have been married for several years. Frequently couples go through a stage in which a gradual decrease in shared experience is brought about by such responsibilities as child care and community activities, since these responsibilities may involve long working hours, large distances between work and home, the segregation of occupational and family life, fatigue, mistrust, vocabulary-language barriers, educational differences, role differentiation, and periods of separation. The result is often an undesired decrease in the couple's bonds. When this is experienced it is possible for the couple to develop ways to

---

thus rationally derived, and a part of a complex theory, but has not been thoroughly tested by rigorous empirical data. Those who limit their thinking to empirically tested ideas will thus want to be skeptical of this principle, but those who have more confidence in social science as an analytic, interpretive, rational process will want to have considerable confidence in this principle. If readers are like the author, they will give credence to both the empirical and the analytic approach and accept, tentatively, ideas from either.

maintain sharing, such as providing a time for talking, establishing regular family rituals and traditions, making plans for being together, engaging in joint recreation or education, and writing notes and letters. The net effect, assuming that the principle is valid, is that bonds are enhanced.

It is usually easy to see the effects of shared experience when relationships have relatively low bondedness. Thus, in a relationship in which two individuals are just getting acquainted and the bonds are still fairly low, a marked increase or decrease in the amount of shared experience usually has a visible effect on bondedness.

Changes in shared experience can also have a marked effect on a marital relationship that has become so routine, taken for granted, and everydayish that many of the bonds have gradually withered away. In such a relationship bondedness is low and a substantial change in the amount of shared experience can very quickly have a discernible effect on the bonds. It is considerably more difficult to observe the effects of changes in shared experience when a relationship has fairly strong bonds, because the bonds are so complex and slow to change that increases or decreases in shared experience usually have no immediately discernible effect on the bonds in the relationship.

Although changes in the amount of shared experience usually do not have a dramatic effect on the bonds in most established marital relationships, it should not be assumed that they have no effect. If this principle is valid, a long-term decrease or increase in the shared experience of a married couple can still be expected to bring about a change in the bonds. However, the change in the bonds will be gradual, and it may take months or even years before the couple suddenly realizes that their "ties" to each other are different. It seems likely that this point is truer for decreases than for increases in shared experience, because usually there are so many bond-producing things in marital relationships other than shared experience that a drop in shared experience has little immediate, visible impact, while marked increases in shared experience, even in established, complex relationships, can create visible changes in bonds in a fairly short period of time.

The following two exercises are designed to create situations in which changes in shared experience in a relationship have an effect on the bonds in the relationship. Since changes in shared experience tend to have less immediate, visible impact on bonds in established relationships, these exercises frequently have a discernible effect only on relationships with relatively weak bonds. This is not always the case, however, as occasionally couples with rather intense bonds find that activities such as these change the bonds enough so that they can tell the difference.

INCREASING SHARED EXPERIENCE

Goal: To increase the bonds in a relationship by increasing the amount of shared experience.

1. Identify a relationship in which you want to increase the strength of the bonds.

2. Each day for a week deliberately plan to do one of the following two things:

    a. Engage in some pleasant activity that you have not previously done together. Do it as a pair only—no one else with you. This can involve such ordinary things as visiting a neighbor, one helping the other with some schoolwork, engaging in a new leisure activity such as miniature golf or billiards, visiting a museum, etc.

    b. Discuss some previous experience in your life or lives that you have not talked about before. Try to select something that is or was fairly important, and remember that the object is for the other person, in a sense, to share the experience.

3. At the end of the week both of you try to identify whether there are differences in the bonds in your relationship.

DECREASING SHARED EXPERIENCE

Goal: To decrease the bonds in a relationship by decreasing the amount of shared experience.

1. Select a relationship in which you want to decrease the bonds permanently or in which a temporary reduction in the bonds would not be a problem in the relationship.

2. Carry a notebook or a piece of paper for one week—in your pocket, purse, etc.

3. During the week try to identify experiences you are now having or have had in the past that you have not and will not let the other person know about, become involved in, or in any other way share with you. Number these experiences, and describe them briefly in writing. (Experiences with this exercise indicate that if you are doing this only as an experiment and you plan to share these things with the other person after the week, you may not experience a discernible decrease in the bonds. The more you plan to eventually share these things with the other person the

less likely it is that this exercise will decrease the bonds you feel.)

4. At the end of the week, review the list of experiences and evaluate how much this exercise has increased your independence from the other person.

Incomplete action

THE INCOMPLETE ACTION PRINCIPLE: The amount of investment in incomplete action influences the bonds in a relationship, and this is a positive relationship.

Incomplete action occurs when a couple have already invested time, energy, thought, or planning on something that requires both of them for its completion. It is possible to have relatively little or a great deal of incomplete action in a relationship, and most couples in most of the forms of marriage usually have a large amount of incomplete action. There is probably less incomplete action in Temporary marriages and the first stage of Two-Step marriages than in most of the other forms of marriage. The incomplete action marriage ranges from no incomplete action to a very large amount, as shown below.

Amount of incomplete action

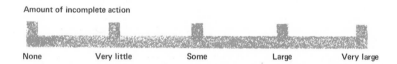

None   Very little   Some   Large   Very large

This idea is implicit in Mead's (1934, 1938) social philosophy and is more thoroughly developed in Faris' (1937) analysis of human nature. Turner (1970, pp. 80–81), however, made the principle explicit. The principle has not been tested with quantified empirical data, but it is probably defensible to tentatively accept it as valid because it is an integral part of symbolic interactionist thought and because it seems to be consistent with everyday reality.

This principle is relevant for dating and marital relationships because the amount of incomplete action in these relationships can easily be increased or decreased. When couples want to use this principle to enhance their bonds they can plan things they would like to do in the immediate future, such as take a vacation or re-model their home, or even plan much later activities, such as what they will do after retirement. Probably one of the reasons that children provide additional bonds between a couple is that so much of the parental role includes the expectation of guiding and rearing the childern.

This principle can also be used to reduce bonds in such situations as breaking an engagement, terminating a relationship with someone other than one's spouse, or adjusting to the death of a loved one. The principle suggests that the fewer incomplete joint activities there are the weaker the bonds, and the way to use this principle to decrease bonds is to decrease these uncompleted activities by completing them or by changing plans. For example, a clear-cut break with daily routines and rituals, rearranging the furniture, or moving to a new house disrupts the expected interaction patterns with someone, and such changes seem to help cope with bereavement.

The following exercise is one way of implementing this principle, and it can be done by married couples or in relationships that are as transient as those of classmates in a marriage course.

INCREASING INCOMPLETE ACTION

Goal: To increase bonds by increasing the amount of incomplete action in a relationship.

1. Select a relationship in which you want to increase the bonds between you and the other person.

2. Think up several things to do that (a) cannot be done unless both members of the couple are involved in them and (b) will take a relatively long period of time. These could include such diverse activities as joining a bridge or dance club; playing musical duets; working on a committee; collaborating on something, such as writing or decorating; planning now what to do on next year's vacation; starting a new tradition, such as going out on a certain date each month or having breakfast in bed every rainy Saturday; or assuming a parent surrogate role for a rehabilitation or prison system where both a husband and wife are needed. Be creatve in thinking up novel or exotic things.

3. Select one of the ideas in step #2 and implement it. After you have become involved in it enough to have really invested yourself in the experience, take some time to evaluate whether you have experienced any change in the bondedness in the relationship. (Theoretically, you're supposed to.)

The amount of reserve

Another of the principles developed by Turner (1970, pp. 85–87) has to do with the amount of "reserve" in relationships. Turner points out that most "communication is hedged about by a certain amount of reserve—some concern about how freely one ought to speak on certain subjects, how best to state the matter to avoid misunderstanding, or what kind of reaction to anticipate from the other person" (1970, pp. 85–86). Usually when we decrease this reserve with someone it is a very gradual process, and it is done by selecting one or two areas at a time in which we can relax our ordinary defenses and become more uninhibited. As the reserve decreases a sense of privacy tends to develop in that particular relationship, and the bonds between the individuals become stronger.

The independent variable in this principle is never clearly labeled by Turner. He refers to it as a condition of "adjusted communication," and uses such terms as *reserve, defenses, guard, free expression,* and *spontaneity* in describing this factor. He used the word *reserve* most frequently, however, so it is suggested here that the best label for this variable is the *amount of reserve* in a relationship. As shown below, this is apparently a continuous variable rather

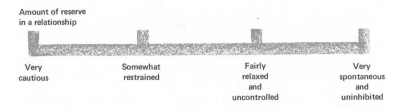

Amount of reserve
in a relationship

Very cautious   Somewhat restrained   Fairly relaxed and uncontrolled   Very spontaneous and uninhibited

than a dichotomous variable, since the amount of reserve in a relationship may range all the way from a relationship in which virtually all interaction is highly reserved—as is likely to be the case with the policeman who has just stopped someone for speeding—to a relationship with very low reserve, such as that between old friends and some couples who have been married for a long time. The principle is:

THE RESERVE PRINCIPLE: The amount of reserve in a relationship influences the strength of the bonds in that relationship, and this is an inverse relationship.

Turner does not analyze empirical data in developing this principle, as it is apparently derived from the symbolic interaction school of thought. The idea is thus rationally rather than empirically derived. The idea also seems to be intuitively reasonable, but at present it should not be viewed as a very thoroughly proven scientific principle.

This principle has a number of practical implications for courtship and marriage. As individuals interact and spend time together they become familiar with the variety of ways in which they react to each other and learn how to interpret what each of these reactions means. The new bride learns that her husband's gruffness in response to her cheery good morning is not meant as rejection but indicates that he isn't awake enough for cheer. Also, a person learns not only what the responses mean—he also learns ways to deal with them. The boy who has inadvertently offended his girlfriend has experience in helping resolve her offended feelings. Should she be offended again, he knows a little more about how to handle the situation. He may also have less need to "walk on tiptoe" in order to avoid the possibility of offending.

The freedom to express ourselves with little reserve can apply to the serious expression of our strong feelings or the ideas we champion, and it can also include the freedom to engage in silly spontaneities or to use nonverbal codes. There is, for example, the husband who puts the ingredients of a treat he would like his wife to make in a strategic place on the kitchen counter. She knows what a package of marshmallows placed in front of an open box of Rice Krispies means. Other forms of relaxed, uninhibited communication, such as being able to say, "You know what I mean," and realizing that your partner really does know, and being free to say things just as they come to mind, tend to create feelings of cohesion and integration in dating, marital, and family relationships.

Another aspect of the Reserve principle is that it is difficult for most people to develop low reserve quickly in their relationships with other people. In fact it is difficult for some of us to ever be unreserved with others. What this means is that most of us who want to acquire an unreserved type of relationship have to develop it gradually by dropping our "guards" a little at first and seeing what happens. Frequently the other person will respond by also taking a chance and dropping some of his reserve. This will probably lead to learning new things about each other and learning new ways to interact, and when we are comfortable with the new relationship we can then drop reserve in other areas. It is probably wise to have some gradualness in this process, because if we were to drop all of our reserve very quickly the chances are fairly high that we wouldn't know how to interact with the other person comfortably, and the relationship would be disrupted or uncomfortable. It is thus a process of dropping reserve *and* learning how to interact rather than just dropping reserve. There is probably an optimum amount of reserve in all relationships, and each of us can gradually discover the amount we are comfortable with in different relationships. For some of us there will be very few areas of reserve in some relationships, but others will be most comfortable with more reserve. For example, some people may want to be tactful, considerate of others' feelings, and polite most of the time, and such restrictions are forms of reservedness. Other people are comfortable with fairly formal relationships in which much of their private lives and selves are "reserved."

The Reserve principle can be used to either increase or decrease bonds. During courtship and the early stages of marriage most couples want to increase their bonds and the principle provides a method for doing this—for decreasing the reserve in the relationship. The two "Decreasing Reserve" exercises below are designed to help learn ways to accomplish this.

DECREASING RESERVE—1

Goal: To increase the strength of the bonds in a relationship by decreasing the reserve in the interaction.

1. Identify a relationship in which (*a*) you want to increase the strength of the bonds and (*b*) you can spend several hours more time visiting with this person in the next week or so than you have in the recent past.

2. Most of the time we interact with other people in certain "roles," and we have to be proper and conform to the expectations that we and others have for ourselves in those roles. Some of these fairly "ceremonial" roles are: being a spectator at a concert or a sporting event; being a dancing partner for an evening; being a parent, where we have all kinds of responsibilities that have to be carried out in a "proper" or "right" manner; and going hunting. What you are to do in this exercise is spend some time (several hours if possible) with the other person during which you mostly just talk and visit with him or her as a "person"—as a person in a whole or total sense rather than as someone who is supposed to be doing something or going someplace with you. This is a good time to talk about such things as wants, wishes, aspirations, memories, tender moments, goals, and, especially, how you and the other person "feel" about these things. The more you can

"get away" from things that have to be done and the more informal you can be during these hours the better.

Most of the time we need to be "doing" something with someone in some role (often we use these roles as a sort of crutch so that we don't have to relate to the person as a person), so you may be a little uncomfortable at first. To help this you may want to spend only a little while together on the first few occasions, and then gradually spend more and more time together.

3. At the end of a week or so, has your tendency to be "reserved" with the other person decreased? Also, does the exercise seem to have had any effect on the bonds of your relationship? If not . . . these exercises don't work for everyone . . . you may be able to devise some better ways to decrease the reserve in your relationship.

DECREASING RESERVE—2

Goal: To increase the strength of the bonds in a relationship by decreasing the reserve in the interaction.

1. Identify a relationship in which (a) you want to increase the strength of the bonds and (b) you can talk with the other individual about the various ways you are "reserved" in your interaction.

2. Set aside a half hour or so in which to do the four following things with this other person.

   a. Briefly write down five to ten ways in which you are "reserved" (guarded, controlled, inhibited) in your interaction with each other. Don't evaluate or discuss these ways while you are trying to identify the other ways because this would probably interfere with identifying other ways in which you are reserved.

   b. Evaluate the ways in which you are reserved and determine which one or two of them you think it would be best to eliminate or change. (These should be ways in which you want to change and ways in which it would be fairly easy to change.)

   c. Talk about whether there is anything either of you will need to do differently for you to feel safe or comfortable with the lessened reserve. There may be nothing to change, or one of you may need to change something, such as "Don't make fun of me when . . ." or "Hold me close when . . ."

   d. Try this for several days.

3. After trying it, evaluate whether or not the "reserve" in your relationship is different . . . and . . . whether or not you can see any difference in your bonds.

At other stages of life couples may want to decrease the strength of their bonds, and there are many ways in which this too can be accomplished. The communication can be changed so that it is more formal, more guarded, and less spontaneous, and if the principle is correct this will decrease bonds and probably prevent other bonds from appearing that might have developed otherwise. When couples are terminating a marriage this strategy is frequently used. The individuals restrict their areas of communication, talk only at certain times, and on occasion talk to each other only through a third person, such as their lawyer. The conversations usually become businesslike, to the point, and unemotional, and this very quickly builds reserve . . . and decreases bonds. The "Increasing Reserve" exercise below is designed to help accomplish this.

INCREASING RESERVE IN A RELATIONSHIP

Goal: To decrease the bonds in a relationship by increasing the reserve in the interaction.

1. Select a relationship in which you want to decrease the strength of the bonds.

2. Change your method of communicating with the other person for a period of time by doing as many of the four following things as you can.

    a. Limit your interaction with the other person so that it is confined to things that need to be done or accomplished.

    b. When you do interact with the other person, confine your interaction (talking, spending time together, etc.) to some narrow aspect of life, such as a certain role or a specific activity. Be "businesslike" in your manner by being precise, formal, clear, and efficient.

    c. Avoid talking about how you "feel" about things or letting your actions reveal your emotions.

    d. Be suspicious about the other person's motives.

3. After a period of time, evaluate the amount of reserve in the relationship and whether or not there has been a change in the bonds.

As people become involved with one another, their living patterns become intermeshed and their roles become interlocked. Some of this interlocking is due to their taking complementary roles in the division of the tasks that must be done. Some, however, is due to interdependence in more emotional and personal matters, like a wife coming to depend on her husband for humor in a tight spot or a husband learning to depend on his wife for intellectual stimulation. The following example from the life of a well-known evangelist illustrates the interlocking of roles and the effect this has on bonds.

The inter-dependence of roles

> When I was first married, I had no real experience or deep interest in church affairs. I knew nothing of board meetings or committee functions. I certainly could not see myself presiding over one. But it soon became apparent that this was an area where I could be of great use to Norman. Studying him made me realize that this sort of activity was not one of his strong points. Organizational work left him impatient and restless. He was at his best when he was preaching or writing, or dealing with the emotional difficulties of individuals. I began to see that if I could take some of the organizational work off his back, go to the committee meetings, report back, summarize, simplify, help Norman make the big decisions and spare him from having to make the little ones, I would be making an enormous contribution—one that would make me even more indispensable to him (Peale, 1971, p. 35).

The interdependence of roles is a continuous variable, as it is possible to have very little interdependence—as in a marriage

Interdependence of roles

| None | Little | High amount | Very high amount |

between two very independent people in which each relinquishes few tasks to the other and each satisfies many needs by himself or with others outside the relationship. It is also possible to have a great deal of interdependence—as in a marriage between partners in which one or the other, but not both, do most tasks and in which the couple's personal needs are fulfilled largely by each other. The relevant generalization is:

THE INTERDEPENDENCE OF ROLES PRINCIPLE: The amount the roles in a relationship are interdependent influences the strength of the bonds in the relationship, and this is a positive relationship.

Waller and Hill (1951, pp. 328–33) described ways in which interdependence is important in marital relationships. The variables involved, however, were not clearly described until Turner's (1970, p. 83) analysis of the effects of interdependence on bonds. The principle is based on qualitative analysis of what goes on in relationships rather than on quantified, empirical data, and hence it should be accepted with tentativeness until more research is done.

One way this principle can be employed in everyday life is to learn ways to increase or decrease the amount roles interlock, and there are innumerable ways in which such changes can be made. Examples of things couples can do to increase the meshing of their roles are: to have one member of the couple be primarily responsible for handling the finances for both; to turn to each other rather than to parents or friends for support in times of difficulty; to have one member do such things as type up the other's papers; to have one member assume responsibility for the maintenance of the other member's car; to help each other with occupational problems; and to divide up household jobs so that each member becomes increasingly dependent on the other one for getting certain things done. A side effect of some of these activities may be to decrease shared experience, and when this occurs the net effect may be no change in bondedness. Examples of things that can be done to decrease the interlocking of roles are: to seek companionship outside the marriage; to have such jobs as ironing clothes or repairing household gadgets done by persons other than the spouse; and to turn to friends or relatives rather than to one's spouse for companionate and/or supportive experiences. If we want to increase the strength of bonds by increasing the interlocking of some roles we can use the "Action Plan" outline on pages 164–65 to devise ways to do this. It is fairly difficult to devise a brief Action Plan that will make a substantial difference in bondedness in a relationship that has been established for a long period of time because bondedness changes so slowly. However, a long-term Action Plan can make a major difference in bondedness. Those of us who are just starting a relationship or whose bonds have virtually disappeared can expect a short-term Action Plan to make substantial changes in bonds by changing the amount roles are interlocked.

Support

Another principle that Turner (1970) argues makes a substantial difference in bonds can be termed the *Support* principle. The independent variable in this principle is the extent to which a person's

behavior enhances another person's self-esteem.[3] High supportiveness exists when a person does a great deal that enhances the other
person's self-esteem and relatively little to decrease that person's
self-esteem. Low supportiveness exists when the net effect of a
person's behavior is to decrease the other person's self-esteem.
Supportiveness occurs, for example, when one person's interaction
reinforces a favorable impression of another, shows that the person
likes to be around him or her, shows admiration or affection, or
shows concern and caring. Supportive communication says, "You are
important to me"; "You are what you want to be, and it is OK";
"You are worthwhile." We have all noticed the different ways we
feel about our own self in the presence of different responses. When
a person looks at us rather than away or down at his or her work,
when a person acknowledges our thinking by relevant comments, or
when a person shows delight in being around us, we are ex-

Amount of supportiveness

None   Low   High   Very high

periencing supportiveness, and we usually feel pleasant. Supportiveness is a continuous variable, as diagramed below, and the main
idea in this principle is that changes in supportiveness tend to bring
about changes in the bonds in a relationship. The principle is:

**THE SUPPORT PRINCIPLE: The amount of support in a re-
lationship influences the strength of the bonds in that relationship, and this is a positive relationship.**

It is likely that of all the independent variables dealt with in this
chapter this is the most manipulable, and if that is the case it is the
variable that probably gives us the greatest amount of control over
the bonds in our dating and marital relationships. We can learn to increase or decrease our supportiveness relatively easily, and we can

---

[3] A number of different terms could be used instead of *supportiveness*.
Turner, for example, uses the term *responsiveness* (1970, p. 65). Another term
that has wide usage is *warmth* (Sears, Maccoby, and Levin, 1957). The term
support is used here because it seems to this author to be the best label and
because it has probably been the most widely used term in the prior literature
(Straus, 1964; Becker, 1964).

do this in such a wide variety of situations that it can make a substantial difference. The following exercise is designed to help us acquire and/or enhance skill at certain kinds of supportive behavior. No exercises are provided to help learn how to decrease supportiveness because that skill is so pervasively learned in our society that most of us are already pretty adept at it. Supportive behavior usually takes effort or energy, and if we were to get in situations in which we wanted to decrease bonds we could just stop behaving supportively.

EVALUATING AND INCREASING SUPPORT

Goal: To identify situations in which supportiveness occurred and did not occur in a relationship, and to increase supportiveness.

1. In a long-term relationship, such as one with a spouse, fiancé(e), friend, or sibling, find the time for a 30-minute discussion about supportiveness in the relationship.

2. Identify five recent situations in which you were supportive. List these on a piece of paper. If you are interested in increasing the supportiveness of the other person, also complete steps 2, 3, and 4 for that person. Some situations in which supportiveness may have occurred are:

   a. When one person did something to make the other feel better about herself or himself.

   b. When one person was feeling low or discouraged and needed someone to turn to.

   c. When one person *encouraged* the other.

   d. When one person showed *confidence* in the other.

   e. When one person did something that showed he or she *cared* about the other.

3. Identify three situations in which you could have been more supportive than you were. List these on a piece of paper.

4. Select one way in which you could be more supportive, and develop an Action Plan. See pages 164–65 for the outline for Action Plans. You may want to select one of the behaviors mentioned in step #3, or you may want to select some other behavior.

Identification

We often hear the expressions "I can identify with that" or "I identify with her." What does it mean to "identify"? To identify is to internalize something by copying it from someone else. We feel embarrassed if someone we know is in an embarrassing spot (if, for example, he approaches the cafeteria cashier with a full tray and finds he has no money with him). We feel proud if someone we know is in a prestigious position (if, for example, she is on the city council or is the obvious leader at a group meeting). We identify with such people as other members of our race, other members of our student body, other members of our religion, other members of our family, and other members of our friendship group. This can even be noticed on casual dates. For example, we feel chagrin if our partner is rude to someone who seems to have taken our seats at a ball game or we feel proud if we are introduced to someone who obviously admires our date.

Turner (1970, pp. 65–72) points out that a person's self-esteem may be enhanced or damaged through identification, and the independent variable in this principle is the extent to which identification enhances self-esteem. This is a continuous variable, and its highest point is a condition in which a person's self-esteem is greatly

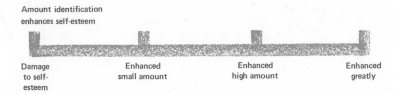

enhanced by identification with another person. Its lowest point is a condition in which identification damages self-esteem. The idea that relates the two variables is:

THE IDENTIFICATION PRINCIPLE: The amount that the identification of partners with each other enhances their self-esteem influences the strength of the bonds in the relationship, and this is a positive relationship.

This principle has many implications for everyday life. Popular advice encouraging teenage girls to cultivate their talents, improve their appearance, and involve themselves in worthwhile activities is at least partly aimed at helping them increase the possibility that a boyfriend's self-esteem will be enhanced through association with them, and thus make cohesion more likely. When a woman or a man hunts for a job that the other member of the couple will feel proud of, one effect may be that the self-esteem of the woman or the man will be enhanced through the connection, and thus the cohesion of the couple may be enhanced. The person who plans her or his hairstyle and wardrobe to have "the look of success" is also probably increasing the possibility of cohesion with her or his spouse.

SUMMARY

This chapter dealt with factors that influence the bonds in marital relationships. Six generalizations were identified, and various ways to apply these hypotheses were discussed. The first principle discussed was the *Shared Experience* principle, (1) which asserts that a positive relationship exists between the common experiences of two individuals and their bondedness. The second principle discussed was the *Incomplete Action* principle, (2) which asserts that the greater the amount of investment someone has in activities that are not yet completed and that involve someone else the greater the bonds with the other person. The *Reserve* principle (3) asserts that the less the need to behave in controlled, careful ways in a relationship the stronger the bonds in the relationship. The *Inter-*

Causal model for principles in Chapter 13

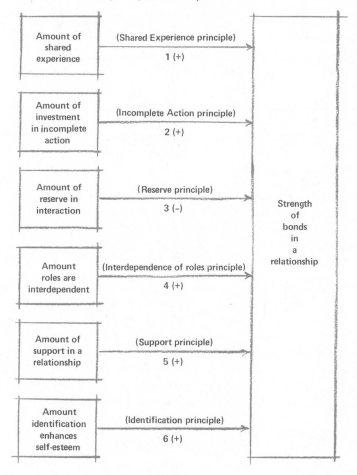

dependence of Roles principle (4) suggests that the more two individuals rely on or need each other to perform various activities the stronger the bonds and, conversely, the more independent they are of each other the weaker the bonds. The *Support* principle (5) states that the more two individuals engage in supportive or warm behaviors with each other the greater the bonds. The *Identification* principle (6)—the last principle discussed—asserts that when identification with someone else enhances one's self-esteem this tends to increase the bondedness in the relationship, while when identification detracts from one's self-esteem this tends to decrease the bondedness. All of these principles are diagramed in the causal model in Figure 13–1.

SUGGESTIONS FOR FURTHER STUDY

Goode, William J.   1956. *After Divorce*. Glencoe, Ill.: Free Press.

Turner, Ralph H.   1970. *Family Interaction*. New York: Wiley, chaps. 3–4.

Waller, Willard, and Hill, R. L.   1951. *The Family: A Dynamic Interpretation*. Rev. ed. New York: Dryden, chap. 16.

14

External roles and marriage

TWO FACTORS that are important in most marriages are (*a*) the amount of companionship the spouses have with each other and (*b*) the relationships of spouses with others outside the marriage, such as friends, neighbors, and relatives. One study that demonstrated the value of companionship in marriage was Blood and Wolfe's (1960, pp. 150–51) study of over 700 Detroit wives. They found that 48 percent of the wives chose "companionship in doing things together with the husband" as the most valuable aspect of marriage, and that companionship far outstripped the four other aspects of marriage (love, understanding, standard of living, and the chance to have children) that it was compared with. The relationships we have with people other than our spouse are important because none of us live in a social vacuum. We interact in a "social network" of other people and organizations, and this network influences our marital relationships in a number of ways. The classic example of how relationships outside a marriage influence what occurs inside the marriage is the "triangle," in which the spouse becomes romantically involved with a third person, and . . . there are frequently all kinds of repercussions. Such situations have intrigued poets, novelists, and playwrights for centuries, and in addition to forming the basis for plots in fiction they often occur in real life.

Even though most of us recognize that our relationships outside marriage are important, we know fairly little about what effects our *routine nonmarital relationships,* such as interaction with friends and neighbors, have on our marital situation. And most of us know still less about how we can use our nonmarital relationships to help us attain our marital goals. Social scientists also know relatively little about this, but a few principles have been discovered that seem potentially useful in helping us increase or at least maintain acceptable levels of satisfaction with our marital situations. This chapter identifies one of the principles about how relationships with friends influence marital satisfaction and discusses several ways to apply this principle.

The other main factor that is dealt with in this chapter is the amount of *companionship* in a marital relationship. At first glance most of us probably think that the relationship between companionship and marital satisfaction is positive and linear—the more companionship the greater the satisfaction with the marriage, and the less companionship the less satisfaction. Some recent research, however, suggests that the relationship between companionship and marital satisfaction is considerably more complex than this. In most marriages, apparently, there is such a thing as too little *and* too much companionship. In addition the relationship between companionship and satisfaction can apparently be understood only when our involvement with friends outside the marriage is considered at the same time. This latter point is the reason that the two factors of companionship with friends *and* companionship with our spouse are discussed in the same chapter.

CONCEPTUAL CLARIFICATION

Before the principles about companionship and marital satisfaction can be identified it is first necessary to define several terms. The first two concepts that must be identified are the *connectedness* of the friendship network and the *companionship* in the marital relationship. Elizabeth Bott (1957) was the first to describe the connectedness variable, and she defined it as the "extent to which the people known by a family, know and meet one another independently of the family. I use the word '*close-knit*' to describe a network in which there are many relationships among the component units, and the word '*loose-knit*' to describe a network in which there are few such relationships" (1957, p. 56). Connectedness is apparently a continuous variable that ranges between two extremes rather than a dichotomy, and this variable is diagramed below. Bott describes the close-knit and loose-knit extremes in the following manner:

Connectedness of social network

Very low   Low   Medium   High   Very high

Close-knit networks are most likely to develop when husband and wife, together with their friends, neighbors, and relatives, have grown up in the same local area and have continued to live there after marriage. Many people know one another and have known one another since childhood. Women tend to associate with women and men with men. The only legitimate forms of heterosexual relationship are those between kin and between husband and wife. Friendship between a man and a woman who are not kin is suspect.

In such a setting, husband and wife come to marriage each with his own close-knit network. Each partner makes a considerable emotional investment in relationships with the people in his network. Each is engaged in reciprocal exchanges of material and emotional support with them. Each is very sensitive to their opinions and values, not only because the relationships are intimate, but also because the people in the network know one another and share the same norms so that they are able to apply consistent informal sanctions to one another. The marriage is superimposed on these pre-existing relationships. . . .

Networks become loose-knit when people move from one place to another or when they make new relationships not connected with their old ones. If both husband and wife have moved considerably before marriage, each will bring an already loose-knit network to the marriage. Many of the husband's friends will not know one another; many of the wife's friends will not know one another. Although they will continue to see some old friends after marriage, they will meet new people too, who will not necessarily know the old friends or one another. In other words, their external relationships are relatively discontinuous both in space and in time. Such continuity as they possess lies in their relationship with each other rather than in their external relationships (1957, pp. 92–96).

Thus, in close-knit networks the individuals all interact with one another, and there is more total interaction with the extramarital associates. In loose-knit networks a person may interact with several friends, but the friends do not form a group, and the person has less total nonmarital interaction with friends than he or she would have in a close-knit network.

The *amount of companionship* is a fairly commonsense variable. It refers to the amount of friendly, informal interaction two people have in their marital relationship. It usually involves such fellowship-promoting activities as visiting with each other, taking walks, pursuing leisure-time activities together, and enjoying each other as friends. This can be diagramed as a continuous variable, ranging from no companionship at all to very high amounts of companionship.

Amount of companionship

None   Small   Large   Very high

Some marriages have a great deal of companionship, and some have very little. Many scholars (Burgess et al., 1963) have argued that one of the significant changes in the marriage institution in the past century has been an increase in the amount of companionate interaction that people expect in marriage, and studies have found that companionship is indeed important to most married couples (Blood and Wolfe, 1960, p. 150).

THE SOCIABILITY PRINCIPLE

Nelson (1966) has demonstrated that the relationship between companionship and marital satisfaction cannot be accurately understood unless the connectedness of the social network is also simultaneously taken into account. One way to take both of these variables into account at the same time is to use a two-by-two table, as is done in Figure 14–1. This creates four different cells, each of

Figure 14–1

The amount of marital satisfaction according to the amount of companionship and the connectedness of the social network

| | | Amount of companionship | |
		Low	High
Connectedness of the social network	High	Low companionship in the marriage and high involvement outside the marriage (HIGH SATISFACTION)	High companionship in the marriage and high involvement outside the marriage (LOW SATISFACTION)
	Low	Low companionship in the marriage and low involvement outside the marriage (LOW SATISFACTION)	High companionship in the marriage and low involvement outside the marriage (HIGH SATISFACTION)

which describes a different life situation. The upper left-hand cell describes a situation in which there is low companionship in the marriage and high informal interaction outside the marriage. The upper right-hand cell describes a situation in which there is high companionship in the marriage and high involvement outside the marriage. The lower left-hand cell describes a situation in which there is low companionship in the marriage and little contact with friends and associates outside the marriage, and the lower right-hand cell describes a situation in which there is high companionship in the marriage and low involvement outside the marriage. The companionship principle indicates which of these life situations seem to be conducive to marital satisfaction and which of them seem to detract from marital satisfaction. Nelson's data suggest that there are two cells in which people tend to be satisfied with their marital situation and two in which people tend to be dissatisfied. Since most people in contemporary society want a high amount of companionship in their marriage, most usually expect the two "high companionship" situations (the right-hand cells) to be the ones in which marital satisfaction is highest. This, however, is only half right, according to Nelson's data. Most people who have high companionship and low connectedness have high satisfaction in their marriages, but most people who have high companionship and high involvement with friends are much less satisfied with their marriage. The surprising finding is that people who have low companionship in their marriage and high involvement outside the marriage also have high marital satisfaction.

Nelson's explanation of these fairly unanticipated findings is that people apparently need a certain amount of companionate interaction with others and they can get it with various combinations of companionateness inside *or* outside their marriage. If they have low companionship in their marriage and low involvement with friends outside the marriage, they tend to be too lonely and are unsatisfied with their marriage. Apparently, if they get companionship either with their spouse *or* with someone outside the marital relationship this increases their satisfaction with their marital situation. If, however, they are highly companionate with their spouse *and* have high amounts of involvement with friends outside the marriage, this apparently tends to create competing and overburdening demands, and the net effect is less satisfaction with the marital relationship.

It is difficult to state Nelson's idea in a principle when companionship and connectedness are separate variables. It is, however, possible to state this idea as a general principle if these two variables are combined into a more inclusive variable. When these two factors are combined into one variable the more inclusive factor can be called the total *amount of sociability* in a person's life.[1] This more inclusive variable refers to the variation in the amount of companionship in the marriage *and* the amount of involvement with friends outside the marriage. It is a continuous variable, and ap-

---

[1] Nelson discusses a "fund of sociability." He argues that people have a certain amount of this fund and that too little opportunity to expend it or too many demands on it are disruptive. The formulation suggested here adopts most of Nelson's ideas, but it omits the "fund" aspect and deals only with the amount of sociability that occurs. It should probably also be mentioned that people undoubtedly differ in the amount of sociability that is optimal for them, but it still seems reasonable that the curvilinear hypothesis suggested by Nelson operates. It is just that the optimal amount of social interaction is higher for some than it is for others.

parently it can range from very little to very high amounts of informal interaction, as shown below:

Amount of sociability

Very low   Low   Medium   High   Very high

When this more inclusive variable is defined in this manner it is possible to use Nelson's findings to state the following principle:

THE SOCIABILITY PRINCIPLE: The amount of sociability in a person's life influences the person's marital satisfaction in a curvilinear manner.

The curvilinearity in this relationship is diagramed in Figure 14–2 and, as that figure shows, increases in the amount of interaction tend to increase marital satisfaction—up to a point. However, after a certain amount of companionate interaction has been attained, additional increases tend to decrease marital satisfaction. Thus, there seems to be an optimum amount of informal companionate interaction, and either too much or too little creates problems in most marital relationships.

There is not a great deal of empirical evidence for the Sociability principle, but two empirical studies provide data that argue for its validity. One of them is Nelson's (1966) study. His data were

Figure 14–2

The relationship between the total amount of informal interaction and marital satisfaction

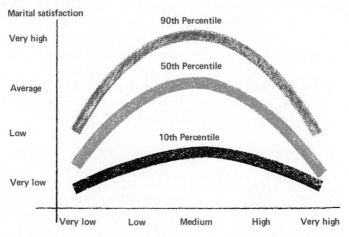

gathered from a working-class sample of 131 wives, and the findings in that study were consistent with the principle. Blood and Wolfe (1960, p. 260) measured the amount of companionship in the marital relationship, but they did not measure the connectedness of the social network. However, they found a similar curvilinear relationship between companionship and marital satisfaction. They differentiated between five levels of companionship (none, slight, moderate, considerable, and intense), and they found that the highest marital satisfaction scores were obtained when considerable companionship was present. Either low or intense amounts of companionship were associated with lower satisfaction scores, and considerable companionship was associated with the highest satisfaction. Another finding in the Blood and Wolfe (1960, p. 183) study is also relevant. They found that wives who had alternative resources outside the home for meeting their emotional needs felt that the husband's "understanding" was less important to them than did wives who lacked external sources of emotional support. This finding also adds support for the sociability principle, as it is consistent with the idea that there are ways to meet our companionate needs other than having a highly companionate-supportive marital relationship.

There are a number of ways in which the Sociability principle can be applied in daily life. One way is that this principle provides a basis for coping with a marital situation in which one person is dissatisfied with a marriage because his or her spouse is not as companionate or friendly as the person wants the spouse to be. The Sociability principle suggests that there are several different ways in which a couple could probably cope with this problem. One obvious way is for the less companionate spouse to change his or her behavior, and a second obvious way is for the dissatisfied spouse to change his or her expectations. Most couples learn, however, that changing this type of behavior in a spouse or in oneself is usually quite difficult, and that frequently it is impossible, even when the person wants to change. Another alternative solution to this problem that is suggested by the Sociability principle is for the lonely spouse to solve his or her dissatisfaction with the marriage by becoming more involved in nonmarital relationships that provide friendship and companionship. The wife has such options as joining service organizations where there is a closeness and camaraderie among the participants or increasing her involvement in neighborhood study groups, coffee breaks with neighbors, or recreational

*Practical
implications
of the
Sociability
principle*

groups, such as bowling leagues. The husband can foster friendships with co-workers or join service, social, or sports clubs. When a person prefers that companionate activity be with his or her spouse these substitutes may be slightly less desirable, but they may be the most desirable solution when it is not possible to change other aspects of the marital situation, and apparently such nonmarital substitutes can genuinely improve the marital situation.

Two skills are involved in using the Sociability principle in this way. One is being able to analyze or diagnose one's own situation to determine whether companionship or friendship is deficient, and the other is being able to increase or decrease the amount of companionate interaction in one's life when a need is perceived. The two following exercises are designed to help increase these abilities.

EVALUATING SOCIABILITY

Goal: To determine how adequate one's marital companionship and one's nonmarital friendly relationships are.

1. One effective way to evaluate our situation is to discuss it with someone we trust and feel comfortable around. Decide who would be an effective confidant(e) and ask that person to help you evaluate this particular part of your life. (Sometimes a spouse is useful, and in other situations the best person may be a friend, a religious leader, or a relative.)

2. Discuss with this other person the various aspects of your companionship in your marriage and your friendly, informal involvement with others outside the marriage.

    As you look at this part of your life, try to determine which of the following statements best describes you:

    a. I try to have more informal interaction than I should. I really can't do justice to all of the relationships I try to maintain.

    b. I am slightly overinvolved, compared to what I think would be ideal.

    c. The informal relationships aspect of my life is about right.

    d. I would like to have a little more involvement with either friends outside my marriage *or* with my spouse.

    e. I would like to have considerably more friendly-companionate-informal but fairly intimate involvement with others.

3. Some other questions you might discuss are such things as: Am I able to share my joys and satisfactions with others as much

as I would like? Do I have someone to turn to when I'm low or down, and do I want to have that type of relationship? Are my friendships interfering with my marriage, or is my marriage interfering with my friendships? Do I feel lonely too often?

4. Hopefully, you will emerge from this analysis with a more accurate and carefully thought-out opinion about the adequacy of the sociability in your life.

CHANGING THE AMOUNT OF SOCIABILITY

Goal: To either increase or decrease informal involvement with others (either spouse or outside the marriage).

Getting ready: An important part of this exercise is thinking up new ideas, and an effective way to do this is to use a group. To do this, use a discussion group in a class or get together with one or two other couples. In the group discussion, identify which individual or couple you are trying to help. (If you try to help everyone at the same time, there will probably be more chaos than help.)

1. Of the five steps in this exercise, the hardest step is this first one. It is to IDENTIFY A SET OF REALISTIC ALTERNATIVES TO EITHER INCREASE OR DECREASE INFORMAL INTERACTION. To do this, select one person to write down suggestions, and classify the suggestions according to whether they involve a possible change (1) with the spouse or (2) with a person or group outside the marriage. Try to list at least three or four suggestions in each category.

2. The second step is to SELECT ONE ALTERNATIVE as the one to try. A group is of limited utility for this step, as this is often done better by an individual or a couple rather than by a group.

3. After one alternative has been selected, IDENTIFY A "PLAN OF ACTION" that describes how to accomplish the alternative selected. A group can be useful in helping think up a plan and keeping it realistic.

4. Implement the plan.

5. After the plan has been implemented long enough for some changes to have occurred, evaluate how effective the plan was. If it was effective, repeat the preceding "Evaluating Sociability" exercise. If the plan was not effective, and you still want to expend the energy it will take to change this aspect of your life, look

over the list of alternatives you acquired in step 1 of this exercise. If one of them looks like a good possibility, select it and go on to step 3 of this exercise. If none of them look realistic, try to get some help from others, such as friends, religious leaders, or a marriage counselor, to get a better list of alternatives.

The Sociability principle also has practical relevance when a couple are making a major change in their life, such as a change of residence. If they move very far they will decrease their interaction with their previous social network. This usually means that friendships will be terminated—except for occasional letters or visits—and it is possible to use the Sociability principle to make several predictions about how this will influence the marital relationship. If the couple's level of involvement was so high that the decrease in *total sociability* is a decrease from a very high amount, it is likely that the decrease will have positive benefits in the marriage. If, however, the move decreases the couple's total informal interaction to a fairly low amount it is likely that the decrease will be a frustrating experience. And it is likely that this is one reason that moving is frequently a disruptive, undesirable experience for families.[2] However, Nelson's ideas also provide a basis for possible solutions to these frustrations. Couples might find it useful to consciously increase their marital and parent-child companionate interaction during such periods to a level that is higher than usual. They might find that this increase in intrafamilial involvement would cushion some of the discomforts of changing to a new location. They would probably not want to have so much intrafamilial interaction as to preclude the development of new extrafamilial companionships if their preferred style of life includes a good deal of nonfamily interaction, but even in fairly Utilitarian marriages that have relatively little companionship they might benefit from temporary increases in marital companionship.

The Sociability principle also seems to have relevance in student marriages. In many student marriages the schedule of the student-spouse is extremely demanding when he or she works part- or full-time while "finishing up" at school. Moreover, this intensely demanding period usually occurs right after the wedding, at a time when most couples are accustomed to having considerable companionship with each other and want to maintain this high level of interaction. It isn't uncommon for the nonstudent spouse (usually

---

[2] The May 1973 issue of the *Journal of Marriage and the Family* is a special issue devoted to the effects of moving, and several of the articles discuss this point.

the wife) to develop frustrations over playing second fiddle to the "books" or feeling less important than she was before the marriage, and for the husband to have so many demands that he feels overwhelmed. According to the Sociability principle, the wife is having too little sociability and the husband too much. The husband's involvement is not usually companionship outside the marriage, but the net effect seems to be much the same. There are several ways to cope with such situations when they are viewed from the perspective provided by the sociability principle. One solution is for the couple to make the demands less intense by taking a longer time to finish the schooling. Another way to accomplish the same end is for the nonstudent spouse to acquire nonmarital forms of involvement during this period of their life and then to terminate those involvements when the couple leave the "married student" status and have a more settled style of life. The non-student spouse could probably achieve an appropriate balance of involvements through any of a variety of activities, ranging from artistic creativity, employment, continuing his or her own education, church service, or friendships. Employment is a choice many young couples opt for, partly because this has the added benefit of enabling the student-spouse to be less involved in providing income.

The Sociability principle is also relevant when the children leave home and there are fewer parental responsibilities, when the husband or the wife either goes to work or retires, and when couples move away from or back to areas in which they have relatives they are expected to interact with. At each of these times couples can use the principle to reestablish a desirable equilibrium in their informal involvements with each other and with acquaintances outside their marriage.

SUMMARY

This chapter has dealt with ways in which companionship with our spouse and interaction in the social network outside marriage influence the satisfaction we have with our marriage. The most recent thinking in the social sciences argues that it is impossible to understand the effects of either of these two variables on marital satisfaction unless both are taken into account simultaneously. Because of this the two variables are combined into a more inclusive variable in the *Sociability* principle, which states that there is a curvilinear relationship between our social involvement and marital satisfaction—that there is an optimum level of involvement in informal interaction and that either too little or too much involvement creates problems in the marital relationship. Figure 14–3 diagrams this principle and also illustrates a deduction from the principle that

Figure 14–3

The Sociability principle and a more specific deduction
from it

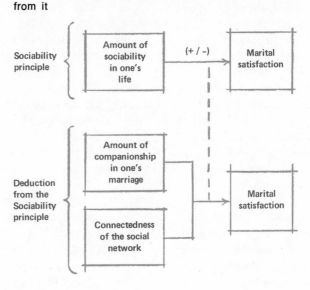

shows the joint influence of marital companionship and connectedness of social networks on marital satisfaction. After the Sociability
principle was identified, several ways to implement it in practical,
everyday situations were discussed.

SUGGESTIONS FOR FURTHER STUDY

Blood, Robert O., Jr.   1969. *Marriage*. Rev. ed. Glencoe, Ill.: Free
   Press, chap. 12.

Bott, Elizabeth   1957. *Family and Social Network*. London: Tavistock.

Bowman, Henry A.   1970. *Marriage for Moderns*. 6th ed. New York:
   McGraw-Hill, chap. 10.

Turner, Ralph H.   1970. *Family Interaction*. New York: Wiley, chaps.
   17 and 18.

Udry, J. Richard   1966. *The Social Context of Marriage*. Philadelphia:
   Lippincott, pp. 393–98.

15

Sexuality in marriage

THE SEXUAL RELATIONSHIP is an important part of the total marital experience for a number of reasons. A pleasant sexual relationship can create meaning and commitment and foster several different types of interpersonal intimacy. It can also provide physical sensory pleasure so unique and intense that it defies verbal description, and it can be the source of emotional and interpersonal pleasures that are among the most rewarding experiences known. It is impossible to know how many couples are able to experience the various potential pleasures and benefits that can result from the sexual aspect of their relationship, but this chapter is written in the expectation that some information about several aspects of human sexuality can help couples increase their chances of experiencing those pleasures and benefits. Sexuality is such a complicated part of life and marriage, however, that one chapter in one book cannot provide a comprehensive analysis of marital sexuality, and because of this most readers would benefit from exposing themselves to some of the additional readings listed at the end of the chapter.

This chapter is divided into four main sections. The first is a brief discussion of some anatomical and physiological aspects of human sexuality. This section is included because sexual adequacy in marriage is a complex interplay of physiological, psychological, emotional, and interpersonal processes, and a lack of information or misinformation about physiological aspects of sexuality seems to be a source of sexual problems for many couples. The second section briefly discusses the cycle of sexual responsiveness, and the third presents several general principles that are potentially useful in creating a satisfying sexual relationship. The last section provides

some correct information about several widely believed sexual
myths.

HUMAN SEXUAL ANATOMY

The male

Married couples can have a pleasant and satisfying sexual relationship without knowing nearly as much about sexual anatomy
and physiology as a physician does. It does help, however, to have a
basic vocabulary about what males and females are like and how
they differ sexually if couples plan to communicate about this part
of the marital relationship.

The male's basic reproductive organs are diagramed in Figure
15–1. The *penis* and *scrotum* project from the lower abdomen. The
scrotum is a thin-skinned sac that hangs between the legs. It contains several important organs. The largest of these are the two
testicles, ovoid organs that are about two inches long. They consist
of several thousand feet of very small tubules in which the *sperm*
are produced. As the sperm mature they move toward the *vas
deferens.* Since sperm must be developed and stored in a temperature several degrees cooler than the normal body temperature, the

Figure 15–1
Male genital organs in cross-sectional view

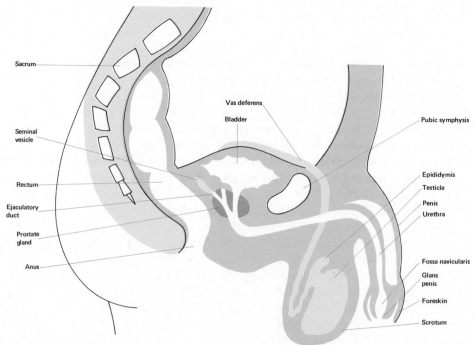

scrotum adjusts its temperature by becoming slightly longer in high temperatures and then contracting when it is cooler. The vas deferens, connects to the urethra just below the *bladder*. The testicles are the tenderest part of the male's sexual anatomy, and even minor jolts or blows to the testicles can be very painful.

Two other parts of the male's internal sexual anatomy are the *prostate gland* and the *seminal vesicle*. These secrete a relatively viscous milky substance called *seminal fluid* or *semen,* and this fluid is stored in the seminal vesicle. The sperm are stored in the lower part of the vas deferens, where they can remain at a lower temperature. When the male becomes sexually aroused the sperm are pushed up the vas deferens by muscular contractions or by a contraction-shortening process of the vas deferens, and the sperm eventually enter the urethra where they are mixed with the seminal fluid. At that time the sperm become active and begin propelling themselves through a whiplike action of their tails. During periods of sexual excitement the opening from the bladder into the urethra is closed so that urine cannot enter the urethra, and when the male reaches the peak of the cycle of sexual stimulation muscular contractions expel the seminal fluid in rhythmic ejaculations. Most of the stored seminal fluid is expelled in the first several contractions, and the total volume expelled is usually about a teaspoonful. The sperm are actually a very small part of the total volume of the semen, even though a normal ejaculation contains several hundred million sperm.

The *penis* is the elongated projection in front of the scrotum. Usually it hangs limply in front of the scrotum, but during periods of sexual excitement it increases in size and becomes erect. When the penis is fully erect it projects outward from the body and curves upward. The average length of an erect penis is usually about six inches, the average diameter about an inch and a half. Erection is caused by constrictions in the blood vessels that lead from the penis. These constrictions cause the spongy tissue in the penis to become filled with blood and hence to become larger and fairly firm. The *glans,* or "head" of the penis, has a very high concentration of sexually relevant nerve endings, and it is stimulation of these nerve endings that gradually increases the male's sexual excitement to its peak and brings about the ejaculation of the semen. The *corona,* a crownlike ridge at the back of the glans, usually has the highest concentration of nerve endings. The *foreskin* is a usually loose fold of skin that partially protrudes over the glans, but during erection the skin over the entire penis becomes smooth and taut. Males develop the capacity to ejaculate at puberty, which usually occurs around age 13 or 14.

The female   Figure 15–2 shows a cross-sectional view of most of the female
sexual and reproductive organs. A front view of some of these
organs is in Figure 17–1, illustrated later. The *vagina* is an elastic
passageway that leads from the exterior genitalia to the uterus, and
is the part of the female into which the penis is inserted during
coitus. Recent research by Masters and Johnson (1966, chap. 6)
has discovered that the vaginal cavity becomes considerably longer
and considerably larger in diameter when a woman is sexually
excited, and that the vaginal tissues are sufficiently elastic to permit
a normal vagina to accommodate a penis much larger than the
average penis. In their research of over 400 women they found only
two women whose vaginas were so small that it would be difficult
for the vagina to accommodate a male penis, and in both cases
when the women were highly sexually aroused the vagina became
sufficiently enlarged to permit coitus with ease. If a woman is not
sexually aroused, however, and she is apprehensive or tense when
intercourse is attempted, the tissues around the vagina contract and
the size of the vagina is considerably reduced. Under those circumstances attempts to insert the penis into the vagina usually are
painful.

The *uterus, ovaries,* and *fallopian tubes* have little to do with
sexual activity, but they have a central role in the reproductive

Figure 15–2

Female genital organs in cross-sectional view

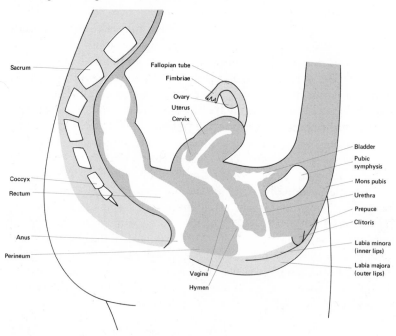

process. *Ova* are produced in the ovaries, and when they are mature they are expelled into the abdominal cavity. This usually occurs on about the 14th day before a menstrual period would normally begin, and somehow the expelled ova get into the fallopian tubes. If an ovum is fertilized while it is in the upper part of one of the fallopian tubes, it later becomes attached to the side of the uterus and a pregnancy begins. When an ovum is not fertilized, it continues through the fallopian tube and into the uterus, but the tissues which were prepared to receive the fertilized egg are sloughed off as the menstrual discharge. The *cervix* is the part of the uterus that projects into the vagina, and during sexual excitement the cervix, along with virtually all of the other tissue in the genital area, becomes slightly larger as a result of a greater concentration of blood in the tissue.

There are several areas with large concentrations of sensitive nerve endings that provide sexual excitement when they are stimulated. The walls of the vagina have relatively few nerve endings, but the tissue surrounding the vaginal opening is surrounded by several layers of skin, called *lips*—or *labia*, if one prefers Latin. The labia minora, or inner lips, especially the parts close to the vaginal opening, are one of the most sensitive areas for most women. There is also a high concentration of nerve endings in the *clitoris*. The clitoris is a small projection in the front part of the external genitalia. It has a shaft and head, and the head is so sensitive that most women find it uncomfortable if the head is manipulated very much directly. Indirect stimulation of the clitoris, however, by stimulating the shaft, or *mons pubis*, is usually very sexually exciting, and the female usually achieves *orgasm*, or sexual climax, through the combined stimulation of the labia minora and the clitoris that occurs with the joint movement of the male and the female during intercourse. It is possible for many women to experience an orgasm by stimulating only one of these areas, but this is less common. It is also possible for some women to achieve an orgasm through stimulation of other parts of the body, such as the nipples of the breast, or through fantasy, but these conditions are very rare.

The *hymen* partially covers the vaginal opening in many women until it is stretched or surgically treated. The smaller diagrams in Figure 15–3 show several variations in the way the hymen can cover the vaginal opening. In some situations the hymen is so thin that it can be stretched or torn with very minor pressure and little pain. The hymen is occasionally very thick and tough, however, and when it is it can only be removed surgically. If a woman had one of the hymenal conditions shown as (c), (d), and (e), a couple would experience difficulty in intercourse, and if they persisted by trying to stretch the tissues the woman would have pain and bleeding.

Figure 15–3

External view of female genitalia

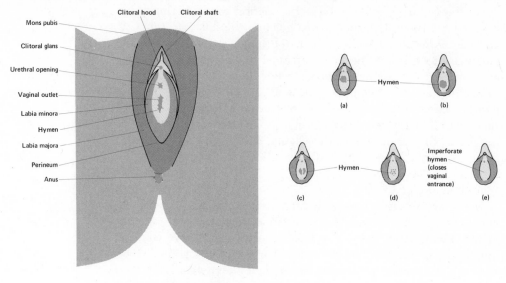

Examination of the hymen is thus one reason it is usually wise for a woman to have a thorough medical examination before she begins to have sexual intercourse.

There is a fairly predictable cycle in the way most people respond to sexual stimulation, and an awareness of what this cycle is can facilitate sexual compatibility and satisfaction. On the other hand, a lack of awareness of how we or our spouse responds to sexual excitement can lead to endless frustration, dissatisfaction, and bitterness. For example, some couples do not realize that it is common for women to take longer than men to become sexually aroused, and they establish a pattern of sexual activity in which the male reaches the peak of his sexual cycle—orgasm—before the female has become sexually aroused. Since the male usually loses interest in sexual activity fairly soon after reaching orgasm, this can become frustrating and disappointing to the female, and when it does, this often leads to serious problems in the couple's relationship. Since this is only one of many ways in which a lack of familiarity with the sexual response cycle can create problems in a marital relationship, the inescapable conclusion is that it is useful to become acquainted with the sexual response cycle.

THE SEXUAL RESPONSE CYCLE

Physiologists and sexologists have discovered many subtle aspects of the human sexual response cycle, but the four-phase cycle de-

Figure 15–4

Typical cycles of female sexual response

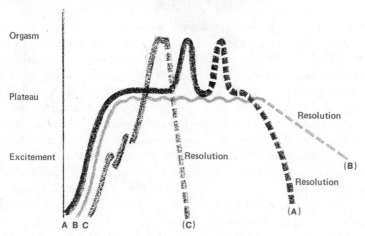

scribed by Masters and Johnson (1966, pp. 3–8) is sufficiently detailed for the purposes of this book. Masters and Johnson divide the cycle into the excitement, plateau, orgasmic, and resolution phases. Several examples of these cycles for females are diagramed in Figure 15–4, and two variations in the cycle for males are shown in Figure 15–5. These illustrations are attempts to show common cyclic responses, but as Masters and Johnson state, "It always should be borne in mind that there is wide variation in the duration and intensity of every specific physiologic response to sexual stimulation" (1966, p. 7).

Figure 15–5

Typical cycles of male sexual response

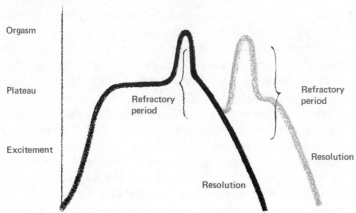

The excitement phase is the period when an individual becomes increasingly sexually excited. It begins when some stimulus arouses sexual or erotic feelings, and several physiological responses usually occur during this phase. The male's penis becomes erect, and a sex flush may begin to appear. The sex flush is a mild reddening of the skin, and it usually appears first on the breast. It may or may not spread to other areas. The breasts of the female usually become discernibly fuller, and the nipples become more erect. Usually the pulse and breathing rate also tend to rise as excitement increases. The entire genital area of the female becomes somewhat larger because of the increased blood supply, and this "tumescence" causes the labia to move apart and turn slightly outward. The walls of the vagina begin to secrete a liquid in a "sweating" fashion, and the volume of the liquid usually increases as excitement increases. Inserting the penis into the vagina early in the excitement phase may be uncomfortable for the female, but toward the end of this phase the increased size, elasticity, and lubrication of the vagina, and heightened sexual interest, create an optimal situation for inserting the penis into the vagina.

Several emotional or psychic processes usually accompany sexual excitement. There is generally a feeling of warmth and pleasantness, and progressively less attention is paid to nonsexual parts of one's environment. There is an elation and thrill that is affectively very pleasant, and there is usually a heightened awareness of the senses that are involved in the sexual relationship—of touching and being touched. A mild euphoria is gradually replaced by a more intense feeling of excitement and thrill.

Many different stimuli can begin this excitement process and provide the additional stimulation that is necessary to reach the plateau phase. Physical stimulation of erogenous zones of the body, such as lips, breasts, thighs, anus, or genitals, are usually sufficiently effective, and various combinations of pictures, movies, jokes, comments, glances, music, and thoughts have different effects on different people. Traditionally in the American society it has been believed that men are aroused by a wider variety of phenomena than are women, and that men are usually aroused more quickly. A variety of explanations have been suggested for this. One theory suggests that since the male's genitals are more external than the female's they receive more stimulation. Two other explanations are that there are innate differences in the way men and women respond to sexual stimuli, and that men and women learn to respond differently to sexual stimuli as they learn other ways of behaving, feeling, thinking, and responding. If the last explanation is the reason for the differences in sexual arousal that have traditionally existed between men and women it is likely that the sexual freedoms that are emerging in the contemporary American society and the gradual erosion of many gender distinctions may eliminate those differences.

The excitement phase is usually one of the longer phases of the sexual response cycle. It usually lasts at least several minutes, and it may last several hours—especially among individuals who are still learning how to respond openly and freely to their sexual feelings.

The plateau phase is a stage in which an individual who is highly aroused sexually can remain for some time without becoming appreciably more or less sexually excited. The length of the plateau phase is largely dependent on the motivation to achieve orgasm and the effectiveness of the stimuli used. If an individual wishes to remain in the plateau phase for a long period of time, intermittent or mild stimulation can be used, and if the desire is to move to a climax quickly, continuous and intense stimulation of the genital area usually brings the person to orgasm.

The plateau phase

The orgasmic phase is usually the shortest of the four stages, as it seldom lasts more than a few seconds. It is the period when the peak of sexual excitement occurs, and this sensation is a subjective awareness of very intense sensory pleasure, located primarily in the "clitoral body, vagina, and uterus of the female and in the penis, prostate, and seminal vesicles of the male" (Masters and Johnson, 1966, p. 6). During orgasm there are also rhythmic involuntary muscular contractions. These contractions are most intense in the pelvic area, but virtually all of the skeletal muscles of the body become involved in an intense orgasm, and it becomes an experience of the entire body. In the male the contractions and sensual awareness are accompanied by an ejaculation of semen from the penis. The female does not experience anything comparable to the male's ejaculation, even though the increased secretion of the vaginally originating liquid (lubrication) during periods of heightened sexual excitement have led many women to think there was some type of ejaculation.

The orgasmic phase

The end of the orgasmic phase in the male tends to occur because of an involuntary sexual exhaustion rather than a general muscular exhaustion. In the female, however, the termination of the orgasmic phase is more a generalized muscular fatigue. This permits many females to learn to return to the plateau phase for a short rest period, as shown by line A in Figure 15–4, and then, if they wish, attain additional orgasms before entering the resolution phase. The male tends to move immediately into the resolution phase. Even though the average duration of an orgasm is usually three to four seconds, women can occasionally experience much longer climaxes —up to 40–60 seconds.

The resolution phase

The resolution phase is a period of gradual decrease in sexual excitement. In the male most of this resolution is usually involuntary, and it begins to occur within a few seconds after ejaculation. The entire resolution phase may be over for the male in 10–15 seconds. He then usually enters a period of sexual satiation, and, with few exceptions, his physiological and psychological ability to respond to restimulation is low for a period of time. The female typically moves through the resolution phase more slowly than the male, especially if a more generalized response of love and emotional involvement accompanied the sexual experience. Many women may also return to the plateau stage at any time during the resolution if there is appropriate stimulation.

THREE PRINCIPLES ABOUT SEXUALITY

At present there are very few general principles about human sexuality, and there are two major reasons for this. First, neither the considerable scientific research being done about sexuality nor the vast amounts of unscientific literature about sex have tried to discover "general principles"—as that term is used in the scientific community and in this book. Most of the scientific research either investigates the proportion of people who engage in various sexual activities, or it is biological and physiological research that deals with bodily processes, and both of these types of research are descriptive rather than principle-seeking. The massive unscientific literature is equally devoid of principles because its goal is either to provide sexual stimulation or to give advice. The advice-laden volumes are useless as sources of principles because the basis for the advice is always a "philosophy of sex" that is unique to a certain cultural or subcultural perspective rather than defensible theory or research. These different philosophies of sexuality include such diverse perspectives as the following: (*a*) sexual participation should be only for reproduction; (*b*) sexuality is evil; (*c*) sexuality should be a playboy or playgirl style of activity; (*d*) sexuality can be for fun and recreation and for reproduction, but there should be different norms for the different uses; (*e*) sexuality is sacred; and (*f*) people are entitled to choose which view of sexuality or which sexual lifestyle they wish to have. Each of these views of sexuality leads to different sets of prescriptions and proscriptions, and at present there is no way to determine in any absolute manner which of the perspectives are more or less defensible. The result is that the vast amount of contradictory, advice-laden literature provides no "general principles" that social scientists could agree on.

A second reason there are very few general principles about sexuality is that a large number of dependent variables are of interest to scientists, but scientists have not yet focused on any one variable long enough to discover and justify defensible principles. Fisher (1973, p. 394) illustrates this dilemma by listing some of the numerous dimensions of sexuality about which principles could be discovered. His list includes:

Attitudes toward sexual gratification
Amount of excitement
Amount of sexual tension
Amount of sexual release
Gross "satisfaction"
Feelings of tenderness and love toward the sex partner
Feelings of unique intimacy
Satisfaction from body nudity and display
Enjoyment in being an object of admiration
Satisfaction from being sexually competent
Sensations of a unique kind of self-release
Empathetic definition of one's sex identity
Fantasy and imaginative role playing (for example,
    pretending to have a novel sex partner)
Satisfaction related to the act of creation and
    reproduction
Enjoyment of muscular and kinesthetic variations
Frequency of achieving orgasm
Sexual responsiveness

The net result is that there are very few, *if any,* defensible principles at the present time, and it is unlikely that there will be very many in the near future. Nonetheless, it seems useful to try to extract from the voluminous literature on sexuality several ideas that may be defensible principles. This is done here in the hope that those *tentative* ideas will be useful to readers and that they will stimulate other scholars in the field to try to improve the ones identified here and discover and justify others. With these goals in mind three generalizations are discussed on the following pages.

One part of Masters and Johnson's research program has focused on strategies for helping couples cope with what has been termed *sexual inadequacy,* and they have described their therapeutic pro-

The spectator role

gram in a volume entitled *Human Sexual Inadequacy* (1970).[1] One of the ideas they have introduced is that assuming a "spectator role" in a marital sexual relationship seems to interfere with a person's sexual adequacy. It may be that this idea should be identified as a principle in the following way:

THE SPECTATOR PRINCIPLE: Assuming a spectator role during coitus tends to interfere with sexual adequacy.

The two variables in this principle are *assuming a spectator role* and *sexual adequacy.* The spectator variable is apparently a dichotomy, in that a person can either be or not be in the spectator role, as shown in the following diagram. When persons are spectators this means that they are conscious of themselves as par-

ticipants and are concerned about "what" they are doing, "how" they are doing it, and what their reactions are. They are observers of themselves, of their partners, and of what is occurring. This contrasts with simply allowing natural feelings, inclinations, and actions to occur without being conscious of them or of oneself. The non-spectator role involves spontaneous, unconcerned, relaxed, and active participation in an experience—being lost or caught up in the situation—and hence being unconcerned about or unaware of it.

The dependent variable in the Spectator principle is difficult to define. Masters and Johnson use the term *sexual inadequacy* to describe a wide variety of conditions because they treat a number of specific sexual difficulties. These include premature ejaculation, ejaculatory incompetence, primary and secondary impotence, orgasmic dysfunction in women, vaginismus, and painful intercourse. They seem, however, to view the spectator role as something that is related to sexual adequacy or inadequacy *in general* rather than as something specific to certain types of inadequacy. Thus, they seem to be dealing with a general factor of adequacy-inadequacy that is itself a variable. They do not define this variable precisely, and they do not specify how it varies. It is suggested here, however, that it could be defined as the ability to participate in a meaningful sexual

---

[1] *Human Sexual Inadequacy* was written for a professional audience, but several books describe the program for lay readers. Belliveau and Richter's (1970) paperback was commissioned by Masters and Johnson, and Lehrman's (1970) book integrates highlights from both of Masters and Johnson's books and publishes additional information about their work.

relationship that is part of a total interpersonal relationship. The
sexual interaction would include sexual intercourse, and it would be
pleasurable and satisfying to the individuals involved. It is likely
that this variable has more than the two categories, adequate and
inadequate. It is probably a continuous variable, as shown below.
Apparently the best term for this variable is *sexual adequacy*.

Sexual adequacy

| Very | Marginally | Marginally | Very |
| inadequate | inadequate | adequate | adequate |

   It is difficult to assess how much confidence can be placed in the
Spectator principle. The principle is implicit in many of the marriage manuals. Also, Masters and Johnson seem to believe that it is
essential in their therapy program, and their fantastic success rate,
about 80 percent, seems to argue for its validity. There has not,
however, been any systematic research that has focused specifically
on this idea. Thus, there is some evidence that this principle is
valid, but the evidence is unsystematic and meager.

   One way to use the Spectator principle would be for a couple to
discuss whether either of them tends to assume a spectator role
during highly erotic sexual activity, and then, if one or the other
does, to try identify what they could do to change this tendency.
There is, however, an interesting irony in trying to do something
about this because we would have to assume the spectator role to
determine whether we assume the role, and we would also have to
take this role if we wanted to help ourselves. It is an understatement
to observe that this paradox seems to make it difficult to use the
Spectator principle. It may be, however, that there is an effective
strategy for using this idea. It may be that most of us do who adopt
the spectator role define the sexual experience as a situation in
which certain things need to be "done" or certain "behaviors" or
"acts" are "optimal" if we are to be successful, adequate sex partners. It may be that changing the definition of the sexual situation
would change the tendency to adopt the spectator role. If we could
define sexual participation as an experience to be felt, or experienced, for whatever it is, we could then forget about what we are
doing or not doing and spontaneously experience and feel. This

change in the definition might help create an ability to "lose one-self" in the experience. It may be that it would be useful to adopt a spectator role long enough to determine whether it is a problem in our own relationship, and then, if it is, to try to redefine the way we view sexual activity, so that we will play the role less.

Pleasurizing   Another principle that can probably be extracted from Masters and Johnson's research and treatment program is:

THE PLEASURIZING PRINCIPLE: The greater the sensory pleasurizing in a relationship—exclusive of coitus—the greater the sexual adequacy, and vice versa.

The independent variable in this principle employs the concept of "sensate focus," and it refers to the amount of sensory gratification that is acquired through such activities as touching, tracing, massaging, and fondling. As discussed in Chapter 5, touching is a complex, many-faceted form of communication which can be used to share information and to create such experiences as tenderness, affection, solace, understanding, desire, warmth, comfort, and excitement. Foreplay is a widely publicized activity that consists of sexually specific physical stimulation, but when foreplay refers to the stimulation of specific erogenous zones of the body it is a much narrower and more limited activity than the more inclusive phenomenon of providing physical, sensory pleasure in a spontaneous, experiential, giving, and receiving manner—as a style of life rather than as a prelude to intercourse. This sensory pleasurizing is apparently a continuous variable, ranging from no pleasurizing to a high amount of pleasurizing, as shown below. The dependent variable in this hypothesis is the same one as that of the Spectator principle, and it was defined on page 374.

Amount of sensory pleasurizing

None   Low   Moderate   High

The research on this principle has led to the speculation that the relationship between the variables in the Pleasurizing principle is curvilinear rather than linear. Masters and Johnson (1970) found that couples who have difficulty with their sexual functioning tend to have little pleasurizing in their relationship. They also observed that there can be many reasons for this hesitancy about pleasurizing, and that these reasons include unconscious resentments, anxiety about sexual functioning, and conditioning in early life. As the Masters and Johnson couples acquired the ability to create any type of sensory pleasure for and with each other their sexual adequacy seemed to be facilitated, and this finding suggests that variation between no pleasurizing and low or moderate amounts of pleasurizing tends to facilitate sexual functioning. Masters and Johnson did not, however, have any data which dealt with variation between moderate and very high amounts of pleasurizing. Thus, the Masters and Johnson data suggest that the part of the relationship labeled *a* in Figure 15–6 is valid but do not provide any evidence that the parts of the relationship labeled *b* and *c* are valid.

Another body of research suggests that line *b* in Figure 15–6 may be more accurate than line *c*. This research is, in a way, not as good as the Masters and Johnson research because the researchers were dealing with such matters as the "length of sexual foreplay" and the "frequency of a woman attaining orgasm" rather than with the more general and less diffuse variables of pleasurizing and sexual adequacy, but foreplay and orgasm seem to be similar enough to be relevant. The findings of Kinsey and his colleagues (1953) and of Fisher (1973, chap. 7) argue for line *b* rather than line *c*, even though Gebhard's (Shiloh, 1970) further analysis of Kinsey's data tentatively suggests that extended foreplay may help some women attain orgasm who would not otherwise be able to. The net result of these studies is that the present evidence indicates that variation between no pleasurizing and some pleasurizing seems to facilitate sexual adequacy, but that variation between some pleasurizing and a large amount of pleasurizing probably has less effect and perhaps no effect on sexual adequacy. Thus, line *a–b* rather than line *a–c* in Figure 15–6 seems to describe the relationship between pleasur-

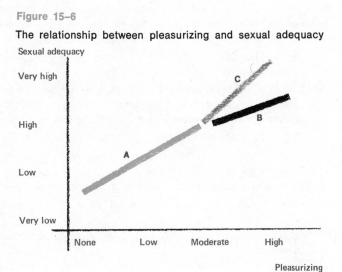

Figure 15–6

The relationship between pleasurizing and sexual adequacy

izing and sexual adequacy. It should probably be reemphasized, however, that the Pleasurizing principle should be viewed as a very tentative idea.

There are two main processes in using the Pleasurizing principle. The first is to determine how much sensual pleasurizing occurs in a relationship, and whether a couple could better attain their goals if pleasurizing were increased. If we have considerable pleasurizing in our relationship, the Pleasurizing principle suggests that we would probably not increase our sexual adequacy if we were to increase the amount of sensory stimulation we provide each other. If, however, we are the type of couple who do not provide much sensual pleasure for each other, we might find our sex life more satisfying if we were to increase the amount of pleasure we receive and provide. The "Recognizing Pleasurizing" exercise that follows is an evaluation of this part of a relationship.

RECOGNIZING PLEASURIZING

Goal: To recognize how much "sensory pleasure" is provided in a relationship.

1. It is possible to provide and receive sensory pleasure that is not specifically related to sexual intercourse, and this step is an attempt to identify how much this is done in a relationship. Evaluate each of the following items according to how often it occurs in your relationship: Never, very seldom, occasionally, or frequently.

   a. Gently touch the skin of the other person in an affectionate, caressing manner.

   b. Kiss in a variety of different ways, such as on the lips and other areas, short and long, gentle and firm, on intimate occasions and at other times, alone and around others, etc.

   c. "Say something" by delicately touching.

   d. Create a feeling in the other person by softly touching ears, neck, closed eyes, cheeks, etc.

   e. Pause and savor a feeling one has for a long, sensing time.

   f. Enjoy, deeply, sensations of different parts of one's body, such as hands, toes, skin.

   g. Completely and totally relax and enjoy whatever sensations occur.

h. Guide the other person's hand to help the other person provide sensory pleasure to any part of one's body.

2. After evaluating each of these possible ways of providing and receiving pleasure, try to identify other ways to evaluate how much "pleasurizing" occurs in your relationship.

3. Discuss your evaluation to determine whether you have an optimal level of pleasurizing, whether you are overemphasizing this part of your relationship, or whether you would benefit from more sensory stimulation.

The second process that is involved in using this principle is being able to increase the amount one can provide or experience sensory pleasure and feel good about it rather than feel uncomfortable or guilty about it.[2] This second process is considerably more difficult than the first, as it involves *changing* something rather than merely *recognizing* what we do. Also, this is a particularly challenging part of life for some of us to change because we may have deeply ingrained fears, anxieties, guilt feelings, or beliefs that prevent us from providing or receiving physical pleasures. The three exercises below provide some suggestions that may be useful to some of us. Others may need to get special help from someone, such as a professional counselor, before they can become as spontaneous as they wish to be. The first two exercises are designed to help us become more aware of and experiencing with our own bodies, and the last is designed to help us become more pleasurizing in a more sexually specific way.

INITIAL BODY AWARENESS EXPERIENCE[3]

Goal: To begin the process of becoming more aware of body parts and movements, and to begin experiencing pleasure from this awareness.

1. Begin by sitting or lying on the floor or sitting in a chair. Take off your shoes; put both feet on the floor. Close your eyes. If

---

[2] As with any principle, it is possible to increase or decrease the independent variable to try to attain one's goals. This author has not, however, been able to identify a situation in which someone would want to decrease this particular independent variable.

[3] This and the following exercise were developed by Otto (1969). He adapted them from the work of Sally McClure and Roberta Lewinson, who had previously studied with Mary Whitehouse at Los Angeles.

you are sitting on the floor, cross your legs or stretch them out in front of you. Do what is comfortable for you.

Now begin to become aware of your body. First feel your breathing. Is it rapid? Is it shallow? Is it deep? Let it be without labeling it, without changing it. If it wants to change, let it change. There is no need to do anything now; just become aware of your breathing, what it says to you, and what it wants to do. (Let time pass.)

Can you now become aware of your spine and back? Become aware of your spine and back where you are carrying your weight. Is the weight hanging heavy, or is it easy? Is it holding you up, or are you holding it up? (Let time pass.)

Now move your spine slightly to become fully aware of where your back is. You can sway back and forth a little or from side to side. Feel your spine and where your center is. Keep your eyes closed. (Let time pass.)

Now let your spine go, or, if you want to, continue to be aware of it, but begin to become aware of your chest. Are you letting it drop down into your belly? Is your chest lifted, or is it relaxed?

Now, feeling your chest and your spine, can you rock your spine and the upper part of your body just a bit to feel yourself sitting where you are sitting? (Let time pass.)

Are you moving your body as a whole, or is your head leading, or are you following your head? Whatever it is, it's OK. (Let time pass.)

Now concentrate your awareness on your contact where you are sitting. Feel your thighs and the soles of your feet. Are they holding you up? Are you pushing? (Let time pass.)

If you are sitting on the floor, are you letting yourself sink into the floor? Or are you forcing yourself into the floor? Hold yourself off, then let yourself sink deep into where you are sitting or lying. (Let time pass.)

Are your thigh muscles relaxed or tense? Let them go; let them sink in. (Let time pass.)

And now bring your awareness to your back, your neck, and your head. Move your back and your head so that your head is somewhat balanced and not hanging. (Let time pass.) Can you tip your head toward your shoulder? Become aware of the weight and carriage of your head. Feel how it affects your spine. (Let time pass.) You can become aware of the small movement of your head through your whole body. Feel your head free on top of your shoulders. (Let time pass.) Tip your head to the other shoulder. Feel the weight. (Let time pass.) Bring it back slowly so that it rests easily on top of your shoulders. Feel it rest there. (Let time pass.) Now slowly let your head drop forward; sense the weight. (Let time pass.) Slowly lift your head until it is back on top of your shoulders. (Let time pass.) Slowly drop your head on your back. Feel the stretch in your neck. (Let time pass.) Now bring the head back slowly. (Let time pass.) Slowly drop your head to one shoulder and hold it there. (Let time pass.) Now slowly roll it to the back and sense it there. (Let time pass.) Gently roll your head to the other shoulder and hold. (Let time pass.) Now slowly roll it to the front and feel what is happening. (Let time pass.) Now reverse, roll your head to the side and hold it. (Let time pass.) Now to the back. (Let time pass.) Now to the other side. (Let time pass.) Now to the front. (Let time pass.) Finally, slowly lift your head until it is sitting easily on top of your shoulders. Sense how you feel. (Let time pass.)

2.   Later, evaluate how adequate you were in receiving pleasure from your body.

TOTAL BODY AWARENESS EXPERIENCE

Goal: To increase one's ability to receive sensory pleasure alone.

1.   First take several minutes to relax thoroughly. Then let consciousness and awareness of all parts of your body float through you. Become aware that all of you is here. (Let time pass.)

As you become aware of your total body, become aware of your face. (Remember to keep your eyes closed.) Begin by tightening your eyes. Then let them go. Repeat. Tighten your mouth—scrunch it together and narrow it in—then let it go. Repeat this. (Let time pass.)

Now feel your forehead. Wrinkle it; let it relax. Become aware of your nose. Move it, wriggle it, tense it, and relax it. (Let time pass.)

Open your face as much as possible. Open it wide. You can feel your forehead broadening, your eyes relaxing. (Let time pass.)

Open your mouth. Let it relax. Tense it again, and let it relax again. Move your lips so that you can really feel them relax. Now move your chin vigorously. Let it relax. (Let time pass.)

See if what you have just done affects the rest of your body. Feel if it changes the way you are sitting. Feel what is going on in your body. (Let time pass.)

Now let your face become relaxed. Let your face speak to you. Some muscles will want to move. Let them. Just wait and let it happen. (Let time pass.)

Your head may want to move with this. There may be practically no movement or some. Don't force or rush it. Just let it happen. Be aware while it happens. (Let time pass.)

See if your lips are moving or if your eyes are tensing or if there is tensional movement in the corners of your mouth. Let it happen. (Let time pass.)

Focus your attention on your hands. Are they relaxed? Are they holding each other? Are they holding you? Can you now let them separate easily and open them up as far as you can. (Let time pass.)

Now lengthen your fingertips so that they reach outward away from you. Shut them; open them. (Let time pass.) Repeat this several times. (Let time pass.)

Now turn your hands over so that your palms are upward. Feel your palm. Become aware of it. (Let time pass.) Now turn your palm any way you want to, but let it curl and relax.

Now let your palms tense and relax. Let them curl hard and relax. Do this several times. (Let time pass.)

See what happens in your arms in the process. Let whatever wants to happen in your arms happen. Let it occur naturally. Feel where your arms are. Are you holding them close? Have they become part of the expression? (Let time pass.)

Now find out what your hands want to do. Relax; don't hold your body. Let your hands do whatever they want to do as if they had a life of their own which you do not have to label or analyze. Just let your hands be. (Pause.) Let your arms become part of this movement. (Pause.) While you are doing this, find out where your elbows are. Do they want to come into this? (Let time pass.)

Let your hands discover each other. Explore your hands. (Let time pass.) Feel your fingers. (Let time pass.) Discover your wrist. (Let time pass.) Now move up and feel your arms. (Let time pass.) Then your elbows. (Let time pass.) Reach up and touch your upper arms. (Let time pass.) Feel how they join the shoulder. (Let time pass.) Now feel your shoulders and your neck. (Let time pass.) Feel how your head sits on your neck. (Let time pass.)

Touch your face. (Let time pass.) Discover the feel of your face, your nose. (Let time pass.) Your eyes, your mouth, your cheeks. (Let time pass.) Your hair and eyes. (Let time pass.) Continue discovering yourself. (Let time pass.) Touch yourself wherever you wish. (Let time pass.) Touch your chest. (Let time pass.) Your stomach, your legs. (Let time pass.) Your buttocks. (Let time pass.) Your back, your sides; wherever you wish. Discover yourself—sense yourself. (Let time pass.)

Now feel what wants to be stretched. (Let time pass.) Stretch it. Sense yourself enjoying stretching. (Let time pass.)

Now being aware of all the parts of your body you want to be aware of, open your legs. Feel the movement. Tense your legs and leave them open. Then close them in again. Now stretch your legs and close them in. Stretch them hard, then relax them. Re-

peat this several times. (Let time pass.) Relax completely and lie
quietly for several minutes, with no thoughts.

2. Later, evaluate how adequate you were in receiving pleasure
    from your body, and, if you wish, design other experiences alone
    or with someone to further increase these skills.

INTERPERSONAL PLEASURIZING[4]

Goal: To increase a couple's ability to provide and receive
       sensory pleasurizing by practicing pleasurizing for several
       days when they will not engage in coitus.

1. *The first day.* During the first day of this exercise, the couple are
    to select two different times during the day when they will ex-
    plore sensory experiences, especially touch, with each other.
    Times of tiredness, stress, or tension should be avoided because
    these feelings or sensations tend to be communicated non-
    verbally, and the goal is to provide and receive pleasure, warmth,
    and closeness. After both partners have taken all their clothes
    off, one partner should be selected who will begin to provide
    "pleasure" and to discover which touching experiences are most
    pleasurable for the other partner. Tracing, massaging, caressing,
    and fondling can be used, and either person can verbally or non-
    verbally give directions about pleasure. The person who is being
    touched is to keep the other person from doing anything un-
    pleasant, distracting, or irritating. It is not necessary to say that
    something feels good unless the expression is spontaneous and
    would help the "giving" partner to learn what will provide pleasure.
    During this day the touching activities can include any parts of
    the body except the breasts or the genitals. This is to help acquire
    the ability to enjoy the less erogenous zones of the body. It may
    be desirable to use pleasant oils or lotions, especially if one
    member of the couple has rough hands. During the course of
    each "pleasurizing session," trade the giving and receiving roles
    at least once. The pleasurizing sessions can be as long as de-
    sired, but, to maximize learning, do not proceed to intercourse
    during this day. Enjoy the pleasurizing as an end in itself.

---

[4] This exercise is an attempt to implement the procedures and sequences
Masters and Johnson use in the first days of their program for sexual inadequacy. Some of the instructions for this exercise are taken from Belliveau
and Richter's (1970, pp. 103–10) descriptions of the Masters and Johnson
program.

2. *The second day.* During the second day, two more pleasurizing sessions should be held. These are to be like the ones held on the first day, with two exceptions. The first change is that the person who receives the "pleasurizing" must participate actively by putting his or her hand over the hand of the "giving" partner to show personal preference by light pressure or change of direction. This will help both members learn more about how to provide pleasure. This is especially useful for men because there is an unfounded myth in our culture that men automatically know all there is to know about sex and that they can naturally divine women's sexual needs. Actually many men and women do not know themselves, what stimulates them most, until they spontaneously experience. The second change is that the touch can be extended to include the genitals and breasts. This, however, is to be done in a manner which will not cause ejaculation or orgasm. Again, the goal is to provide pleasure short of a sexual climax.

3. *The third day.* During the third day, the couple are to have at least one pleasurizing session in which the goal is to provide pleasure and not proceed to intercourse. Then, as part of a later session, they may engage in whatever sexual activity they wish.

4. After the three days, evaluate your ability to provide sensory pleasure to each other, and devise additional strategies for increasing this skill—if you wish you were better at it.

The Security principle

Several major findings emerged from Fisher's (1973) extensive studies of female sexuality, and one of them seems sufficiently clear and well documented to justify a new principle. The idea is:

THE SECURITY PRINCIPLE: The more secure a woman feels about her love object, the more likely she is to attain orgasm.

The independent variable in this principle is *security,* and this variable denotes the extent to which women believe or feel their love objects may easily be lost or may disappear. Many women seem to feel that they can "count on" the stability of their love objects, and seem to invest more of themselves in the sexual experience when they are more likely to attain a sexual climax frequently. Fisher believes that this relationship occurs because of the socialization practices in contemporary society, and that if women were reared differently the relationship would disappear. If that is the case the Security principle is a culture-specific idea and not really a bona fide "general principle," but whether or not this is so will not be known the case until additional research is undertaken.

If Fisher is correct in his speculation that this relationship exists primarily because of cultural factors, it is also likely that the principle only operates for some of us in the contemporary American society. It may be, for example, that the Security principle tends to operate for those of us who prefer the more traditional or conventional styles of marriage, but that it does not operate for those of us who prefer one of the more innovative styles of marriage. The principle may also be relevant in marital situations in which the wife is not experiencing orgasm at all or is experiencing it less frequently than she wishes. The principle suggests that in such situations changes in the security of the marital relationship as a whole have an impact on the quality of the sex relationship, and we may wish (1) to examine the security feelings and then perhaps (2) to do something to alter them.

MYTHS AND REALITIES ABOUT SEX[5]

There are a large number of beliefs, traditions, and opinions about various aspects of sex that persist even though there is growing evidence that many of them are not true. And, to make matters worse, the social and biological sciences have not yet completed enough research to determine whether many of these beliefs are true or false. Many of these beliefs have been stated as *facts* in some or all of the "marriage manuals," and hence it is occasionally possible to quote several different published sources to document a particular belief. All too often, however, when one goes to the original source, one learns that there is no evidence to justify the belief.

For several reasons these myths frequently interfere with pleasant, satisfying sexual interaction. Some of the myths create unrealistic expectations, but since couples don't know that their expectations are unrealistic they become disappointed and resentful when they are not able to achieve them. Some of the myths create the feeling that sexual interaction is an unpleasant, distasteful experience rather than a pleasant, unifying activity, and other myths even lead to the view that sexual interaction is a source of pain and discomfort. It thus seems useful to identify some of the widely held myths about sex and to provide some accurate information that will

[5] This section is highly dependent on McCary's (1971) *Sexual Myths and Fallacies,* and those who wish to have additional documentation on the myths discussed here would find that source useful.

separate fact from fantasy. This is possible in the few areas in which enough good research has been done to establish what the truth is. Since, unfortunately, there are many other areas in which research has not yet determined whether "commonly held beliefs" are myths or realities, we should probably all be cautious about accepting what we read or are told about sexual interaction—especially if the information we are given doesn't seem consistent with our own experience and inclinations.

The following sections identify eleven misconceptions about sex, and attempt to separate facts from fantasies.

Males respond more quickly to sexual stimuli than do females. Masters and Johnson (1966) discovered that the walls of the vagina begin secreting lubricants within 10–15 seconds of an effective sexual stimulus. It may be that in the contemporary American society many women do respond more slowly, physically and emotionally, but it is very possible that this is entirely due to cultural conditioning.

Reaching an orgasm simultaneously is best. This belief has been widely publicized in marriage manuals. When simultaneous orgasm occurs, however, the male usually moves immediately into the resolution phase of the response cycle, and his subsequent loss of interest and of an erection may prevent the wife from attaining subsequent orgasms during that coital experience if she wishes to. Many couples who are able to achieve simultaneous orgasm prefer to reach their climaxes separately.

Women are not completely satisfied with their sex life if they fail to achieve orgasm at least a majority of the times they engage in intercourse. Many couples are taught that unless they "learn how" to have sexual relationships in such a way that the wife attains a climax most or all of the time, the wives are not experiencing an optimal level of gratification. One almost unbelievable aspect of this myth is that some husbands put more stock in the myth than they do in their wives' reports that they enjoy sexual intercourse even when they do not attain a climax. Considerable research (for example, Raboch, 1970; McGuire and Steinhilber, 1970; Hollender, 1971; Wallin and Clark, 1963; and Golden, 1971) has found, however, that many wives report that they are highly satisfied with their sex life even though they seldom or never experience orgasm. There is some evidence (Masters and Johnson, 1966, pp. 119–23) that women experience discomfort if they remain at the plateau stage of the sexual response cycle for several hours without proceeding to the orgasmic phase of the cycle when they are able to attain a climax. This, however, is quite different from participating in intercourse for romantic or personal reasons when not highly aroused sexually, or from being unable to attain a climax.

A vaginal orgasm is better than a clitoral orgasm.   It is widely believed that women experience two different types of orgasm and that one is better than the other. The belief is that a "clitoral" orgasm—one achieved through stimulation of the clitoris—is less desirable than a "vaginal" orgasm—one achieved through stimulation of the vagina. A vaginal orgasm is also supposed to be achievable only by women who are more emotionally mature or physically healthy. Masters and Johnson (1966, pp. 56–67) identified two reasons why this belief is indeed a myth. One reason is that the walls of the vagina have very few nerve endings, and hence a climax attained through stimulation of the vaginal area is attained through stimulation of the tissues surrounding the vagina, primarily the inner lips, rather than through stimulation of the vagina itself. The second reason is that a careful evaluation of physiological and emotional reactions to clitoral and vaginal orgasms found no differences between them. Apparently the orgasmic experience differs in intensity and type from person to person and from time to time, but there are no systematic differences according to whether it results from stimulation of the vagina, the clitoris, both the vagina and the clitoris, from stimulation of other erogenous zones, such as the breasts or the perineum, or from fantasy.

Women cannot participate or are not interested in participating in intercourse after the menopause.   Although there is little research about female sexuality after menopause, the research that has been done (Masters and Johnson, 1966, chap. 15; Kinsey, 1953; Deutsch, 1945; Fisher, 1973) shows conclusively that women can participate in sexual intercourse effectively and with intense pleasure well into their seventies and eighties. After the menopause the tissues in the genital region tend to have less tone and elasticity and to be "thinner," but the female sexual organs continue to function effectively when there is an appropriate interpersonal relationship and normal sexual stimulation. Some women even experience an increase in sexual pleasure after menopause. The reasons for this are not known, but two possibilities that have been suggested are that some women then lose their fear of becoming pregnant and that others experience an increased desire to become pregnant.

People are able to have a certain number of sexual experiences and when those are used up their sexual activity is over.   There are great differences in the amount people participate in sex, but the amount of participation when a person is young is positively correlated with the amount of participation when that person is older, and this indicates that there is no "set" amount of sexual activity for a person. Kinsey (1948, 1953) found that individuals tended to establish a pattern of participation in sexual activity when they were young and that this pattern tended to continue throughout their lives, with a gradual decrease in frequency in males after their late teens and in females after their early thirties.

Coitus should be avoided during pregnancy. Most husbands and wives do not experience any marked change in their sexual interest during the first trimester of pregnancy, and a substantial number of wives experience an increased interest in sex during the second trimester. Both husbands and wives tend to experience a decreased interest in sex during the third trimester (Landis, Poffenberger, and Poffenberger, 1950; Masters and Johnson, 1966, chap. 10). Couples would do well to consult the wife's physician about intercourse during pregnancy because such circumstances as a threatened natural abortion occasionally justify a cessation of sexual activity. In normal circumstances, however, couples can participate in intercourse or manual sexual stimulation as often and with as many variations as their interest and the comfort of the wife permit. Most couples find that certain positions, such as the husband supine, are less comfortable during pregnancy, and hence they tend to use slightly different positions at that time. There are, however, differences of opinion on whether couples should engage in intercourse at certain times during pregnancy. Some scholars (Javert, 1957, 1960) argue that orgasm during coitus may be an important factor in causing miscarriages, especially if the intercourse occurs at about the time a normal menstrual period would begin. The research on this is, however, inconclusive, and, again, the best solution is probably to consult with one's physician about what would be best in one's own situation.

Both highly frequent sexual participation and sexual abstinence are harmful. Little systematic research has been conducted on this issue, but the research that has been done (Masters and Johnson, 1966; McGary, 1967) indicates that no lasting physiological or psychological effects can be attributed to either high or low participation in sexual activity. The male tends to have more nocturnal emissions when his other sources of ejaculation are infrequent. Also, the sperm count in the semen decreases when he has a large number of ejaculations in a short period of time. These, however, are short-term consequences of high or low participation. There is also some evidence (Fisher, 1973) that sexual desire is increased when couples abstain from coitus for short periods of time and that it is decreased by highly frequent participation in coitus, but there is no evidence that either very frequent or very infrequent sexual activity has any systematic harmful effects—physically, mentally, or emotionally.

Women are most interested in sex at the time of ovulation. There is some evidence that many women experience systematic variation in sexual appetite during the menstrual cycle. The evidence suggests, however, that most women are most interested in sex the week before and the week after their menstrual period. Fisher (1973) has suggested that one explanation for this is that most couples have intercourse less frequently or not at all during the menstrual period. The cyclic differences seem to be minor changes in sexual appetite for most women, and not all women experience the same pattern. Some women are most highly motivated sexually during the menstrual flow, and others experience no discernible cyclic changes in their sexual desire.

The size of the penis and foreskin makes a difference in sexual gratification. This myth has many variations, among them the beliefs that a large penis is associated with the female's sexual gratification and the male's sexual virility and physical stature. It is also widely believed that the circumcised male has less control over ejaculation and experiences a more intense orgasm. All of these beliefs are invalid. There is almost no correlation between body size and penile size, and very often small men have a large penis and large men have a small penis. Masters and Johnson (1966) used artificial penises to determine whether penile size was related to gratification in the female, and they found no relationship. This is probably partly because the vaginal walls have an extremely low concentration of sexually relevant nerve endings. Masters and Johnson (1966) also found no relationship between circumcision and sperm count, tendency to premature ejaculation, or any other discernible physiological or psychological reactions.

It is dangerous to have coitus during menstruation. A variety of cultures have had mythical beliefs about the causes of menstruation and the effects of contact with the menstrual fluid and of sexual intercourse during or just after the menstrual period. There are no medical, physiological, anatomical, or sexual reasons to abstain from intercourse during the menstrual period. Some individuals find the presence of the menstrual discharge to be unaesthetic, and the discharge does have a slight odor, but these factors and cultural taboos are the only justifications for abstinence during menstruation.

SUMMARY

The first section of this chapter discussed the basic anatomy and physiology of the male and female sexual organs. This was followed by a discussion of what the normal sexual response cycle is and how a knowledge of that cycle can be helpful in creating a pleasant and satisfying sexual relationship. Three general principles were then presented, and they were the *Spectator, Pleasurizing,* and *Security* principles that are diagramed in Figure 15–7. The last section of

Figure 15–7

Summary diagram of the principles in Chapter 15

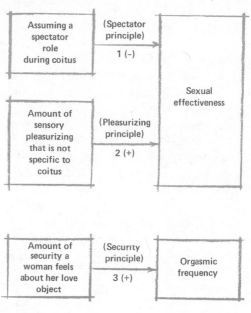

the chapter identified 11 widely believed myths about sex and
explained why they are invalid.

SUGGESTIONS FOR FURTHER STUDY

Bell, Robert R.   1966. *Premarital Sex in a Changing Society.* Engle-
    wood Cliffs, N.J.: Prentice-Hall.

Belliveau, Fred, and Richter, Lin   1970. *Understanding Human Sexual
    Inadequacy.* Boston: Little, Brown.

Bohannan, Paul   1969. *Love, Sex, and Being Human.* Garden City,
    N.Y.: Doubleday.

Cannon, Kenneth and Long, Richard   1971. "Premarital Sexual Be-
    havior in the Sixties." *Journal of Marriage and the Family* 33:36–49
    (February).

Cox, Frank D.   1968. *Youth, Marriage and the Seducing Society.* Du-
    buque, Iowa: Brown.

Crawley, Lawrence Q.; Malfetti, James L.; Stewart, Ernest I.; and
    Vas Dias, Nini   1964. *Reproduction, Sex, and Preparation for Mar-
    riage.* Englewood Cliffs, N.J.: Prentice-Hall.

Francoeur, Anna K., and Francoeur, Robert T.   1974. *Hot and Cool
    Sex: Cultures in Conflict.* New York; Harcourt Brace Jovanovich.

Kogan, Benjamin A.   1973. *Human Sexual Expression.* New York:
    Harcourt Brace Jovanovich.

Lehrman, Nat   1970. *Masters and Johnson Explained*. Chicago: Playboy Press.

McCary, James L.   1967. *Human Sexuality*. New York: Van Nostrand.

McCary, James L.   1971. *Sexual Myths and Fallacies*. New York: Van Nostrand.

Masters, William H., and Johnson, Virginia E.   1966. *Human Sexual Response*. Boston: Little, Brown.

Masters, William H., and Johnson, Virginia E.   1970. *Human Sexual Inadequacy*. Boston: Little, Brown.

Morrison, Eleanor S. and Borosage, Vera   1973. *Human Sexuality: Contemporary Perspectives*. Palo Alto, Calif.: National Press Books.

Pengelley, Eric T.   1974. *Sex and Human Life*. Menlo Park, Calif.: Addison-Wesley.

Petras, John W.   1973. *Sexuality in Society*. Boston: Allyn and Bacon.

Pierson, Elaine C.   1973. *Sex Is Never an Emergency: A Candid Guide for Young Adults*. Philadelphia: Lippincott.

Schwarz, Oswald   1969. *The Psychology of Sex*. Baltimore: Penguin Books.

16

Coping with stress

IT IS POSSIBLE to create a marital and family situation that is rewarding and pleasant most of the time, but even in ideal circumstances some situations are difficult and stressful. Some stressful situations are sudden and unexpected, such as an accident that seriously injures a member of the family or the birth of a child who is mentally subnormal or physically deformed. Other stressful situations, such as bereavement, are as inevitable as the changing of the seasons, and sometimes they are anticipated for long periods of time. Hansen and Hill (1964, pp. 793–94) have classified stressful events according to whether they involve demoralization, the loss of a family member, the acquisition of a family member, changes in a family's social status, or a combination of such events, and their typology is reproduced in Figure 16–1. An examination of their list is a sobering experience, as it demonstrates that a very large number of stressful events happen to families. Extensive as this list is, however, it doesn't include a number of other common crises, such as the sudden loss of a job, chronic illnesses, acute serious illnesses, such as strokes or heart attacks, automobile accidents, houses burning, industrial accidents, and missing persons.

For several reasons it is important to include a chapter on methods of coping with stressful events. One reason is that we experience many of these events as married couples or as families rather than as single individuals. A second reason is that some stressful events are inevitable, and if we learn ways to cope with them their disruptive effects can be minimized. A third reason is that there has been considerable research in this area, and social scientists have gradually learned several important principles that can be used to help cope with stressful events.

Figure 16–1

A classification of family crises of dismemberment, accession, and demoralization

---

Dismemberment only

Death of a child, spouse, or parent
Hospitalization of spouse
War separation

Accession only

Unwanted pregnancy
Return of deserter
Stepfather, stepmother additions
Some war reunions
Some adoptions, aged grandparents, orphaned kin

Demoralization only

Nonsupport
Infidelity
Alcoholism
Drug addiction
Delinquency and events bringing disgrace

*Demoralization plus dismemberment
or accession*

Illegitimacy
Runaways
Desertion
Divorce
Imprisonment
Suicide or homicide
Institutionalization for mental illness
Mental retardation

Types of stresses involving status shifts

Sudden impoverishment
Prolonged unemployment
Sudden wealth and fame
Refugee migrations, political and religious
Disasters, tornadoes, floods, explosions
War bombings, deprivations
Political declassing, denazification

Source: Adapted from Hansen and Hill (1964, pp. 793–
94).

A final reason for including this topic in a marriage course is that
modern society has created a system that tends to insulate children
and young adults from many of the "normal" stressful events that
families encounter (Parsons and Fox, 1952). When people are
seriously ill, mentally unstable, or near death, they are quickly
removed from family situations in which they might be visible to
children or young adults. In addition, parents often try to isolate
their children from stressful events. Because of this partial insulation from many of the tragedies of life, many of us are well into

adulthood before we encounter situations that teach us such things as the inevitability of tragedy or the effects that stresses have on intimate relationships. The result is that when we eventually learn how extensive stressful events really are, this can be a fairly shocking experience in itself. The aim of this chapter is to help the reader to learn about stress in a relatively painless manner and to provide information that can be used to cope with stress.

FOUR KEY TERMS

Before the principles can be communicated clearly it is first necessary to define four key terms. Two of these terms are *stress* and *crisis*. Following Burr's (1973, pp. 199–203) interpretation of the way these terms have been used in previous research, these two concepts are defined differently. *Stresses* are defined here as changes in families that are of sufficient magnitude to potentially produce a crisis. Changes in such things as income, number of family members, goals, processes, values, roles, and boundaries are examples of potentially crisis-producing events. *Crises* are defined here as situations in which the marital or family system is so disrupted or disorganized that it is not able to operate in its routine or usual manner.

When *stress* and *crisis* are defined in this manner it is possible to define the other two major terms in this chapter. One of them is *vulnerability* (Hansen, 1965). This term refers to the differences in the ability of couples or families to keep potentially stressful situations from disrupting the routine, everyday, relatively normal operation of their social system. Couples or families that are usually able to cope with potentially disruptive events by not becoming highly disrupted or disorganized are able to resist stress, and hence are low in vulnerability. On the other hand, couples and families are high in vulnerability when their normal functioning is easily disrupted by stressful events. Family vulnerability to stress is a continuous variable that ranges from low to high vulnerability, and it is represented by the following diagram.

Vulnerability to stress

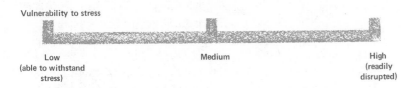

| Low | Medium | High |
| (able to withstand stress) | | (readily disrupted) |

The fourth term is *regenerative power*, which denotes the ability of couples or families to recover from crises (Hansen, 1965). Sometimes it is not possible to keep a stressful event from creating a full-blown crisis, either because the family's vulnerability is high or because the stressful event is highly disruptive. When this happens a couple or family is faced with the need to recover from the crisis, and this is when regenerative power is relevant. At other times it is possible to keep a stressful event from disrupting a social system, and if that is the case no "crisis" ever occurs. In such situations regenerative power is irrelevant. Regenerative power is also a continuous variable, as shown below.

Regenerative power

Low   Medium   High

AVOIDING CRISES

Adaptability

THE ADAPTABILITY PRINCIPLE: The greater the adaptability of a family the less the vulnerability to stress, and vice versa.

Adaptability in this context refers to the ability to change the usual ways of doing things or the roles in the relationship and to easily adopt innovations or new ideas. It is a continuous variable that ranges from very low adaptability to high adaptability. Persons

Family adaptability

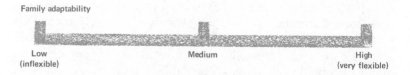

Low   Medium   High
(inflexible)   (very flexible)

low in adaptability resist change and are rigid and inflexible in their opinions and in their ways of doing things; and a family low in adaptability is one that tends to be inflexible and resistant to change. Modern systems theorists have coined a term called *system openness* (Buckley, 1967; Speer, 1970) which refers to how open a system (such as a marital couple or family) is to new information ideas, or ways of doing things. Apparently adaptability and openness are identical concepts.

Not only is this principle intuitively plausible, but there has been considerable research about it and all of the empirical studies have supported it. Most of the evidence was acquired in studies of how families adjusted to the stresses of the economic depression in the 1930s (Angell, 1936; Cavan and Ranck, 1938; Koos, 1946; and Komarovsky, 1940), but additional support has also been found in a study of war separation and reunion (Hill, 1949) and in clinical settings (Speer, 1971).

It is relatively easy to find illustrations of this principle in family life situations. One obvious example is a situation in which a family's primary source of income is lost through an accident, illness, or economic depression. Families that rigidly adhere to a particular set of beliefs, such as the belief that the wife should not work or that the family should not accept help from private or public sources, will usually find this event a more serious crisis than will families that are more adaptable in their style of life. Another example is that parents who have rigid, inflexible beliefs about how to rear their children are probably more vulnerable to the stresses that occur in the adolescent years than are parents who are fairly adaptable in their definitions of their parental role.

Adaptability is apparently not a global personality trait, in the sense that some people are adaptable in all aspects of their lives and that others are unadaptable in most or all aspects of their lives. There is evidence that adaptability is in part a situational process, in that people usually tend to be adaptable in some aspects of their lives and unadaptable in other aspects. Hill (1949), for example, found that the ability to adapt to the stressful events of war separation and war reunion tended to be somewhat exclusive. The wives who were able to adapt easily to war separation tended to have difficulty coping with war reunion and the wives who had difficulty adapting to war separation had less difficulty with war reunion.

If we are more adaptable in some areas than in others, and if stressful events in areas of life in which we are less adaptable tend to create more disruption than stressful events in areas of life in which we are relatively adaptable, it may be useful to determine in which areas we are adaptable and in which areas we are rigid. The following exercise is designed to help us identify these different areas.

ASSESSING ADAPTABILITY

Goal: To identify areas of low and high adaptability.

1. Think of the one view, idea, opinion, value, etc. about marital and family life which you are probably least willing to change. Write it down.

2. Think of the view, etc. about which you are next most unadaptable, and continue doing this until you have a list of the 8 or 10 areas of least adaptability.

3. Think of 8 or 10 views, etc. about marital and family life which you would be quite willing to change, and make a second list.

4. If possible, do this with someone such as your spouse, fianceé(e), or date. Compare the lists and then discuss how each of you feels emotionally about the two lists.

5. The following list will get you started, but it is likely that the subjects that are important to you are not even on this "starter" list. Your lists of role expectations in the "Increasing Consensus" exercise on page 308 may be helpful.

    a. I want to have considerable time to myself.
    b. I want a spouse who is sexually very responsive.
    c. I want to have a career outside the home.
    d. Sex should (should not) be confined to marriage.
    e. Men and women should be completely equal.
    f. My children must be very obedient to their parents.
    g. We will have good music in our home.
    h. I want a very affectionate marital relationship.
    i. I must have an income in the top 10 percent of the population.
    j. I want to engage in outside sports.
    k. I want to spend a great deal of time reading.
    l. We will not have a television set in our home.
    m. A man ought to be able to hit his wife.
    n. Etc.

One way to use this general rule in courtship is for two individuals who are considering marriage to evaluate each other's adaptability and take this into account in deciding whether to marry. Adaptability is, of course, only one of a large number of factors that should be considered, but since we know that it is related to a family's vulnerability to stress it is probably a useful one to take into account. In marital situations, the Adaptability principle is relevant because adaptability can be manipulated. As Burgess and Wallin (1953, pp. 630–55) point out in their extensive discussion of adaptability, this characteristic is probably not determined by genetic or biological factors, and hence we can change our adaptability if we use social situations to help us change it. The following exercise is designed to help readers increase their adaptability by using social situations and capitalizing on a distinction Nye (1967) made between intrinsic and instrumental values. Nye differentiated between things valued as "ends in themselves" and things valued because they are "instrumental" in helping us attain some desirable goal. Nye's distinction is useful because, as he points out (1967, p. 247), instrumental values tend to be less rigid than intrinsic values and can frequently be changed more easily. The goal of the following exercise is thus to find some instrumental values and then to use one's social situation to help change them. The exercise is designed on the assumption that Nye (1967) is correct in concluding that we can change "instrumental" values or beliefs much more easily than "intrinsic" values.

INCREASING ADAPTABILITY

Goal: To increase adaptability.

1. Make a list of 5 to 10 opinions you have about the way things "ought" to be in marriage. (If you did the preceding exercise you can use the list you made there. If you didn't do that exercise you can use its "starter" list of opinions as illustrations of the type of opinions you might list.)

2. Identify which of these opinions you tend to value intrinsically (as ends or goals in themselves) and which you value mostly because they are instrumental in helping you attain some other ends or goals. If none of them are instrumental, then think up instrumental opinions you have about how things ought to be in courtship and marriage. Examples of instrumental opinions might be:

   a. My wife should not work . . . not because working is bad, but because the children need care, and if she worked she couldn't care for them.

   b. I want to continue my art lessons . . . not because art is so important but because it gives me a feeling of independence and a feeling that I'm creating something.

   c. My husband (or wife) should be the one to initiate our lovemaking . . . not because I want him (her) to take the initiative but because this will show that he (she) desires me.

3. Pick the one instrumental opinion you feel least strongly about.

4. Talk to some intimate acquaintance (spouse, good friend, etc.) about your opinion. The aim of your discussion is to find several ways in which your goal or end might be accomplished other than the way you started with. Occasionally this will make you more adaptable than you were previously. Does it? If not, you might try discussing another opinion. If the second discussion doesn't help, try your hand at devising different types of experience that will increase or decrease your adaptability.

Integration   **THE INTEGRATION PRINCIPLE: The amount of family integration influences its vulnerability to stress, and this is an
inverse relationship.**

Integration is defined in a number of different ways in the
scholarly literature. It is defined here, following Angell (1936) and
Hill (1964, p. 144), as the adequacy versus inadequacy of the family organization. If a family is organized "adequately," its members
feel fairly comfortable about the way things are done. There is
coherence and unity in the family; the various family members are
interdependent; and common interests, affectional needs, and personal wishes are taken into account. In families with low integration there are unresolved disagreements about what different members of the family ought to be doing, and the powerful members of
the family usually make sure that the necessary jobs get done. When
there is low integration there also usually tends to be discontent
with the family organization. The level of integration is a continuous and very complex variable that ranges from low to high
integration.

Family integration

Low   Medium   High
(disorganized)   (well organized)

The Adaptability and Integration principles were derived from
and tested in the same body of research (primarily Angell, 1936;
and then Cavan and Ranck, 1938; Komarovsky, 1940; Koos, 1946;
and Hill, 1949). Both principles have considerable empirical support, and hence considerable confidence can be placed in them. The
evidence also suggests that the Adaptability principle probably
makes more difference than the Integration principle (Waller and
Hill, 1951, p. 461), but both principles are apparently important.

The Integration principle can be applied in our personal lives in
a number of different ways. For example, couples who learn this
principle and are not experiencing a stressful event could use the
principle to assess the adequacy of their integration—to determine
whether their level of integration might be a detriment if they were
to experience a stressful event. Unfortunately knowledge in this
area has not progressed to a point at which science knows how

much integration is needed for it to be helpful rather than a hin-
drance in stressful situations, and this means that about all couples
can do is try to determine such things as (1) whether they are con-
spicuously better or worse off than most couples they know, and
(2) whether they are comfortable with the way they are organized
in their own relationship. If the couple are worse off than most couples it is likely that this factor is contributing to high vulnerability,
and if they are as well off or better off than most couples it is likely
that this factor is keeping their vulnerability low. If both members
of the couple tend to be comfortable with the way their life situation
is organized it is likely that their level of integration will help them
when they meet stressful situations. However, if one or both members resent or feel uncomfortable with the way things are organized
this is something they may want to try to change. Occasionally the
more powerful member is satisfied, and the other goes along without really being very comfortable, and there is some evidence (Komarovsky, 1946) that in this type of situation a stressful event will
have a more disruptive impact on the couple's life than if both are
satisfied. The following exercise is designed to help people in a
relationship determine how adequate their integration is and to help
them begin changing it if they think it should be changed.

INTEGRATION IN A RELATIONSHIP

Goal: To determine how adequate the "integration" in a relationship is, and to change the integration if it is not satisfactory.

1. This exercise should be done for a relationship that has considerable permanence. Such situations as a marital relationship, one's
relationship with parents, or a long-term roommate relationship
are best. It is difficult to do this exercise in most dating relationships or in class discussion groups.

2. Set aside 30 minutes to discuss the level of "integration" in a
relationship.

3. During the discussion, your first goal is to determine how satisfied
each person in the relationship is with the way things get done
that need to get done. Some of the issues you may find it useful
to discuss are:

a. Sometimes people in a relationship have a fairly clear picture
of how things should get done, and at other times people are
confused about who ought to be doing what. Some persons
like to have a rigid division of labor, and other persons like to

have people work together, and in either situation there can be clarity or confusion about how things ought to be done. Where do you stand on this issue?

b. How much would each person in the relationship like to see things organized differently in terms of giving those involved more or less leadership, initiative, responsibility, or follow-through in what they are supposed to do?

c. If there is "supervision," how adequate is it? Is more supervision given than is needed, more needed than is given, an optimal amount?

d. How able are you to talk about the way things are organized so that changes can be made if circumstances arise which make changes necessary?

4. If, after this discussion, you are satisfied with the integration in your relationship, you have finished the exercise. If, however, you wish to change the integration, go on to step 5.

5. Each person in the relationship should identify the changes she or he would like to see in its "organization." Then discuss the various suggestions, to agree on one or two modest changes that could probably be made in the near future, and develop an Action Plan to help you accomplish these changes. See pages 164–65 for the Action Plan outline.

Externaliza-
tion of blame

THE EXTERNALIZATION OF BLAME PRINCIPLE: The externalization of blame for a stressful event influences the vulnerability of the family to this event, and this is an inverse relationship.

The externalization of blame should probably be viewed as a dichotomous variable, as shown below. The responsibility for a

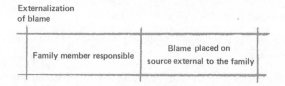

stressful event is placed either on a family member or on an external source. The process involved in this principle can be illustrated by a situation in which chronic unemployment occurs. The principle suggests that when the unemployment occurs because of a major economic disruption in a society, the unemployment will tend to be less disruptive for a family than when it occurs because the father refused to work or was personally responsible in some other way. Of course, the externalization of blame would not eliminate all of the effects of the unemployment, but the principle suggests that it would have some influence on the amount of internal disruption in the family system.

This principle was first explicitly stated by Hansen (1964, p. 209) in his review of factors related to family vulnerability, and it is implicit in earlier work by Cavan and Ranck (1938) and Komarovsky (1946). This means that the body of scientific evidence that supports this principle is not large. Although the principle also seems to have some validity on an intuitive basis, it should probably be viewed with more tentativeness than most of the principles identified in this chapter.

It seems fairly difficult to find ways to "use" this principle, since the only way this author and his students have found to use it is for individuals or couples to make sure they do not blame individuals in the family for a problem when it is possible to find external reasons for that problem. This can be done by deliberately trying to find external reasons whenever someone asks "why" a problem exists. This is not to suggest that people should deny that internal reasons exist, but that they should *actively* search for external reasons when reasons are sought.

One of the things that make this principle so difficult to use is that the independent variable—the externalization of the source responsible for a problem—is so difficult to change, manipulate, or control. Thus, the major value of this principle in dating and marital relations is that it gives some insight into the reasons that frequently make families vulnerable to stress.

Another factor that is thought to be an important variable in determining family vulnerability to a stressful event is the *definition of the severity of the event*. The idea here is that the more serious a family thinks something is the more devastating it actually becomes. This idea has a long tradition in social psychology, as it is a specific instance of the generalization attributed to W. I. Thomas that a situation perceived as real is real in its consequences.

Definition of the severity of the event

The idea in this principle can perhaps best be explained by means of a hypothetical example. Assume that two families encountered the same stressful event—say, their houses burned down. One family viewed this experience as extremely serious, while the other family defined it as much less serious. Even if the actual loss from the two fires were identical, the family that viewed the situation as less serious would probably experience less disruption, chaos, trauma—in other words, less crisis—than the family that viewed the situation as more serious. This principle is:

THE SEVERITY PRINCIPLE: The definition a family makes of the severity of a stressful event influences the family's vulnerability to that event, and this is a positive relationship.

At first glance this generalization seems to be difficult to use in everyday life. However, it is possible to apply the principle in ways that can reduce vulnerability to stress. A vast literature suggests that the way people define things is due in large part to their points of reference (Merton, 1968, chaps. 10, 11). For example, if a blind person were to compare his situation to that of the many sighted people around him he would feel deprived, and think his situation very serious, If, on the other hand, the same person were to compare his situation to others with even more serious life situations than his own, he would usually feel relatively better off, and consider his situation less serious. The same processes operate in many other aspects of life. For example, the veteran confined to a wheelchair will respond to his situation very differently if he focuses on how relatively deprived he is than if he focuses on others in similar situations. The point here is that individuals, couples, or families can manipulate their definitions of the seriousness of stressful events by manipulating their reference points. It would be unrealistic to think that this would produce major changes in a family's vulnerability, but it might make enough difference to be worthwhile. The following exercise is thus designed to help individuals, couples, or families decrease the severity of one of such definitions.

CHANGING DEFINITIONS OF SITUATIONS

Goal: To change the definition of the seriousness of a stressful event so that it is viewed as less serious.

1. Identify an event in your own marital or family situation that you define as fairly serious. (If at all possible, try to think of an event

you are experiencing now, one you have experienced in the past, or one that someone close to you, such as a parent, has experienced.)

2. *Intellectual part.* Think about several marital or family situations that are *more* serious than the one you have identified. After thinking about those other situations and comparing your situation with them, does your own situation seem less severe or less important?

3. *Behavioral part.* Identify one or two marital or family situations that are as serious or more serious than the one you have identified. Locate some people who are experiencing these situations, and become involved with them in a manner that will acquaint you with what they are experiencing. You will want to be extremely tactful in doing this, but there are many places where it could be done. For example, you could offer your services as a temporary volunteer in such institutions as hospitals or health agencies, or in institutions that care for retarded or disabled individuals, and in this way provide a valuable service while gaining a new perspective. You could also inconspicuously observe a hospital emergency room for an afternoon, visit a school for the blind to become familiar with its programs, spend a few hours in a divorce court, visit a welfare office, etc.

4. Evaluate whether step 2 or step 3 had any effect on your definition of the seriousness of the stressful event. They may not, but . . . they just might.

Amount of time

Hansen and Hill have theorized that families are fairly vulnerable when stressful events occur suddenly and without prior warning, and that they tend to be less vulnerable when they are aware that a stressful event is going to occur. These authors argue:

The suddenness with which some stresses hit the family calls for behavior markedly different from that touched off by stresses which have a long history of development. With the increasing problem of alcoholism or loss of control of a child, the family is often forewarned and foreworried about a climax. The child who comes home a delinquent after months of rebellion at home doesn't so much surprise his parents as humiliate them. Quite different is the response of parents whose child "out of the blue" is suddenly involved in a gang fight or car theft.

Even more markedly, the family which loses its life possessions because of a fire or hurricane will often react quite differently from a family which suffers the same losses because of consistent economic reverses over which it has no control. The first instance is unanticipated, the second foreseen (1964, pp. 794–95).

The important variable in this principle is the *amount of time a potentially stressful event is anticipated* and it is diagramed below.

Amount of time
events are anticipated

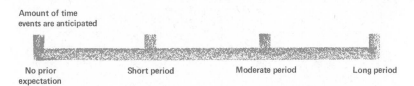

No prior   Short period   Moderate period   Long period
expectation

The relevant principle is:

THE TIME-CRISIS PRINCIPLE: The amount of time that stressful events are anticipated influences vulnerability to to this stress, and this is an inverse relationship.

Hansen and Hill (1964) apparently induced this idea from their analysis of disaster research, but they do not give a detailed analysis of the data on which they based the principle. The principle has an inherent rationality to it because people cannot prepare for stressful events if they don't know they are coming, but they can and frequently do prepare for them when they know these events are coming. We should, however, probably be very tentative in accepting this principle until more systematic analyses of empirical data are made. It may be that there is an optimal anticipation time, and that either very short or very long periods of anticipation are most disruptive. This, however, is only speculation, and we will not know what the shape of this relationship is until additional research is done.

One way this hypothesis can be applied is for couples to try whenever possible to be prepared for stressful events before they occur. This is, of course, impossible with accidents and sudden illnesses, but many stressful events are virtually universal experiences, and we can become somewhat informed about them and then do whatever seems wise to prepare for them. Examples of predictable stressor events would include just about any major role transition (refer to Chapters 11 and 17 for a number of principles that are useful in preparing for and coping with such transitions). Also, the "stage" behaviors that children go through as they mature such as the negativism of the twos, the toilet talk of the fours, and the striving for independence of the teens are all stressful events,

and there are many ways in which we could prepare for these
stresses.

This principle, like many of the others in this book, could be used
unwisely. It would be possible for us to become so preoccupied
with possible future tragedies or stressful situations that we would
miss out on things that we value more than the slight change in
vulnerability this awareness would provide. On the other hand, however, some of us go through life blithely unaware of inevitable
stresses that are fairly obvious, and giving only a little more thought
to such stressful events would make a substantial difference in the
effect they have on us. The point here is, thus, to pay some but not
too much attention to future stresses so that appropriate prepara-
tions can be made. For individuals who want to increase their
awareness of future stresses, the following exercise may be helpful. Those of us who already give an inordinate amount of attention
to such events would probably do well to skip this exercise.

IDENTIFYING POSSIBLE STRESSFUL SITUATIONS

Goal: To increase one's awareness of stressful situations that
        might occur or probably will occur.

1. Find several individuals whose situations are similar to yours.
    These may be fellow class members, friends, or other couples.
    Agree to have a short discussion about future stressor events in
    your lives.

2. Each person make a list of changes that will probably occur in
    the near future that might be difficult to cope with. As each in-
    dividual thinks of a new event, mention it to the others so that
    they can determine whether it is one that they should add to
    their lists. Identify how far in the future (months or years) each
    change will probably occur. Some that you may include are:

    Becoming a parent
    Leaving parents' home
    Graduating from college
    Changing jobs
    Getting married
    Having morning sickness (during pregnancy)
    Getting a divorce
    Moving
    Children leaving home
    Retiring
    Death of a loved one
    Loved one returning after being away

3. After making the list, determine how much attention you should
    give to these changes. Have you been giving them too much, too
    little, or an optimal amount of attention?

*Prior role
learning*

One of the factors discussed in earlier chapters is also useful in
helping keep potentially disruptive events from becoming full-
fledged crises. That factor is *prior role learning.* If a person is able
to learn successful ways of coping with stressful events through such
activities as reading about them, experiencing similar situations,
having a role model to copy, or even in some cases previously experiencing the stress or event and learning from these previous
experiences this can be helpful in coping with the stressful event.
This principle is:

THE PRIOR ROLE LEARNING AND STRESS PRINCIPLE:
The amount of prior learning about a stressful event influences the vulnerability of families to that event, and this
is an inverse relationship.

Several different kinds of evidence support this principle. Some
empirical research, such as Angell's (1936) and Cavan and Ranck's
(1938) studies of the depression and Hill's (1949) study of war
separation and reunion, found that previous successful experience
with a similar stressor event was associated with successful experience in later stressor events. In addition, this principle can be
deduced from several of the major theories of socialization, including Parsons' (1955, chap. 1) functionalism, symbolic interaction

Figure 16–2

The relationship between prior role learning and
family vulnerability to stress

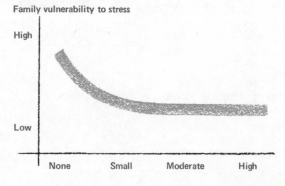

Amount of prior role learning

theory (Stryker, 1964; Rose, 1962), and role theory (Sarbin, 1968). What this means is that great confidence can be placed in this principle. More is also known about the shape of the relationship in this principle than in many of the other principles in this chapter. All that is known about most of the principles in this chapter is that the relationships tend to be positive or negative, but there is evidence (Burr, 1973, chap. 6) that the relationship in the Prior Role Learning and Stress principle is curvilinear. Figure 16–2 diagrams this relationship and shows that small amounts of prior learning probably make considerable difference in vulnerability, while additional increases after a moderate amount of learning make less difference.

This principle is illustrated by the fact that it is much easier to cope with the death of persons close to us the second time than the first time (Fulton, 1965; Glasser and Strauss, 1965), as a great deal of learning seems to occur the first time an individual experiences bereavement. Two other examples that illustrate this principle are the birth of the first child and the launching of children. Research indicates that the first birth and the first launching tend to be more disruptive than later births and later launchings (Deutscher, 1959).

One way to increase our ability to use this principle is to create learning experiences that will prepare us for stressful situations that we will probably experience later in life. Research has demonstrated that several transition points in life, such as the birth of the first child (LeMasters, 1957), the launching of children (Deutscher, 1959), and retirement (Cavan, 1962), are frequently stressful times, and in addition most families will encounter serious illnesses at one time or another, and everyone will experience bereavement. The following exercise is designed to help decrease our vulnerability by increasing prior learning about stressful role changes.

LEARNING ABOUT STRESSFUL ROLE CHANGES

Goal: To increase prior learning about stressful role changes.

1. Select a stressful role change, such as one of those described in the last paragraph.

2. Locate someone, such as a friend, neighbor, relative, or other acquaintance, who has experienced a change of this kind.

3. You will want to be tactful and delicate in discussing the experience, but see whether you can discuss such topics as:

   a. Things the person found difficult about change.

   b. Ways of behaving the person found useful in keeping the event from becoming a crisis.

   c. What the person learned from the experience that he or she would use if the same situation were encountered again.

4. There is a great value in writing these types of things down, so you may benefit from making a list of these three things.

RECOVERING FROM CRISES

The six principles discussed in the previous section of this chapter all dealt with factors that can be used to decrease the chances that a potentially stressful event will create a crisis in a social system. It is, however, unthinkable that families will always be able to prevent stressors from disrupting routine family activity. In other words, even when families are highly adaptable, well integrated, able to externalize the sources of stressor events, apt to define the events as less serious than they really are, able to foresee the events, and in possession of a great deal of prior role learning there will still be situations in which the families will experience disruption, frustration, disorganization—in short *crises*. When this occurs most families want to recover from the disorganized or crisis condition as rapidly as they can, and a second group of principles that have emerged from the family stress literature become very relevant because they identify factors that influence the "regenerative power" of families—the ability of families to recover from crisis situations. This skill is a continuum, as shown below. Six principles concerning

Regenerative power

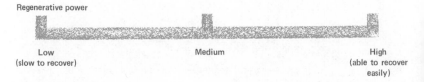

Low	Medium	High
(slow to recover)		(able to recover easily)

regenerative power are identified in the following pages that, hopefully, we can find ways to use in coping with the inescapable stresses of life.

There is considerable evidence that three of the factors that are related to the vulnerability of families to stress are also related to the regenerative power of families. These three factors are the *level of adaptability, level of integration,* and *amount of prior learning,* and the principles that relate these factors to regenerative power are:

Factors related to vulnerability that are also related to regenerative power

THE ADAPTABILITY–REGENERATIVE POWER PRINCIPLE: The amount of family adaptability influences the regenerative power of families, and this is a positive relationship.

THE INTEGRATION–REGENERATIVE POWER PRINCIPLE: The amount of family integration influences the regenerative power of families, and this is a positive relationship.

THE PRIOR ROLE LEARNING–REGENERATIVE POWER PRINCIPLE: The amount of prior role learning about stressful events influences the regenerative power of families, and this is a positive relationship.

There is enough research about these principles to justify placing considerable confidence in them. These principles were central hypotheses in most of the research on the effects of economic depression on the family (Angell, 1936; Cavan and Ranck, 1938; Komarovsky, 1940; Koos, 1946), and they were further substantiated in Hill's (1949) study of war separation and reunion.

The practical implications of these principles are that we can learn something about our ability to cope with crises by determining how adaptable and integrated we are as a couple and as a family and by evaluating the amount we have learned about what to do when crises occur. Those of us who are excessively rigid, poorly organized, and have had no prior contact with crises will probably have a more difficult time recovering from crisis situations than those of us who are fairly flexible in our life-style, are fairly well organized, and have dealt successfully with crises or crisislike situations. This makes the exercises developed earlier in this chapter doubly important because improvements in these three factors have the dual role of helping us to prevent crises and helping us to recover from them.

It is important to note that some types of prior learning about crises are probably detrimental in coping with crises. In studying family reactions to economic reversals, Cavan and Ranck (1938) and later Koos (1964, chap. 14) discovered that families which were unable to deal effectively with a particular type of crisis were less able to deal with that type of crisis when they experienced it later. This suggests that *ineffective* ways of coping with crises are apparently most likely to recur in subsequent crises, and that what is important is learning ways to cope *effectively* with crises. This suggests that as we attempt to learn about crises in families we try to differentiate between effective and ineffective coping strategies. It would, of course, be nice if the social sciences had progressed to a point at which we knew which strategies were effective and which ineffective, but little is known about this at present.

Style of decision making

Hill tried to determine whether the decision-making process in families is related to the ability of families to recover from crises. He found that the relative distribution of control does not make any difference in the ability of families to recover from crises. He divided his sample into husband-dominant, equalitarian, and wife-dominant groups to see whether these groups differed in their ability to recover from crises and found that the three groups did not differ in regenerative ability. He also found, however, that the method that families used in making decisions was related to regenerative power. Those families that used a "family council" type of decision making tended to be better able to cope with crises. Hill's summary of his findings is that "*the consultive process* in the family is more important than the seat of ultimate authority" (1949, p. 224; Hill's italics). These findings were used by Burr (1973, p. 213) as the basis for stating the two following principles:

THE RELATIVE CONTROL PRINCIPLE: The relative amount of control exercised by spouses is not related to the regenerative power of families.

THE CONSULTATION PRINCIPLE: The amount of consultation in decision making influences the regenerative power of families, and this is a positive relationship.

The independent variables in these principles are both continuous variables, and they are diagramed below.

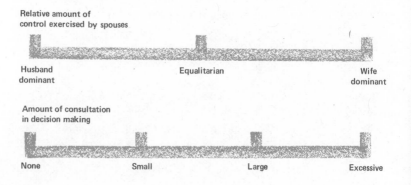

Relative amount of
control exercised by spouses

Husband   Equalitarian   Wife
dominant   dominant

Amount of consultation
in decision making

None   Small   Large   Excessive

The relative amount of control exercised by spouses varies between the two extremes of husband-dominance and wife-dominance,
and the amount of consultation in decision making varies between
none and excessive amounts.

At present the social sciences do not know what the shape of the
relationship is in the Consultation principle, but it could be speculated that it is a curvilinear relationship like the one diagramed in
Figure 16–3. Too little consultation between family members in

Figure 16–3

The relationship between the amount of consultation
in decision making and family regenerative power

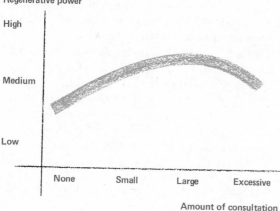

making decisions is associated with low regenerative power, but
there is a point of diminishing returns, and eventually a point is
probably reached at which an increase in consultation actually
decreases regenerative power. The suggestion that this relationship
follows this particular curve is, however, speculative as it is based
only on intuition and reason, and the speculation should be viewed
tentatively until additional research is undertaken to test it.

This is probably one of the most usable principles in this book
because the style of decision making in a family is usually something that can be changed fairly easily. One way to use the principle is to first determine how much consultation usually occurs in
our relationship. Then, if consultation seldom or never occurs, and
we want to increase it, we can change our style of making decisions.
The two following exercises are designed to help us accomplish

these two objectives. The first is designed to help us assess the level of consultation that usually occurs, and the second is designed to help us increase that level.

DETERMINING THE AMOUNT OF CONSULTATION

Goal: To determine how much consultation usually occurs in the decision making in a couple or family.

1. Answer each of the following questions (1) never, (2) seldom, (3) usually, or (4) always.

   a. When there is a decision of moderate importance, is there discussion about alternative solutions (or does one person make the decision alone)?

   b. If there is discussion in making such decisions, do all of the adults or grown children think that they get to fully express their opinions and desires?

   c. Do the decision makers in the family (especially the person who is the "leader" in making decisions) *listen* to the opinions of others rather than do such things as ignore them, pay little attention to them, or belittle them?

   d. Do the least powerful members of the family (ignore very small children) think that others respect and value their opinions—even though they may not get their way?

2. If most of your answers are "seldom" or "never" you probably have far less than average consultation. If all of your answers are "usually" you probably have much more consultation than the average family, and if you marked "always" on all of the questions you are undoubtedly so idealistic that you can't accurately determine how much consultation really occurs.

INCREASING CONSULTATION

Goal: To increase the amount of consultation in decision making.

You will recall from Chapter 6 that consciously or unconsciously we go through a certain sequence of events in making decisions. Some of these are frequently skipped over quickly or ignored, but the sequence is roughly: (1) recognize a problem, (2) identify one or more alternative solutions, (3) evaluate these alternatives, (4) select the "best" alternative and implement it, and (5) evaluate the effectiveness of the solution. The goal of this exercise is to increase the amount of *discussion* that occurs in steps 2 and 3.

1. Identify a close relationship—family, roommates, etc. This activity could also be done as a couple.

2. Discuss the goal of this exercise with the others so they understand what you are trying to accomplish, and then decide to do the following experiment for one week.

   a. In most relationships one person is usually the "leader" in making decisions. Sometimes it is the one who talks the most. If in your relationship one of you usually isn't the leader, then pick that one to be the leader in decision making for the week.

   b. During the week whenever you make a "joint" decision you are to be aware of when you go from step 3 to step 4; and just as you go to step 4 the leader is to interrupt the usual, natural process of making decisions and make a little speech. She or he is to orally ask whether the others want to comment about the alternatives. The object of this is to give the others more of an opportunity to "consult," so it is also important that the leader listen carefully to these additional comments. (Frequently it will be useful for the others to help the leader recognize when her or his little speech is due with such comments as, "Hey, it's time for your little thing . . .")

3. The leader is doing the most work in this experiment, so after there have been 8 or 10 decision-making sequences, she or he is to be rewarded. Keep track by marking the number of sequences on a sheet that is in a conspicuous place, such as a refrigerator door. Agree that after the 8 to 10 session she or he will get something special, such as a favorite dinner, someone else doing the dishes, shopping spree, dinner out, shoes shined, etc.

4. At the end of the week evaluate whether the additional concern with each other's opinions has increased the amount of consultation in decision making in the relationship. Also determine whether the overall decision-making process has improved, because occasionally this change has other benefits and couples or families want to continue the change. Admittedly, consultation makes decision making a little more time-consuming and inefficient, but the other by-products are frequently so valued that they are worth it.

THE SOCIAL ACTIVITY PRINCIPLE: The amount of social activity of wives outside the home is related to the regenerative power of families, and this is a positive relationship.

Social activity of wives

This is a very nontechnical idea, as the key variable is simply *the amount of activity* wives have in nonfamily social roles. This is a continuous variable that ranges between no outside participation and extremely high amounts of activity in nonfamily roles, as diagramed below.

Amount of activity
wife has in nonfamily roles

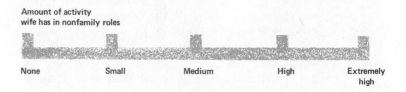

None   Small   Medium   High   Extremely
                                                                                      high

There is enough evidence in support of this principle for it to be accepted with considerable confidence. Duvall (1945) and Hill (1949, p. 205) found evidence for the principle in adjustments to war separation and reunion. Later, Rose (1955) and Deutscher (1962) found that the principle held true for the ability to cope with the launching of children. Little is known about the shape of this relationship, as these research reports were only concerned with whether or not the relationship existed. It seems likely, however, that the relationship is curvilinear, like the one diagramed in Figure 16–4. If it is, then very low and very high participation are associated with low regenerative power, and moderate amounts of participation are associated with high regenerative power. This speculative guess about the shape of this relationship is based only on reason and intuition, so the principle should be regarded as tentative until there is further empirical research.

Figure 16–4

The relationship between wives' nonfamily social activity and regenerative power

Regenerative power

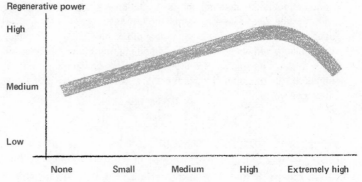

High

Medium

Low

None   Small   Medium   High   Extremely high

Amount of wives' nonfamily social activity

This principle has several practical implications for marital and family relationships. Apparently wives who confine themselves to the four walls of their home decrease the likelihood that they and their families will be able to recover easily from crisis situations. On the other hand, wives who become interested in roles other than their family roles are doing something that increases the ability of their families to cope with stressful events. Such a wide variety of nonfamily roles are available to women in the modern society that the nonfamily roles of wives needn't be confined to service activities or employment. They can also include such things as artistically expressive roles, political roles, furthering one's education, etc. Probably a wise use of this principle would be for each couple to determine how involved the wife is in nonfamily roles and then, depending on her level of activity, make adjustments in a creative, meaningful way. It is likely, however, that couples may need to deal with their attitudes about these nonfamily roles because there is evidence (Orden and Bradburn, 1969) that participating in such roles under pressure is more disruptive than helpful, and couples probably ought to first create a desire in the wife to want to engage in nonfamily activities before trying to decide which ones would be best. It also seems likely that participation merely for the sake of participation would be empty and frustrating, so couples would probably be wise to also find activities that are meaningful, rewarding, and pleasant.

Most of the time people think of satisfaction in marriage as an end or goal rather than as something that influences other things. There is, however, evidence (Angell, 1936; Cavan and Ranck, 1938; Koos, 1946; Hill, 1949) that marital satisfaction is related to the ability of families to recover from crises. It is difficult to know from the previous theorizing and research how the causality in this relationship goes, so the principle is stated here as a covariational rather than a causal principle.

Marital satisfaction

THE SATISFACTION-REGENERATION PRINCIPLE: The amount of marital satisfaction is related to the regenerative power of families, and this is a positive relationship.

Nothing is known about the shape of this relationship, but it is very easy to see its practical implications. Couples who are able to work out harmonious and pleasant marital relationships are usually better able to cope with crises when they come than couples who have troubled marital relationships. The principles in Chapters 13 and 14 that deal with ways to increase marital satisfaction are very relevant in this context, as they are the best ways to vary the satisfaction dimension that are known at present. Individuals who are interested in using the Satisfaction-Regeneration principle to increase their regenerative power should review the exercises developed in those chapters and devise additional similar experiences on their own.

BEREAVEMENT—A SPECIAL CASE

Bereavement is a stressor event that is a natural and inevitable part of life. All of us experience bereavement, no matter how much we may wish to avoid it, and when bereavement involves the death of someone close to us it is virtually always a crisis-type experience. We cannot continue our usual routines of life, and we are usually stunned and overwhelmed by the experience.

Research has found that we usually go through a fairly predictable sequence of events in adjusting to bereavement. These events are usually divided into four stages: (1) the Immediate stage, (2) the Postimmediate stage, (3) the Transitional stage, and (4) the Repatterning stage (Eliot, 1932; Fulcomer, 1942; Nye and Berardo, 1973, chap. 23). The Immediate stage usually lasts for a number of hours, and it is often characterized by a combination of such behaviors as numbness, struggling against the reality of the death, collapse, dazedness, violent and continuous weeping, and a stoic determination to meet the situation quietly and rationally. The Postimmediate stage usually lasts for several days—until after the funeral and burial, when there is a feeling that "it's all over." This stage is also usually characterized by several different types of behavior, such as periods of "low spirits" and despondency, self-absorption, overly active leadership in making plans and arrangements, less frequent and less violent weeping, and at specific times, such as at the burial, by listlessness and a passive conformity to the cultural rituals and ceremonies.

The Transitional stage varies greatly in length, as it is the stage in which the bereaved use a "trial and error" method of arriving at an acceptable stability in their life. The stage is usually characterized by periods of considerable activity in rearranging things, such as furniture and habits, and by periods of depression and despondency. There is usually considerable weeping, wanting others around to talk to, and attention seeking. Gradually there are periods of activity, cheerfulness, and previously typical behavior. The final,

Repatterning stage is marked by a return to the usual roles and duties in life, preservation of mementos, and a selective memory of the past. The individual gradually assumes some of the roles of the deceased—especially if the deceased was the spouse—and they usually experience mental imagery, such as daydreams and nocturnal dreams about the other person. This is usually also a period of heightened independence in which the help of others is increasingly avoided.

Most researchers comment that the reactions to death are so varied that it is difficult to identify the general principles involved. There is, however, considerable agreement among scholars concerning the validity of one of the principles that have been identified (Fulton, 1965; Glasser and Strauss, 1964). That principle deals with the speed of the recovery from bereavement. The *speed of recovery* variable refers to the length of time between a stressful experience, such as a death, and the final recovery from the disruption, disorganization, and discomfort of the crisis. Some people recover very rapidly from such crises as bereavement, and others take considerably longer to get over them. This variable is, of course, continuous, and it ranges from short to long periods of time.

The principle states that the speed of recovery is related to the adequacy or quality of the final adjustment. In most crisis situations the more quickly a couple or family can return to a condition of "normalcy" the better is their adjustment, but this is not true for the crisis of bereavement. With bereavement there is a curvilinear relationship between these two variables like the one diagramed in Figure 16–5. Very rapid recovery from bereavement tends to be

Figure 16–5

The relationship between speed of recovery and quality of the final adjustment to bereavement

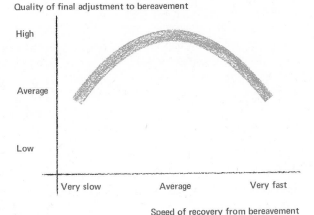

Speed of recovery from bereavement

associated with a less adequate final adjustment than a pattern of recovery that allows for a period of mourning and difficulty before the final adjustment is made. It is also possible that excessively long periods of adjustment are associated with less adequate eventual adjustment, but apparently this possibility has never been tested. These relationships are particularly relevant in this chapter because adjustment to bereavement differs so greatly from adjustment to most of the other crises that families experience, such as financial reverses or the addition or departure of a member of a family. The two principles that state these relationships are:

THE SPEED OF RECOVERY–CRISIS PRINCIPLE: The speed of recovery from most family crises is related to the quality of the readjustment after the crisis, and this is a positive relationship.

THE SPEED OF RECOVERY–BEREAVEMENT PRINCIPLE: The speed of recovery from bereavement is related to the quality of the final adjustment, and this is a curvilinear relationship.

Both of these principles have practical implications for marital and family life. One implication is that if we want to have a complete and comfortable recovery from the death of someone close to us, we will do well to take our time in getting over the pain, frustration, and sense of loss that we experience. If we try to "get back on our feet" too quickly we may later find that we are not really as much "on our feet" as we thought we were. Apparently the folk wisdom that tells us to "take your time in getting over it" and "wait a while for the hurt to go away" is well founded.

Another implication of these principles is that, for most crises, if people wish to make a complete recovery it is best to try to recover as quickly as possible. Apparently, being willing to make adaptations and necessary changes fairly soon after a stressful event will make for a better recovery than will doggedly trying to hold on to old ideas, old ways of doing things, or old roles until there is no hope that they will work.

SUMMARY

Stressful events are inescapable in marital and family life, but a number of things can be done to help prevent those events from becoming full-blown crises and to help us recover from crises when they do come. This chapter has identified six factors that influence the vulnerability of families to such stressful situations. These factors are family adaptability, family integration, externalizing the blame for the stressful event, defining the seriousness of the stressful situation appropriately, anticipating stressful events when possible, and learning ways to successfully cope with stressors before they

Figure 16–6

Causal model of the Principles in Chapter 16

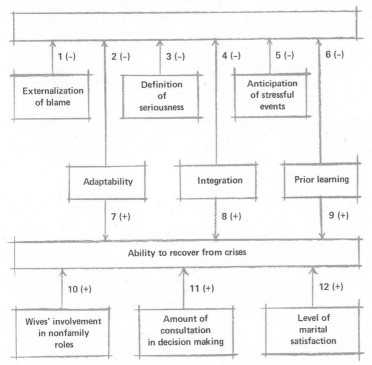

occur. These six generalizations are shown in Figure 16–6 with arrows 1 through 6. Adaptability, integration, prior learning, the amount wives are involved in nonfamily roles, the amount of consultation in decision making, and the level of marital satisfaction influence the regenerative power of families—the ability of families to recover from crises when they occur. These six generalizations are shown in Figure 16–6 as arrows 7 through 12. Bereavement is a unique type of family crisis in several ways, and adjusting to bereavement usually seems to follow a predictable sequence of stages. Attempts to recover from bereavement too quickly tend to produce long-term difficulties, so it is apparently usually better to allow for a period of mourning before trying to resume normal, routine patterns of life. For most family crises, however, the sooner recovery from the crisis situation takes place the better the recovery usually is.

SUGGESTIONS FOR FURTHER STUDY

Angell, R. C.   1936. *The Family Encounters the Depression*. New York: Scribner.

Cavan, Ruth S., and Ranck, Katherine H.   1938. *The Family and the Depression*. Chicago: University of Chicago Press.

Hill, Reuben   1949. *Families under Stress*. New York: Harper.

Kirkpatrick, Clifford   1963. *The Family as Process and Institution*. 2d ed. New York: Ronald Press, chaps. 20–23.

Koos, E. L.   1946. *Families in Trouble*. New York: King's Crown Press.

Nye, F. Ivan   1958. *Family Relationships and Delinquent Behavior*. New York: Wiley.

Waller, Willard, and Hill, R. L.   1951. *The Family: A Dynamic Interpretation*. Rev. ed. New York: Dryden, chaps. 21–24.

Winch, Robert F.   1963. *The Modern Family*. Rev. ed. New York: Holt, Rinehart and Winston, chaps. 22 and 23.

17

Parenthood: Planning and preparing

I T IS very likely that the transition into parenthood is the most complex and dramatic change that most people ever make in their lives. Other major transitions, such as beginning to date, starting one's first job, graduating, marrying, and retiring, all involve some changes, but it is seldom that any of them is as involved as the process of becoming a parent. The coming of a child produces unalterable changes in the marital relationship, creates immense responsibilities for the welfare of a human who is dependent on others for virtually everything, rearranges most of the social and personal rhythms in a couple's life, and creates a variety of new obligations to friends, society, and relatives. In addition, and this may be the most important change of all, it creates new views about and obligations for oneself. Many people find the process of becoming a parent very difficult, and such terms as *baby blues* and *postpartum psychosis* have been used to describe some of the stresses of the process. The following comments by parents further illustrate those stresses:

We had no idea that the baby would bring so many changes. Before the baby was born we used to take off whenever we wanted and go pretty much anyplace. Now we are pretty much tied down, and when we do go there's sort of a nagging feeling that maybe we ought to be home in case something went wrong.

My mother came down and stayed with us for a week, and that really helped out. After she left, though, it seemed like I was always tired. The night feedings, all those diapers, and just the worry about whether the baby was OK and whether I was doing what I was supposed to. I got pretty low after a few weeks of it.

Some of the difficulties of this period are described in vivid detail by two analysts of family life:

No matter how going a concern a marriage may be, the advent of children causes severe strain between parents. Any orderly, smooth, satisfactory relationship carefully worked out between husband and wife is broken up the very first night the child is home from the hospital. The inability of a child to do anything for itself means that demands are made on parents which create a new relationship between husband and wife. Their time and energy are no longer their own for companionship or intimacy. The little tyrant need only raise its voice a tiny bit to break up the parents' closest embrace. The warmth of the adult relationship is forever being disturbed by the child's demands for physical attention. At any hour of the night the newborn youngster can separate husband and wife without repaying them for their loss with even a friendly smile. The child's physical requirements have the right of way over their feelings toward each other and toward the child (Levy and Munroe, 1938, p. 243).

The magnitude of the responsibilities that are assumed when a couple become parents suggests that couples would be wise to give considerable thought to *planning* about parenthood rather than assume that they should automatically become parents because they are expected to. This planning could consist of an examination of such issues as whether they ought to become parents, when it would be wise or unwise to have children, how many children they ought to have, and what methods they ought to use if they wish to control the time of conception. The first section of this chapter examines some of these issues and discusses the methods that are currently available to control conception.

The second section is relevant for those who decide that they want to become parents since it deals with some things couples can do to *prepare* for parenthood. Six different principles are identified, and couples can use them to make the transition into parenthood easier. Couples who decide that they should not become parents will find the second part of this chapter fairly irrelevant to their life situation.

PLANNING ABOUT PARENTHOOD

A sequence of decisions

There seems to be a sequence to the issues that couples face in making decisions about parenthood, and the first and most fundamental decision is whether they should become parents at all. Some couples may find that parenthood is incompatible with such factors as their abilities, temperaments, goals, emotional stability, or preferred life-style, and that they would be much better off not to have children. Other couples may find that becoming parents is the most important part of their lives. Unfortunately the social sciences have thus far discovered very little that can help in making a decision about whether or not to have children. Some research (Burgess and Cottrell, 1939; Christensen and Philbrick, 1952) has shown that couples who have children and do not want them are less happy than are other couples, and there is little question that parenthood is a stressful, demanding, and expensive activity; but these facts are of little help in deciding whether or not to become parents.

Some individuals have the impression that some subcultural groups or religions consider it wrong to even address the question of whether or not to become parents because these groups or religions oppose "birth control." It is true that some religious groups believe that certain methods of controlling conception are immoral, but this author is not aware of any group that considers it inappropriate for a couple to address the question of whether or not they should become parents. In fact, quite to the contrary, even among those who are most vocal in opposing some of the contemporary methods of contraception, couples are admonished to avoid conception under several explicit conditions. These include situations in which the mother's health would be endangered by childbirth, in which the couples are unable to care properly for the children, and in which illnesses would be genetically transferred to the children. Thus, there is universal agreement that under some circumstances individuals should not become parents. There are differences, however, concerning the methods used to control conception.

When couples decide that they wish to become parents they are then faced with several other decisions. These include: (1) when to have children, (2) the number of children they should have, and (3) the desirable methods of controlling conception if they wish to do so. Those couples who decide not to assume the role of parenthood are, of course, only faced with the last of these decisions. Unfortunately the research about the timing of children and the ideal number of children is so inconclusive that it is of little value in decision making. Christensen and his colleagues (1963–69) found that the divorce rate is slightly higher for couples who begin parenthood within the first 6 to 12 months after their marriage and slightly lower for couples who defer parenthood until after 24 months of marriage. There are, however, so many factors involved in these differences that it is difficult to know what the causal factors are, and it is premature to use these research findings to make judgments about the timing of children. Research has also been done on the changes during the 20th century in the preferred number and spacing of children, but this research too is of little value in making a decision about one's own situation. Science and modern technology have, however, made great progress in developing methods of controlling conception, and the next section of this chapter briefly describes these methods. Those who wish to obtain additional information about contraceptive methods would find Hubbard's (1973) volume an excellent source, and most physicians have short books on the subject which they lend to interested patients.

The pill. Oral contraceptives, or "the pill," are now the most widely used medically prescribed method of birth control. They were approved for distribution in 1960, and the Food and Drug Administration estimated that about 8.5 million women were using them by 1969. The pill works by controlling the hormonal balance in the female so that conception is impossible. In the normal menstrual cycle there is a rhythmic change in the amount of estrogen in the body, and the level of estrogen is relatively low just after the menstrual period. When the estrogen level is low the pituitary gland is stimulated to secrete another hormone that causes an ovum-containing follicle to mature on an ovary. When the follicle is mature ovulation occurs—that is, an ovum is expelled into the abdominal cavity. The egg then finds its way into the fallopian tube, as shown in Figure 17–1. Normally, if the egg is fertilized before it proceeds too far toward the uterus, it will become implanted on the

Figure 17–1

The female reproductive organs

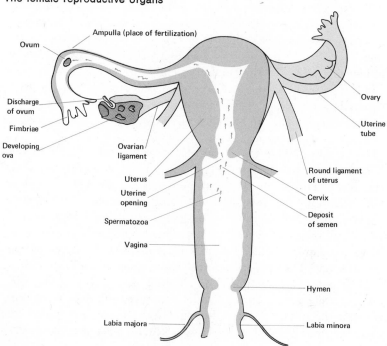

wall of the uterus and pregnancy will occur. The pill, which includes a synthetic form of estrogen, changes this cycle. A woman begins taking the pill four days after the menstrual period starts. The heightened level of estrogen in the bloodstream prevents the pituitary gland from secreting the follicle-stimulating hormone, and the chain of events that leads to ovulation is stopped. The usual pattern is for the woman to continue taking the pill for 20 or 21 days and then stopping. Usually the menstrual flow begins within two or three days. Four days after the flow begins the woman begins taking the pill again.

Oral contraceptives have several advantages and disadvantages in comparison with other contraceptive devices. The advantages are: (1) They are very effective in preventing conception. (2) The times at which they are taken has nothing to do with the times in which a couple have sexual intercourse so that the couple do not have to interrupt their sexual activity to use them. (3) When pregnancy is desired, all that the female needs to do to become fertile again is to stop taking them.

Some of the disadvantages of oral contraceptives are: (1) There is some expense, as the woman should take them under the supervision of a physician and a supply must be purchased each month. (2) They must be taken every day if they are to be effective. (3) Most women who take them experience several known side effects. (4) Research is still inconclusive about several other possible side effects.

For the first several months that they take oral contraceptives many women experience the same symptoms that occur with pregnancy. These usually include such conditions as enlargement and tenderness of the breasts, nausea, weight gains, less evenness of temperament, and mild skin problems. Occasionally the side effects are so severe that the use of the pill has to be discontinued. Oral contraceptives may also tend to increase the incidence of thromboembolic disease (pathological blood clotting). The Medical Research Council of Great Britain initiated a controversy in 1967, when it published a report stating that oral contraceptives are a factor in the production of that disease, and since then there has been a vast amount of research and numerous debates on the subject. At present the research is inconclusive, and there are wide differences of opinion in the research and medical communities. The Pure Food and Drug Administration, however, has directed manufacturers of oral contraceptives to include the following warning with each box of pills.

The oral contraceptives are powerful, effective drugs. Do not take these drugs without your doctor's continuous supervision. As with all effective drugs they may cause side effects in some cases and should not be taken at all by some. Rare instances of abnormal blood clotting are the most important known complications of oral contraceptives. These points were discussed with you when you chose this method of contraception. While you are taking these drugs, you should have periodic examinations at intervals set by your doctor. Tell your doctor if you notice any of the following: 1. Severe headache; 2. Blurred vision; 3. Pain in the legs; 4. Pain in the chest or unexplained cough; 5. Irregular or missed period.

Thus, the pill is a very effective contraceptive that has achieved widespread acceptance in a short time. Its use has some risks, but so does the use of other drugs, such as aspirin, vitamins, and penicillin. The pill also decreases some risks, such as unwanted pregnancy. Hence, each couple must evaluate the various pros and cons, and then, in consultation with their physician, make a decision for themselves.

Intrauterine devices (IUDs). Inserting various plastic or metal devices into the uterus is also very effective in preventing pregnancy. The devices are called IUDs, and most of them are about an inch long. They have a variety of shapes, as shown in Figure 17–2. The devices are not affected by body tissue and may be left in the uterus for years. The processes by which they prevent pregnancy

Figure 17–2

Various styles of IUDs

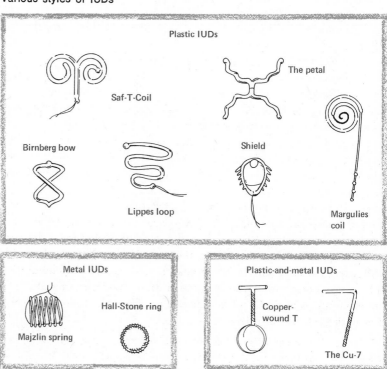

are not currently understood. It may be that the devices alter the muscular activity of the uterus so that fertilized eggs do not become implanted, or it may be that they cause the ovum to proceed through the fallopian tube more quickly than usual, and that this causes the ovum to pass through rather than remain in the uterus. Whatever the process, IUDs are very effective in preventing pregnancy. The ease with which IUDs can be used and their permanence have made them very popular in a number of the less industrialized nations, and they are being used increasingly in the United States.

Among the advantages of IUDs are the following: (1) They are the most effective current contraceptive method except for surgery, abstinence, and the pill. (2) Their side effects are rare, and those that do occur are not serious. (3) They are inexpensive, in that their only cost is the cost of having a doctor or medical specialist insert them. (4) They can be left in the uterus almost indefinitely, though it is a common practice, to remove and clean them after two to three years. (5) They do not interfere with coitus. (6) There is no need to "remember" to use them, as there is with the pill and most other contraceptives.

These are some disadvantages of intrauterine devices: (1) They are occasionally expelled from the uterus, and the woman may not be aware that this has happened. This disadvantage is less of a problem with some models because they have a thread attached to them which enables the woman to check periodically to see whether the device is still intact. (2) They must be inserted by a physician or a medical specialist. (3) Occasionally, especially if the user has not yet given birth to a child, their users experience more cramping and a larger discharge during the menstrual period. (4) In rare cases they seem to contribute to infection.

The condom. The condom is a thin sheath which fits over the erect penis. It controls conception because the seminal fluid that is ejaculated from the penis is retained in the condom rather than discharged into the vagina. Condoms are usually made of rubber, but some are also made from thin animal membranes. The condom is used by unrolling it over the penis before coitus is begun. If the male has normal control over the ejaculation it is possible to begin intercourse before applying the condom, and this may provide more pleasure. This also increases the likelihood of pregnancy, however, because most males discharge a small amount of seminal fluid before the major ejaculation. These preliminary emissions usually contain a low sperm count, and hence there is a low probability that they will cause pregnancy. Delaying the time when the condom is put on also increases the likelihood that the couple will not want to take the time and inconvenience to use it at all.

These are some advantages of condoms: (1) They are readily available, since they can be purchased in most drug stores and from vending machines in such locations as rest rooms and barbershops. (2) They are inexpensive. (3) They are easy to use. (4) They provide a sense of psychological assurance for many people because in the American culture there is a long-established belief in their reliability and because there is a visible containment of the seminal fluid. (5) They can be used without involving a physician. (6) They are moderately effective.

However, condoms have several disadvantages: (1) They decrease sensory pleasure. Most males indicate that condoms interfere with sexual stimulation, and some females indicate that condoms prevent them from feeling the ejaculation process. (2) They tend to interfere with or disrupt lovemaking or intercourse, as time must be taken to put them on. (3) Their users must maintain a continual awareness as to whether an adequate supply is on hand. (4) There is always the possibility of breakage or holes. Actually this is a minor factor, since the risk is very low that microscopic holes would permit enough sperm to escape to cause pregnancy, and the quality control maintained by the Food and Drug Administration makes breakage extremely unlikely when condoms are used properly. This possibility is nonetheless psychologically disconcerting to some couples.

Female occlusive devices. These devices are of two different types. One is the diaphragm, a shallow, cuplike device that is usually made of soft rubber with a springy outer edge. It is inserted into the vagina and covers the cervix. It is usually used with a spermicide, such as a jelly or a cream, and the combination of the shield to keep the sperm from entering the uterus and the spermicide to destroy the sperm prevents conception.

The other type of occlusive device is the cervical cap. The cap is functionally much like the diaphragm, in that its purpose is to create a barrier between the sperm and the egg. The cap, however, is smaller, thicker, and less flexible than the diaphragm, and it fits tightly over the cervix. The diaphragm is usually inserted into the vagina each time intercourse is anticipated, but a plastic cervical cap can be left in place from the end of one menstrual flow to the beginning of another. The cervical cap is more difficult to insert, however, as it must fit tightly over the cervix. Both the diaphragm and the cervical cap must be fitted by a physician, and they must be refitted after a pregnancy, since the size and firmness of the uterus and cervix change with the expansion and contraction that occur in pregnancy and birth.

The occlusive devices have the advantage of being moderately effective in controlling conception, and their effectiveness can be increased by combining spermicides with them and by making sure that they are in place when they are used. This is important for those who cannot use some of the less troublesome devices, such as the pill or IUDs. However, occlusive devices have a number of disadvantages: (1) They must continually be inserted, removed, and cleaned. (2) They must be fitted by a physician. (3) Their insertion may interfere with lovemaking or intercourse. This is not always a problem because when the woman anticipates intercourse it is possible for her to insert the diaphragm several hours prior to coitus. This prior knowledge is, however, not always possible, and it may be very rare with some couples. (4) The size and elasticity of the vaginal tissues changes considerably when women are sexually excited, and a diaphragm that fits snugly when a woman is not sexually aroused may not fit during periods of sexual excitement. These are all minor inconveniences, and occlusive devices have no important medical side effects. Thus, occlusive devices are effective but inconvenient, and many couples who cannot use more effective and convenient methods find them very valuable.

Rhythm. The rhythm method of contraception refers to periodic abstinence from intercourse during the part of the menstrual cycle when conception is most likely. Ovulation usually occurs 14 days before menstruation begins, but it is very common for this to vary two days either way. If allowance is also made for the fact that sperm may remain active for a day or two, this means that there is an eight-day stretch between menstrual periods when the chances of pregnancy are highest. Couples who practice the rhythm method of birth control abstain from intercourse during those eight days. If the menstrual cycle is fairly regular, and if no illnesses or unusual emotionally exciting or depressing events disrupt an ordinarily regular cycle, the rhythm method is fairly effective. In actual practice, however, it is usually not one of the more effective methods. One reason for its ineffectiveness is that occasionally a woman may skip an ovulation, and when this occurs the next ovulation may occur at any time. Studies with artificial insemination (Farris, 1956), for example, have found that pregnancy does occur occasionally very early or very late in the menstrual cycle.

Some advantages of the rhythm method are: (1) It is approved by such religions as Roman Catholicism, whose orthodox position insists on a "natural" method of birth control. (2) It is the only method some couples are able to use effectively. (3) It can be coupled with one or more of the other methods to decrease the likelihood of pregnancy. (4) It involves no expense. (5) It can be used without the aid of a physician.

Among its drawbacks are the following: (1) It places heavy demands on the self-discipline and mental alertness of those using it.

(2) It is less effective as women become older because the regularity of the menstrual cycle decreases. Unfortunately, that is usually the very time when most couples are the most interested in having an effective method. (3) It tends to disrupt the sex life of couples because it demands abstinence for a relatively long time, and couples frequently become interested in sex during the unsafe period.

Chemicals. A variety of chemical substances are used to destroy sperm and thus prevent conception. These are available in many forms, including aerosol spray cans, foaming tablets, creams, jellies, and suppositories. The chemicals must be inserted into the vagina just before, but not too long before, intercourse occurs. These chemicals are most effective when they are combined with one of the other methods, such as the diaphragm, the cervical cap, or the condom, and they have few, if any, advantages when they are used alone. They do, however, have several disadvantages. (1) They cannot be separated from the sex act. (2) They must be applied each time the couple have intercourse, even if intercourse is repeated several times in a short period of time. (3) They limit the female's activity because after they are applied she is not able to walk about or shower without seriously decreasing their effectiveness. (4) They demand considerable mental effort, since a supply must be kept on hand at all times and they must be applied each time the couple become interested in intercourse.

Withdrawal. In this method, frequently called "coitus interruptus," the penis is removed from the vagina just prior to ejaculation. This prevents the seminal fluid from being expelled near the cervix. The method varies greatly in effectiveness, depending on how well the male understands his ejaculatory process, the care taken, and the motivation to be effective. Withdrawal has the advantages of (1) inexpensiveness, (2) simplicity, (3) a long-established tradition of effectiveness, and (4) naturalness. Withdrawal has several drawbacks, however. (1) Males frequently expel small amounts of seminal fluid before the major ejaculation, and occasionally these have high sperm count. These secretions are usually too small to cause conception, but under some conditions they may. (2) Many males and females find the interruption of intercourse undesirable. (3) Considerable self-discipline and concentration are demanded at a time when sexual excitement usually reduces both.

Sterilization. Sterilization can be performed on either the male or the female. In the male it is usually done through a *vasectomy,* which is the process of tying and cutting, or cutting and electrically cauterizing (fulgurating) the vasa deferentia. Usually this is done with a small incision and local anesthesia. In the female, sterilization is usually done through a *tubal ligation,* which is the process of cutting, cauterizing, or clipping the fallopian tubes to interfere with the passage of the ovum into the uterus. Both operations are usually done when a couple wish to become permanently infertile, but it is sometimes possible to perform a second operation that will success-fully restore fertility. Studies (Ehrlich and Ehrlich, 1970; Freund, 1971) report a 15–50 percent success rate in operations attempting to restore fertility after a vasectomy has been performed, and a 25–65 percent success rate in attempts to reverse tubal ligations (Ehrlich and Ehrlich, 1970; Hubbard, 1973, p. 101). The secondary sex characteristics are not affected by either method of birth con-trol, as the structure and function of most of the reproductive organs are not changed. Voluntary sterilization has become in-creasingly popular in recent years, and it has been estimated that over one million sterilization operations are performed in the United States each year (Higgins, 1972).

Some of the advantages of sterilization are: (1) it is permanent; (2) it is highly effective; (3) it does not require concentration or memory; and (4) it is separated from the sex act. Among its dis-advantages are the following: (1) it is fairly expensive; (2) it must be performed by a physician; (3) its effects cannot be easily re-versed if one later wishes to regain fertility; and (4) some in-dividuals find it difficult to adjust to it emotionally.

Other methods.   A variety of other methods can be used to try to control conception, but, as will be discussed later, most of them are fairly ineffective. One of these methods is for the female to *douche* just after intercourse. Douching is the process of washing the vagina, and it is usually accomplished with an enema bag and about a quart of water. Some couples also add a mild spermicide to the water, such as several tablespoons of vinegar, lemon juice, or a soapy mixture. The douche is frequently effective in washing most of the seminal discharge out of the vagina, but it may in some circum-stances actually facilitate conception by providing additional liquid which would make the sperm more mobile. An undetermined num-ber of couples continue to use this method for such reasons as a belief in folk medicine, fear, ignorance of better methods, or the psychological satisfaction of "washing out" the seminal fluid. Most authorities, however, agree that as a method of birth control douch-ing is very ineffective, and that douching is also unnecessary as a hygienic measure, as the vagina naturally excretes foreign substances and maintains a desirable level of cleanliness.

It is also widely believed that a woman cannot become pregnant while she is *breast-feeding,* and numerous couples have learned to their consternation that this too is not accurate. It is true that most women do not experience a menstrual flow until six to eight weeks after a childbirth, and even longer when they breast-feed. Most people do not know, however, that ovulation occurs prior to the first menstrual period, and that it may occur as soon as two weeks after a birth.

Another erroneous belief is that if the woman "holds back" her climax or orgasm this will prevent conception. This process, sometimes called *female reserve,* is ineffective because there is no connection between the female's orgasm and conception. *Coitus reservatus* is also usually classified among the ineffective methods. Here intercourse is stopped at a point near the male orgasm. A couple could have several periods of movement and then relaxation before stopping, but the object is to terminate intercourse before the male ejaculates. This method is usually so unsatisfying for the male that couples have difficulty following it, and hence it is usually both undesirable and ineffective. *Coitus obstructus* is another method that is usually ineffective. Here either the male or the female presses hard on the base of the penis just as the male ejaculates. The theory is that this will cause the seminal fluid to be pushed into the bladder, thus preventing conception. The process is relatively uncomfortable for the male, may actually injure some of the tissues involved, and does not effectively prevent the expulsion of sperm into the vagina if the penis remains in the vagina after ejaculation.

Future possibilities for contraception. A large number of other contraceptive methods are currently being developed and tested. These include procedures that would immunize the female against sperm through an injection, through placing a substance under the skin, and through substances taken orally. Another approach is to develop methods of preventing sperm formation. Some of these, such as an oral contraceptive pill for men, are currently available, but their undesirable side effects, such as feminization of secondary sex characteristics and depression of sex drive (Garcia-Bunuel, 1966), are such that they are not currently being used. Other drugs, such as one which would render the cervical mucus hostile to sperm (Connell, 1966) and pills that are taken within six days after intercourse (Morris and Van Wagenen, 1966), are being experimented with. It thus seems inevitable that contraceptive methods will be developed that will be more effective and will have fewer disadvantages than the devices currently available.

The relative effectiveness of contraceptive methods

There has been enough research on the effectiveness of the various contraceptive devices to permit fairly detailed comparisons of their effectiveness. Table 17–1 shows their relative effectiveness and groups them into these three categories: highly effective, moderately effective, and usually ineffective. The highly effec-

Table 17–1

The relative effectiveness of various contraceptive methods

Method	Expected number of pregnancies among 1,000 married women during one year
Highly effective methods	
Abstinence..	0
Sterilization of male (vasectomy)....................	1–2
Sterilization of female (tubal ligation)..............	1–3
Oral contraceptive (combined regimen)............	1–6
Oral contraceptive (sequential).....................	10–20
Intrauterine devices (IUDs)........................	25–35
Moderately effective methods	
Condom...	100–200
Occlusive devices...............................	100–200
Rhythm..	150–300
Chemicals.......................................	150–400
Withdrawal (coitus interruptus).....................	Varies greatly
Ineffective methods	
Douche..	Fairly high
Lactation (breast-feeding).........................	Fairly high
Female reserve...................................	Fairly high
Coitus reservatus.................................	Fairly high
Coitus obstructus.................................	Fairly high
No protection of any kind	800

Source: The figures are averages derived from Pincus (1965), Drill (1966), Hubbard (1973, chap. 3), and Smith (1973).

tive group includes sterilization, abstinence, the pill, and intra-uterine devices (IUDs). The combined pill is slightly more effective than the sequential one. The moderately effective group includes the condom; occlusive devices, such as the diaphragm or the cervical cap; rhythm; and chemicals. There are differences of opinion about whether withdrawal should be included in the moderately effective or the ineffective group, because its effectiveness varies so much from couple to couple. It is, however, included in the moderately effective group here. The ineffective methods include douching, breast-feeding, female reserve, coitus reservatus, and coitus obstructus. Table 17–1 shows the average pregnancy rate per 1,000 women per year insofar as the available research data permit these estimates. It should also be remembered that several devices can be used in conjunction to increase their effectiveness.

PREPARING FOR PARENTHOOD

Most married couples in the United States want to become parents, and the vast majority of them eventually do so. As was mentioned earlier, however, a sizable number of these couples find that the transition into the parent role is a fairly difficult time. This is illustrated by the findings from two separate studies[1] which found that the birth of the first child was an extensive or severe crisis for a substantial majority of parents and was not disruptive at all for very few parents. In addition many mothers experience what has come to be known as "baby blues" at some time after the birth of their first child, and a few find the experience so difficult that they need psychiatric help. The last half of this chapter identifies and discusses six principles that couples can use to increase the ease of the transition into parenthood and decrease the problems that frequently occur. Three of these principles (Learning about the Parent Role, Normative Changes with Parenthood, and Consensus about Parental Expectations) are integrated with principles that were discussed in Chapter 11. The three other principles (the Role Compatibility, Goal Facilitation, and Activity principles) involve new ideas.

Several later studies, such as Hobbs (1965, 1968), argued that the coming of the first child was not a serious crisis for as many couples as the LeMasters and Dyer studies found, and a controversy (Jacoby, 1969) has persisted about what percentage of couples experience severe stress in this transition. This controversy is irrelevant as far as this chapter is concerned, because some couples experience severe stress, others experience less difficulty, and some have no trouble at all, and what these exact percentages are matters little. The main concerns here are that enough couples experience difficulty for this to be an important issue and that several principles can be identified that can help couples cope with the problem.

Learning about the parent role

One of the principles that was introduced in Chapter 11 states that when people acquire information about the spouse role before they marry this tends to make the transition into marriage easier than if they know little or nothing about marriage. It is possible to use logic to generalize this idea to other roles, and then create a similar principle about making the transition into the parent role. The first step in this logic is to briefly review the principle that was introduced in Chapter 11. It states:

THE LEARNING ABOUT THE SPOUSE ROLE PRINCIPLE: The amount of prior learning about the spouse role influences the ease of making the transition into this role, and this is a positive, curvilinear relationship.

---

[1] LeMasters (1957), and Dyer (1963).

This generalization deals only with the process of making the transition into marriage, but it seems reasonable that the process of learning about a role before one actually begins it would facilitate the transition into virtually any role. If that is true it is possible to view the above as a more specific case of the following more general idea.

THE PRIOR LEARNING PRINCIPLE: The amount of prior learning about a role influences the ease of making the transition into that role, and this is a positive, curvilinear relationship.

It is then possible to make several deductions from this very general principle. One of these deductions is that, if the Prior Learning principle is true, and if there can be variation in the amount of information people can acquire about parenthood before becoming parents, it follows that:

THE LEARNING ABOUT THE PARENT ROLE PRINCIPLE: The amount of prior learning about the parent role influences the ease of making the transition into parenthood, and this is a positive, curvilinear relationship.

The logical interrelationship of these three generalizations is shown in Figure 17–3 on the following page. The Prior Learning principle is the most abstract or general idea and, as the dotted lines show, the Learning about the Spouse Role and the Learning about the Parent Role hypotheses can be deduced from the more general idea. As that figure also shows, it is also possible to make similar deductions about other roles, and this permits us to expect that some learning about other roles such as student, automobile driver, or employee would facilitate the transition into those roles.

The variables in the Learning about the Parent Role principle are both easy to define. The amount of prior learning refers to how much someone knows about the norms, expectations, values, demands, obligations, or other aspects of the parent role before entering that role, and this factor can vary from no learning at all to very large amounts of information. The dependent variable refers to the degree to which there is freedom from difficulty and the presence of easily available resources to make the shift from nonparent to parent. If a person has difficulty in making the step into parenthood this is low ease, and if she or he is able to make this change with little difficulty this is high ease. The curvilinearity that is thought to exist in this relationship (Burr 1972, 1973, p. 125) is diagramed in Figure 17–4 and, as the steep-sloping part of the lines show, when there is no prior learning virtually everyone has low ease. A

Figure 17–3

The logical relationship between several principles about prior learning
and the ease of making role transitions

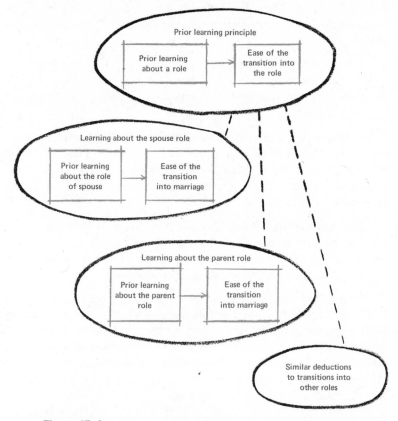

Figure 17–4

The relationship between prior learning and the ease of the
transition into parenthood

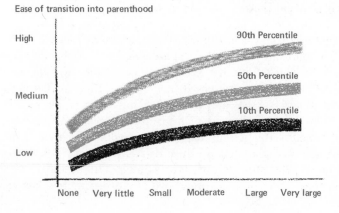

little bit of learning, however, seems to go a long way, because relatively small increments of learning cause rapid increases in the ease of the transition. Then, after moderate amounts of learning have occurred, there seems to be a point of diminishing returns, because additional learning experiences create less and less increase in the ease of the transition.

This principle can be used in many ways to make the transition into parenthood easier, and most of us take advantage of it somewhat without ever realizing it. Routine activities, such as baby-tending and watching parents of infants, provide some insight into what the role of parenthood is like. Also, when newly married couples get together and have the opportunity for informal conversation they frequently begin discussing the various aspects of having and taking care of babies, and this undoubtedly provides some valuable "learning" for many couples. There are also several activities that can be done to consciously use this principle, and five of them are mentioned below.

Take classes. Most communities have several organizations that teach courses on preparation for parenthood, and these classes can provide valuable "prior learning." Frequently these classes are offered through such organizations as the YMCA or YWCA, a hospital, a medical clinic, or a university extension or continuing education center. Some of these classes are relatively short, consisting of four or five sessions that focus on the facilities of a hospital and what to expect and do right after the child is born, and others are more extensive. Many colleges and universities also have classes on child development that can provide valuable information about what to expect as a parent.

Practice parenthood. It is occasionally possible for a newly married couple to find an opportunity to become pseudoparents for a period of time. Most couples who have been married for several years would welcome the opportunity to have a responsible couple take care of their children for a weekend or a week so that they could get away for a vacation. In fact, many couples who are parents would love to have this opportunity, but don't know where they can locate someone or don't have the money to pay someone who would be willing and able to take care of their children. In these situations, if a young couple could move into a home for a short period of time and act as the parents of the children, both couples would benefit. We cannot learn everything about parenthood and how we will respond to having children of our own in this type of experience, but it can provide useful learning for some of us. If nothing else, it can provide us with an opportunity to observe some aspects of parenthood and stimulate some discussion about our reactions to them.

Reading. There is a great deal of literature on infant care and parenthood, and it can provide some prior learning. One good source of information is the pamphlets published by the United States Children's Bureau entitled "Prenatal Care," "Infant Care," and "Your Child from One to Six." Other excellent books are:

Ways to Help Babies Grow and Learn: Activities for Infant Education by Leslie Segner.
The Magic Years by Selma H. Fraiberg.
The Child under Six by James L. Hymes, Jr.
Parents Are Teachers by Wesley C. Becker.
Between Parent and Child by Haim G. Ginott.
Mom and Dad Are Me by Joseph Perez and Alvin Cohan.

Talk to new parents. Most couples who have recently become parents love to talk endlessly about what they are experiencing, and we can take advantage of this to learn more about parenthood. The following exercise explains one way to do it.

TALKING TO PARENTS

Goal: To talk with some new parents to help us learn more about what parenthood is like.

1. Locate friends or relatives who have recently become parents. You can do this as a couple, as an individual, or as a discussion group in a class. Explain to them that you want to learn more about what parenthood is like . . . so you will be better prepared and have realistic expectations. Ask them whether you can visit with them about what it has been like for them and find out what their advice would be to other couples.

2. While talking with them get information from them about the following items . . . as well as about other items you may be interested in.
    a. What surprised them the most?
    b. In what ways were they well prepared and not well prepared?
    c. How has the coming of the child affected their marital relationship?
    d. Who has been the most "help" to them?

> e. What do they wish they had done differently?
>
> f. What things are they glad they did just the way they did them?
>
> g. How do they divide up the care of the child?
>
> h. Who has had to change the most, and in what ways?
>
> i. What advice do they have for other couples?
>
> 3. Do this with at least two couples if you can. Sometimes one couple is so unique that they do not provide a typical perspective, and the more couples you are able to visit with the greater the likelihood that you will be getting typical experiences.

Normative change

Another of the principles introduced in Chapter 11 dealt with the idea that the greater the change in normative expectations when one marries the less the ease of making the transition into marriage. This generalization can also be viewed as a specific case of a more general idea. The more abstract idea is that the amount of normative change when any role is entered will influence the ease of making the transition into that role, and this highly general idea can also be applied to parenthood. Since the logical process of developing this generalization is the same as that of developing the principles discussed in the previous section, it is probably sufficient to merely list the principles and diagram them. They are thus stated below with the most general idea stated first, and they are diagramed in Figure 17–5 on the following page.

THE NORMATIVE CHANGE PRINCIPLE: The amount of normative change that occurs as one assumes a role influences the ease of making this transition, and this is an inverse, curvilinear relationship.

THE NORMATIVE CHANGE WITH MARRIAGE PRINCIPLE: The amount of normative change that occurs as one assumes the role of spouse influences the ease of making this transition, and this is an inverse, curvilinear relationship.

THE NORMATIVE CHANGE WITH PARENTHOOD PRINCIPLE: The amount of normative change that occurs as one assumes the role of parent influences the ease of making this transition, and this is an inverse, curvilinear relationship.

The normative change variable refers to how many changes there are in the interpersonal obligations or the tasks that a person is

Figure 17–5

The logical relationship between several principles about normative
change and the ease of role transitions

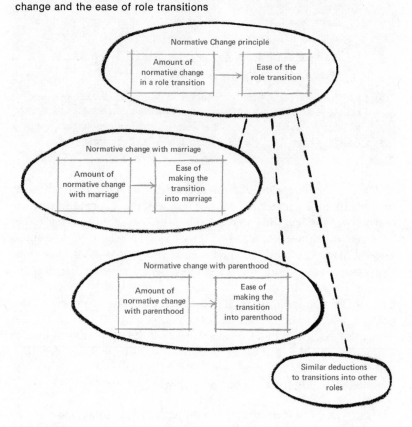

Figure 17–6

The relationship between the amount of normative change and the
ease of making role transitions

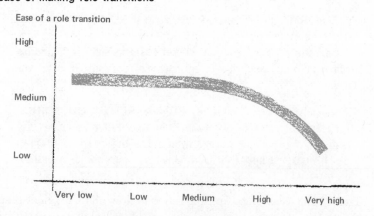

"supposed" to do or not do. In some role transitions there are relatively few changes, and in other transitions there are a great number of changes. Usually quite a few changes occur when a couple become parents, because they assume new responsibilities for the care and rearing of the child, and their style of relating to each other and to friends, relatives, and even employers becomes different. The curvilinearity that is thought to exist in these principles (Burr 1972; 1973, p. 140) is diagramed in Figure 17–6, and the lines show that normative change makes little difference when there is relatively little change. However, when a great deal of change is occurring, variation in the amount of change seems to make considerable difference in the ease of making a shift in one's roles.

Three different skills are involved in applying this principle. The most basic of these is to be aware of the fact that variation in the number of normative changes usually has an effect on how easy or difficult the transition into parenthood is. This awareness provides the basic insight that is necessary for the other skills. The second skill is the ability to evaluate our own situation to determine how many normative changes are occurring. Some of us may be in situations in which relatively few of the norms in our lives will change when we become parents, and others of us may have a great many changes occur at the same time that we become parents. We may, for example, be having our first child at the same time that we are graduating from college, moving, and assuming a new job or profession. If we were to be in that type of situation we would probably be wise to recognize that the enormous changes we are making will create more difficulties in the process of becoming parents.

The third skill that is needed in using this principle is the ability to do something about our situation when this is necessary. If we were in the above situation, we might want to do something to reduce the normative changes that are occurring, or, if we cannot reduce them, to think up some strategies for minimizing the disruptive effects of the changes. Some examples of things that might reduce the changes are:

1. Prepare the baby's room and clothing well in advance of the birth.
2. Try to plan the birth so that it doesn't coincide with other major transitions, such as graduation and changing jobs.
3. Make any changes in "life-styles" well before the baby comes.

This might include such things as having social life become more "home centered" if that is a change we will be making, or rearranging such tasks as shopping, cooking, and cleaning if that will be done after the baby comes.

Some examples of things that might be done to minimize the disruptiveness of changes are:

1. Arrange to have someone, such as the husband's or wife's mother, come and live in the home to help out during the initial adjustment to the parent role.
2. Allow more time than usual for talking about or coping with unforeseen events, feelings, and experiences.
3. Expect that period of life to be more difficult than usual, and be especially supportive, patient, and helpful to each other.
4. Minimize the work load as much as possible with modern conveniences, such as diaper services or disposable diapers, as this will save energy and increase your ability to deal with the situation.
5. Try to take advantage of the other principles identified in this chapter. These principles can help to minimize the difficulties of this period and thus compensate for the large number of changes.

In applying the Normative Change with Parenthood principle we should realize that variation in the number of changes seems to make a difference only when there are a fairly large number of them. Most of us seem to be able to take a sizable number of changes in stride. Thus, if we are in a situation in which we are not expecting an unusually large number of normative changes, we usually would be wise to put our creative energies to work on other aspects of our life situation rather than try to reduce the number of normative changes or minimize their effects.

Consensus about expectations

Another principle introduced in Chapter 11 also seems to be relevant for the transition into parenthood. This is the idea that consensus about expectations about the spouse role influences the ease of the transition into marriage. The principle can be generalized just as the two previous principles were, resulting in the three following principles. The logical interrelationships of these ideas is shown in Figure 17–7.

THE CONSENSUS ABOUT EXPECTATIONS PRINCIPLE: The greater the consensus about expectations for a role the greater the ease of the transition into the role, and vice versa.

Figure 17–7

The logical relationship between several principles about consensus on role expectations and the ease of role transitions

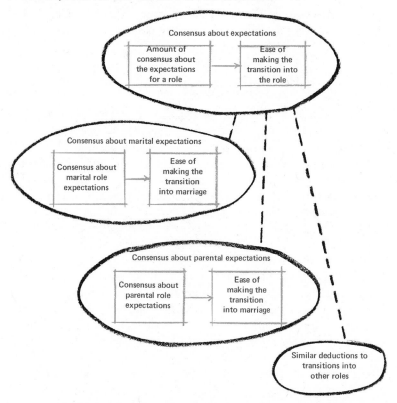

THE CONSENSUS ABOUT PARENTAL EXPECTATIONS PRINCIPLE: The greater the consensus about expectations for the parent role the greater the ease of the transition into parenthood, and vice versa.

THE CONSENSUS ABOUT MARITAL EXPECTATIONS PRINCIPLE: The greater the consensus about expectations for the spouse role the greater the ease of the transition into marriage, and vice versa.

The consensus about expectations variable was defined in detail on pages 203–4, but, briefly, it refers to the amount two or more individuals agree on what they think someone should do or not do in a particular role. It is a continuous variable, ranging from no consensus to a very high level of consensus. There is a considerable amount of research (Cottrell, 1942; Gross et al., 1957; Campbell and Pettigrew, 1959) that supports these principles, so these are ideas in which we should have considerable confidence. Cottrell (1942) and Burr (1972; 1973, pp. 128–31) have also theorized that the relationship is linear, but there is little research upon which to base this speculation. We should thus assume that the relationships in these principles occur, but that we are not sure about their shape.

Several versions of the Consensus about Expectations principle were discussed in earlier chapters, and a variety of techniques were discussed for: (1) knowing what role expectations are (page 203), (2) being able to recognize our own expectations (page 205), (3) being able to recognize the expectations of others (page 206), and (4) being able to resolve conflicts about expectations or to find ways to minimize the disruptive effects of such conflicts (pages 305–8). Those of us who wish to apply these principles to the transition into parenthood can easily adapt the earlier exercises cited to the parental situation.

It seems useful to make several additional comments about using these principles to ease the transition into parenthood. All of us have a number of expectations about how we and our spouse ought to behave as parents, but many of those expectations are unconscious or not fully crystallized before we get close to or into the parental role. Thus, there may be some value in discussing our role expectations at some length as we approach parenthood—even though we may have talked about them considerably before. We may have acquired more fixed opinions, or we may now be aware of opinions of which we were unaware previously. This can be especially true as we talk with friends about what they do and don't do as parents, and as we observe them and interact with them while they are "parenting." Many couples find that the process of discovering what their expectations about parenthood are is a very long process, and they gradually become aware of opinions and feelings as the years pass, the children grow up, and new situations are encountered. It is not uncommon for parents to react very emotionally to something and then, after observing how they have reacted, to become aware of a particular expectation or belief about parenthood that they have not perceived before. Thus, the process of learning about one's own and one's spouse's expectations is frequently a lifelong activity rather than something that can be done with a few lengthy discussions just before or after marriage.

Role compatibility

Role compatibility refers to the degree to which the demands of an individual's various roles are compatible (Cottrell, 1942; Goode, 1960). It varies in a continuous manner from two roles having no compatibility at all to their being highly compatible. For example, after the birth of their first child many women find that if they continue the same work schedule the demands of their career or occupation role and of their mother role are incompatible. In such situations sometimes the couple can change the nature of one of the roles so that the two roles are more compatible. For example, the wife may decide to work part-time or may change her work so that she works at home more. She may also change the way she plays the mother role by having someone else help her in taking care of the child. Or, adaptations can be made in the husband's roles to help reduce the incompatibility. The principle that ties role compatibility to ease of the transition into parenthood is:

THE ROLE COMPATIBILITY PRINCIPLE: The amount of compatibility between the parent role and other roles influences the ease of the transition into the parent role, and this is a positive relationship.

There is little basis for making speculations about the shape of this relationship, but Cottrell (1942) suggests that it is linear. This means that any variation in compatibility will tend to create some change in the ease of the transition.

The implications of this principle are very much like the implications of the Consensus about Expectations principle. If we can learn ways to manipulate the compatibility of our roles this will permit us to influence the ease with which we can move into the parent role. The skills that permit this are: (1) knowing what role compatibility is, (2) being able to recognize it in our own life situation, and (3) being able to consciously change the compatibility of our roles. Some example of things that can be done to increase the compatibility of the parent role with other roles are:[2]

1. *Compartmentalize roles.* This means to separate the time and place of one's various roles. For example, if the parenthood role is incompatible with the creative artist role it might help to move the art studio out of the house and confine one's art to a time when one doesn't have to have parental duties.
2. *Change expectations.* We could change some of our beliefs about what we or someone else ought to do in one or several roles. Perhaps we are too demanding or rigid, and "giving in" would help eliminate the role incompatibility.

---

[2] These are modifications of more general suggestions by Goode (1960).

3. *Eliminate a role.* Sometimes we could just quit doing something, such as participating in a sports club, being a volunteer, working on a job, or engaging in an avocation.
4. *Rearrange obligations.* Sometimes spouses could rearrange their tasks to eliminate role incompatibilities. Many couples have both husband and wife share in various household and child care responsibilities, and another strategy is to divide the tasks in unorthodox ways.

Goal facilitation

A fifth factor that influences how easily people make the transition into parenthood deals with how much the parental role helps them attain their goals. If parenthood helps people attain their goals the transition is easier, and if parenthood prevents people from attaining their goals the transition is harder. The main variable in this principle is the *amount parenthood facilitates goal attainment*. This varies from one extreme at which parenthood prevents attaining a goal to the opposite extreme at which it highly facilitates attaining a goal (Biddle and Thomas, 1966, pp. 60–61; Burr, 1973, p. 134). There is an intermediate point at which parenthood is ir-

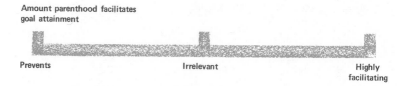

Amount parenthood facilitates
goal attainment

Prevents   Irrelevant   Highly
                                                                                facilitating

relevant to a goal, neither hindering nor helping its achievement. The relevant principle is:

THE GOAL FACILITATION PRINCIPLE: The amount that parenthood facilitates goal attainment influences the ease of the transition into parenthood, and this is a positive relationship.

Little is known about the exact shape of this relationship, so about all that can be said is that it is positive. This means that the greater the facilitation of goals the greater the ease and the less the facilitation of goals the less the ease.

This principle is more abstract and probably more difficult to use than most of the others in this book, but nonetheless it has important practical implications. If we were to assume, for example, that a couple wanted to travel and become financially established before having their first child but that the wife became pregnant very soon after the wedding, this principle permits us to make a prediction about the ease with which this couple will be able to adjust to the parental role. Since the coming of the child interferes with attaining some goals—travel and financial security—the transition will be more difficult than it would have been if the couple had not had those goals. On the other hand, a couple who view parenthood as the most important part of their life would undoubtedly make the transition into parenthood more easily than a couple who do not want children or are indifferent about whether or not they have children.

When we can manipulate our life situation so parenthood facilitates goal attainment we can partially change the ease of adjusting to the role shift. One way to do this is to time the arrival of children so they will not be born at times when there are important competing goals, and to try to have them when this is consistent with our other goals. With the increasing effectiveness of birth control techniques this is, of course, becoming increasingly possible. Another thing we can do is to consciously change the goals in our life situations. This is, in many ways, more difficult to do, but it is frequently possible. If, for example we were to find that we were expecting a child, and that the child would interfere with some important goals, we could try to identify, examine, and perhaps rearrange some of the priorities in our life situation so that the role of parenthood would help rather than hinder us in attaining our goals. One way to help do this would be to find acquaintances or groups of individuals who have a set of goals that we share and then increase our association with them. If it is true, as most social scientists argue, that we tend to become like the people with whom we associate intimately, this will probably lead to some goal shifts.

There are two other things that we could do if we find that parenthood hinders goal achievement. One is to focus on substitute gratifications that parenthood will bring because this process can identify things that may compensate for lost goals. The other is to defer goals or to find other ways to attain them. For example, the couple cited earlier who wanted to travel before becoming parents could perhaps defer their travel plans until after the children are grown and launched, find ways to travel with their children, or use such resources as grandparents to free them to travel without their children.

The last principle in this chapter deals with the effects of certain activities on adjusting to parenthood. This idea was originally discussed by Goode (1960) when he pointed out that occasionally in-

Amount of activity

dividuals occupy so many roles that they can't do everything they are obligated to do. He then pointed out that one solution would be to reduce the amount of things they have to do. This idea can be stated in a principle, but it is first necessary to define the independent variable involved. It can be labeled the *amount of activity*, and can be defined as the total amount of behavior a person is obligated to perform (Goode, 1960; Burr, 1973, p. 132). It ranges from none to very large amounts, and the relevant principle is:

THE ACTIVITY PRINCIPLE: The amount of activity in a person's life influences the ease of the transition into the role of parent, and this is an inverse, curvilinear relationship.

The curvilinearity in this relationship is illustrated in Figure 17–8. As can be seen in this diagram, increases or decreases in the

Figure 17–8

The effect of the activity level on the ease of adjusting to parenthood

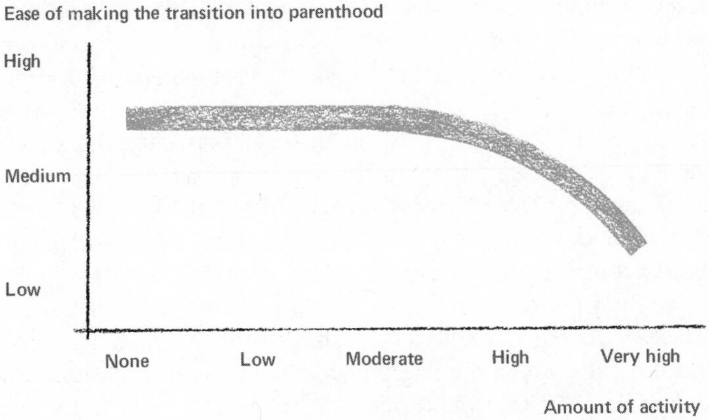

Ease of making the transition into parenthood

amount of activity when the activity level is moderately low do not influence the ease of making the transition into parenthood. However, for people whose levels of activity are high, increases or decreases in the amount of activity probably have a substantial influence on the ease of the transition.

In the contemporary American culture this principle is particularly important for the wife in her shift into the parental role because when the first child is born the usual pattern is for her activity level to increase more than her husband's does. If the wife has a large number of activities, *and she retains them* after the child is born, the birth of the child may increase her total level of activity sufficiently to substantially decrease the ease of making the transition. One solution that some of us may like is fairly easy to accomplish, and it is a solution that frequently receives support from others. This is for the new mother to substantially reduce her involvement in other activities when she has her first child. This need not be a total elimination of other activities, since total elimination would probably have other disadvantages, but it should be enough of a reduction to keep the new demands from making the overall level of activity higher than desirable. This is a fairly "traditional" type of solution, and some of us may prefer other solutions. We may, for example, want to make substantial changes in the husband's role or to arrange a fairly clear schedule about what the husband and wife are to do.

A number of skills are involved in using this principle. One is being able to recognize the amount of activity that we have in our life. A second is being able to tell when we have reached a point at which our demands are high enough to interfere with other things— such as making the transition into parenthood. A third—and more advanced—skill is being able to increase or decrease the amount of our activity. Some of the things that could be done to accomplish this are:

1. Temporarily or permanently stop some activities.
2. Delegate responsibilities to others, such as co-workers, fellow club members, children, or spouse.
3. Hire someone to do part of one's work.
4. Rearrange one's schedule to spread some activities over a longer period.
5. Do some things "less well" for a period of time.
6. Get assistance from someone else, such as a spouse or a friend, in deciding how to curtail one's activities.

SUMMARY

There were two major concerns in this chapter. The first was to discuss the issues that are involved in making plans about parenthood, and the second was to identify a number of things couples could do to prepare for parenthood. In the section that discussed "planning" about parenthood, some of the decisions couples must make were identified and then a variety of different methods of controlling conception were described and compared. In the second part of the chapter six principles were identified which couples could use to maximize the pleasures and minimize the pains of making the transition into parenthood. These principles are all sum-

Figure 17–9

Summary of the principles about the ease of making the transition into parenthood

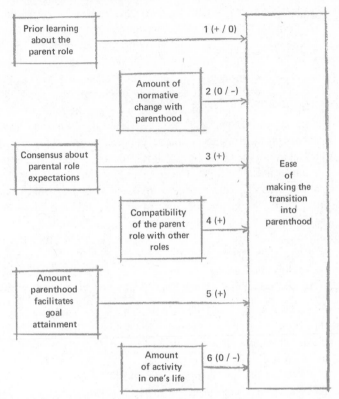

marized in Figure 17–9. The arrow marked 1 is the Learning about the Parent Role principle; the 2 arrow is the Normative Change with Parenthood principle; and arrow 3 is the Consensus about Parental Expectations principle. The relationship between these three principles and the more general ideas from which they can be deduced were explained and diagramed. Arrow 4 illustrates the Role Compatibility principle; arrow 5 shows the Goal Facilitation principle; and arrow 6 shows the Activity principle. The practical implications of those principles and several strategies for applying them were also discussed.

SUGGESTIONS FOR FURTHER STUDY

Blood, Robert O., Jr. 1968. *Marriage*. New York: Free Press, chaps. 19–21.

Bowman, Henry A. 1974. *Marriage for Moderns*. New York: McGraw-Hill, chaps. 10–12.

Burr, Wesley R.   1972. "Role Transitions: A Reformulation of Theory."
    Journal of Marriage and the Family 34:407–16.

Hubbard, Charles W.   1973. *Family Planning Education*. St. Louis:
    Mosby.

Hymes, James L.   1952. *Understanding Your Child*. Englewood Cliffs,
    N.J.: Prentice-Hall.

Patterson, Gerald R.   1971. *Families*. Champaign, Ill.: Research Press.

Udry, J. Richard   1974. *The Social Context of Marriage*. New York:
    Lippincott, chaps. 16 and 17.

Marriage as the years pass

A NUMBER of research studies in the past 40 years have attempted to learn what happens to spouses' feelings toward each other as they become parents and begin the process of raising their children. These studies have fairly conclusively shown that the typical pattern is for love feelings to become less intense and for marriages to become less satisfying and less pleasant during the first 10 to 15 years. This is then frequently followed by a period when marriages become somewhat more pleasant after the children are grown and leave home.

One of the first studies to find that marital happiness decreased during the first years of married life was published in 1938, and it found a slight decrease in marital happiness in the first few years of marriage. Happiness then stayed at about the same level until the couple had been married about 20 years, when there was a slight increase. It would be nice to be able to report that later research has found that the decrease in the early years was unique to marriage in the 1930s, but this isn't the case. Several studies conducted during the 1950s, 60s, and 70s found essentially the same pattern. For example, Blood and Wolfe (1960, p. 232) found that marital satisfaction decreased steadily from early marriage to retirement, as shown in Figure 18–1. Luckey (1966) studied 80 couples who had been married from 2 to 21 years and found that the longer the couples had been married the fewer "favorable personality qualities each saw in his mate, and . . . the less they saw their spouses as admired, grateful, cooperative, friendly, affectionate, considerate, and helpful" (p. 45). The findings from another recent study are presented in Figure 18–2, and this research found essentially the

Figure 18–1

Wife's marital satisfaction, by length of marriage

Average marital satisfaction

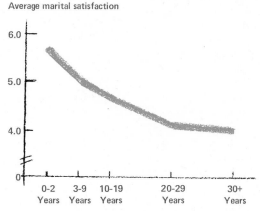

Source: Blood and Wolfe (1960, p. 264).

same pattern. The percentage of couples who thought their marriage was "'very satisfying" decreased dramatically through the stage in their life when they launched their children. About a dozen other research studies have also found essentially this same variation over the life cycle.[1]

Thus, research has demonstrated fairly conclusively that marital happiness for most couples decreases during the first 10 to 15 years of marriage. This finding, however, has to be squared somehow with the fact that *some* couples experience an increase in marital happiness. Virtually everyone has heard couples who have been married for some time make the comment that their love was so much richer, deeper, and more meaningful after several years of marriage, that they weren't *really* in love when they were first married—even though they thought they were at the time. In addition, some couples undoubtedly evaluate their marriage as "different, but not really better or worse than it was when we were first married."

In this author's opinion, there will probably not be any contradiction between these differences when more research is done, because it will probably be found that Figure 18–3 shows what really happens. That figure shows that the vast majority of couples, as indicated by the width of the line, experience a gradual decline in their marital happiness in the first years of the marriage and then a slight increase when the children are grown. A small minority of couples don't go either up or down in their marital satisfaction or happiness, and another small minority actually experience an increase in their marital happiness. If the conclusion suggested in

[1] These studies are reviewed in Burr (1970), Rollins and Feldman (1970), and Rollins and Cannon (1974).

Figure 18–2

Percentage of individuals in each stage of the family life cycle reporting that the marriage is very satisfying

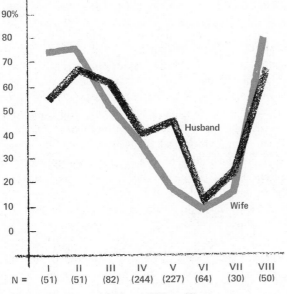

Source: Rollins and Feldman (1970, p. 26).

Figure 18–3 is correct, *this provides a challenge and an opportunity for married couples*. It means that couples can avoid the typical pattern of gradual disillusionment if they can learn what it takes to be among the minority who maintain or enhance their marital re-

Figure 18–3

Proportions of couples experiencing a decrease, stability, or an increase in their marital happiness

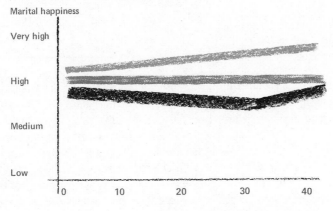

Length of time married (years)

lationship. This last chapter is an attempt to identify ways in which some of the principles discussed in earlier chapters and several new principles can help couples attain this goal.

USING PRINCIPLES IN OTHER CHAPTERS TO ENRICH MARRIAGE AS THE YEARS PASS

It is difficult to know which groups of principles in the earlier chapters are most relevant for maintaining a pleasant, satisfying marital relationship over the years because so many of them can serve this purpose. In this author's opinion, however, the two most relevant groups of principles are probably the ones in Chapter 8 that deal with interaction and the ones in Chapters 3 through 6 that deal with communication and decision making. As a result of this bias (and it is admittedly only a personal preference) only those principles are being discussed here, and it is left to readers to review the other principles and find whether and how they can be useful to them in enriching their marital relationship as the years pass.

Interaction   One principle that seems to be very relevant in this context is the Interaction principle discussed in Chapter 8. It is:

> THE INTERACTION PRINCIPLE: When the interaction between two individuals is profitable, the more they interact the stronger will be their love for each other, and, conversely, the less they interact the less intense their love.

Readers who wish to review how the variables in this principle are defined and how much confidence we should place in it can refer to page 218. Suffice it to say here that this idea was originally stated by Homans (1950), and that there is a vast amount of evidence that it is correct.

One reason this principle seems to be important in maintaining a satisfactory marital relationship over the years is that studies (Blood and Wolfe, 1960) have found that the pattern in most marriages is for the couple to spend less and less time in such activities as sharing precious moments, talking about events that happen to them when they are apart, going out together, and, in general, being close companions and friends. As the children come, and the husband and wife become increasingly involved in careers, housekeeping, PTA, community service, individual leisure activities, etc., couples usually find that their interaction as persons, and as companionate spouses, tends to decrease. And to make matters worse (assuming that the goal is to maintain positive love feelings in the relationship), the interaction that does occur tends to become less and less profitable. It deals with such problems as strains in the budget, getting shoes for the kids, how to relate to aging parents, difficulties at work, and the only time many couples ever have a lengthy conversation is when the problem they are dealing with is a serious one.

We can use the Interaction principle to manipulate our situations so that we can maintain the level of positive feelings (love) toward each other that we wish, and the steps in doing this are: (1) to acquire a sizable repertoire of profitable ways in which we *can* interact; (2) to maintain an optimal level of such profitable interaction, (3) to decrease unprofitable interaction as much as possible; and (4) to increase the profit in the interaction we have. Four exercises on pages 220–23 deal with these four ways to implement this principle, and those of us who are interested in these issues may wish to go back and take more advantage of those exercises than we did earlier . . . or invent some of our own.

It has been said that successful marriage is not so much avoiding problems as being able to deal with the problems encountered in ways that create success. And all couples face a countless number of problems. Those of us, however, who learn how to communicate with each other in ways that are comfortable, open, and reassuring have a skill that will go a long way toward helping us maintain and enrich our marital relationship. If, as the principles in Chapter 3 suggest, we learn how to keep our intense emotions from disrupting our communication and learn how to establish a sense of trust and concern in a relationship, we will probably find that this will help us establish and enhance our marital relationship. Also, if we will employ the principles in Chapter 4 that help us enhance rather than depreciate self-esteem this will help us to do more than just cope with difficulties. It will create a situation in which our marital interaction will be increasingly rewarding and pleasant rather than disillusioning. The many skills that are identified in Chapter 5 can also be used to help us in developing an effective style or pattern of communicating, and even though effective communication is not a panacea that will solve everything in a marriage, it is a resource that is of immeasurable value in enabling us to enrich rather than gradually destroy a pleasant marital relationship.

The principles in Chapter 6 that deal with effective decision making can also be valuable in helping a marriage become what we

Using principles about communication and decision making

want it to be. If we can learn to make decisions that are satisfactory to us and our spouse and that are at least moderately effective, these "coping" skills will clear the way for the development of positive feelings and bonds. If, however, we do not learn how to make satisfying decisions we will probably find that resentments, bitterness, and frustrations gradually build walls and that these get in the way of the parts of our relationship that could help our marriage become what we want it to be.

The conclusion that emerges from this is that those of us who are able to develop habits of effective communication and decision making will usually be better able to create the type of marital relationship we want. And this is probably true whatever the style of marriage we prefer. Whether our marriage is Traditional, Intrinsic, Open, Utilitarian, or any other style we can probably attain the goals of our style better by having moderately effective communication and decision-making patterns. This suggests that those of us who want to enhance and enrich our marriages as the years pass ought to review Chapters 3–6 with the thought in mind of using the information in those chapters to help create a long-term, adequate proficiency in communicating and problem solving.

ONE ADDITIONAL PRINCIPLE

The last principle in this book is one that should be integrated with several of the principles that were discussed in earlier chapters. It will be recalled that the phenomenon of "similarity" has occurred and recurred in earlier chapters, and that the theme in the principles that used it is that the more similar two individuals are, the better off they are probably going to be in their marriage. Specifically, it was stated on page 228 that the amount of similarity influences the intensity of love feelings, and on page 189 it was stated that the amount of similarity influences the probability that a couple will be satisfied with their marriage. And, a more specific case of this latter idea was discussed on page 204, namely, that a particular type of similarity, consensus on role expectations, is probably very important. These three ideas are diagramed in Figure 18–4 together with the following new principle:

THE SOCIAL NETWORKS PRINCIPLE: The more spouses are jointly involved in their social networks the more similar the spouses will become, and vice versa.

The independent variable in the Social Networks principle is the amount spouses are jointly involved in their social networks, and for the sake of brevity this is called *joint involvement*. It is a continuous variable, ranging from a condition in which spouses are in-

Figure 18–4

The relationships between similarity and several other variables

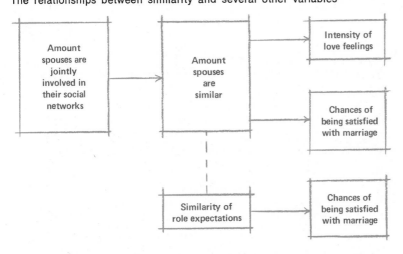

volved in different social networks to a condition in which spouses are involved in the same social networks. Some of the social networks that American couples are usually involved with are relatives, friendship groups, work groups, social clubs, and service organizations. If one spouse is highly involved with one set of relatives or one social group, and the other spouse is highly involved with a different set of relatives or another social group, this would be a condition of low joint involvement. This variable can be diagramed in the following way:

The dependent variable in the Social Networks principle is the amount two spouses are similar in basic values, such as goals, interests, role expectations, and philosophy of life, and in less basic aspects of life, such as leisure-time interests, hobbies, and personal inclinations. This variable was earlier defined and illustrated on page 189.

The relationship in this principle is positive, but there is currently no way to know what shape the relationship has. The principle was first stated by Ackerman (1963), and it has been further elaborated by Scanzoni (1965). Also, as Scanzoni has pointed out, this idea is closely related to and can be deduced from some of the most respected ideas in modern sociology (Coser, 1956; Gibbs and Martin, 1964). This principle is thus one which deserves considerable confidence.

Two skills are involved in using this principle. The *first* is being able to recognize which social groups we and our spouse belong to and to recognize how those groups influence us. Almost all of us belong to some groups, and as our attitudes, beliefs, values, hopes, dreams, and goals gradually change the groups always seem to change. In fact, what seems to occur is that, if we aren't comfortable with the groups we have been identified with, we change groups so we can interact comfortably, and then the new groups influence us. It takes some skill, however, to recognize what these groups are and how they bring about the gradual changes in ourselves and our spouse.

The *second* skill that we need in order to use this principle is to be able to actively do something about these groups. Most of us become involved with different groups at different stages of our adult life. For example, we may be very involved at one stage of our life with groups that are active participants in sporting events, such as car racing, collegiate athletics, beachcombing, or horse racing, but this involvement may last only a few years. Many of us find ourselves participating in groups such as these until we buy a house, have children, and adopt a more sedate style of life. When these latter events occur we find that the groups we are involved with change. Some of us find ourselves increasingly influenced in our adult years by the business community, as we invest more of ourselves in it, gain some prestige, and find that our jobs, careers, or professions assume an importance we didn't previously expect. As these changes in our "group involvement" occur it becomes possible to actively plan and direct some of this activity. One way to do this is to gradually create more or less joint involvement by deliberately becoming more or less involved in some activities.

One very common pattern in the contemporary American scene is for the husband to become highly involved in his career and extrafamilial activities, for the wife to become involved in her motherly and home-oriented concerns, and for both of them to become integrated with different groups. One way of changing this pattern is for the husband to become more involved in the home by spending more time there and by assuming more responsibilities for the supervision and training of the children, the care of the home, and household tasks; and, at the same time, for the wife to become more involved in extrafamilial concerns and groups by giving more emphasis to a career, service activities, artistic creativity, her education, etc. One of the beauties of the contemporary society is that the rigid definitions of what husbands and wives ought to do have now become flexible enough to give most of us considerable freedom in the way we structure our activities and become involved with groups.

It is probably too extreme to believe that couples ought to have joint involvement in all of their nonfamily social groups. In fact it seems reasonable to speculate that the emphasis on individuality in the American culture makes it desirable to have some activities and reference groups that are individual rather than couple activities. The main concern in this principle thus seems to be with (1) the majority of nonfamily associations and (2) with the salient groups that influence our basic values and goals. If our involvement with the majority or virtually all of our groups, especially the salient ones, is as individuals rather than as couples, this principle makes a fairly clear prediction. We will probably grow apart as the years pass. This may occur so slowly and imperceptibly that we will not be aware of it until the divergence cannot be narrowed. On the other hand, if a substantial amount of our involvement is as a couple, this will foster similarity—and all of the consequences that follow from being similar. Another way this principle can be used is to become aware of it and to begin making plans before we are married. Most of us set trends and patterns in our relationships during the formative months, and many of these patterns remain. It would be possible to set a pattern of discussing what our social networks are and how they probably influence us, and to work at creating an optimum amount of "jointness" in these social networks. This type of premarital discussion would set the stage for continuing to be aware of these networks after marriage and, very probably, for enabling most of us to create and maintain an optimal situation relatively easily.

It should probably also be mentioned that some of us undoubtedly want different degrees of joint participation and similarity. Those of us who value our independence and do not want our marriage to be a highly salient part of our lives would not want the same amount of joint involvement that others might want. Those of us who want an Intrinsic marriage probably would be best off if we were to have relatively high amounts of joint activity, while those of us who want an Open or a Utilitarian marriage would probably not need the same degree of commonality. Again, as has been said so many times throughout this book, different people will want to use a principle in different ways in order to attain different marital goals.

SUMMARY

This chapter discussed the fact that most marriages in the contemporary American culture pass through a period of disillusionment, but it was suggested that it is possible to create a relationship that can remain optimal or even become better rather than follow the typical pattern. Several principles were discussed which can probably assist couples in maintaining and enhancing their relationship. Some of these principles were initially presented in earlier chapters, and the discussion centered on how they could be used to enrich marriage as the years pass. One new principle was presented—the Social Networks principle. This states that the more couples share their involvement with nonfamily groups the more similar they will be, and when this is coupled with several other principles that deal with similarity the chain sequence described in Figure 18–5 is identified. Several strategies for using this prin-

Figure 18–5

The chain sequence showing the effects of variation in joint involvement in nonmarital groups

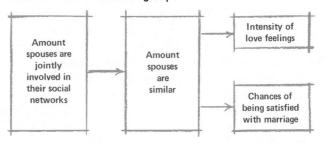

ciple were then discussed. There are also, undoubtedly, many other principles that can be used to maintain and enhance marital relationships as the years pass. For example, couples can use the principles in Chapter 14 on how to change bonds and the principles about love in Chapter 8 to maintain the degree of bondedness and the level of love feelings that they want to have.

SUGGESTIONS FOR FURTHER STUDY

Blood, Robert O., Jr.   1968. *Marriage.* New York: Free Press, chap. 16.
Bott, Elizabeth   1957. *Family and Social Network.* London: Tavistock.
Duvall, Evelyn   1971. *Family Development.* 4th ed. Philadelphia: Lippincott, chaps. 13, 14, 15, and especially 16.

Otto, Herbert   *More Joy in Your Marriage.* New York: Hawthorne Books.

Rollins, Boyd C., and Cannon, Kenneth L.   1974.   "Marital Satisfaction over the Family Life Cycle: A Reevaluation." *Journal of Marriage and the Family* 36:271–83 (May).

Scanzoni, John   1965. "A Reinquiry into Marital Disorganization." *Journal of Marriage and the Family* 27:483–91 (November).

Appendix

Summary of principles in chapter 3

EMOTION AND VERBAL
COMMUNICATION

1. **THE EMOTIONALITY PRINCIPLE:**

    When the intensity of emotions is high, the greater the intensity the less the amount of rational control people have over their behavior, and the less the intensity the greater the control (p. 52).

2. **THE CONTROL PRINCIPLE:**

    The greater the rational control over behavior the greater the quality of verbal communication, and vice versa, and this is a curvilinear relationship (p. 55).

3. **THE TRUST PRINCIPLE:**

    The greater the trust that an individual perceives in a relationship the greater the willingness to communicate about important emotions, and the less the trust the less the willingness (p. 67).

4. **THE CONCERN PRINCIPLE:**

    The greater the concern an individual perceives another person has for him or her the greater the willingness of the individual to communicate about important emotions, and the less the concern the less the willingness (p. 73).

5. **THE NORMS-EMOTION PRINCIPLE:**

    The more a person's norms proscribe communication about emotions the less willing the person is to communicate about important emotions, and vice versa (p. 75).

Diagram of principles in chapter 3

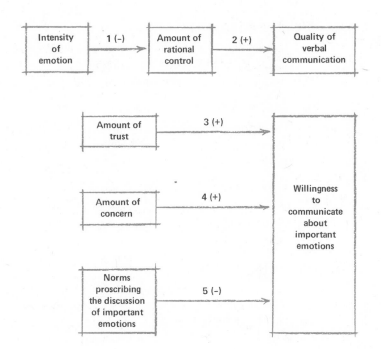

Summary of principles in chapter 4

THE ROLE OF SELF-ESTEEM IN COMMUNICATION

1. **THE SELF-ESTEEM PRINCIPLE:**

    The amount of self-esteem influences the amount of anxiety that individuals experience, and this is an inverse, curvilinear relationship (p. 85).

2. **THE DEFENSIVENESS PRINCIPLE:**

    The amount of anxiety due to lowered self-esteem influences the amount individuals use defensive behaviors called defense mechanisms (p. 86).

3. **THE DEFENSE-COMMUNICATION PRINCIPLE:**

    The use of defense mechanisms frequently has an adverse effect on the quality of the verbal communication (p. 89).

4. **THE ANXIETY PRINCIPLE:**

    The amount of anxiety an individual experiences due to lowered self-esteem influences the amount the person's behavior is rationally controlled, and this is a positive, curvilinear relationship (p. 95).

Diagram of principles in chapter 4

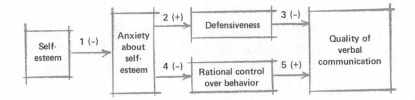

Summary of principles in chapter 6

EFFECTIVE AND SATISFYING DECISION MAKING

1. **THE ALTERNATIVES PRINCIPLE:**

   The number of alternatives considered in decision making influences the quality of the decision making, and this is a curvilinear relationship (p. 149).

2. **THE RATIONALITY PRINCIPLE:**

   The greater the rational control over behavior the better the quality of decision, and vice versa (p. 153).

3. **THE OPENNESS OF COMMUNICATION PRINCIPLE:**

   The more open the communication in a group the better the quality of the decision making (p. 156).

4. **THE LEADERSHIP PRINCIPLE:**

   The greater the degree of consensus among the members of a group about the leader in decision-making situations the better the quality of the decision making, and vice versa (p. 158).

5. **THE QUALITY OF ATTENTION PRINCIPLE:**

   The higher the quality of attention that is given to opinions of others in a group the higher the quality of the decision making, and vice versa (p. 160).

6. **THE RISK PRINCIPLE:**

   The amount of risk taking in decision making influences the quality of the decision making, and this is a curvilinear relationship (p. 161).

7. **THE DECISIVENESS PRINCIPLE:**

   The decisiveness in decision making affects the quality of decisions, and this is a positive relationship (p. 163).

8. **THE AMOUNT OF PARTICIPATION PRINCIPLE:**

   When people have an interest in the outcome of a decision, the more they participate in the decision-making process the more satisfied they usually are with the decision, and vice versa (p. 166).

9. THE CONSENSUS PRINCIPLE:

The more consensus there is about a decision the greater the satisfaction with the decision, and vice versa (p. 169).

Diagram of principles in chapter 6

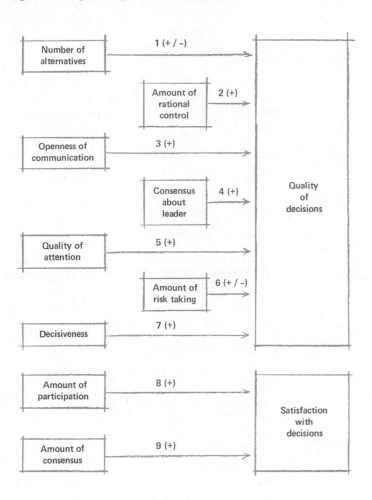

Summary of principles in chapter 7

PREMARITAL RELATIONSHIPS

1. THE MODELING PRINCIPLE:

    The closer an individual's prospective spouse's parents' marital relationships are to the individual's ideal marital relationships the greater the chances that the individual will be satisfied with the marriage, and vice versa (p. 179).

2. THE APPROVAL PRINCIPLE:

    The more that intimate acquaintances approve of a prospective spouse, the greater the chances that a couple will be satisfied with the marriage, and vice versa (p. 185).

3. THE LENGTH OF COURTSHIP PRINCIPLE:

    The length of the courtship that precedes a marriage is positively related to the chances of being satisfied with the marriage (p. 187).

4. THE SIMILARITY PRINCIPLE:

    The more similar two individuals are in any one area of life the greater their chances of being satisfied with their marriage, and, conversely, the more dissimilar they are the lower the chances that they will be satisfied with their marriage (p. 189).

5. THE IMPORTANCE PRINCIPLE:

    The more important a particular similarity or dissimilarity is (personally or in a culture) the greater the influence it has on marital satisfaction, and vice versa (p. 193).

6. THE RELEVANCE PRINCIPLE:

    The more a similarity or dissimilarity is relevant for marital interaction the greater the influence it has on marital satisfaction, and vice versa (p. 195).

7. THE RELATIVE STATUS PRINCIPLE:

    When a couple are dissimilar in an area, and this

difference has status implications, the dissimilarity tends to be more disruptive if the husband is inferior than if the wife is inferior (p. 196).

8. THE CONSENSUS ABOUT EXPECTATIONS PRINCIPLE:

The greater the consensus about marital role expectations the greater the chances of marital satisfaction, and vice versa (p. 204).

Diagram of principles in chapter 7

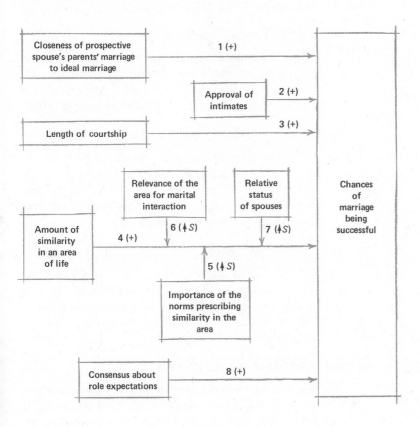

Summary of principles in chapter 8

DEVELOPING AND NURTURING LOVE IN RELATIONSHIPS

1. **THE PROFIT PRINCIPLE:**

   The greater the profit a person experiences in a relationship the greater the love for the other person, and vice versa (p. 217).

2. **THE INTERACTION PRINCIPLE:**

   When the interaction between two individuals is profitable, the more they interact the stronger will be their love for each other, and, conversely, the less they interact the less intense their love (p. 218).

3. **THE SENSE OF IMPORTANCE PRINCIPLE:**

   The more important an individual feels he or she is to someone else the stronger the love feelings will be toward the other person, and, conversely, the less important he or she feels, the less intense the love feelings toward the other person (p. 224).

4. **THE EMOTIONAL HELP PRINCIPLE:**

   The more help a person provides in times of emotional distress the greater the intensity of the love feelings toward this person, and, conversely, the less help a person provides the less intense the love feelings (p. 226).

5. **THE SIMILARITY-LOVE PRINCIPLE:**

   When two individuals have an enduring relationship, the more similar they are to each other the stronger will be their love, and, conversely, the more different they are the less intense will be their love (p. 228).

6. **THE BONDEDNESS PRINCIPLE:**

   The stronger the bonds in a marital relationship the greater the intensity of the love feelings, and, conversely, the weaker the bonds the less intense the love (p. 230).

Diagram of principles in chapter 8

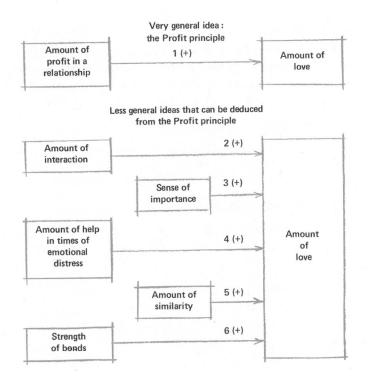

Very general idea:
the Profit principle

| Amount of profit in a relationship | 1 (+) → | Amount of love |

Less general ideas that can be deduced from the Profit principle

Amount of interaction — 2 (+) →

Sense of importance — 3 (+) →

Amount of help in times of emotional distress — 4 (+) →

Amount of similarity — 5 (+) →

Strength of bonds — 6 (+) →

Amount of love

Summary of principles in chapter 9

PERSONAL READINESS
FOR MARRIAGE

1. THE SKILL PRINCIPLE:

    The amount of skill a person has to behave in the ways normatively prescribed for a marital role influences the chances of marital satisfaction, and this is a positive, curvilinear relationship (p. 234).

2. THE AGE AT MARRIAGE PRINCIPLE:

    Age at the time of a person's first marriage is related to the probability of the marriage being satisfying, and this is a positive, curvilinear relationship (p. 237).

3. THE EDUCATION PRINCIPLE:

    The greater the amount of education the greater the chances of marital satisfaction, and vice versa (p. 240).

4. THE DESIRE FOR CHILDREN PRINCIPLE:

    The amount an individual desires children is related to the chances of marital satisfaction, and this is a positive relationship (p. 241).

5. THE CONVENTIONALITY PRINCIPLE:

    The amount of an individual's conventionality is related to the chances of marital satisfaction, and this is a positive relationship (p. 242).

Diagram of principles in chapter 9

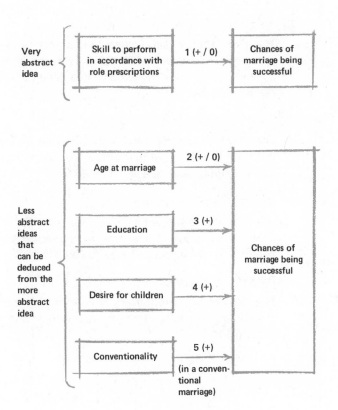

Summary of principles in chapter 10

PREMARITAL SEXUAL ATTITUDES AND BEHAVIOR

1. **THE SEXUAL NORMS PRINCIPLE:**

    The more that social or personal norms proscribe premarital sexual behaviors the greater the negative consequences when these behaviors occur, and vice versa (p. 255).

2. **THE SALIENCE PRINCIPLE:**

    The greater the salience of a group to an individual the more the norms of that group are internalized by that individual, and vice versa (p. 260).

3. **THE RESPONSIBILITY PRINCIPLE:**

    The greater the responsibility one has for other family members the less one's premarital sexual permissiveness, and vice versa (p. 266).

4. **THE PROFIT FROM SEX PRINCIPLE:**

    The greater the profit from sexual stimulation the greater the intensity of sexual motivation, and vice versa (p. 267).

Diagram of principles in chapter 10

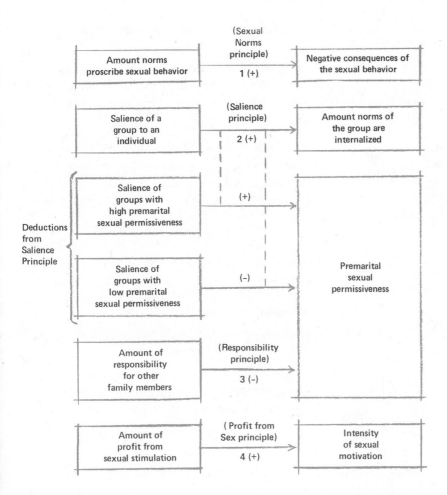

Summary of principles in chapter 11

EASING THE TRANSITION
INTO MARRIAGE

1. THE LEARNING ABOUT THE SPOUSE ROLE
   PRINCIPLE:

   The amount of prior learning about the spouse role
   influences the ease of making the transition into this
   role, and this is a positive, curvilinear relationship
   (p. 276).

2. THE TRANSITION PROCEDURES PRINCIPLE:

   The importance and definiteness of the transition
   procedures for becoming married influence the ease
   of making the transition into marriage, and this is a
   positive relationship (p. 280).

3. THE NORMATIVE CHANGE WITH MARRIAGE PRINCIPLE:

   The amount of normative change that occurs as one
   assumes the role of spouse influences the ease of
   making this transition, and this is an inverse, curvilinear relationship (p. 281).

4. THE CONSENSUS ABOUT MARITAL EXPECTATIONS
   PRINCIPLE:

   The greater the consensus about expectations for
   the spouse role the greater the ease of the transition
   into marriage, and vice versa (p. 287).

Diagram of principles in chapter 11

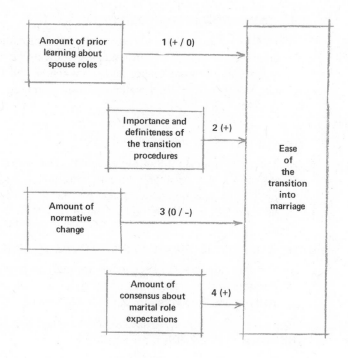

Summary of principles in chapter 12

ACHIEVING SATISFACTION
IN MARITAL ROLES

1. **THE CONGRUENCE PRINCIPLE:**

    The more congruence between role expectations and role behavior, the more satisfied individuals tend to be with their marriage, and, conversely, the less congruence the less satisfied they tend to be (p. 298).

2. **THE IMPORTANCE PRINCIPLE:**

    The more important the role expectations the greater the effect that variation in the congruence of expectations and behavior has on marital satisfaction, and the less important the less effect (p. 299).

3. **THE CONSENSUS ABOUT EXPECTATIONS PRINCIPLE:**

    The greater the consensus about marital role expectations the greater the chances of marital satisfaction, and vice versa (p. 306).

4. **THE ROLE COMPATIBILITY PRINCIPLE:**

    The greater the role compatibility in marriage the greater the marital satisfaction, and vice versa (p. 311).

5. **THE UNDERSTANDING PRINCIPLE:**

    The more accurately spouses understand each other the greater their marital satisfaction, and vice versa (p. 313).

6. **THE POWER-UNDERSTANDING PRINCIPLE:**

    The more power either spouse has the less likely that that spouse's accuracy of understanding is positively related to his or her marital satisfaction, and vice versa (p. 315).

7. THE SIMILARITY-UNDERSTANDING PRINCIPLE:

> When two spouses are similar, accuracy of understanding tends to be positively related to marital satisfaction, but when they are dissimilar the relationship tends to be inverse (p. 317).

8. THE DEPRIVATION-SATISFACTION PRINCIPLE:

> The relative deprivation of one's marriage as a whole influences marital satisfaction, and this is an inverse relationship (p. 319).

Diagram of principles in chapter 12

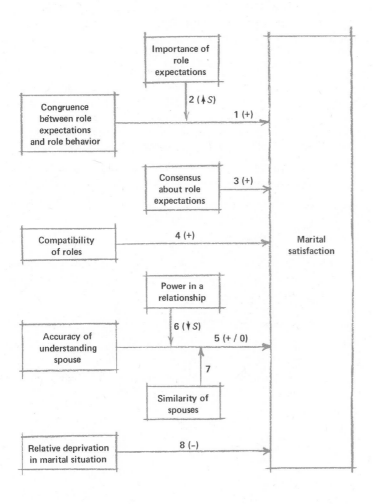

Summary of principles in chapter 13

CONTROLLING BONDS
IN MARRIAGE

1. **THE SHARED EXPERIENCE PRINCIPLE:**

   The amount of shared experience a couple has influences the strength of their bonds, and this is a positive, linear relationship (p. 330).

2. **THE INCOMPLETE ACTION PRINCIPLE:**

   The amount of investment in incomplete action influences the bonds in a relationship, and this is a positive relationship (p. 334).

3. **THE RESERVE PRINCIPLE:**

   The amount of reserve in a relationship influences the strength of the bonds in that relationship, and this is an inverse relationship (p. 336).

4. **THE INTERDEPENDENCE OF ROLES PRINCIPLE:**

   The amount the roles in a relationship are interdependent influences the strength of the bonds in the relationship, and this is a positive relationship (p. 341).

5. **THE SUPPORT PRINCIPLE:**

   The amount of support in a relationship influences the strength of the bonds in that relationship, and this is a positive relationship (p. 343).

6. **THE IDENTIFICATION PRINCIPLE:**

   The amount that the identification of partners with each other enhances their self-esteem influences the strength of the bonds in the relationship, and this is a positive relationship (p. 345).

Diagram of principles in chapter 13

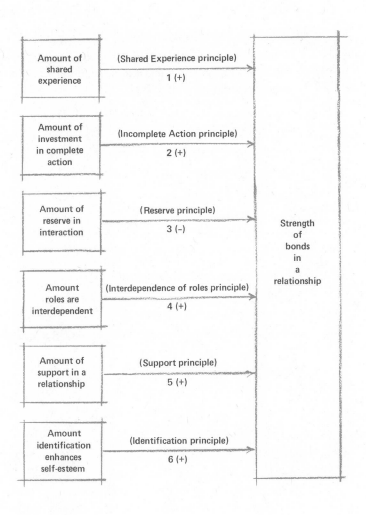

Amount of shared experience	(Shared Experience principle) 1 (+)	
Amount of investment in complete action	(Incomplete Action principle) 2 (+)	Strength of bonds in a relationship
Amount of reserve in interaction	(Reserve principle) 3 (−)	
Amount roles are interdependent	(Interdependence of roles principle) 4 (+)	
Amount of support in a relationship	(Support principle) 5 (+)	
Amount identification enhances self-esteem	(Identification principle) 6 (+)	

Summary of principles in chapter 14

EXTERNAL ROLES AND MARRIAGE

1. THE SOCIABILITY PRINCIPLE:

    The amount of sociability in a person's life in-
    fluences the person's marital satisfaction in a curvi-
    linear manner (p. 354).

Diagram of principles in chapter 14

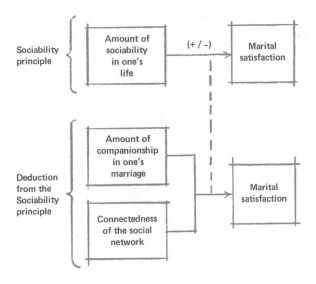

Summary of principles in chapter 15

SEXUALITY IN MARRIAGE

1. **THE SPECTATOR PRINCIPLE:**

    Assuming a spectator role during coitus tends to interfere with sexual adequacy (p. 274).

2. **THE PLEASURING PRINCIPLE:**

    The greater the sensory pleasurizing in a relationship—exclusive of coitus—the greater the sexual adequacy, and vice versa (p. 376).

3. **THE SECURITY PRINCIPLE:**

    The more secure a woman feels about her love object, the more likely she is to attain orgasm (p. 384).

Diagram of principles in chapter 15

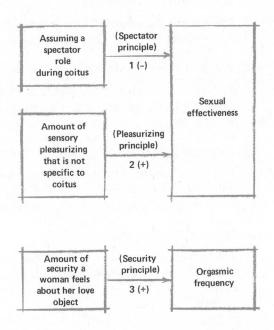

Summary of principles in chapter 16

COPING WITH STRESS

1. THE ADAPTABILITY PRINCIPLE:

   The greater the adaptability of a family the less the vulnerability to stress, and vice versa (p. 396).

2. THE INTEGRATION PRINCIPLE:

   The amount of family integration influences the vulnerability to stress, and this is an inverse relationship (p. 400).

3. THE EXTERNALIZATION OF BLAME PRINCIPLE:

   The externalization of blame for a stressful event influences the vulnerability of the family to this event, and this is an inverse relationship (p. 402).

4. THE SEVERITY PRINCIPLE:

   The definition a family makes of the severity of a stressful event influences the family's vulnerability to that event, and this is a positive relationship (p. 404).

5. THE TIME-CRISIS PRINCIPLE:

   The amount of time that stressful events are anticipated influences vulnerability to this stress, and this is an inverse relationship (p. 406).

6. THE PRIOR ROLE LEARNING AND STRESS PRINCIPLE:

   The amount of prior learning about a stressful event influences the vulnerability of families to that event, and this is an inverse relationship (p. 408).

7. THE ADAPTABILITY-REGENERATIVE POWER PRINCIPLE:

   The amount of family adaptability influences the regenerative power of families, and this is a positive relationship (p. 411).

(Continued on page 496.)

Diagram of principles in chapter 16

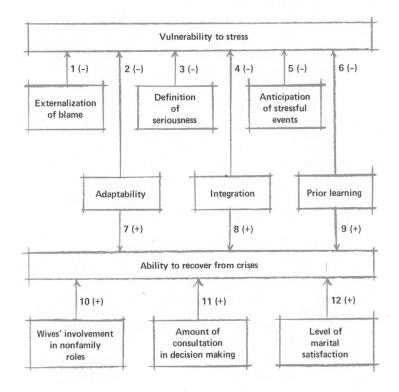

Vulnerability to stress

1 (-) 2 (-) 3 (-) 4 (-) 5 (-) 6 (-)

Externalization of blame

Definition of seriousness

Anticipation of stressful events

Adaptability

Integration

Prior learning

7 (+) 8 (+) 9 (+)

Ability to recover from crises

10 (+) 11 (+) 12 (+)

Wives' involvement in nonfamily roles

Amount of consultation in decision making

Level of marital satisfaction

8. **THE INTEGRATION-REGENERATIVE POWER PRINCIPLE:**

> The amount of family integration influences the regenerative power of families, and this is a positive relationship (p. 411).

9. **THE PRIOR ROLE LEARNING-REGENERATIVE POWER PRINCIPLE:**

> The amount of prior role learning about stressful events influences the regenerative power of families, and this is a positive relationship (p. 411).

10. **THE RELATIVE CONTROL PRINCIPLE:**

> The relative amount of control exercised by spouses is not related to the regenerative power of families (p. 412).

11. **THE CONSULTATION PRINCIPLE:**

> The amount of consultation in decision making influences the regenerative power of families, and this is a positive relationship (p. 412).

12. **THE SOCIAL ACTIVITY PRINCIPLE:**

> The amount of social activity of wives outside the home is related to the regenerative power of families, and this is a positive relationship (p. 415).

13. **THE SATISFACTION-REGENERATION PRINCIPLE:**

> The amount of marital satisfaction is related to the regenerative power of families, and this is a positive relationship (p. 417).

14. **THE SPEED OF RECOVERY–CRISIS PRINCIPLE:**

> The speed of recovery from most family crises is related to the quality of the readjustment after the crisis, and this is a positive relationship (p. 420).

15. **THE SPEED OF RECOVERY–BEREAVEMENT PRINCIPLE:**

> The speed of recovery from bereavement is related to the quality of the final adjustment, and this is a curvilinear relationship (p. 420).

Summary of principles in chapter 17

PARENTHOOD: PLANNING
AND PREPARING

1. **THE LEARNING ABOUT THE PARENT ROLE PRINCIPLE:**

   The amount of prior learning about the parent role influences the ease of making the transition into parenthood, and this is a positive, curvilinear relationship (p. 439).

2. **THE NORMATIVE CHANGE WITH PARENTHOOD PRINCIPLE:**

   The amount of normative change that occurs as one assumes the role of parent influences the ease of making this transition, and this is an inverse, curvilinear relationship (p. 443).

3. **THE CONSENSUS ABOUT PARENTAL EXPECTATIONS PRINCIPLE:**

   The greater the consensus about expectations for the parent role the greater the ease of the transition into parenthood, and vice versa (p. 447).

4. **THE ROLE COMPATIBILITY PRINCIPLE:**

   The amount of compatibility between the parent role and other roles influences the ease of the transition into the parent role, and this is a positive relationship (p. 449).

5. **THE GOAL FACILITATION PRINCIPLE:**

   The amount that parenthood facilitates goal attainment influences the ease of the transition into parenthood, and this is a positive relationship (p. 450).

6. **THE ACTIVITY PRINCIPLE:**

   The amount of activity in a person's life influences the ease of the transition into the role of parent, and this is an inverse, curvilinear relationship (p. 452).

Diagram of principles in chapter 17

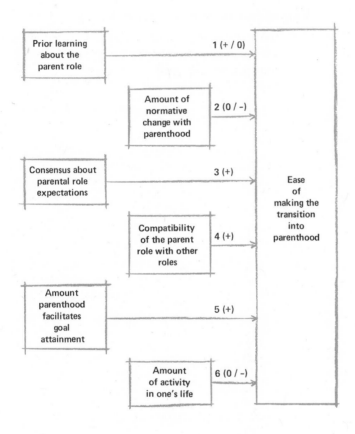

Prior learning about the parent role — 1 (+ / 0) →

Amount of normative change with parenthood — 2 (0 / –) →

Consensus about parental role expectations — 3 (+) →

Compatibility of the parent role with other roles — 4 (+) →

Amount parenthood facilitates goal attainment — 5 (+) →

Amount of activity in one's life — 6 (0 / –) →

Ease of making the transition into parenthood

Summary of principles in chapter 18

MARRIAGE AS THE
YEARS PASS

1. **THE SOCIAL NETWORKS PRINCIPLE:**

   The more spouses are jointly involved in their social networks the more similar the spouses will become, and vice versa (p. 462).

Diagram of principles in chapter 18

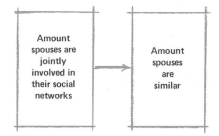

References

Ackerman, Charles "Affiliations: Structural Determinants of Differential Divorce Rates," *American Journal of Sociology,* vol. 69, pp. 12–20, 1964.

Adams, Bert N. "Occupational Position, Mobility and the Kind of Orientation," *American Sociological Review,* vol. 32, no. 3, pp. 364–76, 1967.

Adams, Bert N. *Kinship in an Urban Setting.* Chicago: Markham, 1968.

Adler, Alfred *Problems of Neurosis.* London: Kegan Paul, 1929.

Adler, Alfred "Individual Psychology," in C. Murchison (ed.), *Psychologies of the 1930's,* Worcester, Mass.: Clark University Press, 1930.

Adler, Alfred *What Life Should Mean to You.* Boston: Little, 1931.

Aldous, Joan "Strategies for Developing Family Theory," *Journal of Marriage and the Family,* vol. 32, pp. 250–57, 1970.

Aldous, Joan "A Framework for the Analysis of Family Problem Solving," in Joan Aldous et al. (eds.), *Family Problem Solving.* Chicago: Dryden Press, 1971.

Aldous, Joan, and Hill, Reuben *International Bibliography of Research in Marriage and the Family: 1900–1964.* Minneapolis: University of Minnesota Press, 1971.

Allport, G. W. *Pattern and Growth in Personality.* New York: Holt, Rinehart and Winston, 1961.

Allport, G. W. "The Open System in Personality Theory," *Journal of Abnormal and Social Psychology,* vol. 3, pp. 301–10, 1971.

Anastasi, Thomas E. *Face-to-Face Communication.* Cambridge, Mass.: Management Center of Cambridge, 1967.

Angell, R. C. *The Family Encounters the Depression.* New York: Scribner, 1936.

Argyle, M., and Dean, J. "Eye Contact, Distance, and Affiliation," *Sociometry*, vol. 28, pp. 289–304, 1965.

Arnold, Magda B. *Emotion and Personality*. New York: Columbia University Press, 1960.

Arnold, Magda B. (ed.) *The Nature of Emotion*. Middlesex, England: Penguin Books, 1968.

Axelson, Leland J. "The Marital Adjustment and Marital Role Definitions of Husbands of Working and Nonworking Wives," *Marriage and Family Living*, vol. 25, no. 2, pp. 189–95, 1963.

Baber, Ray E. "A Study of 325 Mixed Marriages," *American Sociological Review*, vol. 2, pp. 705–16, 1937.

Baber, Ray E. *Marriage and the Family*. New York: McGraw-Hill, 1939.

Baber, Ray E. *Marriage and the Family*. 2d ed. New York: McGraw-Hill, 1953.

Bachrach, A. J.; Candland, D. K.; and Gibson, J. T. "Group Reinforcement of Individual Response Experiments in Verbal Behavior," in P. A. Berg and B. M. Bass (eds.), *Conformity and Deviation*. New York: Harper, 1961.

Backman, C. W., and Secord, P. F. "The Effect of Perceived Liking on Interpersonal Attraction," *Human Relations*, vol. 12, pp. 379–84, 1959.

Backman, C. W., and Secord, P. F. "The Compromise Process and the Affect Structure of Groups," *Human Relations*, vol. 17, no. 1, pp. 19–22, 1964.

Bales, Robert F., and Strodtbeck, Fred L. "Phases in Group Problem Solving," *Journal of Abnormal and Social Psychology*, vol. 46, pp. 485–95, 1951.

Bandura, A., and Walters, R. H. *Social Learning and Personality Development*. New York: Holt, Rinehart and Winston, 1963.

Barnett, Larry D. "Interracial Marriage in California," *Marriage and Family Living*, vol. 25, no. 4, pp. 424–27, 1963.

Barnett, Larry D. "Research on International and Interracial Marriages," *Marriage and Family Living*, vol. 25, pp. 105–7, 1963a.

Bartell, Gilbert D. "Group Sex among the Mid-Americans," *Journal of Sex Research*, vol. 6, pp. 113–30, 1970.

Bartell, Gilbert D. *Group Sex*. New York: Wyden, 1971.

Bartz, Karen Winch, and Nye, F. Ivan "Early Marriage: A Propositional Formulation," *Journal of Marriage and the Family*, vol. 32, pp. 258–68, 1970.

Bass, Bernard M. "Amount of Participation, Coalescence and Profitability of Decision-Making Discussions," *Journal of Abnormal and Social Psychology*, vol. 67, pp. 92–94, 1963.

Bates, F. L. "Position, Role and Status: A Reformulation of Concepts," *Social Forces*, vol. 34, pp. 313–21, 1956.

Bauby, Cathrina *OK, Let's Talk about It*. New York: Van Nostrand Reinhold, 1972.

Baughman, E. E., and Welsh, George S. *Personality: A Behavioral Science*. Englewood Cliffs, N.J.: Prentice-Hall, 1962.

Bauman, K. E. "Selected Aspects of the Contraceptive Practices of Unmarried University Students," *American Journal of Obstetrics and Gynecology*, vol. 108, no. 2, pp. 203–9, 1970.

Becker, Wesley C. *Parents Are Teachers*. Champaign, Ill.: Research Press, 1971.

Bell, Howard M. *Youth Tell Their Story*. Washington, D.C.: American Council on Education, 1938.

Bell, Robert R. *Marriage and Family Interaction*. Homewood, Ill.: Dorsey Press, 1963.

Bell, Robert R. *Premarital Sex in a Changing Society*. Englewood Cliffs, N.J.: Prentice-Hall, 1966.

Bell, Robert R., and Buerkle, Jack V. "Mother and Daughter Attitudes to Premarital Sexual Behavior," *Marriage and Family Living*, vol. 23, no. 4, pp. 390–92, 1961.

Bell, Robert R., and Chaskes, Jay B. "Premarital Sexual Experiences among Coeds, 1958 and 1968," *Journal of Marriage and the Family*, vol. 32, no. 1, pp. 81–84, 1970.

Bell, W., and Boat, M. D. "Urban Neighborhoods and Social Participation," *American Journal of Sociology*, vol. 62, pp. 391–98, 1957.

Belliveau, Fred, and Richter, Lin *Understanding Human Sexual Inadequacy*. New York: Bantam Books, 1970.

Benson, Purnell "The Common Interests Myth in Marriage," *Social Problems*, vol. 3, pp. 27–34, 1955.

Berger, Peter, and Hellner, Hansfried "Marriage and the Construction of Reality," *Diogenes*, vol. 46, Summer, pp. 1–24, 1964.

Bernard, Jessie "Factors in the Distribution of Success in Marriage," *American Journal of Sociology*, vol. 40, pp. 49–60, 1934.

Bernard, Jessie *The Future of Marriage*. New York: World, 1972.

Biddle, B. J., and Thomas E. J. *Role Theory: Concepts and Research*. New York: Wiley, 1966.

Blalock, Hubert M., Jr. *Causal Inferences in Non-Experimental Research*. Chapel Hill: University of North Carolina Press, 1964.

Blalock, Hubert M., Jr. *Theory Construction*. Englewood Cliffs, N.J.: Prentice-Hall, 1969.

Blalock, Hubert M., Jr. *Causal Models in the Social Sciences*. Chicago: Aldine-Atherton, 1971.

Blau, Peter M. "Structural Effects," *American Sociological Review*, vol. 25, pp. 178–93, 1960.

Blau, Peter M. *Exchange and Power in Social Life*. New York: Wiley, 1964.

Blau, Peter M.   "A Formal Theory of Differentiation in Organizations," *American Sociological Review,* vol. 35, no. 2, pp. 201–18, 1970.

Blau, Peter M.   "Justice in Social Exchange," in Herman Turk and Richard L. Simpson (eds.), *Institutions and Social Exchange: The Sociologies of Talcott Parsons and George C. Homans.* Indianapolis: Bobbs-Merrill, 1971.

Blood, Robert O., Jr   "Romance and Premarital Intercourse—Incompatibles?" *Marriage and Family Living,* vol. 14, pp. 105–8, 1952.

Blood, Robert O., Jr.   *Marriage.* Glencoe, Ill.: Free Press, 1962.

Blood, Robert O., Jr.   The Husband and Wife Relationship," in F. Ivan Nye and Lois Hoffman, (eds.), *The Employed Mother in America.* Chicago: Rand McNally, 1963.

Blood, Robert O., Jr.   "Long-Range Causes and Consequences of the Employment of Married Women," *Journal of Marriage and the Family,* vol. 27, pp. 43–47, 1965.

Blood, Robert O., Jr., and Hamblin, Robert L.   "The Effect of the Wife's Employment on the Family Power Structure," *Social Forces,* vol. 37 (May), pp. 347–52, 1958.

Blood, Robert O., Jr., and Wolfe, Donald M.   *Husbands and Wives: The Dynamics of Married Living.* Glencoe, Ill.: Free Press, 1960.

Blum, Alan F.   "Social Structure, Social Class, and Participation in Primary Relationships," in William J. Goode (ed.), *The Dynamics of Modern Society.* New York: Atherton Press, 1966.

Blumer, Herbert   "Sociological Analysis and the Variable," *American Sociological Review,* vol. xxi (December), pp. 683–90, 1956.

Bolton, Charles D.   "Mate Selection as the Development of a Relationship," *Marriage and Family Living,* vol. 23, no. 3, pp. 234–40, 1961.

Bolton, Charles D.   "Is Sociology a Behavioral Science?" *Pacific Sociological Review,* vol. vi (Spring), pp. 3–9, 1963.

Bossard, James H. S., and Boll, Eleanor S.   *Sociology of Child Development.* New York: Harper, 1954.

Bossard, James H. S., and Letts, H. C.   "Mixed Marriages Involving Lutherans," *Marriage and Family Living,* vol. 18, pp. 308–10, 1956.

Bott, Elizabeth   *Family and Social Network.* London: Tavistock Publications, 1957.

Bower, Joseph L.   "Group Decision Making: A Report of an Experimental Study," *Behavioral Science,* vol. 10, pp. 277–89, 1965.

Bowerman, Charles E.   "Age Relationships at Marriage, by Marital Status and Age at Marriage," *Marriage and Family Living,* vol. 18, no. 3, pp. 231–33, 1956.

Bowerman, Charles E.   "Prediction Studies," in Harold T. Christensen (ed.), *Handbook of Marriage and the Family.* Chicago: Rand McNally, 1964.

Bowerman, Charles E., and Day, Barbara R. "A Test of the Theory of Complementary Needs as Applied to Couples during Courtship," *American Sociological Review*, vol. 21, pp. 602–5, 1956.

Bowerman, Charles E., and Irish, Donald P. "Some Relationships of Stepchildren to Their Parents," *Marriage and Family Living*, vol. 24, pp. 113–21, 1962.

Bowman, Henry A. *Marriage for Moderns*. 6th ed. New York: McGraw-Hill, 1970.

Bradburn, N. M. "In Pursuit of Happiness," *National Opinion Research Center*, vol. 53, report no. 92 (May), University of Chicago, 1963.

Braithwaite, R. B. *Scientific Explanation*. London: Cambridge University Press, 1959.

Breedlove, William, and Breedlove, Jerrye *Swap Clubs*. Los Angeles: Sherbourne Press, 1964.

Brewer, R. Z., and Brewer, M. B. "Attraction and Accuracy of Perception in Dyads," *Journal of Personality and Social Psychology*, vol. 8, pp. 188–93, 1968.

Bridgman, P. W. *The Logic of Modern Physics*. New York: Macmillan, 1927.

Brim, Orville G. "Family Structure and Sex Role Learning by Children: A Further Analysis of Helen Koch's Data," *Sociometry*, vol. 21, pp. 1–16, 1958.

Brim, Orville G. *Education for Child Rearing*. New York: Russell Sage Foundation, 1959.

Brim, Orville G. *Socialization after Childhood: Two Essays*. New York: Wiley, 1966.

Brown, Hugh B. *You and Your Marriage*. Salt Lake City: Bookcraft, 1960.

Brown, Robert *Explanation in Social Science*. Chicago: Aldine, 1963.

Brown, Roger *Social Psychology*. New York: Free Press, 1965.

Broxton, J. A. "A Test of Interpersonal Attraction Predictions Derived from Balance Theory," *Journal of Abnormal and Social Psychology*, vol. 66, pp. 394–97, 1963.

Buck, John L. *Chinese Farm Economy*. Chicago: University of Chicago Press, 1930.

Buckley, Walter *Sociology and Modern Systems Theory*. Englewood Cliffs, N.J.: Prentice-Hall, 1967.

Buerkle, J. V., and Anderson, T. R. "Altruism, Role Conflict, and Marital Adjustment: A Factor Analysis of Marital Interaction," *Marriage and Family Living*, vol. 1, pp. 2–26, 1961.

Buerkle, J. V., and Badgley, F. R. "Couple Role-Taking: The Yale Marital Interaction Battery," *Marriage and Family Living*, vol. 21, pp. 53–58, 1959.

Burchinal, Lee G. "Marital Satisfaction and Religious Behavior," *American Sociological Review*, vol. 22, pp. 306–10, 1957.

Burchinal, Lee G.   "Maternal Employment, Family Relations, and Selected Personality, School-Related, and Social Development Characteristics of Children," *Research Bulletin,* vol. 497 (Oct.). Ames: Iowa State University Agricultural and Home Economics Experiment Station, 1961.

Burchinal, Lee G.   "The Premarital Dyad and Love Involvement," in Harold T. Christensen (ed.), *Handbook of Marriage and the Family.* Chicago: Rand McNally, 1964.

Burchinal, Lee G., and Bock, Elmer W.   "Religious Behavior, Premarital Pregnancy, and Early Maturity," *Alpha Kappa Deltan,* vol. 29, no. 2, pp. 39–44, 1959.

Burchinal, Lee G., and Chancellor, Loren   "Survival Rates among Religiously Homogamous and Heterogamous Marriages," *Research Bulletin,* vol. 512 (December), Iowa State University Agricultural and Home Economics Experiment Station, 1962.

Burchinal, Lee G., and Chancellor, Loren   "Survival Rates among Religiously Homogamous and Interreligious Marriages," *Social Forces,* vol. 41, no. 4, pp. 353–62, 1963.

Burchinal, Lee G., and Kenkel, William F.   "Ages at Marriage, Occupations of Grooms and Interreligious Marriage Rates," *Social Forces,* vol. 40, no. 4, pp. 348–54, 1961.

Burgess, Ernest W., and Cottrell, Leonard S., Jr.   *Predicting Success or Failure in Marriage,* Englewood Cliffs, N.J.: Prentice-Hall, 1939.

Burgess, Ernest W.; Locke, Harvey J.; and Thomes, Mary Margaret   *The Family.* 3d ed. New York: American, 1963.

Burgess, Ernest W., and Wallin, Paul   *Engagement and Marriage.* Philadelphia: Lippincott, 1953.

Burma, John H.   "Research Note on the Measurement of Interracial Marriage," *American Journal of Sociology,* vol. 57, no. 6, pp. 587–89, 1952.

Burma, John H.   "Interethnic Marriage in Los Angeles, 1948–1959," *Social Forces,* vol. 42, pp. 156–65, 1963.

Burr, Wesley R.   "Marital Satisfaction: A Conceptual Reformulation; Theory and Partial Test of the Theory," unpublished Ph.D. dissertation, University of Minnesota, 1967.

Burr, Wesley R.   "Satisfaction with Various Aspects of Marriage over the Life Cycle: A Random Middle Class Sample," *Journal of Marriage and the Family,* vol. 29, pp. 32–37, 1970.

Burr, Wesley R.   "An Expansion and Test of a Role Theory of Marital Satisfaction," *Journal of Marriage and the Family,* vol. 33, pp. 368–72, 1971.

Burr, Wesley R.   "Role Transitions: A Reformulation of Theory," *Journal of Marriage and the Family,* vol. 34 (August), pp. 407–16, 1972.

Burr, Wesley R. *Theory Construction and the Sociology of the Family.* New York: Wiley, 1973.

Byrne, D. "Interpersonal Attraction and Attitude Similarity," *Journal of Abnormal and Social Psychology,* vol. 62, pp. 713–15, 1961.

Byrne, D. "Response to Attitude Similarity–Dissimilarity as a Function of Affiliation Need," *Journal of Personality,* vol. 30, pp. 164–77, 1962.

Byrne, D.; Clore, G. L.; and Worchel, P. "Effect of Economic Similarity–Dissimilarity on Interpersonal Attraction," *Journal of Personality and Social Psychology,* vol. 4, pp. 220–24, 1966.

Byrne, D. and Griffitt, A. "Developmental Investigation of the Law of Attraction," *Journal of Personality and Social Psychology,* vol. 4, pp. 699–702, 1966.

Byrne, D.; Griffitt, W.; Hudgins, W.; and Reeves, K. "Attitude Similarity–Dissimilarity and Attraction: Generality beyond the College Sophomore," *Journal of Social Psychology,* vol. 79, pp. 155–61, 1969.

Byrne, D., and Nelson, D. A. "Attraction as a Linear Function of Proportion of Positive Reinforcements," *Journal of Personality and Social Psychology,* vol. 1, pp. 659–63, 1965.

Byrne, D., and Rhamey, R. "Magnitude of Positive and Negative Reinforcement as Determinant of Attraction," *Journal of Personality and Social Psychology,* vol. 2, pp. 884–89, 1965.

Cameron, Norman, and Margaret, Ann *Behavior Pathology.* Boston: Houghton Mifflin, 1951.

Campbell, D. A., and Stanley, J. *Experimental and Quasi-Experimental Designs for Research.* Chicago: Rand McNally, 1963.

Campbell, E. Q., and Pettigrew, T. F. "Racial and Moral Crisis: The Role of Little Rock Ministers," *American Journal of Sociology,* vol. 64, pp. 509–16, 1959.

Cartwright, Dorwin and Zander, Alvin (eds.) *Group Dynamics.* 3d ed. New York: Harper and Row, 1968.

Casler, Lawrence *Is Marriage Necessary?* New York: Human Sciences Press, 1973.

Catton, William R., Jr., and Smirich, R. J. "A Comparison of Mathematical Models for the Effect of Residential Propinquity on Mate Selection," *American Sociological Review,* vol. 29, pp. 522–29, 1964.

Cavan, Ruth Shonle "Self and Role in Adjustment during Old Age," in Arnold M. Rose (ed.), *Human Behavior and Social Processes.* Boston: Houghton Mifflin, 1962.

Cavan, Ruth Shonle *The American Family.* 3d ed. New York: Thomas Y. Crowell, 1969.

Cavan, Ruth Shonle and Ranck, Katherine H. *The Family and the Depression.* Chicago: University of Chicago Press, 1938.

Chancellor, Loren E., and Monahan, Thomas P. "Religious Preference and Interreligious Mixtures in Marriages and Divorces in Iowa," *American Journal of Sociology*, vol. 41, pp. 233–39, 1955.

Charters, W. W., Jr., and Newcomb, T. M. "Some Attitudinal Effects of Experimentally Increased Salience of a Membership Group," in E. Maccoby, T. M. Newcomb, and E. L. Hartley (eds.), *Readings in Social Psychology*. New York: Holt, Rinehart and Winston, 1958.

Cheng, C. K., and Yamamura, Douglas S. "Interracial Marriage and Divorce in Hawaii," *Social Forces*, vol. 36, no. 1, pp. 77–84, 1957.

Christensen, Harold T. "Cultural Relativism and Premarital Sex Norms," *American Sociological Review*, vol. 25, pp. 31–39, 1960.

Christensen, Harold T. "A Cross-cultural Comparison of Attitudes toward Marital Infidelity," *International Journal of Comparative Sociology*, vol. 3, pp. 124–37, 1962.

Christensen, Harold T. "Child Spacing Analysis via Record Linkage: New Data plus Summing Up from Earlier Reports," *Marriage and Family Living*, vol. 25, pp. 272–80, 1963.

Christensen, Harold T. "Normative Theory Derived from Cross-cultural Family Research," *Journal of Marriage and the Family*, vol. 31 (May), pp. 209–22, 1969.

Christensen, Harold T., and Barber, Kenneth E. "Interfaith versus Intrafaith marriages in Indiana," *Journal of Marriage and the Family*, vol. 29, pp. 461–69, 1967.

Christensen, Harold T., and Carpenter, George "Timing Patterns in Premarital Sexual Intimacy: An Attitudinal Report on Three Modern Western Societies," *Marriage and Family Living*, vol. 24, no. 1, pp. 30–35, 1962.

Christensen, Harold T., and Gregg, Christina F. "Changing Sex Norms in America and Scandinavia," *Journal of Marriage and the Family*, vol. 32, no. 4, pp. 616–27, 1970.

Christensen, Harold T., and Meissner, Hanna H. "Studies in Child Spacing: III. Premarital Pregnancy as a Factor in Divorce," *American Sociological Review*, vol. 18, no. 6, pp. 641–44, 1953.

Christensen, Harold T., and Philbrick, Robert E. "Family Size as a Factor in the Marital Adjustment of College Couples," *American Sociological Review*, vol. 17, pp. 306–12, 1952.

Clarke, Alfred C. "An Examination of the Operation of Residential Propinquity as a Factor in Mate Selection," *American Sociological Review*, vol. 17, pp. 17–22, 1952.

Clements, William H. "Marital Interaction and Marital Stability: A Point of View and a Descriptive Comparison of Stable and Unstable Marriages," *Journal of Marriage and the Family*, vol. 29, pp. 697–702, 1967.

Cohen, M., and Nagel E. *An Introduction to Logic and Scientific Method*. New York: Harcourt, 1934.

Coleman, James C. *Abnormal Psychology and Modern Life.* Chicago: Scott, Foresman, 1956.

Connell, Elizabeth *Science News,* May 21, 1966.

Constantine, Larry L., and Constantine, Joan M. "Report on Ongoing Research in Group Marriage," presentation to January meeting, Society for the Scientific Study of Sex, New York, 1971.

Cooley, C. H. *Human Nature and the Social Order.* New York: Scribner, 1902.

Cooley, C. H. *Social Organization.* New York: Scribner, 1909.

Coombs, Robert H. "Reinforcement of Values in the Parental Home as a Factor in Mate Selection," *Marriage and Family Living,* vol. 24, no. 2, pp. 155–57, 1962.

Corsini, Raymond J. "Understanding and Similarity in Marriage," *Journal of Abnormal and Social Psychology,* vol. 52, no. 3, pp. 326–32, 1956.

Corsini, Raymond J. "Multiple Predictors of Marital Happiness," *Marriage and Family Living,* vol. 18, pp. 240–42, 1956a.

Coser, Lewis A. *The Functions of Social Conflict.* New York: Free Press, 1956.

Costner, Herbert L. "Theory, Deduction, and Rules of Correspondence," *American Journal of Sociology,* vol. 75, no. 2, pp. 245–63, 1969.

Costner, Herbert L., and Leik, Robert K. "Deductions from 'Axiomatic Theory,' " *American Sociological Review,* vol. 29 (December), pp. 819–35, 1964.

Cottrell, L. S., Jr. "Roles and Marital Adjustment," *Publications of the American Sociological Society,* vol. 27 (May), pp. 108–15, 1933.

Cottrell, L. S., Jr. "The Adjustment of the Individual to His Age and Sex Roles," *American Sociological Review,* vol. 7 (October), pp. 617–20, 1942.

Crawford, Thomas J., and Naditch, Murray P. "Relative Deprivation, Powerlessness, and Militancy: The Psychology of Social Protest," *Psychiatry,* vol. 33, no. 2 (February), pp. 208–33, 1970.

Cuber, John F., and Harroff, Peggy B. *The Significant Americans: A Study of Sexual Behavior among the Affluent.* New York: Appleton-Century-Crofts, 1966.

Culbert, S. A. "The Interpersonal Process of Self-Disclosure: It Takes Two to See One," *Explorations in Applied Science,* no. 3, 1967.

Cumming, Elaine et al. "Disengagement—A Tentative Theory of Aging," *Sociometry,* vol. 23 (March), pp. 23–35, 1960.

Davis, Fred *Passage through Crisis: Polio Victims and Their Families.* Indianapolis: Bobbs-Merrill, 1963.

Davis, James A. "A Formal Interpretation of the Theory of Relative Deprivation," *Sociometry,* vol. 22, no. 4 (December), pp. 280–96, 1959.

Davis, Katherine B. *Factors in the Sex Life of Twenty-Two Hundred Women.* New York: Harper, 1929.

Davis, Kingsley "Extreme Social Isolation of a Child," *American Journal of Sociology,* vol. 45 (January), pp. 554–65, 1940.

Davis, Kingsley "Final Note on a Case of Extreme Isolation," *American Journal of Sociology,* vol. 52, no. 5, pp. 432–37, 1947.

Davis, Kingsley *Human Society.* New York: Macmillan, 1949.

Davis, Kingsley "The Role of Class Mobility in Economic Development," *Population Review,* vol. 6 (July), pp. 67–73, 1962.

Davis, K., and Blake, J. "Social Structure and Fertility: An Analytical Framework," *Economic Development and Cultural Change,* vol. 4, (April), pp. 211–35, 1956.

Davitz, Joel R. *The Language of Emotion.* New York: Academic Press, 1969.

Day, Barbara R. "A Comparison of Personality Needs of Courtship Couples and Same Sex Friendships," *Sociology and Social Research,* vol. 45, no. 4, pp. 435–40, 1961.

Dean, Dwight G. "Romanticism and Emotional Maturity: A Preliminary Study," *Marriage and Family Living,* vol. 23 (February), pp. 44–45, 1961.

Dean, Dwight G. "Romanticism and Emotional Maturity: A Further Exploration," *Social Forces,* vol. 42, pp. 298–303, 1964.

DeBurger, J. E. "Selected Factors in Premarital Experience Related to Marital Adjustment," unpublished master's thesis, Indiana University, 1961.

Deutsch, Morton "Cooperation and Trust: Some Theoretical Notes," in M. R. Jones (ed.), *Nebraska Symposium on Motivation.* Lincoln: University of Nebraska Press, 1962.

Deutsch, Morton *The Resolution of Conflict.* New Haven: Yale University Press, 1973.

Deutsch, Helene *Psychology of Women.* Vol. 2. New York: Grune and Stratton, 1945.

Deutscher, Irwin *Married Life in the Middle Years.* Kansas City, Mo.: Community Studies, 1959.

Deutscher, Irwin "Socialization for Postparental Life," in Arnold M. Rose (ed.), *Human Behavior and Social Processes.* Boston: Houghton Mifflin, 1962.

Dittman, Allen T. *Interpersonal Messages of Emotion.* New York: Springer, 1972.

Doby, J. T. *An Introduction to Social Research.* New York: Appleton-Century-Crofts, 1967.

Dosey, M. A., and Meisels, M. "Personal Space and Self-Protection," *Journal of Personality and Social Psychology,* vol. 11, pp. 93–97, 1969.

Douglas, J. W. B., and Bloomfield, J. M. "Children under Five," in Ruth and David Glass (eds.). Boston: *Studies in Society,* Allyn and Bacon, 1938.

Douvan, Elizabeth "Employment and the Adolescent," in F. Ivan Nye and Lois Hoffman (eds.), *The Employed Mother in America.* Chicago: Rand McNally, 1963.

Drill, Victor A. *Oral Contraceptives.* New York: McGraw-Hill, 1966.

Dubin, Robert *Theory Building.* Glencoe, Ill. Free Press, 1969.

Duncan, Otis Dudley "Axioms or Correlations?" *American Sociological Review,* vol. 28 (June), pp. 452, 1963.

Dunn, Marie S. "Marriage Role Expectations of Adolescents," *Marriage and Family Living,* vol. 22 (May), pp. 99–111, 1960.

Durkheim, Emile *The Division of Labor in Society.* New York: Free Press, 1933. (First published in French in 1893.)

Duvall, Evelyn "Loneliness and the Serviceman's Wife," *Marriage and Family Living,* vol. 7 (August), pp. 77–82, 1945.

Duvall, Evelyn *Family Development.* 4th ed. Philadelphia: Lippincott, 1971.

Dyer, Everett D. "Parenthood as Crisis: A Re-study," *Marriage and Family Living,* vol. 25 (May), pp. 196–201, 1963.

Dyer, William G., and Urban, Dick "The Institutionalization of Equalitarian Family Norms," *Marriage and Family Living,* vol. 20, pp. 53–58, 1958.

Dymond, Rosalind "A Scale for the Measurement of Empathetic Ability," *Journal of Consulting Psychology,* vol. 13, pp. 127–33, 1949.

Dymond, Rosalind "The Relation of Accuracy of Perception of the Spouse and Marital Happiness," *American Psychologist,* vol. 8, pp. 344, 1953.

Easterlin, Richard A. "Does Money Buy Happiness?" *Public Interest,* no. 30, pp. 310, 1973.

Ehrlich, H. J. "Attitudes and Behavior and the Intervening Variables," *American Sociologist,* vol. 4 (February) pp. 29–34, 1969.

Ehrlich, Paul, and Ehrlich, Anne H. *Population, Resources, Environment: Issues in Human Ecology.* San Francisco: Freeman, 1970.

Ehrmann, Winston W. *Premarital Dating Behavior.* New York: Holt, 1959.

Elder, Glen H., Jr. "Structural Variations in the Child-Rearing Relationships," *Sociometry,* vol. 25, pp. 241–62, 1963.

Elder, Glen H., Jr. "Parental Power Legitimation and Its Effect on the Adolescent," *Sociometry,* vol. 26, pp. 50–65, 1963.

Eliot, Thomas D. "The Bereaved Family," *Annals of the American Academy of Political and Social Science,* vol. 160 (March), pp. 184–90, 1932.

Ellis, Robert A., and Lane, Clayton W. "Social Mobility and Social Isolation: A Test of Sorokin's Dissociative Hypothesis," *American Sociological Review*, vol. 32 (April), pp. 237–53, 1967.

Erikson, Erik H. *Childhood and Society*. New York: Norton, 1951.

Essig, May, and Morgan, D. H. "Adjustment of Adolescent Daughters of Employed Mothers to Family Life," *Journal of Educational Psychology*, vol. 33 (April), pp. 219–33, 1945.

Fane, R. M. *Transmission of Information: A Statistical Theory of Communications*. Cambridge, Mass.: MIT Press, 1961.

Farber, Bernard "An Index of Marital Integration," *Sociometry*, vol. 20 (June), pp. 117–34, 1957.

Faris, Ellsworth *The Nature of Human Nature*. New York: Harper, 1937.

Farris, Edmond J. *Human Ovulation and Fertility*. Philadelphia: Lippincott, 1956.

Feldman, Julian, and Kantor, Herschel E. "Organizational Decision Making," in James G. Marsh (ed.), *Handbook of Organizations*. Chicago: Rand McNally, 1965.

Festinger, Leon "The Analysis of Sociograms Using Matrix Algebra," *Human Relations*, vol. 2, pp. 153–58, 1949.

Festinger, Leon "A Theory of Social Comparison Processes," *Human Relations*, vol. 7, pp. 117–40, 1954.

Fisher, Seymour *The Female Orgasm*. New York: Basic Books, 1973.

Foote, Nelson "Family Living as Play," *Marriage and Family Living*, vol. 17 (November), pp. 297–305, 1955.

Foote, Nelson "Matching of Husband and Wife in Phases of Development," *Transactions of the Third World Congress of Sociology, International Sociological Association*, vol. 4, pp. 24–34, 1956.

Foote, Nelson, and Cottrell, L. S. *Identity and Interpersonal Competence*. Chicago: University of Chicago Press, 1955.

Fraiberg, Selma H. *The Magic Years*. New York: Scribner, 1959.

Francis, R. G. *Some Elementary Logic: An Introduction to Social Research*. New York: Appleton-Century-Crofts, 1967.

Freedman, R. "The Sociology of Human Fertility: A Trend Report and Bibliography," *Current Sociology*, vol. 11, pp. 35–121, 1962.

French, John R. P., and Raven, Bertram "The Basis of Social Power," in D. Cartwright and A. Zander, *Group Dynamics: Research and Theory*. 2d ed. Evanston, Ill.: Row, Peterson, 1960.

Freud, Anna *The Ego and the Mechanisms of Defense*. New York: International Universities Press, 1946.

Freud, Sigmund, and Breuer, Joseph *On the Psychical Mechanisms of Hysterical Phenomena*. 1893.

Freund, Matthew "Reversibility of Vasectomy and the Role of the Frozen Semen Bank," *Medical Counterpoint*, vol. 3 (November), pp. 15–27, 1971.

Fromm, Erich   *Escape from Freedom.* New York: Rinehart, 1941.

Fromm, Erich   *Man for Himself.* New York: Rinehart, 1947.

Fromm, Erich   *The Sane Society.* New York: Rinehart, 1955.

Fromm, Erich   *The Art of Living.* New York: Harper, 1956.

Fulcomer, David M.   "The Adjustive Behavior of Some Recently Bereaved Spouses: A Psycho-Sociological Study," unpublished Ph.D. dissertation, Northwestern University, 1942.

Fullerton, Gail Putney   *Survival in Marriage.* New York: Holt, Rinehart and Winston, 1972.

Fulton, Robert   (ed.)   *Death and Identity.* New York: Wiley, 1965.

Furstenberg, Frank F., Jr.   "Industrialization and the American Family: A Look Backward," *American Sociological Review,* vol. 39, pp. 326–37, 1966.

Garcia-Bunuel, Rafael   "New and Experimental Methods of Fertility Control," *Current Medical Digest,* vol. 33, no. 6, pp. 889–99, 1966.

Garner, W. R., and Jake, H. W.   "The Amount of Information in Absolute Judgments," *Psychological Review,* vol. 58, pp. 446–59, 1951.

Gianopoulos, Artie and Mitchell, Howard E.   "Marital Disagreement in Working Wife as a Function of Husband's Attitude toward Wife's Employment," *Marriage and Family Living,* vol. 19 (November), pp. 373–78, 1957.

Gibbs, Jack P., and Martin, Walter J.   *Status Integration and Suicide.* Eugene: University of Oregon Books, 1964.

Gibney, Frank   "The Strange Ways of Staphorst," *Life,* vol. 27 (September), pp. 2–8, 1938.

Gibson, Q.   *The Logic of Social Enquiry.* New York: Humanities Press, 1960.

Ginott, Haim G.   *Between Parent and Child.* New York: Macmillan, 1965.

Glasser, B., and Strauss, A.   *Awareness of Dying.* Chicago: Aldine, 1960.

Glazer, B. G., and Strauss, A. L.   *The Discovery of Grounded Theory: Strategies for Qualitative Research.* Chicago: Aldine, 1967.

Glick, Paul C.   *American Families.* New York: Wiley, 1957.

Glueck, S., and Glueck, E.   "Working Mothers and Delinquency," *Mental Hygiene,* vol. 41, pp. 327–52, 1957.

Goffman, Erving   *The Presentation of Self in Everyday Life.* Garden City, N.Y.: Doubleday Anchor Books, 1959.

Gold, M. A.   *A Social Psychology of Delinquent Boys.* Ann Arbor, Mich.: Institute of Social Research, 1961.

Golden, Boris A.   "Honeymoon Sexual Problems," *Medical Aspects of Human Sexuality,* vol. 5, no. 5, pp. 139–52, 1971.

Golden, Joseph   "Patterns of Negro-White Intermarriage," *American Sociological Review,* vol. 19, no. 2, pp. 144–47, 1954.

Goode, William J.   *After Divorce.* Glencoe, Ill.: Free Press, 1956.

Goode, William J. "The Theoretical Importance of Love," *American Sociological Review,* vol. 24, pp. 38–47, 1959.

Goode, William J. "A Theory of Role Strain," *American Sociological Review,* vol. 25 (August), pp. 488–96, 1960.

Goode, William J. "Illegitimacy, Anomie, and Cultural Penetration," *American Sociological Review,* vol. 26, no. 6, pp. 910–25, 1961.

Goode, William J. "Norm Commitment and Conformity to Role Status Obligations," *American Journal of Sociology,* vol. 66, pp. 250–59, 1963.

Goode, William J. *World Revolution and Family Patterns.* New York: Free Press, 1963a.

Goode, William J.; Hopkins, Elizabeth; and McClure, Helen *Social Systems and Family Patterns: A Propositional Inventory.* Indianapolis: Bobbs-Merrill, 1971.

Goody, Jack "A Comparative Approach to Incest and Adultery," *British Journal of Sociology,* vol. 7, no. 4, pp. 286–305, 1956.

Gordon, Thomas *Parent Effectiveness Training.* New York: Wyden, 1970.

Gould, Julius P., and Kolb, William L. *A Dictionary of the Social Sciences,* New York: Free Press, 1964. Quoted in Richard Evans and Norman R. Smith, "A Selected Paradigm of Family Behavior," *Journal of Marriage and the Family,* vol. 31, pp. 512–17, 1964.

Gross, N., et al. *Explorations in Role Analysis: Studies of the School Superintendency Role.* New York: Wiley, 1957.

Guetzkow, H., and Dill, W. R. "Factors in Organizational Development of Task-oriented Groups," *Sociometry,* vol. 20, pp. 175–204, 1957.

Guetzkow, H., and Simon, H. A. "The Impact of Certain Communication Nets upon Organization and Performance in Task-oriented Groups," *Management Science,* vol. 1, pp. 233–50, 1955.

Guilford, J. P. *Psychometric Methods,* 2d ed. New York: McGraw-Hill, 1954.

Hage, Jerald *Techniques and Problems of Theory Construction in Sociology.* New York: Wiley Interscience, 1972.

Halbwachs, Maurice *La Mémoire Collective.* Paris: Presses Universitaires de France, 1950.

Hall, Calvin S., and Lindzey, Gardner *Theories of Personality.* New York: Wiley, 1957.

Hamblin, Robert L., and Blood, Robert O., Jr. "Premarital Experience and the Wife's Sexual Adjustment," *Social Problems,* vol. 3, pp. 122–30, 1956.

Hamilton, Gilbert V. *A Research in Marriage.* New York: A. and C. Boni, 1929.

Hansen, Donald A. "Personal and Positional Influence in Formal Groups: Propositions and Theory for Research on Family Vulnerability to Stress," *Social Forces,* vol. 44, pp. 202–10, 1965.

Hansen, Donald A., and Hill, Reuben "Families under Stress," in Harold T. Christensen (ed.), *Handbook of Marriage and the Family*, Chicago: Rand McNally, 1964.

Hanson, Norwood R. *Patterns of Discovery*. London: Cambridge University Press, 1958.

Hanson, Norwood R. "The Logic of Discovery," *Journal of Philosophy*, vol. 25 (December) pp. 1073–89, 1958a.

Hardy, Kenneth "An Appetitional Theory of Sexual Motivation," *Psychological Review*, vol. 66, pp. 1–18, 1964.

Harper, Robert A. "Communication Problems in Marriage and Marriage Counseling," *Marriage and Family Living*, vol. 20 (May), pp. 107–12, 1958.

Hartley, Ruth E. "Some Implications of Current Changes in Sex Role Patterns," *Merrill Palmer Quarterly*, vol. 6, no. 3, Baltimore: pp. 153–64, 1960.

Hartman, Carl G. *Science and the Safe Period*. Williams and Wilkins, 1962.

Hastorf, A. H., and Bender, I. E. "A Caution Respecting the Measurement of Empathetic Ability," *Journal of Abnormal and Social Psychology*, vol. 45, pp. 469–76, 1954.

Hatch, Gary L. "Factors Involved in Attitudes towards Patterns of Affection in College Campuses in Utah," unpublished PhD. dissertation, Brigham Young University, 1973.

Hawkins, James L., and Johnson, Kathryn "Perception of Behavioral Conformity, Imputation of Consensus, and Marital Satisfaction," *Journal of Marriage and the Family*, vol. 31, no. 3, pp. 507–11, 1969.

Hawley, Amos H. *Human Ecology*. New York: Ronald Press, 1950.

Hays, W. L. *Statistics for Psychologists*. New York: Holt, Rinehart and Winston, 1963.

Heaps, Richard A., and Rohde, Norma. *Interpersonal Communication: A Skill Development Workbook*. Provo, Utah: Brigham Young University Publications, 1974.

Heer, David M. "Dominance and the Working Wife," in Lois Hoffman and R. Ivan Nye (eds.). *The Employed Mother in America*. Chicago: Rand McNally, 1958.

Heer, David M. "The Measurement and Bases of Family Power: An Overview," *Marriage and Family Living*, vol. 25 (May), pp. 133–39, 1963.

Heer, David M. "Reply," *Marriage and Family Living*, vol. 25, (November), pp. 477–78, 1963a.

Heer, David M. "Negro-White Marriage in the United States," *Journal of Marriage and the Family*, vol. 28, no. 3, pp. 262–73, 1966.

Heider, F. "Social Perception and Phenomenal Causality," *Psychological Review*, vol. 51, pp. 358–74, 1944.

Heider, F. *The Psychology of Interpersonal Relations.* New York: Wiley, 1958.

Heiss, Jerold S. "Premarital Characteristics of the Religiously Inter-married in an Urban Area," *American Sociological Review,* vol. 25, pp. 47–55, 1960.

Heiss, Jerold S. "Interfaith Marriage and Marital Outcomes," *Marriage and Family Living,* vol. 23, pp. 228–33, 1961.

Heiss, Jerold S. "Degree of Intimacy and Male–Female Interaction," *Sociometry,* vol. 25, pp. 196–208, 1962.

Heltsley, Mary E., and Broderick, Carlfred B. "Religiosity and Pre-marital Sexual Permissiveness: Reexamination of Reiss's Tradition-alism Proposition," *Journal of Marriage and the Family,* vol. 31, no. 3, pp. 441–43, 1969.

Henry, A. F. "Sibling Structure and Perception of the Disciplinary Roles of Parents," *Sociometry,* vol. 20, pp. 67–74, 1957.

Herbait, J. F. *A Textbook in Psychology.* New York: Appleton-Century-Crofts, 1891.

Herbst, P. G. "Analysis and Measurement of a Situation: The Child in the Family," *Human Relations,* pp. 113–40, 1953.

Herzog, Elizabeth "Children of Working Mothers." U.S. Dept. of Health, Education, and Welfare, Social Security Administration, Children's Bureau.

Heshka, S., and Nelson, Y. "Interpersonal Speaking Distance as a Function of Age, Sex and Relationship," *Sociometry,* vol. 35, pp. 491–98, 1972.

Hess, Robert D., and Handel, Gerald "The Family as a Psychosocial Organization," in Gerald Handel (ed.), *The Psychosocial Interior of the Family.* Chicago: Aldine-Atherton, 1967.

Hill, Reuben *Families under Stress.* New York: Harper, 1949.

Hill, Reuben "Sociology of Marriage and Family Behavior, 1945–56: A Trend Report and Bibliography," *Current Sociology,* vol. 7, pp. 1–98, 1958.

Hill, Reuben "Decision Making and the Family Life Cycle," in Ethel Shanas and Gorden F. Streib (eds.), *Social Structure and the Family.* Englewood Cliffs, N.J.: Prentice-Hall, 1965.

Hill, Reuben "Contemporary Developments in Family Theory," *Journal of Marriage and the Family.* vol. 28, pp. 10–25, 1966.

Hill, Reuben "Payoffs and Limitations of Contemporary Strategies for Family Theory Systematization," paper presented at the National Council on Family Relations meetings in Estes Park, Colorado, August 1971.

Hill, Reuben, and Hansen, Donald A. "The Identification of Con-ceptual Frameworks Utilized in Family Study," *Marriage and Family Living,* vol. 22, pp. 299–311, 1960.

Hill, Reuben, and Hansen, D. A. "The Family in Disaster," in G. Baker and D. Chapman (eds.), *Man and Society in Disaster,* New York: Basic Books, 1962.

Hill, Reuben, and Rodgers, R. H. "The Developmental Approach," in Harold T. Christensen (ed.), *Handbook of Marriage and the Family,* Chicago: Rand McNally, 1964.

Hill, Reuben et al. "An Inventory of Marriage and Family Research," *Marriage and Family Living,* 19 (February) pp. 89–92, 1957.

Hillman, James *Emotion: A Comprehensive Phenomenology of Theories and Their Meanings for Therapy.* London: Routledge and Kegan Paul, 1960.

Hillman, Karen G. "Marital Instability and Its Relation to Education, Income, and Occupation: An Analysis Based on Census Data," in R. F. Winch, R. McGinnis, and H. R. Barringer (eds.), *Selected Studies in Marriage and the Family.* Rev. ed. New York: Holt, Rinehart and Winston, 1962.

Himes, Joseph S. "Value Consensus in Mate Selection among Negroes," *Marriage and Family Living,* vol. 14, pp. 317–21, 1952.

Himes, Joseph S. "The Interrelation of Occupation and Spousal Roles in a Middle Class Negro Neighborhood," *Journal of Marriage and the Family,* vol. 22, pp. 362–63, 1960.

Hobart, Charles "Disagreement and Non-Empathy during Courtship— A Re-study," *Marriage and Family Living,* vol. 18, pp. 317–22, 1956.

Hobart, Charles and Clausner, William "Some Social Interactional Correlates of Marital Role Disagreement and Marital Adjustment," *Marriage and Family Living,* vol. 21, pp. 256–63, 1959.

Hobart, Charles W., and Lindholm, Laura Lee "The Theory of Complementary Needs: A Re-examination," *Pacific Sociological Review,* vol. 6, no. 2, pp. 73–79, 1963.

Hobbs, Daniel F. "Parenthood as Crisis: A Third Study," *Journal of Marriage and the Family,* vol. 27 (August), pp. 367–72, 1965.

Hobbs, Daniel "Transition to Parenthood: A Replication and an Extension," *Journal of Marriage and the Family,* vol. 30 (August), pp. 413–17, 1968.

Hodge, Robert W. et al. "Occupational Prestige in the United States, 1925–1963," *American Journal of Sociology,* vol. 70 (November), pp. 286–302, 1964.

Hoffman, Lois W. "Parental Coerciveness, Child Autonomy, and Child's Role at School," *Sociometry,* vol. 23, pp. 15–22, 1960.

Hoffman, Lois W. "Effects of the Employment of Mothers on Parental Power Relations and the Division of Household Tasks," *Marriage and Family Living,* vol. 22, no. 1, pp. 27–35, 1961.

Hoffman, Lois W. "Effects of Maternal Employment on the Child," *Child Development,* vol. 32, pp. 187–97, 1961a.

Hoffman, Lois W. "Mother's Enjoyment of Work and Effects on the Child," in Hoffman and F. Ivan Nye (eds.), *The Employed Mother in America."* Chicago: Rand McNally, 1963.

Hoffman, L. Richard "Group Problem Solving," in Leonard Berkowitz (ed.), *Advances in Experimental Psychology.* Vol. 2, New York: Academic Press, 1965.

Hoffman, L. Richard; Harberg, E.; and Maier, Norman F. "Differences and Disagreement as Factors in Creative Group Problem Solving," *Journal of Abnormal and Social Psychology,* vol. 64, pp. 206–14, 1962.

Hogan, Richard "The Development of a Measure of Client Defensiveness in the Counseling Relationship," unpublished Ph.D. dissertation, University of Chicago, 1948.

Hollender, Marc H. "Women's Wish to Be Held: Sexual and Nonsexual Aspects," *Medical Aspects of Human Sexuality,* vol. 5, no. 10, pp. 12–26, 1971.

Hollingshead, August B. *Elmtown's Youth.* New York: Wiley, 1949.

Hollingshead, August B. "Cultural Factors in the Selection of Marriage Mates," *American Sociological Review,* vol. 15, pp. 619–27, 1950.

Homans, George C. *The Human Group.* New York: Harcourt, Brace, 1950.

Homans, George C. "Social Behavior as Exchange," *American Journal of Sociology,* vol. 63, pp. 597–606, 1958.

Homans, George C. *Social Behavior: Its Elementary Forms.* New York: Harcourt, Brace and World, 1961.

Homans, George C. "Contemporary Theory in Sociology," in R. E. L. Faris (ed.), *Handbook of Modern Sociology.* Chicago: Rand McNally, 1964.

Homans, George C. "Bringing Men Back In," *American Sociological Review,* vol. 29 (December), pp. 809–18, 1964a.

Horney, Karen *Self-Analysis.* New York: Norton, 1942.

Horney, Karen *Our Inner Conflicts.* New York: Norton, 1945.

Hubbard, Charles W. *Family Planning Education.* St. Louis: Mosby, 1973.

Huntington, Robert M. "The Personality–Interaction Approach to Study of the Marital Relationship," *Marriage and Family Living,* vol. 20, pp. 43–46, 1958.

Hurowitz, Jacob I.; Zander, Alvin F.; and Hymovitch, Bernard "Some Effects of Power on the Relations among Group Members," in D. Cartwright and Zander (eds.), *Group Dynamics.* Evanston, Ill.: Row, Peterson, pp. 483–92, 1953.

Hyman, Herbert H. "The Psychology of Status," *Archives of Psychology,* no. 269, 1942.

Hyman, Herbert H. "Reference Groups," *International Encyclopedia of the Social Sciences,* vol. 13, 1968.

Hymes, James L., Jr. *The Child under Six.* Englewood Cliffs, N.J.: Prentice-Hall, 1964.

Ikeda, Yoshisuke, and Sasaki, Eiji "The Circle of Intermarriage in the Contemporary Huge Urban Society," *Japanese Sociological Review* vol. 7, no. 2, pp. 52–58, 1957.

Jackson, Jay M. "Structural Characteristics of Norms," in B. J. Biddle and E. J. Thomas (eds.), *Role Theory: Concepts and Research,* Wiley, pp. 113–25, 1966.

Jacobson, Alver H. "Conflict of Attitudes toward the Roles of the Husband and Wife in Marriage," *American Sociological Review,* vol. 17, pp. 146–50, 1952.

Jacobson, Paul Harold *American Marriage and Divorce.* New York: Rinehart, 1959.

Jacoby, Arthur P. "Transition to Parenthood: A Reassessment," *Journal of Marriage and the Family,* vol. 31 (November), pp. 720–27, 1969.

James, William *Principles of Psychology,* vol. 2. New York: Holt, 1890.

Johnson, David W. *Reaching Out.* Englewood Cliffs, N.J.: Prentice-Hall, 1972.

Jourard, S. M. *The Transparent Self.* New York: Van Nostrand Reinhold, 1971.

Jules, Henry *Jungle People.* New York: Vintage Books, 1964.

Kanin, Eugene J. and Howard, David H. "Postmarital Consequences of Premarital Sex Adjustments," *American Sociological Review,* vol. 23, no. 5, pp. 556–62, 1958.

Kaplan, Abraham *The Conduct of Inquiry.* San Francisco: Chandler, 1964.

Karlen, Arno "The Unmarried Marrieds on Campus," *New York Times Magazine* (January), pp. 28–29, 1969.

Karlsson, Georg *Adaptability and Communication in Marriage: A Swedish Predictive Study of Marital Satisfaction.* Uppsala: Almqvist and Wiksells, 1951.

Karlsson, Georg *Adaptability and Communication in Marriage.* Totowa, N.J.: Bedminister Press, 1963.

Katz, Alvin, and Hill, Reuben "Residential Propinquity and Marital Selection," *Marriage and Family Living,* vol. 20, pp. 27–35, 1958.

Kelley, E. Lowell "Concerning the Validity of Terman's Weights for Predicting Marital Happiness," *Psychological Bulletin,* vol. 36 (March), pp. 202–3, 1939.

Kelley, E. Lowell "Consistency of the Adult Personality," *American Psychologist,* vol. 10, pp. 659–81, 1955.

Kelley, E. Lowell "The Reassessment of Specific Attitudes after Twenty Years," *Journal of Social Issues,* vol. 17, pp. 29–37, 1961.

Kelley, Harold H. "Communications in Experimentally Created Hierarchies," *Human Relations,* vol. 4, pp. 39–56, 1951.

Kemper, T. D. "Reference Group, Socialization, and Achievement," *American Sociological Review,* vol. 22, no. 1, pp. 31–45, 1968.

Kennedy, Ruby Joe Reeves "Subjective Factors in Mate Selection: An Exploratory Study," *Sociology and Social Research,* vol. 35, pp. 391–98, 1944.

Kephart, William M. "The Duration of Marriage," *American Sociological Review*, vol. 19 (June), pp. 287–95, 1961.

Kephart, William M. *The Family, Society, and the Individual*. Boston: Houghton Mifflin, 1961a.

Kerckhoff, Alan C. "Notes and Comments on the Meaning of Residential Propinquity as a Factor in Mate Selection," *Social Forces* vol. 34, no. 3, pp. 207–13, 1956.

Kerckhoff, Alan C. "Patterns of Homogamy and the Field of Eligibles," *Social Forces*, vol. 42, pp. 289–97, 1964.

Kerckhoff, A. C., and Davis, Q. E. "Value Consensus and Need Complementarity in Mate Selection," *American Sociological Review*, vol. 27, no. 3, pp. 295–303, 1962.

Kerlinger, Fred N. *Foundations of Behavioral Research*. New York: Holt, Rinehart and Winston, 1964.

Kernodle, W. "Some Implications of the Homogamy–Complementary Needs Theories of Mate Selection for Sociological Research," *Social Forces*, vol. 38, pp. 145–52, 1959.

Kimura, Yukiko "War Brides in Hawaii and Their In-Laws," *American Journal of Sociology*, vol. 63, pp. 70–76, 1957.

King, Charles E. "A Research Technique of Marital Adjustment Applied to a Southern Urban Minority Population Group," from "Factors Making for Success or Failure in Marriage Among 466 Negro Couples in a Southern City," unpublished Ph.D. dissertation, University of Chicago, 1951.

King, Charles E. "The Burgess-Cottrell Method of Measuring Marital Adjustment Applied to a Non-white Southern Urban Population," *Marriage and Family Living*, vol. 14 (November), pp. 280–85, 1952.

Kinsey, Alfred C. et al. *Sexual Behavior in the Human Male*. Philadelphia: Saunders, 1948.

Kinsey, Alfred C., and Gebhard, Paul H. *Sexual Behavior in the Human Female*. Philadelphia: Saunders, 1953.

Kirkendall, Lester A. *Premarital Intercourse and Interpersonal Relations*. New York: Julian Press, 1961.

Kirkpatrick, Clifford *The Family as Process and Institution*. 2d ed. New York: Ronald Press, 1963.

Kirkpatrick, Clifford, and Hobart, Charles "Disagreement, Disagreement Estimate, and Nonempathetic Imputation for Intimacy Groups Varying from Favorite Date to Married," *American Sociological Review*, vol. 19, no. 1, pp. 10–19, 1964.

Klemer, Richard H. *Marriage and Family Relationships*. New York: Harper and Row, 1970.

Kligler, Deborah H. "The Effects of the Employment of Married Women on Husband and Wife Roles," unpublished Ph.D. dissertation, Yale University, 1954.

Kogan, Kate L., and Jackson, Joan K. "Perceptions of Self and Spouse: Some Contaminating Factors," *Journal of Marriage and the Family*, vol. 26, pp. 60–64, 1964.

Kolb, William L. "Sociologically Established Family Norms and Democratic Values," *Social Forces*, vol. 26 (May), pp. 451–56, 1948.

Kolers, P. A. "Subliminal Stimulation in Problem Solving," *American Journal of Psychology*, vol. 70, pp. 437–41, 1957.

Koller, Marvin R. "Residential Propinquity of White Mates at Marriage in Relation to Age and Occupation of Males," *American Sociological Review*, vol. 13 (October), pp. 613–16, 1948.

Komarovsky, Mirra *The Unemployed Man and His Family*. New York: Dryden Press, 1940.

Komarovsky, Mirra *Blue-Collar Marriage*. New York: Random House, 1962.

Koos, E. L. *Families in Trouble*. New York: King's Crown Press, 1946.

Koos, E. L. *Marriage*. New York: Holt, 1953.

Kotlar, Sally L. "Middle Class Roles . . . Ideal and Perceived in Relation to Adjustment in Marriage," unpublished Ph.D. dissertation, University of Southern California at Los Angeles, 1961.

Lajewski, Henry C. "Child Care Arrangements of Full Time Working Mothers," U.S. Department of Health, Education, and Welfare, Children's Bureau, 1959.

Landis, Judson T. "Marriages of Mixed and Non-Mixed Religious Faith," *American Sociological Review*, vol. 14, pp. 401–7, 1949.

Landis, Judson T. "The Women Kinsey Studied," *Social Problems*, vol. 1, no. 4, pp. 139–42, 1954.

Landis, Judson T. "The Pattern of Divorce in Three Generations," *Social Forces*, vol. 34, no. 3, pp. 201–7, 1956.

Landis, Judson T. "Religiousness, Family Relationships, and Family Values in Protestant, Catholic, and Jewish Families," *Marriage and Family Living*, vol. 22, no. 4, pp. 341–47, 1960.

Landis, Judson T. "A Comparison of Children from Divorced and Nondivorced Unhappy Marriages," *Family Life Coordinator*, vol. 11, no. 3, pp. 61–65, 1962.

Landis, Judson T. "Social Correlates of Divorce or Nondivorce among the Unhappy Married," *Marriage and Family Living*, vol. 25 (May), pp. 178–80, 1963.

Landis, Judson, and Landis, Mary G. "Length of Time Required to Achieve Adjustment in Marriage," *American Sociological Review*, vol. 11 (December), pp. 666–77, 1946.

Landis, Judson, and Landis, Mary G. *Building a Successful Marriage*. 5th ed. Englewood Cliffs, N.J.: Prentice-Hall, 1968.

Landis, Judson T.; Poffenberger, Thomas; and Poffenberger, Shirley "The Effects of First Pregnancy upon the Sexual Adjustment of 212 Couples," *American Sociological Review*, vol. 15, pp. 766–72, 1950.

Landis, Paul H. "Sequential Marriage," *Journal of Home Economics*, vol. 42, pp. 625–27, 1950.

Lange, Carl George *The Emotions*. Baltimore: Williams and Wilkins, 1922.

Lansing, J. B., and Kish, L. "Family Life Cycle as an Independent Variable," *American Sociological Review*, vol. 22, pp. 512–19, 1957.

Lantz, Herman R., Snyder, Eloise C., Britton, Margaret, and Schmitt, Raymond "Pre-industrial Patterns in the Colonial Family in America: A Content Analysis of Colonial Magazines," *American Sociological Review*, vol. 33, pp. 413–26, 1968.

Lanval, Marc "Is Early Marriage a Remedy for Conjugal Unrest?" *International Journal of Sexology*, vol. 2, pp. 18–20, 1948.

Lazarsfeld, Paul F. "Interpretation of Statistical Relations as a Research Operation," in Lazarsfeld and Morris Rosenberg (eds.), *The Language of Social Research*. New York: Free Press, 1955.

Leach, Edmund R. "Adolescence: II. Sins or Rules?" *New Society*, vol. 1, pp. 13–15, 1963.

Leavitt, Harold J. "Some Effects of Certain Communication Patterns on Group Performance," *Journal of Abnormal and Social Psychology*, vol. 46, pp. 38–50, 1951.

Lederer, William J., and Jackson, Don D. *The Mirages of Marriage*. New York: Norton, 1968.

Lehrman, Nat *Masters and Johnson Explained*. Chicago: Playboy Press, 1970.

LeMasters, E. E. "Parenthood as Crisis," *Marriage and Family Living*, vol. 19, pp. 352–55, 1957.

Lenski, G. "Status Crystallization: A Nonvertical Dimension of Social Status," *American Sociological Review*, vol. 19, pp. 405–13, 1954.

Lerner, D. *Cause and Effect*. New York: Free Press, 1965.

Leslie, Gerald R. *The Family in Social Context*. New York: Oxford University Press, 1967.

Leslie, Gerald R., and Richardson, Arthur H. "Family versus Campus Influences in Relation to Mate Selection," *Social Problems*, vol. 55, no. 2, pp. 117–21, 1956.

Levinger, George "Note on Need Complementarity in Marriage," *Psychological Bulletin*, vol. 61, pp. 153–57, 1964.

Levy, John, and Munroe, Ruth *The Happy Family*. New York: Knopf, 1945.

Lewis, Oscar *Village Life in Northern India*. Urbana: University of Illinois Press, 1958.

Lewis, Richard W. "The Swingers," *Playboy*, vol. 16. pp. 149–228, 1969.

Lindsey, Ben B. "The Companionate Marriage," *Redbook*, (March), 1927.

Linton, Ralph *The Study of Man*. New York: Appleton-Century, 1936.

Linton, Ralph "The Natural History of the Family," in Ruth Nanda Anshen (ed.), *The Family: Its Function and Destiny*. New York: Harper, 1959.

Liska, Allen E. "Emergent Issues in the Attitude–Behavior Consistency Controversy," *American Sociological Review*, vol. 39, pp. 261–72, 1974.

Little, K. B. "Personal Space," *Journal of Experimental Social Psychology*, vol. 1, pp. 237–47, 1965.

Litwak, Eugene "Occupational Mobility and Extended Family Cohesion," *American Sociological Review*, vol. 25 (February), pp. 9–21, 1960.

Litwak, Eugene "Geographic Mobility and Extended Family Cohesion," *American Sociological Review*, vol. 25 (June), pp. 385–94, 1960a.

Lively, Edwin "Toward Concept Clarification: The Case of Marital Interaction," *Journal of Marriage and the Family*, vol. 31 (February), pp. 108–14, 1969.

Livingstone, Frank B. "A Formal Analysis of Prescriptive Marriage Systems among the Australian Aborigines," *Southwestern Journal of Anthropology*, vol. 15, no. 4, pp. 261–372, 1959.

Locke, Harvey J. "Predicting Marital Adjustment by Comparing a Divorced and a Happily Married Group," *American Sociological Review*, vol. 12 (April), pp. 187–91, 1947.

Locke, Harvey J. *Predicting Adjustment in Marriage: A Comparison of a Divorced and a Happily Married Group*. New York: Holt, 1951.

Locke, Harvey J. "Correlates of Primary Communication and Empathy," *Research Studies of the State College of Washington*, vol. 24, pp. 116–24, 1956.

Locke, Harvey J. and Karlsson, Georg "Marital Adjustment and Prediction in Sweden and the United States," *American Sociological Review*, vol. 17 (February), pp. 10–17, 1952.

Locke, Harvey J. and Klausner, William "Prediction of Marital Adjustment of Divorced Persons in Subsequent Marriages," *Research Studies of the State College of Washington*, vol. 16, pp. 30–33, 1948.

Locke, Harvey J., and Mackenprang, Muriel "Marital Adjustment and the Employed Wife," *American Journal of Sociology*, vol. 18, pp. 536–38, 1949.

Locke, Harvey J.; Sabagh, Georges; and Thomes, Mary M. "Correlates of Primary Communication and Empathy," *Research Studies of the State College of Washington*, vol. 24, pp. 116–24, 1956.

Locke, Harvey J., and Wallace, Karl M. "Short Marital Adjustment and Prediction Tests: Their Reliability and Validity," *Marriage and Family Living*, vol. 21 (August), pp. 250–55, 1959.

Locke, Harvey J. et al. "Interfaith Marriages," *Social Problems*, vol. 4, no. 4, pp. 329–33, 1957.

Luckey, Eleanore B. "Marital Satisfaction and Its Association with Congruence of Perception," *Marriage and Family Living*, vol. 22, pp. 49–54, 1960.

Luckey, Eleanore B. "Perceptual Congruence of Self and Family Concept as Related to Marital Interaction," *Sociometry*, vol. 24, pp. 234–50, 1961.

Luckey, Eleanore B. "Number of Years Married as Related to Personality Perception and Marital Satisfaction," *Journal of Marriage and the Family*, vol. 28, pp. 44–48, 1966.

Lund, Frederick H. *Emotions: Their Psychological, Physiological and Educative Implications*. New York: Ronald Press, 1939.

Lundy, Richard M. "Self-Perceptions Regarding Masculinity–Femininity and Descriptions of Same and Opposite Sex Sociometric Choices," *Sociometry*, vol. 21, pp. 231–46, 1958.

Lyman, S. M. and Scott, M. B. "Territoriality: A Neglected Sociological Dimension," *Social Problems*, vol. 15, pp. 236–49, 1967.

Maccoby, Eleanor "Children and Working Mothers," *The Child*, vol. 3, no. 3, pp. 83–89, 1958.

Maccoby, Eleanor "Effects upon Children of Their Mother's Outside Employment," from National Manpower Council, *Work in the Lives of Married Women*. New York: Columbia University Press, 1958a.

MacCurdy, John T. *The Psychology of Emotion: Morbid and Normal*. London: Kegan Paul, Trench, Trubner, 1925.

Mace, David R. *Getting Ready for Marriage*. New York: Abdingdon Press, 1972.

Macklin, Eleanor D. "Heterosexual Cohabitation among Unmarried College Students," *Family Coordinator*, vol. 21, pp. 463–72, 1972.

MacLean, R. "Trial Marriage among Peruvian Aborigines," *Mexican Sociology*, vol. 1, pp. 25–33, 1941.

Magoun, F. Alexander *Love and Marriage*. New York: Harper, 1948.

Maier, Norman R. F. *Problem-Solving Discussions and Conferences*. New York: McGraw-Hill, 1963.

Maier, Norman R. F., and Hoffman, L. Richard "Using Trained Developmental Discussion Leaders to Improve Further the Quality of Group Decisions," *Journal of Applied Psychology*, vol. 44, pp. 247–251, 1960.

Malinowski, Bronislaw *The Sexual Life of Savages*. London: Routledge, 1929.

Mangus, A. R. "Role Theory and Marriage Counseling," *Social Forces*, vol. 35 (March), pp. 209–20, 1957.

Manheim, Henry L. "A Socially Unacceptable Method of Mate Selection," *Sociology and Social Research*, vol. 45, no. 2, pp. 182–87, 1961.

Marshall, Alfred *Principles of Economics*. 9th ed. New York: Macmillan, 1961.

Martindale, Don *The Nature and Types of Sociological Theory.* Boston: Houghton Mifflin, 1960.

Martinson, Floyd M. "Ego Deficiency as a Factor in Marriage: A Male Sample," *Marriage and Family Living,* vol. 21. pp. 48–52, 1959.

Martinson, Floyd M. *Marriage and the American Ideal.* New York: Dodd, Mead, 1960.

Marx, Melvin H. (ed.) *Theories in Contemporary Psychology.* New York: Macmillan, 1963.

Masters, William H., and Johnson, Virginia E. *Human Sexual Response.* Boston: Little, Brown, and Company, 1966.

Masters, William H., and Johnson, Virginia E. *Human Sexual Inadequacy.* Boston: Little, Brown, and Company, 1970.

Matson, Floyd *The Human Dialogue.* New York: Free Press, 1967.

McCary, James *Human Sexuality.* New York: Van Nostrand, 1967.

McCary, James L. *Sexual Myths and Fallacies.* New York: Van Nostrand Reinhold, 1971.

McClelland, D. C. *Personality.* New York: Sloane, 1951.

McDougall, W. "Emotion and Feeling Distinguished," in M. C. Reymort (ed.), *Feelings and Emotions.* Worcester, Mass.: Clark University Press, 1928.

McDougall, W. *Energies of Men.* New York: Scribner, 1933.

McGinnis, Robert "Campus Values in Mate Selection: A Repeat Study," *Social Forces,* vol. 36, no. 4, pp. 368–73, 1958.

McGuire, Terence F., and Steinhilber, Richard M. "Frigidity, the Primary Female Sexual Dysfunction," *Medical Aspects of Human Sexuality,* vol. 4, no. 10, pp. 108–23 (October), 1970.

Mead, George H. *Mind, Self, and Society.* Chicago: University of Chicago Press, 1934.

Mead, George H. *The Philosophy of the Act.* Chicago: University of Chicago Press, 1938.

Mead, Margaret *Sex and Temperament in Three Primitive Societies.* New York: Morrow, 1935.

Mead, Margaret "Marriage in Two Steps," *Redbook,* vol. 127 (July), pp. 48–49, 1966.

Mering, Fay Higher von "Professional and Non-professional Women as Mothers," *Journal of Social Psychology,* vol. 42 (August) pp. 21–34, 1955.

Merton, Robert K. "The Ambivalence of Scientists." *Bulletin of the Johns Hopkins Hospital,* vol. 11 (February), pp. 77–97, 1963.

Merton, Robert K. *Social Theory and Social Structure.* Enlarged ed. New York: Free Press, 1968.

Merton, Robert K. and Kitt, Alice S. "Contributions to the Theory of Reference Group Behavior," in Merton and Paul F. Lazarsfeld (eds.), *Continuities in Social Research: Studies in Scope and Method of the American Soldier.* Glencoe, Ill.: Free Press, 1950.

Meyerowitz, Joseph H., and Feldman, Harold "Transition to Parenthood," *Psychiatric Research Reports,* vol. 20, pp. 78–84, 1966.

Michel, Andree "Comparative Data concerning the Interaction in French and American Families," *Journal of Marriage and the Family,* vol. 29 (May), pp. 337–44, 1967.

Middleton, Russell, and Putney, Snell "Dominance in Decisions in the Family: Race and Class Difference," *American Journal of Sociology,* vol. 45 (May), pp. 605–9, 1960.

Mitchell, Howard E. et al. "Areas of Marital Conflict in Successfully and Unsuccessfully Functioning Family," *Journal of Health and Human Behavior,* vol. 3, pp. 88–93, 1962.

Monahan, Thomas P., and Kephart, William M. "Divorce and Desertion by Religious and Mixed Religious Groups," *American Journal of Sociology,* vol. 59, pp. 454–65, 1954.

Monahan, Thomas P. "Are Interracial Marriages Really Less Stable?" *Social Forces,* vol. 48, pp. 461–73, 1970.

Morris, John McL., and van Wagenen, Gertrude *Science News,* May 21, 1966.

Morris, Richard R. "A Typology of Norms," *American Sociological Review,* (October), pp. 610–13, 1956.

Mortensen, C. David *Advances in Communication.* New York: Harper and Row, 1972.

Mullins, Nicholas C. *The Art of Theory Construction and Use.* New York: Harper and Row, 1971.

Murdock, George P. *Social Structure.* New York: Macmillan, 1949.

Murdock, George P. "Family Stability in Non-European cultures," *Annals,* vol. 272, pp. 195–201, 1950.

Murdock, George P. "World Ethnographic Sample," *American Anthropologist* vol. 20, no. 4, pp. 664–87, 1957.

Murray, H. A. Explorations in Personality. New York: Oxford University Press, 1938.

Murstein, Bernard I. "The Complementary Need Hypothesis in Newlyweds and Middle-aged Married Couples," *Journal of Abnormal and Social Psychology,* vol. 63, no. 1, pp. 194–97, 1961.

Nagel, E. *The Structure of Science.* New York: Harcourt, Brace and World, 1961.

National Office of Vital Statistics *Special Reports,* vol. 46, No. 4, 1957.

Nelson, Joel I. "Clique Contacts and Family Orientations," *American Sociological Review,* vol. 31, pp. 663–72.

Newcomb, Theodore M. "The Prediction of Interpersonal Attraction," *American Psychologist,* vol. 11, pp. 575–86, 1956.

Newcomb, Theodore M. *The Acquaintance Process.* New York: Holt, Rinehart and Winston, 1961.

Nichols, Ralph G. *Listening and Speaking: A Guide to Effective Oral Communication.* Dubuque, Iowa: Brown, 1954.

Nickell, Paulena, and Dorsey, Jean Muir *Management in Family Living.* New York: Wiley, 1967.

Nimkoff, M. F., and Middleton, Russell "Types of Family and Types of Economy," *American Journal of Sociology,* vol. 66, pp. 215–25, 1960.

Nirenberg, Jesse S. *Getting Through to People.* Englewood Cliffs, N.J.: Prentice-Hall, 1963.

Nye, F. Ivan "Adolescent–Parent Adjustment: Age, Sex, Sibling Number, Broken Homes, and Employed Mothers as Variables," *Marriage and Family Living,* vol. 14 (November), pp. 327–32, 1952.

Nye, F. Ivan "Child Adjustment in Broken and in Unhappy Unbroken Homes," *Marriage and Family Living,* vol. 17, pp. 356–61, 1957.

Nye, F. Ivan *Family Relationships and Delinquent Behavior.* New York: Wiley, 1958.

Nye, F. Ivan "Employment Status of Mothers and Adjustment of Adolescent Children," *Marriage and Family Living,* vol. 20, pp. 240–44, 1959.

Nye, F. Ivan "Values, Family, and a Changing Society," *Journal of Marriage and the Family,* vol. 29 (May), p. 241–48, 1967.

Nye, F. Ivan, and Bayer, A. E. "Some Recent Trends in Family Research," *Social Forces,* vol. 41, pp. 290–301, 1963.

Nye, F. Ivan, and Berardo, Felix M. (eds.) *Emerging Conceptual Frameworks in Family Analysis.* New York: Macmillan, 1966.

Nye, F. Ivan, and Berardo, Felix *The Family: Its Structure and Interaction.* New York: Macmillan, 1973.

Nye, F. Ivan, and Hoffman, Lois (eds.) *The Employed Mother in America.* Chicago: Rand McNally, 1963.

Nye, F. Ivan et al. "Anxiety and Anti-social Behavior in Preschool Children," in Nye and L. Hoffman (eds.), *The Employed Mother in America.* Chicago: Rand McNally, 1963.

Ogburn, W. F., and Nimkoff, M. F. *Technology and the Changing Family.* Boston: Houghton Mifflin, 1955.

O'Neill, George C., and O'Neill, Nena "Patterns in Group Sexual Activity," *Journal of Sex Research,* vol. 6 (May), pp. 101–12, 1970.

O'Neill, George C., and O'Neill, Nena *Open Marriage.* New York: Evans, 1972.

Orden, Susan R., and Bradburn, Norman M. "Dimensions of Marriage Happiness," *American Journal of Sociology,* vol. 73 (May), pp. 715–31, 1968.

Orden, Susan R., and Bradburn, Norman M. "Working Wives and Marriage Happiness," *American Journal of Sociology,* vol. 74 (January), pp. 392–407, 1969.

Ort, Robert S. "A Study of Role-Conflicts as Related to Happiness in Marriage," *Journal of Abnormal and Social Psychology,* vol. 45, (October), pp. 691–99, 1950.

Otto, Herbert A.   *More Joy in Your Marriage.* New York: Hawthorn Books, 1969.

Otto, Herbert A.   *The Family in Search of a Future.* New York: Appleton–Century–Crofts, 1970.

Packard, Vance   *The Sexual Wilderness.* New York: McKay, 1968.

Palson, Chuck, and Palson, Rebecca Markle   "Swinging: The Minimizing of Jealousy." Mimeographed Paper. Philadelphia, 1970.

Parsons, Talcott   "The Kinship System of the Contemporary United States," *American Anthropologist,* vol. 45, (January–March), pp. 22–38, 1943.

Parsons, Talcott   *The Social System.* Glencoe, Ill.: Free Press, 1951.

Parsons, Talcott, and Bales, Robert F.   *Family: Socialization and Interaction Process.* Glencoe, Ill.: Free Press, 1955.

Parsons, Talcott, and Fox, Renee   "Illness, Therapy, and the Modern Urban American Family," *Journal of Social Issues,* vol. 8, pp. 1–44, 1952.

Patchen, Martin   "A Conceptual Framework and Some Empirical Data regarding Comparisons of Social Rewards," *Sociometry,* vol. 24, no. 2, pp. 136–56, 1961.

Pavela, Todd H.   "An Exploratory Study of Negro–White Intermarriage in Indiana." *Journal of Marriage and the Family,* vol. 26, pp. 209–11, 1964.

Peale, Ruth S.   *The Adventure of Being a Wife.* Englewood Cliffs, N.J.: Prentice-Hall, 1971.

Perez, Joseph F., and Cohan, Alvin I.   *Mom and Dad Are Me.* Belmont, Calif.: Brooks/Cole, 1969.

Perry, Joseph B., Jr.   "The Mother Substitute of Employed Mothers: An Exploratory Inquiry," *Marriage and Family Living,* vol. 23, no. 4, pp. 362–67, 1961.

Peterson, Evan T.   "The Impact of Maternal Employment on the Mother–Daughter Relationship," *Marriage and Family Living,* vol. 23, no. 4, pp. 353–61, 1958.

Phillips, Bernard S.   *Social Research Strategy and Tactics.* New York: Macmillan, 1966.

Pincus, Gregory   *The Control of Fertility.* New York: Academic Press, 1965.

Pineo, Peter C.   "Disenchantment in Later Years of Marriage," *Marriage and Family Living,* vol. 23, pp. 3–11, 1961.

Popenoe, Paul   "A Study of 738 Elopements," *American Sociological Review,* vol. 3, pp. 1–4, 1938.

Popenoe, Paul   *Modern Marriage.* New York: Macmillan, 1940.

Popper, Karl R.   *The Logic of Scientific Discovery.* London: Hutchison, 1959.

Porter, Blaine R.   *The Latter-Day Saint Family.* Salt Lake City: Deseret, 1968.

Powell, Kathryn Summers "Maternal Employment in Relation to Family Life," *Marriage and Family Living,* vol. 23, no. 4, pp. 340–49, 1961.

Price, Richard "Trial Marriage in the Andes," *Ethnology,* vol. 4, pp. 310–22, 1965.

Pruitt, D. G. "Reciprocity and Credit Building in a Laboratory Dyad," *Journal of Personality and Social Psychology,* vol. 8, pp. 143–47, 1968.

Raboch, Jan "Studies in the Sexuality of Women," trans. by Coling Bearne, in Paul H. Gebhard, Jan Raboch, and Hans Giese (eds.), *The Sexuality of Women.* New York: Stein and Day, 1970.

Ramey, James W. "Emerging Patterns of Innovative Behavior in Marriage," *Family Coordinator,* vol. 21 (October), pp. 435–56, 1972.

Ramsøy, Natalie Rogoff "Assortive Mating and the Structure of Cities," *American Sociological Review,* vol. 31, (December), pp. 773–85, 1966.

Rapoport, Rhonda "The Transition from Engagement to Marriage," *Acta Sociologica,* vol. 8, pp. 36–55, 1964.

Rapoport, Robert, and Rapoport, Rhonda "Work and Family in Contemporary Society," *American Sociological Review,* vol. 30, pp. 381–393, 1965.

Reed, Robert "The Interrelationship of Marital Adjustment, Fertility Control, and Size of Family," *Milbank Memorial Fund Quarterly,* vol. 25 (October), pp. 382–425, 1947.

Reevy, William R. "Premarital Petting Behavior and Marital Happiness Prediction," *Marriage and Family Living,* vol. 21 (November), pp. 349–55, 1959.

Reiss, Ira L. "The Treatment of Premarital Coitus in Marriage and the Family Tests," *Social Problems,* vol. 4, no. 4, pp. 334–38, 1957.

Reiss, Ira L. *Premarital Sexual Standards in America.* New York: Free Press, 1960.

Reiss, Ira L. "Sexual Codes in Teen-age Culture," *Annals of the American Academy of Political and Social Science,* vol. 338, pp. 53–62, 1961.

Reiss, Ira L. "The Scaling of Premarital Sexual Permissiveness," *Journal of Marriage and the Family,* vol. 26 (May), pp. 188–98, 1964.

Reiss, Ira L. "Social Class and Premarital Sexual Permissiveness—A Reexamination," *American Sociological Review,* vol. 30, pp. 747–56, 1965.

Reiss, Ira L. *The Social Context of Premarital Sexual Permissiveness.* New York: Holt, Rinehart and Winston, 1967.

Reiss, Ira L., and Miller, Brent C. *A Theoretical Analysis of Heterosexual Permissiveness.* Minneapolis: Minnesota Family Study Center, 1974.

Reymert, Martin L. *Feelings and Emotions.* New York: McGraw-Hill, 1950.

Reynolds, Paul Davidson   *A Primer in Theory Construction.* Indianapolis: Bobbs-Merrill, 1971.

Rodgers, Roy H.   "Toward a Theory of Family Development," *Journal of Marriage and the Family,* vol. 25, no. 3, pp. 262–70, 1964.

Rodman, Hyman   "Marital Power in France, Greece, Yugoslavia, and the United States: A Cross–National Discussion," *Journal of Marriage and the Family,* vol. 29 (May), pp. 320–24, 1967.

Rogers, Carl R.   *Client-Centered Therapy.* Boston: Houghton Mifflin, 1951.

Rogers, Everett M., and Sebald, Hans   "Familism, Family Integration, and Kinship Orientation," *Marriage and Family Living,* vol. 24, no. 1, pp. 25–29, 1962.

Rollins, Boyd C., and Cannon, Kenneth L.   "Marital Satisfaction over the Family Life Cycle: A Re-evaluation," *Journal of Marriage and the Family,* vol. 36 (July), 1974.

Rollins, Boyd C., and Feldman, Harold   "Marital Satisfaction over the Life Cycle," *Journal of Marriage and the Family,* vol. 32, pp. 20–28, 1970.

Rose, Arnold M.   *Theory and Method in the Social Sciences.* Minneapolis: Lund Press, 1954.

Rose, Arnold M.   "Factors Associated with the Life Satisfaction of Middle Class, Middle-aged Persons," *Marriage and Family Living,* vol. 17 (February), pp. 15–19, 1955.

Rose, Arnold M.   *Human Behavior and Social Processes.* Boston: Houghton Mifflin, 1962.

Rosenthall, R.   "Covert Communication in the Psychological Experiment," *Psychological Bulletin,* vol. 67, pp. 356–67, 1967.

Rosow, Irving   "Issues in the Concept of Need-Complementarity," *Sociometry,* vol. 20, pp. 216–33, 1957.

Rossi, Alice   "Transition to Parenthood," *Journal of Marriage and the Family,* vol. 30, pp. 25–39, 1968.

Roth, Julius, and Peck, Robert F.   "Social Class and Social Mobility Factors Related to Marital Adjustment," *American Sociological Review,* vol. 16, pp. 478–87, 1951.

Roy, Prodipto   "Maternal Employment and Adolescent Roles: Urban Differentials," *Marriage and Family Living,* vol. 23, no. 5, pp. 340–49, 1961.

Ruesch, Harold L.; Berry, William A.; Hertel, Richard K.; and Swain, Mary Ann   *Communication Conflict and Marriage.* San Francisco: Jossey-Bass Publishers, 1974.

Runciman, W. G.   *Relative Deprivation and Social Justice.* London: Routledge and Kegan Paul, 1966.

Russell, Bertrand   *Marriage and Morals.* New York: Liveright Publishing Company, 1929.

Safilios-Rothschild, Constantina "The Study of Family Power Structure: A Review, 1960–1969," *Journal of Marriage and the Family,* vol. 32, no. 4, pp. 539–49, 1970.

Sarason, I. G. "Empirical Findings and the Theoretical Problems in the Use of Anxiety Scales," *Psychology Bulletin,* vol. 56, pp. 403–15, 1960.

Sarason, Seymore V. et al. *Anxiety in Elementary School Children: A Report of Research.* New York: Wiley, 1960.

Sarbin, T. R., and Allen, V. L. "Role Theory," in G. Lindzey and E. Aronson (eds.), *The Handbook of Social Psychology.* 2d ed., vol. 1. Reading, Mass: Addison-Wesley, 1968.

Satir, Virginia "Marriage as a Statutory Five Year Renewable Contract," paper presented at the American Psychological Association annual meetings in Washington, D.C., 1967.

Satir, Virginia *Peoplemaking.* Palo Alto, Calif.: Science and Behavior Books, 1972.

Saul, Leon *Emotional Maturity.* Philadelphia: Lippincott, 1947.

Saxton, Lloyd *The Individual, Marriage, and the Family.* 2d ed. Belmont, Calif.: Wadsworth, 1972.

Scanzoni, John "A Reinquiry into Marital Disorganization," *Journal of Marriage and the Family,* vol. 27, pp. 483–91, 1965.

Schellenberg, J. A., and Bee, L. S. "A Re-examination of the Theory of Complementary Needs in Mate Selection," *Marriage and Family Living,* vol. 22, pp. 227–32, 1960.

Schnepp, Gerald J., and Johnson, Mary Margaret "Do Religious Factors Have Predictive Value?" *Marriage and Family Living,* vol. 14 (November), pp. 301–4, 1952.

Scoresby, A. Lynn; Apolonio, Franklin J.; and Hatch, Gary "Action Plans: An Approach to Behavior Change in Marriage Education," *Family Coordinator,* vol. 23 (October), pp. 343–48, 1974.

Sears, Robert R.; Maccoby, Eleanor E.; and Levin, Harry *Patterns of Child Rearing.* Evanston, Ill.: Row, Peterson, 1957.

Secord, Paul F., and Backman, Carl W. *Social Psychology.* New York: McGraw-Hill, 1964.

Secord, Paul F. and Backman, Carl W. *Social Psychology.* 2d ed. New York: McGraw-Hill, 1974.

Segner, Leslie *Ways to Help Babies Grow and Learn: Activities for Infant Education.* Denver, Colo.: World Press, 1970.

Sherif, C. W.; and Sherif, M. (eds.) *Attitude, Ego-Involvement, and Change.* New York: Wiley, 1967.

Sherif, C. W.; Sherif, M.; and Nebergall, R. E. *Attitude and Attitude Change: The Social Judgment–Involvement Approach.* Philadelphia: Saunders, 1965.

Shibutani, Tomotsu   *Society and Personality*. Englewood Cliffs, N.J.: Prentice-Hall, 1961.

Shiloh, A. (ed.)   *Studies in Human Sexual Behavior: The American Scene*. Springfield, Ill.: Thomas, 1970.

Shulman, Alix Kates   *Memoirs of an Ex-Prom Queen*. New York: Knopf, 1972.

Siegel, A. E., and Siegel, S.   "Reference Groups, Membership Groups, and Attitude Change," *Journal of Abnormal and Social Psychology*, vol. 55, pp. 360–64, 1957.

Siegel, A. E. et al.   "Dependence and Independence in the Children of the Working Mothers," *Child Development*, vol. 30, pp. 533–46, 1959.

Silverman, William, and Hill, Reuben   "Task Allocation in Marriage in the United States and Belgium," *Marriage and the Family*, vol. 29, no. 2, pp. 353–59, 1967.

Simenson, William, and Geis, Gilbert   "Courtship Patterns of Norwegian and American University Students," *Marriage and Family Living*, vol. 18, pp. 334–38, 1956.

Simon, H. A.   *Models of Men*. New York: Wiley, 1951.

Simpson, George   "A Durkheim Fragment," *American Journal of Sociology*, vol. 70, no. 5, pp. 527–36, 1965.

Simpson, R. L.   *Theories of Social Exchange*. Morristown, N.Y.: General Learning Press, 1972.

Skinner, B. F.   *Science and Human Behavior*. New York: Macmillan, 1953.

Slater, Phillip E.   "Some Social Consequences of Temporary Systems," in W. G. Bennis and Slater: *The Temporary Society*. New York: Harper and Row, 1968.

Smith, Carl E.   "Negro–White Intermarriage—Forbidden Sexual Union," *Journal of Sex Research*, vol. 2, pp. 169–73, 1966.

Smith, Dennis   "Techniques of Conception Control," in Donald V. McCalister, Victor Thiessen, and Margaret McDermott (eds.), *Readings in Family Planning*. St. Louis: Mosby, 1973.

Smith, James R., and Smith, Lynn G.   "Co-marital Sex and the Sexual Freedom Movement," *Journal of Sex Research*, vol. 5, pp. 131–42, 1970.

Sommer, R.   "The Distance for Comfortable Conversation: A Further Study," *Sociometry*, vol. 25, pp. 111–16, 1962.

Sommer, R.   *Personal Space: The Behavioral Basis of Design*. Englewood Cliffs, N.J.: Prentice-Hall, 1969.

Sorokin, P. A. et al.   *A Systematic Sourcebook in Rural Sociology*. Vol. 2. Minneapolis: University of Minnesota Press, 1931.

Speer, D. C.   "Family Systems: Morphostasis and Morphogenesis, or 'Is Homeostasis Enough?'" *Family Process*, vol. 9, pp. 259–77, 1970.

Speilberger, Charles D. *Anxiety and Behavior*. New York: Academic Press, 1966,

Springborn, B. A. "Some Determinants and Consequences of the Locus of Evaluation in Small Group Problem Solving," unpublished Ph.D. dissertation, University of Michigan. Cited in Richard L. Hoffman, "Group Problem Solving," in Leonard Berkowitz (ed.), *Advances in Experimental Psychology*. Vol. 2, New York: Academic Press, 1966.

Steinmetz, Suzanne K., and Straus, Murray A. *Violence in the Family*. New York: Dodd, Mead, 1974.

Steinzor, B. "The Spatial Factor in Face-to-Face Discussion Groups," *Journal of Abnormal and Social Psychology*, vol. 45, pp. 552–55, 1950.

Stevens, Peter H. *Emotional Crisis*. New York: Odyssey Press, 1965.

Stewart, C. M. "Future Trends in the Employment of Married Women," *British Journal of Sociology*, vol. 12, no. 4, pp. 1–11, 1957.

Stewart, Daniel K. *The Psychology of Communication*. New York: Funk and Wagnalls, 1969.

Stinchcombe, Arthur L. *Constructing Social Theories*. New York: Harcourt, Brace and World, 1968.

Stolz, Lois Meek "Effects of Maternal Employment on Children: Evidence from Research," *Child Development*, vol. 21 (December), pp. 479–82, 1960.

Stouffer, Samuel A., et al. *The American Soldier: Studies in Social Psychology in World War II*. 2 vols. Princeton, N.J.: Princeton University Press, 1949–50.

Straus, Murray A. "Power and Support Structure of the Family in Relation to Socialization," *Journal of Marriage and the Family*, vol. 26 (August), pp. 318–26, 1964.

Straus, Murray A. "Communication, Creativity, and Problem-Solving Ability of Middle and Working Class Families in Three Societies," in Marvin Sussman (ed.), *Sourcebook in Marriage and the Family*. Boston: Houghton Mifflin, pp. 15–26, 1968.

Straus, Murray A. "Leveling, Civility, and Violence in the Family," *Journal of Marriage and the Family*, vol. 36 (February), pp. 13–26, 1974.

Strauss, Anselm "The Ideal and Chosen Mate," *American Journal of Sociology*, vol. 51, pp. 204–8, 1946.

Strauss, Anselm *The Social Psychology of George Herbert Mead*. Chicago: University of Chicago Press, 1956.

Strodtbeck, Fred L., Jones, Rita M., and Hawkins, C. "The Congruity Principle Revisited: Studies in the Reduction, Induction, and Generalization of Persuasion," in Leonard Berkowitz (ed.), *Advances in Experimental Social Psychology*. Vol. 3. New York: Academic Press, 1957.

Stryker, Sheldon   "Role-taking Accuracy and Adjustment," *Sociometry*, vol. 20, pp. 286–96, 1957.

Stryker, Sheldon   "Symbolic Interaction as an Approach to Family Research," *Marriage and Family Living*, vol. 21, pp. 111–19, 1959.

Stryker, Sheldon   "The Interactional and Situational Approaches," in Harold Christensen (ed.), *Handbook of Marriage and the Family*. Chicago: Rand McNally, 1964.

Stuart, Irving R.   "Complementary vs. Homogeneous Needs in Mate Selection: A Television Program Situation," *Journal of Social Psychology*, vol. 56, pp. 219–300, 1962.

Stuart, Richard B.   "Operant-Interpersonal Treatment for Marital Discord," *Journal of Consulting and Clinical Psychology*, vol. 33, pp. 675–81, 1969.

Stuckert, Robert P.   "Role Perception and Marital Satisfaction—A Configurational Approach," *Marriage and Family Living*, vol. 25 (November), pp. 415–19, 1963.

Sullivan, Harry S.   *The Interpersonal Theory of Psychiatry*. New York: Norton, 1953.

Sumner, W. G.   *Folkways: A Study of the Sociological Importance of Usages, Manners, Customs, Mores, and Morals*. New York: Dover, 1906.

Sundal, A. P., and McCormich, T. C.   "Age at Marriage and Mate Selection: Madison, Wisconsin, 1937–1943," *American Sociological Review*, vol. 16 (February), pp. 37–48, 1951.

Sussman, Marvin B.   "Needed Research on the Employed Mother," *Marriage and Family Living*, vol. 23 (November), pp. 368–73, 1961.

Sussman, Marvin B. and Burchinal, Lee   "Kin Family Network: Unheralded Structure in Current Conceptualizations," *Marriage and Family Living*, vol. 24 (August), pp. 231–40, 1962.

Tagiuri, R.; Kogan, N.; Long, L. M. K.   "Differentiation of Sociometric Choice and Status Relations in a Group," *Psychological Reports*, vol. 4, pp. 523–26, 1958.

Tallman, Irving   "The Family as a Small Problem Solving Group," *Journal of Marriage and the Family*, vol. 32, pp. 94–104, 1970.

Taysom, Alice L.   "The Effects of Relative Resources, Normative Prescription of Power, and Flexibility of Norms on Conjugal Power," unpublished master's thesis, Brigham Young University, 1973.

Terman, Lewis M., and Oden, Melita H.   *The Gifted Child Grows Up: Twenty-Five Years Follow-up of a Superior Group*. Stanford, Calif.: Stanford University Press, 1947.

Terman, Lewis M. et al.   *Psychological Factors in Marital Happiness*. New York: McGraw-Hill, 1938.

Tharp, Roland G.   "Psychological Patterning in Marriage," *Psychological Bulletin*, vol. 60, pp. 97–117, 1963.

Thibaut, J. W., and Kelley, H. H. *The Social Psychology of Groups.* New York: Wiley, 1959.

Thomas, John L. "The Factor of Religion in the Selection of Marriage Mates," *American Sociological Review,* vol. 16, pp. 487–91, 1951.

Turner, Ralph H. *Family Interaction.* New York: Wiley, 1970.

Udry, J. Richard "Complementarity in Mate Selection: A Perceptual Approach," *Marriage and Family Living,* vol. 25 (August), pp. 281–88, 1963.

Udry, J. Richard *The Social Context of Marriage.* Philadelphia: Lippincott, 1966.

Udry, J. Richard "Marital Instability by Race, Sex Education, Occupation, and Income, Using 1960 Census Data," in Robert Winch et al., *Selected Studies in Marriage and the Family.* 3d ed. New York: Holt, Rinehart and Winston, 1968.

Udry, J. Richard *The Social Context of Marriage.* 3d ed. Philadelphia: Lippincott, 1974.

Udry, J. Richard; Nelson, Harold A.; and Nelson, Ruth O. "An Empirical Investigation of Some Widely Held Beliefs about Marital Interaction," *Marriage and Family Living,* vol. 23, pp. 388–90, 1961.

Vernon, Glenn M. "Bias in Professional Publications concerning Interfaith Marriage," *Religious Education,* vol. 55, pp. 261–64, 1960.

Vernon, Glenn M., and Stewart, Robert L. "Empathy as a Process in the Dating Situations," *American Sociological Review,* vol. 22, no. 1, pp. 48–52, 1957.

Vincent, Clark E. *Unmarried Mothers.* New York: Free Press, 1962.

Vital Statistics Bulletin *Divorce Statistics Analysis: United States, 1964 and 1965,* series 21, no. 17, Public Health Service, U.S. Department of Health Education and Welfare, 1968.

Wallen, J. L. "Mutual Value-Prediction of Husbands and Wives," unpublished Ph.D. dissertation, Ohio State University, 1957.

Waller, Willard "The Rating and Dating Complex," *American Sociological Review,* vol. 2, pp. 727–34, 1937.

Waller, Willard, and Hill, R. L. *The Family: A Dynamic Interpretation.* Rev. ed. New York: Dryden, 1951.

Wallin, Paul "Religiosity, Sexual Gratification, and Marital Satisfaction," *American Sociological Review,* vol. 22, pp. 300–305, 1957.

Wallin, Paul, and Clark, Alexander "Marital Satisfaction and Husbands' and Wives' Perception of Similarity in Their Preferred Frequency of Coitus," *Journal of Abnormal and Social Psychology,* vol. 57, pp. 370–73, 1958.

Wallin, Paul, and Clark, Alexander "A Study of Orgasm as a Condition of Women's Enjoyment of Coitus in the Middle Years of Marriage," *Human Biology,* vol. 35, pp. 131–39, 1963.

Warren, H. C. (ed.) *Dictionary of Psychology*. Boston: Houghton Mifflin, 1934.

Watzlawick, Paul; Beaven, Janet Lemick; and Jackson, Don D. *Pragmatics of Human Communication*. New York: Norton, 1967.

Weeks, H. Ashley "Differential Divorce Rates by Occupation," *Social Forces,* vol. 21, pp. 336, 1943.

Wells, J. Gibson *Current Issues in Marriage and the Family*. New York: Macmillan, 1975.

Westermarck, Edward *History of Human Marriage*. 3 vols. New York: Allerton Press, 1891.

Whitehurst, Robert "The Unmalias on Campus," paper presented at annual meetings of the National Council on Family Relations, 1969.

Wicker, A. W. "Attitudes versus Actions: The Relationship of Verbal and Overt Behavioral Responses to Attitude Objects," *Journal of Social Issues,* vol. 25 (Autumn), pp. 41–78, 1969.

Widtsoe, John A. *Priesthood and Church Government*. Salt Lake City: Deseret, 1945.

Willis, F. N., Jr. "Initial Speaking Distance as a Function of the Speaker's Relationship," *Psychonomic Science,* vol. 5, pp. 221–22, 1966.

Winch, Robert F. "The Theory of Complementary Needs in Mate Selection: Final Results on the Test of the General Hypothesis," *American Sociological Review,* vol. 20, pp. 552–55, 1955.

Winch, Robert F. *Mate Selection: A Study of Complementary Needs*. New York: Harper, 1958.

Winch, Robert F. *The Modern Family*. Rev. ed. New York: Holt, Rinehart and Winston, 1963.

Winch, Robert F., and Blumberg, Rae Lesser "Societal Complexity and Familial Organization," in Winch and L. W. Goodman (eds.), *Selected Studies in Marriage and the Family*. New York: Holt, Rinehart and Winston, 1968.

Winch, Robert F.; Greer, Scott; and Blumberg, Rae Lesser "The Theory of Complementary Needs in Mate Selection: An Analytic and Descriptive Study," *American Sociological Review,* vol. 19, no. 3, pp. 241–49, 1954.

Yarrow, Marian Radke "Changes in Family Functioning as Intermediary Effects of Maternal Employment," in Alberta Engvall Siegel (ed.), *Research Issues Related to the Effects of Maternal Employment on Children*. University Park, Pa.: Social Science Research Center, 1961.

Yaukey, David "On Theorizing about Fertility," *American Sociologist,* vol. 4 (May), pp. 100–105, 1969.

Young, Michael, and Wilmott, Peter *Kinship and Family in East London*. Glencoe, Ill.: Free Press, 1957.

Young, Paul T. *Emotion in Man and Animal.* Huntington, N.Y.: Krieger, 1973.

Zetterberg, Hans L. *On Theory and Verification in Sociology.* 2d ed. Totowa, N.J.: Bedminster Press, 1963.

Zetterberg, Hans L. *On Theory and Verification in Sociology.* 3d ed. Totowa, N.J.: Bedminister Press, 1965.

Zimmerman, Carle E., and Cerbantes, Lucius F. *Successful American Families.* New York: Pageant, 1960.

Indexes

Author index

Subject index

This book has been set in 10 point and 9 point Caledonia, leaded 2 points. Section titles and chapter titles are in 36 point and 24 point Goudy Old Style italic. Chapter numbers are in 72 point Caslon Old Style #540 italic. The size of the type page is 32 by 46½ picas.